HOLT MATHEMATICS

Holt, Rinehart and Winston, Publishers
New York · Toronto · London · Sydney

Eugene D. Nichols
Distinguished Professor of Mathematics
Education and Lecturer
Mathematics Department
Florida State University
Tallahassee, Florida

Paul A. Anderson
Elementary School Teacher
Clark County School District
Las Vegas, Nevada

Leslie A. Dwight
Former Head of the Department
and Professor of Mathematics
Southeastern Oklahoma State University
Durant, Oklahoma

Frances Flournoy
Professor of Elementary Education
University of Texas
Austin, Texas

Joella Hardeman-Gipson
Professor and Program Director
College of Education
Wayne State University
Detroit, Michigan

Sylvia A. Hoffman
Resource Consultant in Mathematics
Illinois Office of Education
State of Illinois

Robert Kalin
Professor of Mathematics
Florida State University
Tallahassee, Florida

John Schluep
Professor of Mathematics
State University College
Oswego, New York

Leonard Simon
Former Assistant Director
Planning and Curriculum
New York City Board of Education
New York, New York

Cover Art by Gil Cohen. See page 410 for art and photo credits.

ISBN 0-03- 050526-7

4   5   6   7   8   9   032   9   8   7

TABLE OF CONTENTS

EVERY CHAPTER HAS
Maintenance: Keeping Fits/Basic Facts Checks/Basic Skills Checks
Review and Testing: Mid-Chapter Reviews/Chapter Reviews/Chapter Tests
Enrichment: Special Topics/Find Outs!/Activities

Off to the Races!

There were **6** drivers in the race.
Juan finished **first**.
The number on Duke's go-cart is **5**.

Numbers can tell *how many*.

1. How many of the drivers are wearing hats?

2. How many of the drivers are wearing jackets?

3. How many of the drivers have four letters in their names?

4. How many drivers are behind Esther?

Numbers can tell *which ones*. Complete.

5. __?__ finished first in the race.

6. Christine finished __?__ in the race.

7. Roy finished __?__ in the race.

8. Susan finished __?__ in the race.

CHAPTER
USING NUMBERS **1**

Numbers can be used as a *name*. Complete.

9. Another name for Christine is number __?__ .

10. Another name for Juan is number __?__ .

11. Another name for Esther is number __?__ .

12. Another name for Duke is number __?__ .

Does the number tell *how many*, tell *which one*, or *name* something?

13. Juan won two medals for the race.

14. The number on Roy's car is 3.

15. The race was on the third day of September.

16. There were 253 people watching the race.

Numbers to 9,999

The length of the Colorado River is about 2,310 km.
This place-value chart shows the first 4 places in our system.

thousands 1,000	hundreds 100	tens 10	ones 1
2	3	1	0

Read: 2 thousand, 310.

A. Read.

  1. 3,500   **2.** 4,085   **3.** 6,001   **4.** 8,204   **5.** 9,218

B. Write standard numerals.

  6. Seven hundred fifty-five   **7.** Six thousand, seventy-one

C. Write word names.

Example	Standard Numeral	Word Name
	42	forty-two

  8. 20   **9.** 33   **10.** 156   **11.** $1.89   **12.** $2.50

Write standard numerals.

1. Two hundred ninety-one

2. One thousand, eight hundred four

3. Three thousand, thirty

4. Nine thousand, five hundred ten

Write word names.

5. 11   **6.** 21   **7.** 36   **8.** 50   **9.** 73

10. 146   **11.** 198   **12.** 207   **13.** $3.62   **14.** $387

★ **15.** How many different three-digit numerals can be written using the digits 1, 2, and 4 one time each?

Basic Facts Review

Add.

1. 0 $+ 7$	**2.** 7 $+ 1$	**3.** 1 $+ 1$	**4.** 9 $+ 0$	**5.** 4 $+ 5$	**6.** 3 $+ 8$	**7.** 2 $+ 2$
8. 1 $+ 0$	**9.** 1 $+ 6$	**10.** 6 $+ 3$	**11.** 4 $+ 8$	**12.** 7 $+ 5$	**13.** 3 $+ 4$	**14.** 8 $+ 2$
15. 5 $+ 5$	**16.** 9 $+ 2$	**17.** 4 $+ 7$	**18.** 7 $+ 3$	**19.** 1 $+ 3$	**20.** 3 $+ 6$	**21.** 8 $+ 3$
22. 4 $+ 6$	**23.** 5 $+ 0$	**24.** 2 $+ 9$	**25.** 9 $+ 3$	**26.** 6 $+ 2$	**27.** 5 $+ 6$	**28.** 6 $+ 6$
29. 6 $+ 5$	**30.** 4 $+ 3$	**31.** 8 $+ 7$	**32.** 7 $+ 7$	**33.** 6 $+ 9$	**34.** 5 $+ 9$	**35.** 8 $+ 8$
36. 7 $+ 6$	**37.** 4 $+ 9$	**38.** 8 $+ 5$	**39.** 9 $+ 5$	**40.** 5 $+ 8$	**41.** 6 $+ 8$	**42.** 6 $+ 7$
43. 7 $+ 9$	**44.** 8 $+ 6$	**45.** 7 $+ 8$	**46.** 8 $+ 9$	**47.** 9 $+ 6$	**48.** 9 $+ 9$	**49.** 9 $+ 7$

Numbers to 999,999

The area of Pennsylvania is about 117,870 km².

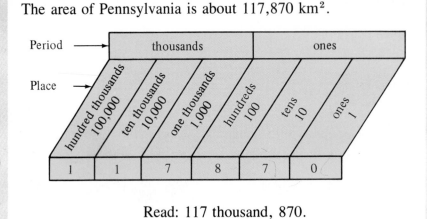

Read: 117 thousand, 870.

A. Look at the place-value chart above.

    1. What digits are in the thousands period?

    2. What digit is in the ten thousands place?

    3. What digit is in the hundreds place?

B. Read.

    4. 10,092   **5.** 25,504   **6.** 104,655   **7.** 452,794

C. In which place is each underlined digit?

    8. 3<u>2</u>,185   **9.** 1<u>3</u>6,498   **10.** <u>3</u>82,055   **11.** 94<u>8</u>,439

> In 389,406, the 8 is in the ten thousands place. The value of the 8 is 8 × 10,000, or 80,000.

D. What is the value of each underlined digit?

    12. 4<u>1</u>,738   **13.** 237,<u>6</u>65   **14.** 5<u>2</u>2,706   **15.** <u>9</u>64,810

E. Write standard numerals.

    Example   Standard Numeral   Expanded Numeral
                529,003   500,000 + 20,000 + 9,000 + 0 + 0 + 3

  16. 900 + 70 + 2   **17.** 40,000 + 2,000 + 0 + 20 + 4

Practice

In which place is each underlined digit?

1. 1$\underline{2}$,813   **2.** 27,$\underline{1}$20   **3.** 38,54$\underline{1}$ **4.** $\underline{4}$2,796

5. 168,$\underline{1}$05   **6.** 2$\underline{5}$1,837   **7.** 394,$\underline{2}$99   **8.** 450,6$\underline{2}$8

9. $\underline{3}$79,281   **10.** 427,$\underline{9}$00   **11.** 6$\underline{2}$1,392   **12.** 898,$\underline{5}$49

What is the value of each underlined digit?

13. 2,2$\underline{6}$0   **14.** $\underline{1}$,506   **15.** $\underline{5}$,184   **16.** 7,83$\underline{8}$

17. $\underline{1}$8,167   **18.** 456,3$\underline{2}$1   **19.** 574,9$\underline{3}$8   **20.** $\underline{9}$0,782

Write standard numerals.

21. 600 + 80 + 3

22. 1,000 + 400 + 30 + 9

23. 80,000 + 0 + 100 + 40 + 4

24. 900,000 + 60,000 + 0 + 0 + 30 + 7

★ **25.** 40 + 9,000 + 0 + 900

★ Write 2 expanded numerals for each.

    Example   283 = 200 + 80 + 3
              283 = (2 × 100) + (8 × 10) + (3 × 1)

26. 486   **27.** 1,572

28. 23,409   **29.** 987,061

Millions and Billions

The planet Neptune is about 4,465,657,600 km from the sun.

billions			millions			thousands			ones		
hundred billions 100,000,000,000	ten billions 10,000,000,000	one billions 1,000,000,000	hundred millions 100,000,000	ten millions 10,000,000	one millions 1,000,000	hundred thousands 100,000	ten thousands 10,000	one thousands 1,000	hundreds 100	tens 10	ones 1
		4	4	6	5	6	5	7	6	0	0

Read: 4 billion, 465 million, 657 thousand, 600.

A. In which place is each underlined digit?

1. 17**5**,387,392

2. 402,30**1**,500

3. 263,928,6**1**0,000

4. 7**4**9,281,131,039

B. Read each numeral in Items 1–4.

These are the word names for the standard numeral 24,000,000,000.

Short Word Name: 24 billion.
      Word Name: twenty-four billion

C. Write the standard numeral.

5. 12 million

6. 64 million

7. 90 million

8. 46 billion

9. 673 billion

10. 1 billion

11. Ninety-seven million, four hundred twenty-five thousand

12. Four billion, seven hundred forty million, fifty-six

In which place is each underlined digit?

1. 776,2<u>4</u>9,618   **2.** 8<u>4</u>2,542,221   **3.** <u>3</u>04,235,380

4. 674,231,2<u>7</u>8   **5.** 5<u>9</u>0,204,481   **6.** <u>4</u>00,369,186

7. 424,068,<u>6</u>00,342   **8.** 569,701,5<u>6</u>0,000   **9.** 701,2<u>3</u>6,501,271

Write standard numerals.

10. 6 million   **11.** 59 million   **12.** 241 million   **13.** 306 million

14. 57 billion   **15.** 60 billion   **16.** 91 billion   **17.** 806 billion

18. Three million, sixty thousand, thirty-seven

19. Seventy-six million, eight hundred seventy thousand

20. Two hundred fifty million, six hundred fifty-four

21. Fifty-two billion

22. Ninety billion, ninety million

23. Six hundred twenty-eight billion

★ **24.** In 568,793,845, what is the value of the 6?

 ★ Solve.

25. Earth is about
100,000,000 + 40,000,000 + 8,000,000 + 800,000 + 0 + 0 + 0
+ 0 + 0 km from the sun. Write this as a standard numeral.

Write word names. *(2)*

1. 38 **2.** 45 **3.** $6.97 **4.** 403

In which place is each underlined digit? *(4, 6)*

5. 54,3<u>1</u>9 **6.** 2<u>7</u>0,841 **7.** 5<u>3</u>,417,598 **8.** <u>2</u>31,470,472

Write standard numerals.

9. Eight hundred sixty-two
(2)

10. Three thousand, eighty
(2)

11. 5,000 + 300 + 30 + 9
(4)

12. 200,000 + 40,000 + 0 + 600 + 40 + 2
(4)

13. 416 million
(6)

14. 29 million
(6)

15. 506 billion
(6)

16. 87 billion
(6)

Basic Facts Review

Subtract.

1. 12 − 3 **2.** 10 − 1 **3.** 3 − 2 **4.** 10 − 6 **5.** 6 − 2 **6.** 11 − 6 **7.** 9 − 3

8. 4 − 1 **9.** 9 − 2 **10.** 11 − 5 **11.** 7 − 6 **12.** 10 − 8 **13.** 6 − 3 **14.** 10 − 7

15. 12 − 4 **16.** 7 − 5 **17.** 9 − 7 **18.** 3 − 0 **19.** 6 − 4 **20.** 12 − 7 **21.** 9 − 5

22. 7 − 7 **23.** 11 − 4 **24.** 8 − 5 **25.** 12 − 8 **26.** 5 − 2 **27.** 6 − 5 **28.** 8 − 4

29. 14 − 6 **30.** 18 − 9 **31.** 13 − 5 **32.** 15 − 6 **33.** 14 − 7 **34.** 16 − 9 **35.** 13 − 8

36. 13 − 6 **37.** 14 − 8 **38.** 15 − 8 **39.** 13 − 9 **40.** 17 − 8 **41.** 15 − 9 **42.** 16 − 8

Playing with Numbers

Materials: paper, pencil, scissors, tape

Trace this pattern for a cube.
Cut along the solid lines.
Fold along the dotted lines.
Then tape the corners.

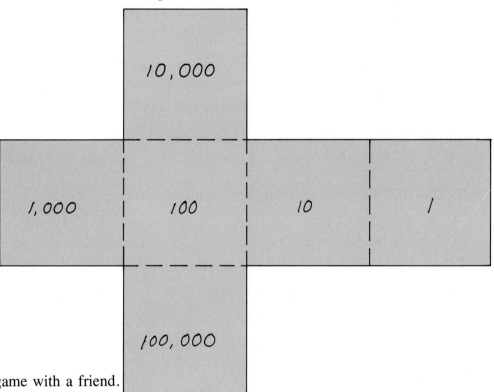

Play this game with a friend.

1. Make a score sheet like the one shown.

2. Each player tosses the cube 6 times. The other player keeps score using tally marks.

3. Find the total score for each player. The player with the highest score wins.

Players	100,000	10,000	1,000	100	10	1	Total
John		I	II	I	I	I	12,111
Linda	I		I	I	I II		101,130

Problem Solving

Dan sold 25 birthday cards and 19 valentine cards. How many cards did he sell in all?

Which number sentence fits the problem?

25 + 19 = □   25 − 19 = □   25 × 19 = □

PLAN: Which operation should be used? Addition
So, 25 + 19 = □ fits the problem.

A. Helen bought ornaments for $3.56 and string for $1.36. What was the total amount of her purchase?

   1. PLAN: Which operation should be used?

   2. Which number sentence fits the problem?
      $3.56 − $1.36 = □ $3.56 + $1.36 = □ $3.56 × $1.36 = □

B. Choose the number sentence that fits the problem.

   3. There are 9 cups in a box. There are 3 boxes. How many cups are there in all?

      9 × 3 = □
      9 + 3 = □
      9 ÷ 3 = □

   4. There were 24 birthday candles in a box. Lee used 12 candles. How many candles are there in the box now?

      24 − 12 = □
      24 × 12 = □
      24 + 12 = □

Choose the number sentence that fits the problem.

1. Baseball cards cost 25¢ for each package. What is the cost of 9 packages?

    25¢ + 25¢ + 25¢ = □
    25¢ × 9 = □
    25¢ ÷ 9 = □

2. Roy is buying party favors that cost $1.98 plus $0.13 tax. What is the total cost?

    $1.98 + $0.13 = □
    $1.98 ÷ $0.13 = □
    $1.98 − $0.13 = □

3. There are 48 calculators in a case. There are 6 cases. How many calculators are there in all?

    48 × 6 = □
    48 + 6 = □
    48 − 6 = □

4. Tracy bought 3 pens for $1.77. Each pen was the same price. How much did each pen cost?

    $1.77 × 3 = □
    $1.77 + $1.77 = □
    $1.77 ÷ 3 = □

5. 128 Sunday newspapers were delivered to the store. 109 were sold. How many were left?

    128 + 109 = □
    128 − 109 = □
    128 × 109 = □

6. Martha bought 3 flashlights. Each one cost $1.20. How much did they cost in all?

    $1.20 + 3 = □
    $1.20 + $1.20 = □
    $1.20 × 3 = □

Comparing Numbers

Mrs. O'Hara is planning a trip. The distance from her house to Orlando, Florida, is about 3,234 km. The distance from her house to Miami, Florida, is about 3,504 km. Which is the greater distance?

Compare:
┌─These are the same.─┐
3,234   3,504
└─These are different.─┘
Compare them.

2 is less than 5, so
3,234 is less than 3,504.

Write: 3,234 < 3,504

The distance to Miami, Florida, is the greater distance.

A. Look at the numbers: 24,679
                             25,342

  1. Are the ten thousands the same?

  2. Are the thousands the same?

  3. Which number is greater?

B. Replace ≡ with >, <, and =.

  4. Compare 4 6,5 9 2 and 4 6,1 4 5.
      5 > 1, so 46,592 ≡ 46,145

  5. Compare 1 2 3,1 3 6 and 1 2 8,0 0 1.
      3 < 8, so 123,136 ≡ 128,001

> **THINK**
>
> 5 > 1
> 5 is greater than 1.
>
> 3 < 8
> 3 is less than 8.

C. Compare. Use >, <, and =.

  6. 354 ≡ 321   **7.** $58.72 ≡ $59.78   **8.** 8,305 ≡ 8,305

  9. 17,247 ≡ 17,427   **10.** 456,292 ≡ 454,384   **11.** 603,451 ≡ 603,218

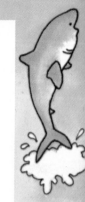

Compare. Use >, <, and =.

1. 78 ▤ 74

2. 35 ▤ 43

3. 629 ▤ 604

4. 957 ▤ 956

5. 5,276 ▤ 5,294

6. 1,056 ▤ 1,056

7. $62.48 ▤ $79.62

8. 3,345 ▤ 3,435

9. 30,276 ▤ 28,796

10. 44,692 ▤ 44,623

11. $732.98 ▤ $772.98

12. 34,118 ▤ 34,112

13. 297,284 ▤ 297,290

14. 688,484 ▤ 688,384

15. 276,450 ▤ 267,450

16. 347,050 ▤ 307,050

★ Solve.

17. Mrs. O'Hara drove 413 km the first day. The second day she drove 429 km. Which day did did she drive farther?

18. During the last 5 years, Mrs. O'Hara has spent $1,269, $1,301, $1,390, $1,290, and $1,260 for vacations. Order the amounts from largest to smallest.

Rounding Numbers

Lisa counted 370 model airplanes at the hobby show.

370 is an exact number found by counting. Numbers are rounded to tell **about** how many. 370 can be rounded to the nearest hundred.

There were **about** 400 airplanes at the show.

A. Look at the number line.

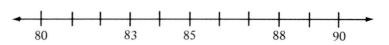

1. Is 83 closer to 80 or 90?
   83 rounded to the nearest ten is 80.

2. Is 88 closer to 80 or 90?
   88 rounded to the nearest ten is 90.

3. Is 85 closer to 80 or 90?

   ▶ A number halfway between two numbers is rounded up to the greater number.
   85 rounded to the nearest ten is 90.

B. Round to the nearest ten or ten cents.

4. 19   5. 24   6. $0.58   7. 65   8. $0.72

C. Round to the nearest hundred or dollar.

[HINT: Use the underlined digit where shown to help you.]

9. 2<u>3</u>8   10. 5<u>89</u>   11. $6.<u>1</u>6   12. 851   13. $9.47

D. Round to the nearest thousand.

[HINT: Use the underlined digit where shown to help you.]

14. 2,<u>3</u>64   15. 3,<u>1</u>78   16. 5,<u>6</u>25   17. 7,738   18. 9,972

Round to the nearest ten or ten cents.

1. 31   **2.** 52   **3.** 49   **4.** $0.26   **5.** 85   **6.** 63

7. 78   **8.** $0.19   **9.** 58   ★ **10.** 145   ★ **11.** 273   ★ **12.** 355

Round to the nearest hundred or dollar.

13. 135   **14.** 256   **15.** $3.22   **16.** 351   **17.** $4.16

18. 409   **19.** 967   ★ **20.** 1,523   ★ **21.** 1,786   ★ **22.** 3,777

Round to the nearest thousand.

23. 1,385   **24.** 2,531   **25.** 2,876   **26.** 3,978   **27.** 6,423

28. 4,321   **29.** 7,508   ★ **30.** 13,139   ★ **31.** 15,732   ★ **32.** 17,196

★ What digits would make these true?

33. 5 ☐ 4 would be rounded to 600.   **34.** 8 ☐ 2 would be rounded to 800.

Basic Facts Review

Multiply.

1. 3×4 **2.** 8×2 **3.** 1×7 **4.** 4×6 **5.** 2×2 **6.** 7×3 **7.** 5×1

8. 6×3 **9.** 3×5 **10.** 4×7 **11.** 5×6 **12.** 0×9 **13.** 3×8 **14.** 2×5

15. 5×5 **16.** 2×0 **17.** 3×1 **18.** 4×4 **19.** 9×2 **20.** 9×3 **21.** 4×0

22. 4×5 **23.** 6×5 **24.** 8×3 **25.** 4×8 **26.** 7×6 **27.** 8×8 **28.** 9×5

29. 8×7 **30.** 9×9 **31.** 8×9 **32.** 7×9 **33.** 8×6 **34.** 6×6 **35.** 5×8

Rounding Larger Numbers

Look at this chart.

	Number	Is the digit to the right 5 or larger?	Round to
Round to the nearest ten thousand.	4̲8,953	48,953 YES	50,000
Round to the nearest hundred thousand.	3̲28,491	32̲4,491 NO	300,000
Round to the nearest million.	2̲6,831,208	26,831,208 YES	27,000,000

A. Round to the nearest ten thousand.

    1. 52,978   **2.** 87,342   **3.** 33,000   **4.** 89,000

    5. 165,000   **6.** 258,163   **7.** 384,062   **8.** 426,008

    9. 596,000   **10.** 628,951   **11.** 792,861   **12.** 798,001

B. Round to the nearest hundred thousand.

    13. 275,953   **14.** 749,353   **15.** 670,000   **16.** 809,487

    17. 1,346,008   **18.** 1,886,001   **19.** 2,364,022   **20.** 3,806,042

    21. 4,006,000   **22.** 5,521,933   **23.** 6,782,097   **24.** 7,962,581

C. Round to the nearest million.

    25. 3,485,739   **26.** 5,781,564   **27.** 8,241,963

    28. 16,592,350   **29.** 21,422,344   **30.** 28,986,000

    31. 32,061,552   **32.** 39,016,446   **33.** 55,592,000

Round to the nearest ten thousand.

1.
17,594

2.
33,914

3.
35,225

4.
58,296

5.
139,901

6.
192,954

7.
255,913

8.
387,007

Round to the nearest hundred thousand.

9.
241,531

10.
318,459

11.
370,225

12.
678,902

13.
1,541,839

14.
1,796,813

15.
2,689,690

16.
4,386,920

Round to the nearest million.

17.
2,867,500

18.
3,486,156

19.
5,734,200

20.
6,388,000

Roman Numerals

The ancient Romans used numerals different than ours.

Roman Numerals	I	V	X	L	C	D	M
Our Numerals	1	5	10	50	100	500	1,000

A. Write our numerals.

Example　M　CCC　L　XXX　V
$\downarrow$　$\downarrow$　$\downarrow$　$\downarrow$　$\downarrow$
1,000 + 300 + 50 + 30 + 5　or　1,385

1. CVIII

2. MCCCLXI

3. MMI

4. MMMCCXXX

The Romans used subtraction in six special cases.
Here are four of them.

IV means 5 − 1, or 4.　　　XL means 50 − 10, or 40.
IX means 10 − 1, or 9.　　　CM means 1,000 − 100, or 900.

B. Here are the other two cases. Complete.

5. XC means 100 − 10, or __?__ .

6. CD means 500 − 100, or __?__ .

Here is how to use the special cases.

　　　　MCMLXIX

M　(CM)　L　X　(IX)
1,000 + 900 + 50 + 10 + 9
　　　　1,969

Steps

1. Circle special cases.
2. Show our numeral.
3. Add.

C. Write our numerals.

7. CCLXXIV

8. DCCIX

9. CMXLII

D. Write Roman numerals for our numerals.

Example　2,197 is written as MMCXCVII

10. 604

11. 1,565

12. 2,979

13. 3,433

Write our numerals.

1. VII   2. IX   3. XI   4. XV

5. XXXIX   6. XLIX   7. XCV   8. LXI

9. CLXIV   10. CCLXX   11. DCC   12. DXC

13. MCDII   14. MCMLXV   15. MCMIX   16. MCDXLIX

Write Roman numerals.

17. 4   18. 8   19. 26   20. 38

21. 53   22. 48   23. 90   24. 99

25. 143   26. 150   27. 405   28. 966

29. 1,400   30. 1,982   31. 2,979   32. 3,027

Solve.

33. The date on the cornerstone is MCMLXX. When was the building built?

Basic Facts Review

Divide.

1. $5\overline{)5}$ 2. $4\overline{)16}$ 3. $6\overline{)24}$ 4. $4\overline{)8}$ 5. $3\overline{)27}$ 6. $2\overline{)0}$

7. $8\overline{)24}$ 8. $8\overline{)0}$ 9. $3\overline{)18}$ 10. $1\overline{)8}$ 11. $2\overline{)6}$ 12. $4\overline{)28}$

13. $6\overline{)12}$ 14. $4\overline{)24}$ 15. $2\overline{)16}$ 16. $3\overline{)3}$ 17. $3\overline{)24}$ 18. $3\overline{)12}$

19. $1\overline{)4}$ 20. $6\overline{)30}$ 21. $4\overline{)32}$ 22. $5\overline{)25}$ 23. $7\overline{)28}$ 24. $9\overline{)18}$

25. $6\overline{)36}$ 26. $7\overline{)42}$ 27. $9\overline{)63}$ 28. $7\overline{)49}$ 29. $5\overline{)40}$ 30. $8\overline{)72}$

31. $7\overline{)56}$ 32. $5\overline{)35}$ 33. $4\overline{)36}$ 34. $7\overline{)35}$ 35. $9\overline{)54}$ 36. $8\overline{)56}$

Problem Solving • Librarians

Topic	Number of Books	Number of Books Borrowed
Mathematics Games	219	190
Hobbies	2,342	1,349
Sports	2,337	1,954
Biographies	852	852
Science Fiction	3,804	3,698
Travel	683	650

Solve. Use the table.

1. Mr. Sanchez, the school librarian, keeps a record of the number of books borrowed. How many books on travel were borrowed? Write a word name for this number.

2. How many biographies were borrowed at least once? Round this number to the nearest hundred.

3. Mr. Sanchez ordered plastic covers for all the science fiction books. He rounded the number of science fiction books to the nearest thousand. How many plastic covers did he order?

4. Which area has the greater number of books—hobbies or sports?

5. Class 6A had a total of $105 in fines for overdue books. Write this amount in words.

Write word names. *(2)*

1. 18   **2.** 41   **3.** 367

In which place is each underlined digit? *(4, 6)*

4. 26,4̲23   **5.** 6̲8,352   **6.** 7,695̲,321

What is the value of each underlined digit? *(4)*

7. 3̲,601   **8.** 8,48̲7   **9.** 9̲0,450

Write standard numerals.

10. Three hundred sixty-four
(2)

11. Three thousand, fifty
(2)

12. 80,000 + 0 + 200 + 40 + 5
(4)

13. 600,000 + 0 + 3,000 + 0 + 60 + 3
(4)

14. 6 million
(6)

15. 42 million
(6)

Compare. Use >, <, and =. *(12)*

16. 927 ☰ 954   **17.** 32,140 ☰ 32,145

18. Round 857 to the nearest hundred.
(14)

19. Round 2,787 to the nearest thousand.
(14)

20. Round $6.06 to the nearest dollar.
(14)

Write our numerals *(18)*

21. XXIV   **22.** LIX   **23.** XCVI

Solve. *(20)*

24. Alan read 29 books during summer vacation. Write a word name for this number.

25. One book for the library cost $8.89. Round this number to the nearest dollar.

Write word names. *(2)*

1. 27   **2.** $9.50   **3.** 2,750

In which place is each underlined digit? *(4, 6)*

4. 4̲3,158   **5.** 2̲79,414   **6.** 2̲,539,134

What is the value of each underlined digit? *(4)*

7. 5,6̲29   **8.** 34̲,523   **9.** 89̲2,450

Write standard numerals.

10. Two hundred eighty-one
(2)

11. Ninety-nine thousand
(2)

12. 8,000 + 0 + 60 + 2
(4)

13. 700,000 + 0 + 4,000 + 500 + 0 + 6
(4)

14. 36 million
(6)

15. 5 billion
(6)

Compare. Use >, <, and =. *(12)*

16. 8,529 ≡ 8,530   **17.** 45,299 ≡ 42,599

18. Round 624 to the nearest hundred.
(14)

19. Round 4,726 to the nearest thousand.
(14)

20. Round $4.57 to the nearest dollar.
(14)

Write our numerals. *(18)*

21. XLII   **22.** LXVI   **23.** XVIII

Solve. *(20)*

24. The librarian received $89.71 in fines for overdue books last
month. Write this amount in words.

25. The library has 89 books on science fiction. Round this number
to the nearest ten.

Basic Skills Check

1.

$$\begin{array}{r} 17 \\ +\ 2 \\ \hline \end{array}$$

A 9   B 19
C 29   D 39

2.

$$\begin{array}{r} 29 \\ -\ 4 \\ \hline \end{array}$$

E 22   F 23
G 25   H 27

3.

$$\begin{array}{r} 42 \\ \times\ 2 \\ \hline \end{array}$$

A 44   B 48
C 84   D 88

4.

$30 \div 6 = \underline{\quad?\quad}$

E 3   F 5
G 6   H 10

5.

$7\overline{)49}$

A 5   B 6
C 7   D 8

6.

$34 + 5 = \underline{\quad?\quad}$

E 38   F 39
G 54   H 93

7.

$40 \times 2 = \underline{\quad?\quad}$

A 20   B 24
C 42   D 80

8.

$98 \times 1 = \underline{\quad?\quad}$

E 1   F 89
G 98   H 108

9.

$$\begin{array}{r} 28 \\ -\ 16 \\ \hline \end{array}$$

A 11   B 12
C 14   D 22

10.

$5\overline{)25}$

E 3   F 4
G 5   H 20

11.

$$\begin{array}{r} 88 \\ +\ 3 \\ \hline \end{array}$$

A 38   B 81
C 91   D 98

12.

$6\overline{)36}$

E 3   F 6
G 12   H 13

13.

$$\begin{array}{r} 63 \\ -\ 56 \\ \hline \end{array}$$

A 7   B 16
C 17   D 27

14.

$$\begin{array}{r} 35 \\ -\ 6 \\ \hline \end{array}$$

E 28   F 29
G 31   H 38

15.

$6 \times 6 = \underline{\quad?\quad}$

A 36   B 48
C 66   D 72

Adding on a Nomograph

In addition, the numbers that are added are called **addends**. The answer is called the **sum**. This nomograph can be used to find the sum of two addends.

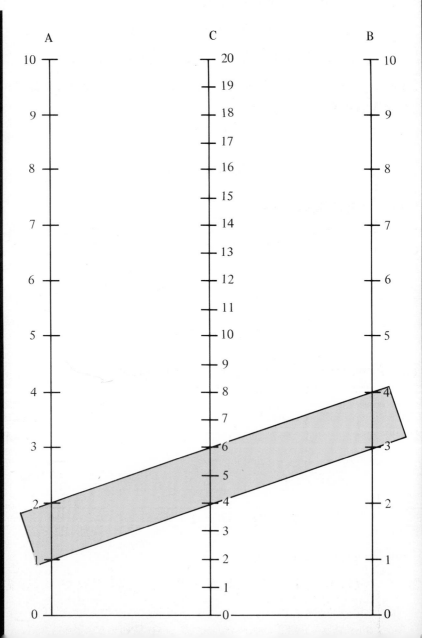

To find 2 + 4 using the nomograph:

1. Find 2 on the A scale. Find 4 on the B scale.

2. Put the edge of a ruler along these two points as shown.

3. Read the sum on the C scale. The edge of the ruler crosses the C scale at 6.

$$2 + 4 = 6$$
$$\uparrow \quad \uparrow \quad \uparrow$$
$$\text{addends} \quad \text{sum}$$

Find each sum, using the nomograph.

1. 6 + 7	**2.** 2 + 3	**3.** 9 + 6	**4.** 7 + 8	**5.** 5 + 6
7 + 6	3 + 2	6 + 9	8 + 7	6 + 5

▶ Changing the order of the addends does not change the sum. This is called the **commutative property of addition.**

$$9 + 8 = 8 + 9$$

Find the sum of the three addends, using the nomograph.
[HINT: Do the work in the parentheses first.]

6. (2 + 1) + 3	**7.** (4 + 1) + 2	**8.** (1 + 3) + 5	**9.** (4 + 1) + 3
2 + (1 + 3)	4 + (1 + 2)	1 + (3 + 5)	4 + (1 + 3)

▶ Changing the grouping of the addends does not change the sum. This is called the **associative property of addition.**

$$(2 + 3) + 4 = 2 + (3 + 4)$$

Find each sum, using the nomograph.

10. 0 + 2   **11.** 0 + 4   **12.** 5 + 0   **13.** 7 + 0   **14.** 8 + 0

▶ When adding 0 and a number, the sum is that number. This is called the **property of zero for addition.**

RACE TIME

Add.

1. 3 + 1	**2.** 5 + 3	**3.** 2 + 2	**4.** 6 + 2	**5.** 4 + 4	**6.** 1 + 5	**7.** 4 + 9
8. 7 + 7	**9.** 8 + 5	**10.** 3 + 8	**11.** 9 + 1	**12.** 5 + 9	**13.** 6 + 7	**14.** 3 + 5
15. 1 + 9	**16.** 8 + 1	**17.** 9 + 9	**18.** 1 + 1	**19.** 6 + 4	**20.** 9 + 5	**21.** 7 + 1
22. 6 + 9	**23.** 9 + 7	**24.** 0 + 2	**25.** 1 + 6	**26.** 2 + 4	**27.** 7 + 3	**28.** 1 + 7
29. 4 + 6	**30.** 5 + 0	**31.** 8 + 9	**32.** 8 + 2	**33.** 4 + 1	**34.** 2 + 9	**35.** 3 + 2
36. 5 + 4	**37.** 7 + 5	**38.** 5 + 1	**39.** 7 + 9	**40.** 4 + 7	**41.** 2 + 6	**42.** 3 + 9
43. 6 + 3	**44.** 9 + 4	**45.** 5 + 7	**46.** 9 + 6	**47.** 2 + 7	**48.** 6 + 5	**49.** 0 + 6
50. 8 + 6	**51.** 7 + 8	**52.** 4 + 2	**53.** 6 + 8	**54.** 4 + 5	**55.** 8 + 7	**56.** 6 + 6
57. 6 + 0	**58.** 5 + 8	**59.** 3 + 6	**60.** 4 + 3	**61.** 3 + 4	**62.** 8 + 3	**63.** 4 + 8
64. 2 + 5	**65.** 0 + 0	**66.** 2 + 8	**67.** 9 + 3	**68.** 5 + 5	**69.** 1 + 8	**70.** 8 + 4
71. 5 + 2	**72.** 9 + 8	**73.** 7 + 2	**74.** 3 + 3	**75.** 2 + 3	**76.** 1 + 4	**77.** 7 + 6
78. 3 + 7	**79.** 2 + 1	**80.** 7 + 4	**81.** 5 + 6	**82.** 8 + 8	**83.** 1 + 3	**84.** 9 + 2

Knowing the basic facts makes addition easier.

If you know:

$$\begin{array}{r} 7 \\ + 8 \\ \hline 15 \end{array}$$

Then you know:

$$\begin{array}{r} 1\ 7 \\ +\ \ 8 \\ \hline 2\ 5 \end{array} \qquad \begin{array}{r} 2\ 7 \\ +\ \ 8 \\ \hline 3\ 5 \end{array} \qquad \begin{array}{r} 3\ 7 \\ +\ \ 8 \\ \hline 4\ 5 \end{array} \qquad \begin{array}{r} 4\ 7 \\ +\ \ 8 \\ \hline 5\ 5 \end{array} \qquad \text{and more.}$$

Practice

Complete.

1.	2.	3.	4.	5.	6.
$\begin{array}{r} 5 \\ +7 \\ \hline 1 \end{array}$	$\begin{array}{r} 15 \\ +\ 7 \\ \hline 2 \end{array}$	$\begin{array}{r} 35 \\ +\ 7 \\ \hline 4 \end{array}$	$\begin{array}{r} 65 \\ +\ 7 \\ \hline 2 \end{array}$	$\begin{array}{r} 75 \\ +\ 7 \\ \hline 2 \end{array}$	$\begin{array}{r} 95 \\ +\ 7 \\ \hline 2 \end{array}$

7.	8.	9.	10.	11.	12.
$\begin{array}{r} 9 \\ +8 \\ \hline 7 \end{array}$	$\begin{array}{r} 29 \\ +\ 8 \\ \hline 7 \end{array}$	$\begin{array}{r} 49 \\ +\ 8 \\ \hline 7 \end{array}$	$\begin{array}{r} 69 \\ +\ 8 \\ \hline 7 \end{array}$	$\begin{array}{r} 89 \\ +\ 8 \\ \hline 7 \end{array}$	$\begin{array}{r} 99 \\ +\ 8 \\ \hline 10 \end{array}$

Add.

13.	14.	15.	16.	17.	18.
$\begin{array}{r} 5 \\ +8 \end{array}$	$\begin{array}{r} 25 \\ +\ 8 \end{array}$	$\begin{array}{r} 35 \\ +\ 8 \end{array}$	$\begin{array}{r} 45 \\ +\ 8 \end{array}$	$\begin{array}{r} 65 \\ +\ 8 \end{array}$	$\begin{array}{r} 85 \\ +\ 8 \end{array}$

19.	20.	21.	22.	23.	24.
$\begin{array}{r} 7 \\ +9 \end{array}$	$\begin{array}{r} 17 \\ +\ 9 \end{array}$	$\begin{array}{r} 37 \\ +\ 9 \end{array}$	$\begin{array}{r} 57 \\ +\ 9 \end{array}$	$\begin{array}{r} 87 \\ +\ 9 \end{array}$	$\begin{array}{r} 97 \\ +\ 9 \end{array}$

Column Addition

Mark returned 4 mystery books, 2 poetry books, 6 novels, and 8 biographies to the library. How many books did he return?

To add these numbers, Mark looked for sums of 10.

4
2 ⟩10
6 ⟩10
+ 8
———
20

REMEMBER: Changing the order and grouping of addends does not change the sum.

He returned 20 books.

A. Add $7 + 2 + 3 + 4 + 8$.

Three students found the sum using different ways.

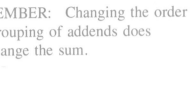

Dot		*Betsy*		*Mark*	
7		7 ↑ 24		7 ⟩10	
2	9	2 | 17		2	
3	12	3 | 15		3	
4	16	4 | 12		4 ⟩10	
+ 8	↓ 24	+ 8 |		+ 8	
24		24		24	

1. Dot added down. What was her sum?

2. How did Betsy find the sum?

3. How did Mark find the sum?

B. Add.

4.	**5.**	**6.**	**7.**	**8.**
6	4	5	3	3
9	3	4	5	8
+ 4	6	9	5	6
	+ 2	8	2	5
		+ 1	+ 8	7
				+ 0

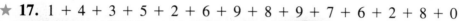

Add.

1.	**2.**	**3.**	**4.**	**5.**	**6.**	**7.**
3	6	7	9	1	4	1
9	6	5	5	5	9	3
+ 7	+ 4	+ 2	8	9	7	4
			+ 2	+ 7	+ 6	+ 6

8.	**9.**	**10.**	**11.**	**12.**	**13.**	**14.**
5	9	3	2	4	2	1
5	8	9	7	2	9	4
2	9	8	8	6	0	8
5	9	7	5	5	8	2
+ 3	+ 6	+ 5	+ 3	4	3	9
				+ 3	+ 1	+ 6

15. 4 + 2 + 5 + 4 + 6 + 9

16. 1 + 5 + 9 + 8 + 6 + 2

★ **17.** 1 + 4 + 3 + 5 + 2 + 6 + 9 + 8 + 9 + 7 + 6 + 2 + 8 + 0

Solve.

18. Betsy and Mark worked on a project together. They used 4 history books, 8 science books, and 3 encyclopedias. How many books did they use in all?

19. Betsy and Mark worked together 4 hours on Monday, 2 hours on Tuesday, 5 hours on Wednesday, 2 hours on Thursday, and 3 hours on Friday. How many hours did they work in all?

Renaming in Addition

Add 39 + 46.

THINK

ADD ONES
RENAME 15

Tens	Ones
1	
3	9
+ 4	6
	5

ADD TENS

Tens	Ones
1	
3	9
+ 4	6
8	5

WRITE

```
  1
  39
+ 46
  85
```

15 = 1 ten and 5 ones

A. Find 175 + 263. Complete.

1. Add ones. 5 + 3 = __?__

2. Add tens. 7 + 6 = __?__ tens

3. Rename 13 tens. __?__ hundred and __?__ tens

4. Add hundreds. 1 + 1 + 2 = ____ hundreds

5. What is the sum?

WRITE
```
   1
  175
+ 263
  438  ← Sum
```

Here is how to add $8.25 + $2.59.

Step 1 Add.

```
    1
$ 8.25
+ 2.59
  10 84
```

Step 2 Place the money notation.

```
    1
$ 8.25
+ 2.59
$10.84
```

B. Add.

6. $ 1.25	**7.** $ 4.67	**8.** $ 8.79	**9.** $ 9.28	**10.** $ 3.68	**11.** $ 0.86
+ 3.48	+ 3.51	+ 2.14	+ 2.75	+ 7.56	+ 4.01

C. Add.

12. 48	**13.** 125	**14.** $ 2.15	**15.** 847	**16.** 69	**17.** 386
+ 23	+ 236	0.26	92	723	4
		+ 5.40	+ 400	+ 45	+ 87

Add.

1. 65
  + 28

2. 74
  + 16

3. 97
  + 74

4. $ 0.73
  + 0.69

5. 637
  + 145

6. 784
  + 106

7. 619
  + 29

8. $ 3.94
  + 0.55

9. 363
  + 719

10. 629
  + 288

11. 492
  + 938

12. $ 2.24
  + 9.78

13. 38
   14
  + 31

14. 29
   21
  + 33

15. 61
    8
  + 19

16. $ 0.42
   0.18
  + 0.80

17. 293
   183
  + 561

18. 169
   240
  + 369

19. 368
   514
  + 175

20. $ 3.86
   6.49
  + 3.19

21. 862
   81
  + 614

22. 460
   275
  + 624

23. 401
    7
  + 83

24. $ 3.94
   0.57
  + 7.36

25. 47
  + 64

26. 146
   371
  + 258

27. $ 7.84
  + 3.65

28. 47
   39
  + 26

29. $ 3.79
   0.92
  + 1.12

30. 98
   37
  + 8

★ Find the missing digits.

31. 9 5
   1 ?
  + ? 6
  ─────
   1 8 9

32. 5 1 9
   6 ? 1
  + ? 7 2
  ───────
   2,1 3 2

33. 6 7 6
   8 ? ?
  + ? 8 7
  ───────
   2,0 6 7

34. ? 9 6
   8 ?
  + 9 ? 8
  ───────
   1,1 4 6

35. 8 6 7
   ? 9 ?
  + 4 ? 2
  ───────
   2,1 4 2

36. 9 ? 3
   ? 4 6
  + 8 6 ?
  ───────
   2,5 7 1

Solve.

37. In three days, Dan spent $9.75, $8.75, and $9.80. How much did he spend in all?

38. Dan bowled three games on Saturday. He scored 186, 93, and 154. What was his total score for that day?

Add. *(28, 30)*

1.	2.	3.	4.	5.	6.	7.
5	6	9	6	8	1	7
9	4	2	7	2	5	6
+ 2	+ 3	2	1	9	2	8
		+ 4	+ 2	2	5	4
				+ 3	+ 8	3
						+ 9

8. 4 + 6 + 7 + 1 **9.** 7 + 8 + 9 + 2 + 3

10.	11.	12.	13.	14.	15.
27	$ 0.79	461	547	829	784
+ 89	+ 0.43	+ 372	+ 629	+ 943	+ 975

16.	17.	18.	19.	20.	21.
46	87	65	75	86	7
35	92	59	5	7	36
+ 18	+ 12	+ 90	+ 56	+ 9	+ 9

22.	23.	24.	25.	26.	27.
$ 0.78	647	$ 5.47	987	$ 4.50	975
0.42	223	3.98	26	0.85	362
+ 0.95	+ 781	+ 1.25	+ 5	+ 2.46	+ 98

Find Out!

Calculator Activity

Find the important dates according to the code. Use only addition.

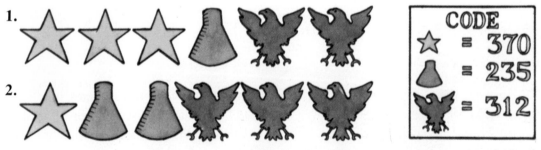

CODE
☆ ≡ 370
🔺 ≡ 235
🦅 ≡ 312

What important events happened in each of these years?

What is the value of each underlined digit?

1. 694,789   **2.** 53,806   **3.** 37,199,694

4. 160,715,436   **5.** 2,595,378   **6.** 474,088,152

Write standard numerals.

7. 80 + 6   **8.** Thirty-four   **9.** Ninety-seven

10. 66 million   **11.** 2,000 + 0 + 0 + 5   **12.** 15 billion

13. Five hundred sixty-three   **14.** 70,000 + 9,000 + 200 + 40 + 8

15. Four hundred twenty-five million   **16.** Thirty-six billion

17. Twenty-one million, thirty-eight thousand

Write our numerals.

18. C   **19.** X   **20.** V   **21.** L

22. M   **23.** D   **24.** IX   **25.** XXVI

26. XL   **27.** LXIX   **28.** XC   **29.** XCV

Compare. Use >, <, or = .

30. 71 ≡ 75   **31.** 93 ≡ 84   **32.** 109 ≡ 111   **33.** 472 ≡ 468

34. 6,014 ≡ 6,020   **35.** 87,312 ≡ 88,326

36. 226,344 ≡ 226,506   **37.** 719,948 ≡ 721,032

Round to the nearest hundred.

38. 359   **39.** 619   **40.** 281   **41.** 850

Round to the nearest thousand.

42. 9,498   **43.** 4,619   **44.** 3,337   **45.** 7,901

46. 5,250   **47.** 8,536   **48.** 2,893   **49.** 6,715

Round to the nearest dollar.

50. $6.49   **51.** $4.90   **52.** $9.13   **53.** $3.61

Problem Solving

There were 23 circus posters on one wall. There were 9 posters on another wall. How many posters were there in all? Write a number sentence that fits the problem.

Step 1   READ
How many posters on one wall?   23
How many posters on the other wall?   9
What is asked?   How many in all?
Step 2   PLAN
What operation should be used?   Addition

Write a number sentence.
23 + 9 = □

A. The circus traveled 1,219 km in May and 853 km in June. How many kilometers did the circus travel in all?

   1. How many kilometers did the circus travel in May?

   2. How many kilometers did the circus travel in June?

   3. What is asked?

   4. Write a number sentence that fits the problem.

B. One of the elephants is 4,172 kg. Another elephant is 3,309 kg. Find the difference.

   5. How many kilograms is one of the elephants?

   6. How many kilograms is the other elephant?

   7. What is asked?

   8. Write a number sentence that fits the problem.

Write number sentences.

1. On Monday, 1,532 tickets were sold. One Tuesday, 2,156 tickets were sold. How many tickets were sold in all?

2. Alan sold 89 programs. Kathy sold 152 programs. How many more programs did Kathy sell?

3. The acrobats practiced 2 hours a day for 5 days. How many hours did they practice in all?

4. In the center ring, there were 12 acrobats, 8 clowns, and 9 jugglers. How many performers were in the ring?

5. Mrs. O'Gara spent $18.96 for 3 tickets. How much was each ticket?

6. Phineas T. Barnum formed a circus in the United States in 1871. How many years ago was this circus formed?

7. There were 432 students at the circus one day. The next day there were 589. How many students saw the circus during the two days?

Find Out!
Brainteaser

Use the digits 1, 3, and 4 and a plus sign only once to write a name for each of these numbers.

1. 35   2. 17   3. 44

Flow Charting

A flow chart shows how to do something. Each shape indicates a simple step. This flow chart shows how to go to the library on a bus.

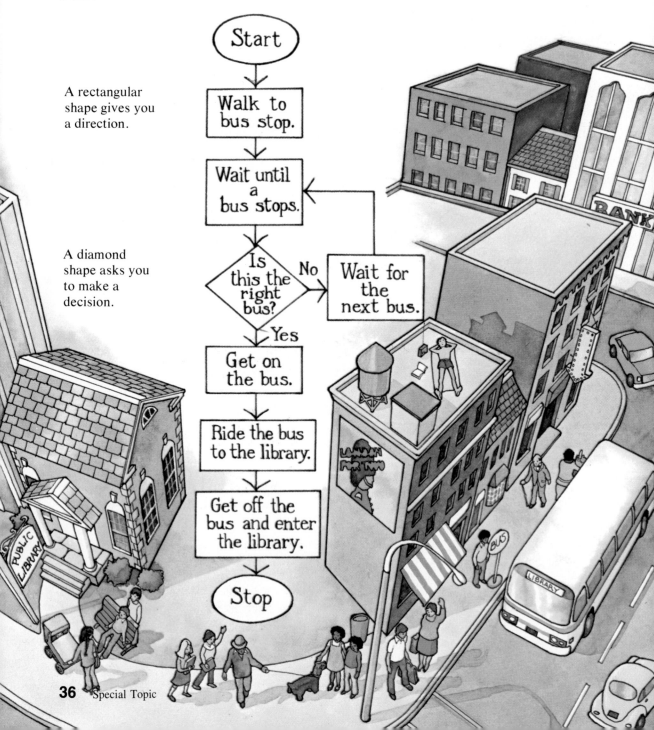

A rectangular shape gives you a direction.

A diamond shape asks you to make a decision.

Start

Walk to bus stop.

Wait until a bus stops.

Is this the right bus? — No → Wait for the next bus.

Yes

Get on the bus.

Ride the bus to the library.

Get off the bus and enter the library.

Stop

Use the flow chart for taking a bus to answer these questions.

1. What is the next step after walking to the bus stop?

2. The wrong bus stops. What is the next step?

3. These are steps for heating a can of soup. Put them in the correct order. Then make a flow chart.

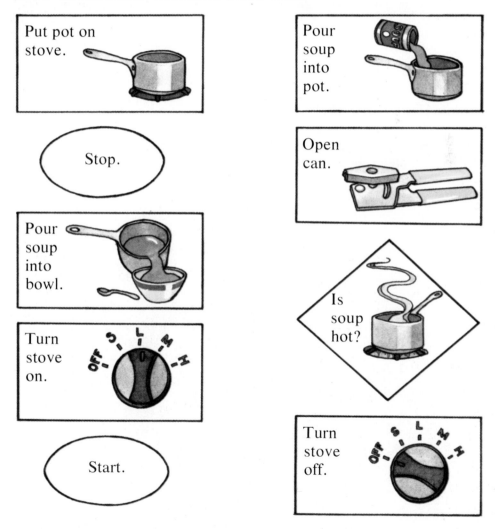

★ 4. Make a flow chart for preparing a grilled cheese sandwich.

Adding Larger Numbers

Add 4,569 + 1,852. Follow these steps.

Step 1 ADD ONES	Step 2 ADD TENS	Step 3 ADD HUNDREDS	Step 4 ADD THOUSANDS
1 4,5 6 9 + 1,8 5 2 ——— 1	1 1 4,5 6 9 + 1,8 5 2 ——— 2 1	1 1 1 4,5 6 9 + 1,8 5 2 ——— 4 2 1	1 1 1 4,5 6 9 + 1,8 5 2 ——— 6,4 2 1

A. Complete.

1. $\overset{1}{}$ $ 92.35
   + 24.06
   ———
   6.41

2. $\overset{1}{}$ 62,842
   + 79,321
   ———
   163

3. $\overset{1}{}$ 14,922
   + 30,455
   ———
   377

4. $\overset{1}{}$ 83,910
   + 1,650
   ———
   560

5. $\overset{1}{}$ 27,406
   + 3,517
   ———
   3

B. Add. First write the addends in vertical form. Be sure to line up the numbers correctly.

Example   47,365 + 2,345 + 4,892

$$\begin{array}{r} \overset{1\;1\;\;2\;1}{47,365} \\ 2,345 \\ +\;\;4,892 \\ \hline 54,602 \end{array}$$

6. 43,651 + 29,327 + 1,420

7. 48,296 + 345 + 6,728

We can check addition by adding up.

ADD DOWN	ADD UP
12,795	12,795
59,234	59,234
+ 23,817	+ 23,817
———	———
95,846	95,846

C. Add and check by adding up.

8. 3,789
   + 2,558
   ———

9. $ 452.35
   + 614.64
   ———

10. 36,253
    11,998
    + 20,456
    ———

11. $ 724.12
    14.73
    + 39.53
    ———

12. 75,873
    4,914
    + 6,895
    ———

Add.

1. 8,154
   + 1,306

2. 9,145
   + 1,832

3. 6,428
   + 345

4. $ 26.87
   + 84.25

5. 5,629
   + 398

6. 32,345
   + 26,061

7. 17,840
   + 2,695

8. 35,864
   + 96,289

9. $ 520.36
   + 849.50

10. 48,341
   + 2,785

11. 2,654
   4,201
   + 1,004

12. 3,357
   2,140
   + 2,891

13. 32,610
   14,056
   + 18,317

14. $ 473.57
   21.46
   118.95
   + 21.05

15. 5,154
   1,068
   6,007
   + 7,996

16. 4,752
   + 3,896

17. 14,257
   1,874
   + 62,501

18. 22,821
   + 6,475

19. $ 660.78
   + 212.11

20. 55,626
   41,910
   + 69,784

21. 42,687
   5,421
   3,485
   + 5,253

22. 3,597
   8,620
   + 5,810

23. 6,428
   2,051
   + 328

24. 22,955
   + 31,035

25. $ 623.12
   + 354.49

26. 5,548 + 2,206 + 112 + 1,050   **27.** 23,098 + 54,896 + 4,922

Solve.

★ **28.** 13 + □ = 12 + 13   ★ **29.** (□ + 42) + 54 = 36 + (42 + 54)

30. Marie bought a bike that cost $157.95 and a bike rack that cost
$21.75. How much did she spend in all?

Adding Hundred Thousands

A galaxy ship patrols three space stations. There are 326,486 people living on the first station. There are 494,527 people on the second and 684,423 people on the third. What is the total number of people living on the three space stations?

▶ To add larger numbers, follow the steps in addition. Remember to rename where necessary.

```
 211 11
 326,486
 494,527
+ 684,423
1,505,436
```

There are 1,505,436 people living on the three space stations.

A. Complete.

1.
```
   11
 245,346
+100,587
   5,933
```

2.
```
 349,902
+114,364
     66
```

3.
```
    1
 275,463
+ 38,621
     084
```

4.
```
    11
 596,031
+822,589
      20
```

5.
```
  1 11
 789,543
 142,679
+459,346
     568
```

6.
```
 1 11
 504,388
 140,847
+ 27,341
     576
```

7.
```
 1 1
 728,400
  65,796
+ 23,241
     437
```

8.
```
 1  1
 826,302
   8,468
+ 29,723
     493
```

B. Add.

9.
```
$2,009.46
+    14.53
```

10.
```
 456,609
+325,211
```

11.
```
 724,926
+558,950
```

12.
```
$4,278.04
+6,966.55
```

13.
```
 643,535
   2,309
+ 32,144
```

14.
```
 704,592
 633,921
+452,780
```

15.
```
$  145.67
 4,028.65
+8,458.22
```

16.
```
 625,983
  42,576
+ 78,698
```

Add.

1.   546,214
   + 213,185

2. $ 9,645.10
  +   140.59

3.   864,567
   + 231,432

4.   378,401
   + 45,295

5. $ 4,295.51
  + 5,824.48

6.   695,347
   + 244,556

7.   834,235
   +   6,968

8. $ 7,864.69
  + 2,159.83

9.   594,372
   +   7,648

10. $ 4,728.86
   + 2,967.34

11.   387,968
   + 54,952

12.   764,558
   + 359,965

13.   127,395
    237,064
   + 143,826

14.   456,802
     48,795
   + 600,278

15.   348,268
      6,496
   + 25,820

16.   902,579
      4,362
   + 176,784

17.   845,252
     76,041
   + 50,778

18.   578,943
    147,623
   + 204,224

19. $ 7,482.74
     80.92
  +   609.55

20. $ 2,774.15
   3,520.79
  + 1,751.82

21. $ 7,936.11
    425.35
  +   24.79

22.   49,604
   821,456
   + 24,872

23. $ 6,532.10
   4,697.32
  +   59.05

24.   404,219
   280,809
   + 924,267

25.   87,005
     2,321
   + 672,408

26. $ 4,039.74
      56.12
  + 2,113.86

27.   234,597
   + 837,098

28.   225,434
   627,984
   + 38,093

29.   432,624
   129,678
   + 45,238

30.   908,254
   + 684,937

★ **31.**   11,459,210
    42,172,649
   +   2,988

★ **32.**   26,174,355
    16,628,398
   +   2,657

33. 826,945 + 289,259 + 8,927

34. 655,254 + 489,978 + 64,997

Solve.

35. Space station Alpha ordered supplies. They needed 1,152 solar shields, 101,520 drums of fuel, and 5,040 laser drills. How many supplies did they order in all?

36. Last year the galaxy ship Gemini made 432,147 patrols. This year it made 527,572 patrols. How many patrols did it make in two years?

Estimating Sums

Paula's Record Shop received 3 boxes of the latest albums. The boxes contained 50, 48, and 75 albums. Paula estimated the sum by rounding each addend. Then she added to find the total number of albums.

Estimate	50	Exact	50
	50		48
	+ 80		+ 75
	180		173

Look at the sums. Since the sums are close, the exact sum is reasonable.

A. Look at the example, then complete.

Estimate	300	Exact	301
	+ 700		+ 731
	1,000		1,032

1. 301 is rounded to __?__ .

2. 731 is rounded to __?__ .

3. The estimated sum is __?__ .

4. The exact sum is __?__ .

5. Is the exact sum reasonable?

B. Manuel has $14.00 and wants to buy 3 records. They cost $4.25, $6.79, and $0.98. Manuel estimates the total cost.

Step 1 Round the addends to the nearest dollar.
Step 2 Add the rounded addends.

$ 4.25	Estimate	$ 4.00
6.79		7.00
+ 0.98		+ 1.00

6. Does he have enough money?

C. Estimate the sum.

7.	**8.**	**9.**	**10.**	**11.**	**12.**
37	348	359	1,492	605	$ 4.15
+ 25	+ 498	+ 442	+ 2,357	478	+ 8.84
				+ 370	

Estimate the sum.

1. 35 + 48	**2.** 58 + 27	**3.** 25 61 + 47	**4.** 46 11 + 13	**5.** 85 72 + 59	**6.** 34 42 + 18
7. 126 + 455	**8.** 516 + 401	**9.** 1,755 + 2,850	**10.** 350 789 + 478	**11.** 621 843 + 668	★ **12.** 475 310 689 + 999

Round each addend to the nearest dollar. Estimate the sum.

13. $ 8.47 + 1.29	**14.** $ 3.78 + 4.50	**15.** $ 6.95 5.49 + 7.13	**16.** $ 8.50 9.25 + 7.68	**17.** $ 5.50 9.43 + 8.79	**18.** $ 4.50 7.48 + 0.95

Solve.

19. Fran wanted to buy two record racks. They cost $5.89 and $5.29. Estimate the total cost.

20. Joe added 23 + 42 + 55 on his calculator. The answer was 120. What is the estimated sum? Was the calculator answer reasonable?

21. David has $15.00. He wants to buy 3 records for $4.98, $5.65, and $6.39. Estimate the cost of the three records. Does he have enough money?

22. Ellie added 785 + 643 + 379 on her calculator. The answer was 1,807. What is the estimated sum? Was the calculator answer reasonable?

Problem Solving

Solve.

1. In January, 32,384 people visited the museum. In February, 31,375 people came. In which month did more people visit the museum? [HINT: Compare.]

2. There were 105,364 samples in the museum's rock and mineral collection. The director ordered 2,340 more. How many samples will there be in all?

3. Last year the museum spent $15,573 to repair exhibits. This year $18,465 was spent. In which year did the museum spend more?

4. Last year, the museum spent $35,480 to prepare new exhibits. This year it spent $47,565. How much did the museum spend in the two years?

5. The Martino family spent $7.50 on admission, $3.75 on guide books and $9.35 on lunch. Estimate the total expense to the nearest dollar.

6. The museum bookshop had 5,342 books on natural history. The manager received an order of 271 new books. What is the total number of books in stock now?

7. The City Natural History Museum has 15,891 exhibits about animals and 12,983 exhibits about plants. Estimate the total number of exhibits.

8. The museum's busiest days are on the weekend. One weekend 14,605 people came on Friday, 18,423 came on Saturday, and 16,689 came on Sunday. How many people came that weekend?

Add.

1. 8
(28) 5
   + 2
   ___
   15

2. 6
(28) 7
   1
  + 5
  ___
  19

3. 2
(28) 9
   7
   6
  + 3
  ___
  27

4. 7
(28) 4
   8
   9
  + 9
  ___
  37

5. 8
(28) 1
   7
   2
   6
  + 2
  ___
  26

6. 78
(30) + 24
   ____
   102

7. 492
(30) + 765
   _____
   1257

8. $ 5.43
(30) 0.78
   + 6.45
   _____
   12.67

9. 207
(30) 456
   + 53
   _____
   1716
   1221

10. $ 5.26
(30) 8.29
   + 7.43
   _____
   20.48

11. $ 86.51
(38) + 27.48
   _____
   113.99

12. 52,769
(38) + 67,536
   _____
   120 305

13. 82,684
(38) 75,923
   + 30,490
   _____
   199101

14. 67,946
(38) 72,902
   4,521
   + 5,206
   _____
   150 675

15. 735,894
(40) + 326,643
   _____
   1062537

16. 585,276
(40) + 23,340
   _____
   608616

17. $ 1,264.37
(40) + 5,926.81
   _____
   729118

18. 485,237
(40) 12,056
   + 3,748
   _____
   501041

19. 345,461 + 2,342 + 51,654
(40)

20. 238,074 + 69,946 + 472
(40)

Estimate the sum. *(42)*

21.   875 900
     + 801 800
     ____ ____
           1700

22.   76 80
     48 50
    + 79 80
    ____ ____
          200

23.   579 600
     442 400
    + 613 600
    ____ ____
          1600

Write a number sentence. *(34)*

24. The clowns practiced 3 hours a day for 5 days. How many hours did they practice? 15

Solve. *(44)*

25. Mrs. Jackson bought items that cost $7.85, $4.25, and $5.95 at the gift shop. How much did she spend in all?

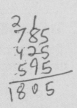

7.85
4.25
5.95
_____
18.05

Add.

1.   2
(28)   9
    + 8

2.   5
(28)   2
     4
    + 7

3.   8
(28)   4
     8
     3
    + 9

4.   6
(28)   7
     5
     3
    + 4

5.   9
(28)   2
     1
     5
    + 6

6.   37
(30)   + 74

7. $ 3.27
(30)   + 4.19

8.   627
(30)   489
   + 86

9. $ 5.67
(30)   4.91
   + 6.73

10.   247
(30)   105
   + 314

11. $ 56.52
(38)   + 34.78

12.   84,754
(38)   + 28,259

13.   3,920
(38)   2,043
  + 42,143

14.   82,341
(38)   75,238
    6,427
  + 2,875

15.   592,347
(40)   + 646,348

16.   824,561
(40)   + 324,492

17. $ 4,843.75
(40)   7,452.69
  + 4,837.19

18.   347,620
(40)   83,896
  + 46,283

19. 82,341 + 575,238 + 6,427
(40)

20. 407,653 + 8,114 + 36,585
(40)

Estimate the sum. (42)

21.   357
    + 258

22.   43
     52
    + 98

23.   529
     286
    + 105

Write a number sentence. (34)

24. There were 5 lions, 8 elephants, and 6 dogs in the center ring.
How many animals were in the ring?

Solve. (44)

25. The museum has 39 paintings on the first floor. There are 34
paintings on the second floor and 28 on the third floor. Find the
total number of paintings.

1.

$$\begin{array}{r} 32 \\ + 75 \\ \hline \end{array}$$

  A 107
  B 106
  C 97
  D 67

2.

$$\begin{array}{r} 564 \\ - 324 \\ \hline \end{array}$$

  E 424
  F 420
  G 240
  H 220

3.

$$\begin{array}{r} 334 \\ \times 2 \\ \hline \end{array}$$

  A 868
  B 768
  C 686
  D 668

4.

3)180

  E 50
  F 56
  G 60
  H 600

5.

$$\begin{array}{r} \$ 6.52 \\ - 3.11 \\ \hline \end{array}$$

  A \$3.31
  B \$3.34
  C \$3.41
  D \$9.63

6.

$$\begin{array}{r} 843 \\ - 536 \\ \hline \end{array}$$

  E 106
  F 206
  G 207
  H 307

7.

$$\begin{array}{r} \$0.21 \\ \times 3 \\ \hline \end{array}$$

  A \$0.24
  B \$0.36
  C \$0.43
  D \$0.63

8.

$$\begin{array}{r} 21 \\ 39 \\ 12 \\ + 12 \\ \hline \end{array}$$

  E 48
  F 84
  G 104
  H 124

9.

$$\begin{array}{r} 494 \\ - 66 \\ \hline \end{array}$$

  A 328
  B 428
  C 432
  D 560

10.

6)769

  E 12r8
  F 111r3
  G 128r1
  H 134r5

11.

$$\begin{array}{r} \$ 0.64 \\ + 0.05 \\ \hline \end{array}$$

  A \$0.39
  B \$0.69
  C \$0.96
  D \$0.99

12.

$$\begin{array}{r} 432 \\ \times 3 \\ \hline \end{array}$$

  E 1,696
  F 1,296
  G 864
  H 435

13.

$99 + 5 = $ _?_

  A 14
  B 94
  C 104
  D 495

14.

5)1,560

  E 321
  F 320
  G 312
  H 12

15.

$$\begin{array}{r} 423 \\ \times 3 \\ \hline \end{array}$$

  A 420
  B 426
  C 1,069
  D 1,269

Subtracting

Here is 21¢ worth of stamps. There are 2 ten-cent stamps and 1 one-cent stamp.

This is also 21¢ worth of stamps. There are 1 ten-cent stamp and 11 one-cent stamps.

A. Here is 32¢ worth of stamps. There are 3 ten-cent stamps and 2 one-cent stamps.

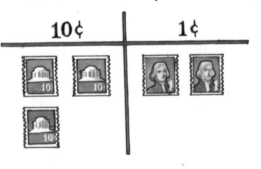

10¢   1¢

1. This can be traded to 2 ten-cent stamps and ___?___ one-cent stamps.

Rename:
3 tens and 2 ones =
2 tens and 12 ones.

B. Rename tens.

Example   ⁴¹⁷ $\cancel{5}\cancel{7}$

2. 49   **3.** 87   **4.** 92   **5.** 146   **6.** 255

C. Rename hundreds.

Examples   ²¹⁸ $\cancel{3}\cancel{8}7$ ⁶¹³ $2,\cancel{7}\cancel{3}6$

7. 365   **8.** 407   **9.** 796   **10.** 1,542   **11.** 2,809

Practice

Rename tens.

1. 53   **2.** 62   **3.** 87   **4.** 357   **5.** 462

Rename hundreds.

6. 412   **7.** 506   **8.** 756   **9.** 1,271   **10.** 3,786

Subtract.

1. 7
  2
	2. 16
	  9
		3. 10
		  7
			4. 6
			  3
				5. 11
				  3
					6. 10
					  1
						7. 5
						  4

8. 6
  0
	9. 15
	  9
		10. 8
		  4
			11. 18
			  9
				12. 9
				  8
					13. 6
					  5
						14. 12
						  9

15. 9
  6
	16. 7
	  5
		17. 5
		  3
			18. 9
			  3
				19. 15
				  8
					20. 14
					  7
						21. 17
						  9

22. 14
  6
	23. 7
	  0
		24. 4
		  3
			25. 10
			  5
				26. 8
				  8
					27. 10
					  2
						28. 5
						  1

29. 17
  8
	30. 7
	  1
		31. 13
		  5
			32. 9
			  4
				33. 8
				  6
					34. 10
					  8
						35. 9
						  5

36. 14
  5
	37. 9
	  7
		38. 8
		  5
			39. 11
			  5
				40. 6
				  6
					41. 11
					  7
						42. 12
						  7

43. 13
  6
	44. 7
	  3
		45. 6
		  2
			46. 9
			  1
				47. 10
				  6
					48. 11
					  8
						49. 9
						  2

50. 8
  3
	51. 9
	  9
		52. 15
		  7
			53. 12
			  6
				54. 6
				  4
					55. 4
					  1
						56. 12
						  8

57. 8
  7
	58. 2
	  2
		59. 13
		  4
			60. 4
			  2
				61. 8
				  1
					62. 10
					  4
						63. 10
						  3

64. 15
  6
	65. 7
	  4
		66. 14
		  8
			67. 11
			  4
				68. 6
				  1
					69. 4
					  4
						70. 13
						  9

71. 16
  7
	72. 3
	  3
		73. 8
		  2
			74. 12
			  3
				75. 7
				  7
					76. 13
					  7
						77. 12
						  5

Renaming in Subtraction

Subtract 74 − 58.

THINK					WRITE

CAN'T SUBTRACT ONES	RENAME	SUBTRACT ONES	SUBTRACT TENS	WRITE

Tens	Ones
7	4
− 5	8

	Tens	Ones
	6	14
	7̶	4̶
−	5	8

	Tens	Ones
	6	14
	7̶	4̶
−	5	8
		6

	Tens	Ones
	6	14
	7̶	4̶
−	5	8
	1	6

$$\begin{array}{r} 6\ 14 \\ 7̶\,4̶ \\ -\ 5\,8 \\ \hline 1\,6 \end{array}$$

A. Find 337 − 154. Complete.

   1. Subtract ones. 7 − 4 = ___?___

   2. Rename. 3 hundreds and 3 tens =
          2 hundreds and ___?___ tens

   3. Subtract tens. 13 − 5 = ___?___

   4. Subtract hundreds. 2 − 1 = ___?___

   5. What is the difference?

WRITE

$$\begin{array}{r} {\scriptstyle 2\ 13} \\ 3̶\,3̶\,7 \\ -\ 1\,5\,4 \\ \hline 1\,8\,3 \end{array}$$ ← Difference

B. Subtract.

6. 53	**7.** 86	**8.** 735	**9.** 354	**10.** 658
− 6	− 38	− 27	− 219	− 465

Practice

Subtract.

1. 76	**2.** 45	**3.** 35	**4.** 56	**5.** 91
− 7	− 9	− 19	− 37	− 44

6. 341	**7.** 987	**8.** 854	**9.** 428	**10.** 563
− 26	− 58	− 639	− 277	− 371

Subtracting Numbers

Subtract 625 − 397. Follow these steps.

Step 1	**Step 2**	**Step 3**
SUBTRACT ONES	SUBTRACT TENS	SUBTRACT HUNDREDS

$$\begin{array}{r} {}^{1}\!\!\:{}^{15} \\ 6\,2\,\cancel{5} \\ -\,3\,9\,7 \\ \hline 8 \end{array} \qquad \begin{array}{r} {}^{11} \\ 5\,\cancel{1}\,15 \\ \cancel{6}\,\cancel{2}\,\cancel{5} \\ -\,3\,9\,7 \\ \hline 2\,8 \end{array} \qquad \begin{array}{r} {}^{11} \\ 5\,\cancel{1}\,15 \\ \cancel{6}\,\cancel{2}\,\cancel{5} \\ -\,3\,9\,7 \\ \hline 2\,2\,8 \end{array}$$

A. Complete.

1.
$$\begin{array}{r} 6\,9\,7 \\ -\,2\,8\,4 \\ \hline 1\,3 \end{array}$$

2.
$$\begin{array}{r} {}^{8}\,{}^{13} \\ 7\,\cancel{9}\,\cancel{3} \\ -\,3\,5\,6 \\ \hline 7 \end{array}$$

3.
$$\begin{array}{r} {}^{3}\,{}^{4}\,{}^{12} \\ \cancel{4}\,\cancel{5}\,\cancel{2} \\ -\,1\,6\,5 \\ \hline 7 \end{array}$$

4.
$$\begin{array}{r} {}^{2}\,{}^{11}\,{}^{4}\,{}^{14} \\ 3,\cancel{1}\,\cancel{5}\,\cancel{4} \\ -\,\ \ 2\,4\,9 \\ \hline 0\,5 \end{array}$$

5.
$$\begin{array}{r} {}^{15} \\ {}^{4}\,{}^{11}\,\cancel{5}\,{}^{11} \\ 5,2\,\cancel{6}\,\cancel{1} \\ -\,3,4\,7\,8 \\ \hline \end{array}$$

B. Subtract dollars and cents.

Example	**Step 1** Subtract.	**Step 2** Place the money notation.
$\begin{array}{r}\$\,47.41\\-\,12.25\\ \hline\end{array}$	$\begin{array}{r}{}^{3}\,{}^{11}\\ \$\,47.\cancel{4}\,\cancel{1}\\-\,12.25\\ \hline 3\,5\,1\,6\end{array}$	$\begin{array}{r}{}^{3}\,{}^{11}\\ \$\,47.\cancel{4}\,\cancel{1}\\-\,12.25\\ \hline \$\,35.16\end{array}$

6.
$$\begin{array}{r} \$\,4.82 \\ -\,2.97 \\ \hline \end{array}$$

7.
$$\begin{array}{r} \$\,98.84 \\ -\,\ \ 0.66 \\ \hline \end{array}$$

8.
$$\begin{array}{r} \$\,75.65 \\ -\,\ \ 1.79 \\ \hline \end{array}$$

9.
$$\begin{array}{r} \$\,23.42 \\ -\,19.38 \\ \hline \end{array}$$

10.
$$\begin{array}{r} \$\,53.26 \\ -\,43.57 \\ \hline \end{array}$$

We add to check subtraction. Look at this example.

$$\begin{array}{r} 6\,4\,3 \\ -\,4\,2\,6 \\ \hline 2\,1\,7 \end{array} \quad \xrightarrow{compare} \quad \begin{array}{r} 4\,2\,6 \\ +\,2\,1\,7 \\ \hline 6\,4\,3 \end{array}$$

C. Subtract. Check by adding.

11.
$$\begin{array}{r} 7\,1\,5 \\ -\,6\,5\,2 \\ \hline \end{array}$$

12.
$$\begin{array}{r} 5,846 \\ -\,\ \ 408 \\ \hline \end{array}$$

13.
$$\begin{array}{r} 6,172 \\ -\,3,249 \\ \hline \end{array}$$

14.
$$\begin{array}{r} \$\,22.51 \\ -\,14.70 \\ \hline \end{array}$$

15.
$$\begin{array}{r} \$\,83.72 \\ -\,44.95 \\ \hline \end{array}$$

Subtract.

1. 755 − 200	**2.** 989 − 378	**3.** $ 6.74 − 2.15	**4.** 396 − 98
5. 458 − 269	**6.** 842 − 94	**7.** $ 2.63 − 1.78	**8.** 525 − 478
9. 343 − 76	**10.** 964 − 577	**11.** $ 68.97 − 25.93	**12.** 2,876 − 765
13. 4,484 − 2,067	**14.** 3,929 − 1,946	**15.** $ 56.65 − 17.37	**16.** 6,578 − 1,869
17. 5,214 − 4,078	**18.** 5,633 − 2,495	**19.** $ 82.35 − 54.59	**20.** 4,664 − 777
21. 3,542 − 654	**22.** $ 6.28 − 1.59	**23.** 732 − 58	**24.** 5,214 − 1,155
25. $ 67.92 − 28.79	**26.** 864 − 275	**27.** 3,862 − 77	**28.** 526 − 37

★ Find the missing digits.

29. 724 − ?5? = 65

30. 2?3? − 1,376 = 1,459

Solve.

31. Tom learned 745 lines for the play. Jane learned 678 lines. How many more lines did Tom learn than Jane?

32. Costumes cost $73.72. Scenery costs $52.89. How much more do the costumes cost than the scenery?

Zero in Subtraction

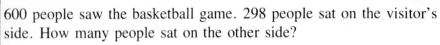

600 people saw the basketball game. 298 people sat on the visitor's side. How many people sat on the other side?

CAN'T SUBTRACT ONES	RENAME	SUBTRACT
600 − 298	9 5 10 10 6̸ 0̸ 0̸ − 2 9 8	9 5 10 10 6̸ 0̸ 0̸ − 2 9 8 3 0 2

There were 302 people on the other side.

A. Complete.

1.
$$
\begin{array}{r}
^{3\ 10}\\
4\!\!\!/\ 0\!\!\!/\ 8\\
-\quad 4\ 7\\
\hline
1
\end{array}
$$

2.
$$
\begin{array}{r}
^{9}\\
^{5\ 10\ 15}\\
6\!\!\!/\ 0\!\!\!/\ 5\!\!\!/\\
-\ 2\ 4\ 9\\
\hline
5\ 6
\end{array}
$$

3.
$$
\begin{array}{r}
^{9}\\
^{2\ 10\ 10}\\
6,3\!\!\!/\ 0\!\!\!/\ 0\!\!\!/\\
-\ 1,2\ 7\ 8\\
\hline
2
\end{array}
$$

Look at this shortcut.

CAN'T SUBTRACT ONES	RENAME	SUBTRACT
4,000 − 2,943	3 9 9 10 4,0̸0̸0̸ − 2,9 4 3	3 9 9 10 4,0̸0̸0̸ − 2,9 4 3 1,0 5 7

B. Complete.

4.
$$
\begin{array}{r}
^{7\ 9\ 13}\\
8\!\!\!/\ 0\!\!\!/\ 3\!\!\!/\\
-\ 4\ 5\ 8\\
\hline
4\ 5
\end{array}
$$

5.
$$
\begin{array}{r}
^{4\ 9\ 9\ 16}\\
5,0\!\!\!/0\!\!\!/6\!\!\!/\\
-\ 4,4\ 2\ 9\\
\hline
7\ 7
\end{array}
$$

6.
$$
\begin{array}{r}
^{6\ 9\ 9\ 10}\\
7,0\!\!\!/0\!\!\!/0\!\!\!/\\
-\ 3,1\ 4\ 5\\
\hline
5
\end{array}
$$

7.
$$
\begin{array}{r}
^{3\ 9\ 9\ 10}\\
4,0\ 0\ 0\!\!\!/\\
-\ 2,0\ 8\ 3
\end{array}
$$

C. Subtract.

8.
$$
\begin{array}{r}
902\\
-\ 32
\end{array}
$$

9.
$$
\begin{array}{r}
600\\
-\ 378
\end{array}
$$

10.
$$
\begin{array}{r}
8,009\\
-\ 2,191
\end{array}
$$

11.
$$
\begin{array}{r}
2,000\\
-\ 1,669
\end{array}
$$

12.
$$
\begin{array}{r}
7,000\\
-\ 4,546
\end{array}
$$

Subtract.

1. 470 – 148	**2.** 703 – 555	**3.** 505 – 371	**4.** 602 – 274	**5.** 801 – 287
6. 406 – 238	**7.** 700 – 345	**8.** 900 – 729	**9.** 200 – 154	**10.** 600 – 26
11. 500 – 162	**12.** 300 – 142	**13.** 7,040 – 525	**14.** 7,070 – 5,267	**15.** 4,030 – 2,125
16. 6,005 – 269	**17.** 7,008 – 1,749	**18.** 6,003 – 4,325	**19.** 8,400 – 6,147	**20.** 3,200 – 946
21. 2,000 – 1,141	**22.** 4,000 – 1,454	**23.** 6,000 – 2,195	**24.** 7,000 – 5,392	**25.** 9,000 – 8,543
26. 9,300 – 572	**27.** 7,104 – 4,245	**28.** 900 – 726	**29.** 808 – 49	**30.** 1,000 – 577
31. $ 62.40 – 50.20	**32.** $ 7.00 – 0.33	**33.** $ 6.07 – 4.38	**34.** $ 50.00 – 24.57	**35.** $ 30.04 – 1.45
36. 6,700 – 492	**37.** $ 3.04 – 0.79	**38.** 8,000 – 7,276	**39.** 802 – 699	**40.** 3,000 – 999

★ Find the answer. Do the work inside the parentheses first.

41. $79 + (18 - 9)$

42. $90 - (14 + 25)$

43. $416 - (318 + 24)$

44. $725 + (155 - 110)$

45. $1,589 - (422 + 159)$

46. $9,822 - (486 - 20)$

Solve.

47. An auditorium has 7,000 seats. 5,225 seats are taken. How many seats are empty?

48. This year, a ticket to the game costs $4.00. Last year it cost $3.35. How much more does the ticket cost this year?

Subtracting Larger Numbers

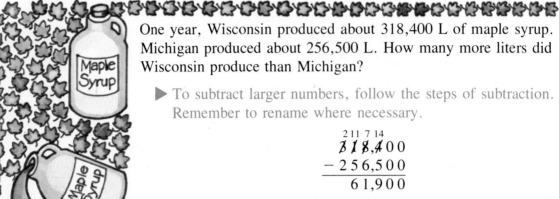

One year, Wisconsin produced about 318,400 L of maple syrup. Michigan produced about 256,500 L. How many more liters did Wisconsin produce than Michigan?

▶ To subtract larger numbers, follow the steps of subtraction. Remember to rename where necessary.

$$\begin{array}{r} {\scriptstyle 2\;11\;7\;14} \\ \cancel{3}1\cancel{8},\cancel{4}00 \\ -\;256,500 \\ \hline 61,900 \end{array}$$

Wisconsin produced 61,900 L more than Michigan.

A. Study the examples. Complete.

Examples

$$\begin{array}{r} {\scriptstyle 14\;15\;11} \\ {\scriptstyle 1\;\cancel{4}\;\cancel{5}\;\cancel{7}\;12} \\ \cancel{2}\cancel{5},\cancel{6}\cancel{2}\cancel{2} \\ -\;\;\;8,957 \\ \hline 16,665 \end{array}$$

$$\begin{array}{r} {\scriptstyle 12\;11} \\ {\scriptstyle 5\;\cancel{2}\;\cancel{1}\;16} \\ \cancel{6}\cancel{3},\cancel{2}\cancel{6}8 \\ -\;25,874 \\ \hline 37,394 \end{array}$$

$$\begin{array}{r} {\scriptstyle 14\;13\;15} \\ {\scriptstyle 6\;\cancel{4}\;\cancel{5}\;\cancel{5}\;11} \\ \cancel{7}\cancel{5},\cancel{4}\cancel{6}\cancel{1} \\ -\;49,976 \\ \hline 25,485 \end{array}$$

1.
$$\begin{array}{r} {\scriptstyle 6\;14\;8\;10} \\ 2\cancel{8}\cancel{7},\cancel{4}\cancel{9}\cancel{0} \\ -\;\;\;69,713 \\ \hline 77 \end{array}$$

2.
$$\begin{array}{r} {\scriptstyle 2\;16} \\ 495,5\cancel{3}\cancel{6} \\ -\;126,798 \\ \hline 8 \end{array}$$

3.
$$\begin{array}{r} {\scriptstyle 0\;12} \\ \$7,43\cancel{1}.\cancel{2}1 \\ -\;6,787.50 \\ \hline 1 \end{array}$$

B. Subtract. First write the problem in vertical form. Be sure to line up the numbers correctly.

Example   369,548 − 28,719

$$\begin{array}{r} {\scriptstyle 8\;\;15\;3\;18} \\ 36\cancel{9},\cancel{5}\cancel{4}\cancel{8} \\ -\;\;\;28,719 \\ \hline 340,829 \end{array}$$

4. 452,435 − 30,457

5. 73,224 − 9,547

6. 62,173 − 7,328

C. Subtract.

7.
$$\begin{array}{r} 48,981 \\ -\;\;5,649 \\ \hline \end{array}$$

8.
$$\begin{array}{r} \$324.99 \\ -\;177.68 \\ \hline \end{array}$$

9.
$$\begin{array}{r} 278,942 \\ -\;149,735 \\ \hline \end{array}$$

10.
$$\begin{array}{r} 929,755 \\ -\;593,948 \\ \hline \end{array}$$

11.
$$\begin{array}{r} 843,347 \\ -\;\;\;7,828 \\ \hline \end{array}$$

12.
$$\begin{array}{r} 673,408 \\ -\;81,573 \\ \hline \end{array}$$

13.
$$\begin{array}{r} 285,100 \\ -\;134,217 \\ \hline \end{array}$$

14.
$$\begin{array}{r} 923,755 \\ -\;593,948 \\ \hline \end{array}$$

Subtract.

1. 87,877
  − 68,036

2. 59,256
  − 8,081

3. 74,357
  − 3,249

4. $ 304.31
  − 23.20

5. 99,253
  − 8,942

6. 66,852
  − 45,478

7. 47,524
  − 34,632

8. 59,765
  − 6,871

9. $ 493.00
  − 131.56

10. 85,854
  − 7,931

11. 82,365
  − 10,476

12. 86,666
  − 29,987

13. 75,012
  − 8,256

14. 40,001
  − 9,872

15. 56,071
  − 9,893

16. 939,523
  − 577,954

17. $ 2,246.34
  − 388.76

18. 322,603
  − 244,754

19. 582,500
  − 297,963

20. $ 654.83
  − 69.94

21. 50,531
  − 12,684

22. 921,238
  − 340,327

23. 465,115
  − 7,328

24. 953,421 − 98,215

25. 43,243 − 19,958

Find Out!
Brainteaser

Here are 4 islands, 8 bridges, and the mainland. Starting anywhere on the map, cross **all 8 bridges one time** and end up on the mainland.

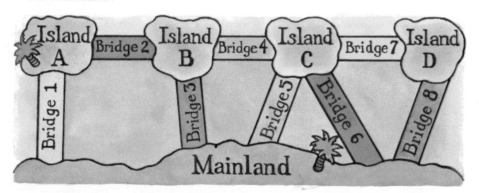

Remember, you can't go over a bridge more than once. You can go over the mainland and islands as many times as you like.

Subtract.

1. 78
(51) − 39
39 ✓

2. 52
(51) − 13
79

3. $6.24
(51) − 3.07
3.17

4. 456
(51) − 129

5. $ 9.84
(52) − 0.68

6. 731
(52) − 388
343

7. 254
(52) − 168

8. 6,914
(52) − 3,956

9. $ 52.14
(52) − 7.31

10. 1,526
(52) − 519

11. $ 60.00
(54) − 12.45
47.55

12. 702
(54) − 534

13. 400
(54) − 155

14. 8,090
(54) − 3,456

15. 3,004
(54) − 2,768

16. 34,620
(56) − 16,846
17.774

17. 91,565
(56) − 3,273
3,273

18. 432,813
(56) − 378,944

19. 753,356
(56) − 269,119

Solve. (56)

20. San Diego Stadium has 52,568 seats. Cleveland Stadium has 80,233 seats. How many more seats does Cleveland Stadium have than San Diego Stadium?

21. Attendance for one baseball season was 715,394. Next season, the attendance was 626,178. What was the difference?

Find Out!

Calculator Activity

Amy gave Sam 1¢ on November 1. On November 2, she gave him 2¢.

On November 3, she gave him 4¢.

Each day she gives him double the amount she gave him the day before. What amount will she give him on November 20? What amount will she give him on November 30?

60¢

Finding Patterns

A **sequence** is formed by a pattern or rule.
Look at these numbers.

The rule here is to ADD 7.

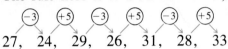

2, 9, 16, 23, 30, 37

The rule here is to SUBTRACT 3, ADD 5.

27, 24, 29, 26, 31, 28, 33

A. Use the rules to complete.

Rules

1. ADD 9. 8, __?__, __?__, __?__, __?__

2. SUBTRACT 9, ADD 6. 76, __?__, __?__, __?__, __?__

B. Complete.

3. 90, 87, 84, 81, _78?_, _75?_, _72_, __?__

4. 45, 51, 57, 63, __?__, __?__, __?__, __?__

5. 100, 91, 101, 92, __?__, __?__, __?__, __?__

Practice

Complete.

1. 84, 82, 80, __?__, __?__, __?__, __?__

2. 62, 59, 56, __?__, __?__, __?__, __?__

3. 34, 31, 41, 38, 48, __?__, __?__, __?__, __?__

4. 500, 510, 506, 516, 512, __?__, __?__, __?__, __?__

Estimating Differences

Last year, 2,809 new trees were planted. A fire destroyed 1,753 of the trees. How many new trees were left?

	Estimate		Exact	
	3,000		2,809	
	− 2,000		− 1,753	
	1,000		1,056	

Look at the differences. Since the differences are close, the exact difference is reasonable.

A. Look at the example, then complete.

	Estimate	Exact
	300	318
	− 200	− 186
	100	132

1. 318 is rounded to __?__ .　　　**2.** 186 is rounded to __?__ .

3. The exact difference is __?__ .　　**4.** The estimated difference is __?__ .

5. Is the exact difference reasonable?

B. Estimate the answer. Complete.

6.　379　ESTIMATE　__?__　　**7.**　8,286　ESTIMATE　8,000
　　− 198　　　　　　　− 200　　　　　− 6,907　　　　　　　__?__
　　　　　　　　　　　　　　__?__

C. Emma has $9.25. She wants to rent a campsite for $4.75.
Emma estimated to find how much change she should receive.

Step 1　Round to the nearest dollar.　　　$ 9.25　　Estimate　$ 9.00
Step 2　Subtract the rounded amounts.　　− 4.75　　　　　　　− 5.00

8. Emma should receive about __?__ .

D. Estimate the answers.

9.　713　　**10.**　476　　**11.**　$ 5.24　　**12.**　7,982　　**13.**　9,445
　　− 234　　　　− 317　　　　− 1.41　　　　− 5,076　　　　− 3,636

Estimate the answers.

1.	423 − 185	**2.**	692 − 359	**3.**	935 − 576
4.	265 − 143	**5.**	414 − 309	**6.**	912 − 736
7.	7,246 − 1,432	**8.**	8,145 − 6,256	**9.**	3,588 − 1,017

Round each to the nearest dollar.
Estimate the answers.

10.	$ 7.63 − 2.75	**11.**	$ 9.24 − 4.32	**12.**	$ 4.07 − 1.15
13.	$ 3.99 − 2.40	**14.**	$ 4.81 − 3.27	**15.**	$ 6.38 − 1.89

Solve.

16. There were 493 campers last week. This week there are 207 campers. Estimate how many more campers there were last week than this week.

17. Mr. Allen did 676 − 234 on his calculator. The answer was 442. What is the estimated answer? Was the calculator answer reasonable?

18. Ellen did 5,826 − 4,309 on her calculator. The answer was 1,517. Was the calculator answer reasonable?

19. Joel has $7.15. He bought a flashlight for $2.99. Estimate to find if he has enough money left to buy a fishing hat for $5.89.

★ **20.** The Nature Club raised $79.55 for a hike. They spent $47.85. Estimate to the nearest ten dollars to find how much money they have left.

★ **21.** Henry has $50.00 He wants to buy a new sleeping bag for $39.25. Estimate to the nearest ten dollars to find how much change he should receive.

Solving Number Sentences

Look at these two number sentences.

1. $6 + 2 = \square$
$8 = \square$
The answer is 8.

2. $33 - 10 = n$
$23 = n$
The answer is 23.

A. Complete to solve.

1. $24 + 18 = \square$
   $\underline{\quad ? \quad} = \square$

2. $8 \times 7 = \triangle$
   $\underline{\quad ? \quad} = \triangle$

3. $48 \div 6 = n$
   $\underline{\quad ? \quad} = n$

4. $157 - 133 = n$
   $\underline{\quad ? \quad} = n$

5. $n = 10 + 10$
   $n = \underline{\quad ? \quad}$

6. $45 + 23 + 18 = n$
   $\underline{\quad ? \quad} = n$

B. Solve.

7. $19 + 7 = \square$

8. $24 \div 3 = n$

9. $116 - 97 = n$

10. $n = 149 - 39$

11. $305 + 16 + 27 = n$

12. $45 \div 9 = n$

Practice

Solve.

1. $7 + 6 = \triangle$

2. $23 + 15 = \triangle$

3. $12 + 41 + 6 = \square$

4. $89 - 45 = \square$

5. $83 - 21 = \square$

6. $35 - 27 = n$

7. $n = 67 - 18$

8. $14 - 6 = n$

9. $4 \times 7 = n$

10. $n = 8 \times 9$

11. $7 \times 4 = n$

12. $n = 6 \times 6$

13. $12 \div 3 = n$

14. $56 \div 8 = n$

15. $n = 72 \div 9$

16. $45 \div 5 = n$

17. $n = 175 + 43$

18. $63 \div 9 = n$

19. $43 + 18 + 9 = n$

20. $173 - 88 = n$

21. $n = 49 \div 7$

22. $n = 325 + 78$

23. $315 - 185 = n$

24. $n = 81 - 16$

★ 25. $n = 898 + 321$

★ 26. $9 + 9 + 9 = n \times 9$

★ 27. $\square + 9 = 7 + 16$

★ 28. $\triangle + 9 = 4 + 86$

★ 29. $40 \div 5 = 6 + n$

★ 30. $\square + 2 = 9 \times 4$

Problem-Solving Steps

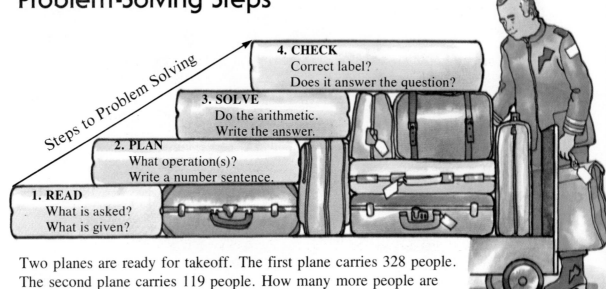

4. CHECK
Correct label?
Does it answer the question?

3. SOLVE
Do the arithmetic.
Write the answer.

2. PLAN
What operation(s)?
Write a number sentence.

1. READ
What is asked?
What is given?

Steps to Problem Solving

Two planes are ready for takeoff. The first plane carries 328 people.
The second plane carries 119 people. How many more people are
on the first plane than on the second plane?

A. Follow the steps and answer these questions.

READ
   1. How many people are on the first plane?

   2. How many people are on the second plane?

   3. What is asked?

PLAN
   4. What operation should be   **5.** Write a number sentence.
   used?

SOLVE
   6. $328 - 119 = n$ **7.** What is the label?
          $\underline{\quad ? \quad} = n$

CHECK
   8. There are $\underline{\quad ? \quad}$ more people on the first plane.

B. Solve. Use the four steps.

   9. There are 375 seats on the plane. The plane is carrying 290
   passengers. How many empty seats are on the plane?

Solve.

1. An airport has a runway that is 4,260 m and a clear zone that is 815 m. What is the total length of the runway and clear zone?

2. In the late 1920's, there were about 1,000 airports in the United States. Today, there are about 13,000. How many more airports are there today?

3. In New York, the temperature is 22°C. In Chicago, it is 15°C. What is the difference in the two temperatures?

4. The largest airship ever built was the Hindenburg. When it crashed, there were 97 people aboard. 36 people lost their lives. How many people survived the crash?

5. An air traffic controller worked 10 hours a day for 7 days. How many hours did she work?

6. Three people ate lunch in the airport cafeteria. In total, the cost was $18. They each paid the same amount. How much did each person pay?

Inequalities

Number sentences with the signs $>$ or $<$ are called **inequalities**.

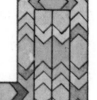

$7 > 3$ Seven is greater than three.
$3 < 5$ Three is less than five.
$4 + 5 > 7$ Four plus five is greater than seven.

A. Make true. Replace $\equiv$ with $>$ or $<$.

  1. $8 \equiv 2$ **2.** $7 - 4 \equiv 5$

  3. $8 + 7 \equiv 10$ **4.** $14 - 9 \equiv 8 - 2$

  5. $13 + 5 \equiv 19 - 7$ **6.** $13 + 7 \equiv 12 + 6$

B. Solve. Use whole numbers less than 10.

     Example $n < 3$
                     $0 < 3$
                     $1 < 3$
                     $2 < 3$
                     The solutions
                     are 0, 1, and 2.

  7. $n > 6$ **8.** $n < 8$ **9.** $n > 2$ **10.** $n < 6$

Practice

Make true. Use $>$ or $<$.

  1. $15 \equiv 52$ **2.** $39 \equiv 41$ **3.** $17 \equiv 94$ **4.** $173 \equiv 231$

  5. $25 + 32 \equiv 53 - 35$ **6.** $85 - 19 \equiv 92 - 35$ **7.** $23 - 14 \equiv 53 - 41$

Solve. Use whole numbers less than 10.

  8. $n < 4$ **9.** $n < 12$ **10.** $n < 5$ **11.** $n < 13$

  12. $n > 8$ **13.** $n > 5$ **14.** $n > 3$ **15.** $n > 1$

  16. $n < 9$ **17.** $n > 7$ **18.** $n > 4$ **19.** $n < 10$

Keeping Fit

Write standard numerals.

1. Ninety thousand, forty-two

2. 13 million

3. $600,000 + 0 + 5,000 + 0 + 30 + 9$

4. Fifteen thousand, two hundred sixty

Round to the nearest hundred.

5. 578   **6.** 193   **7.** 324   **8.** 462

Round to the nearest thousand.

9. 4,824   **10.** 1,176   **11.** 3,296   **12.** 8,845

Add.

13. $5 + 6 + 7 + 5 + 9$ **14.** $5 + 9 + 8 + 3 + 2 + 6$

15. 13 + 40	**16.** 96 + 27	**17.** 289 + 86	**18.** 428 + 94	**19.** $ 6.92 + 8.48
20. 2,401 + 79	**21.** $ 35.46 + 3.91	**22.** 6,290 + 4,914	**23.** 7,194 + 3,046	**24.** 39,036 + 9,978
25. 61,704 + 6,496	**26.** $ 385.70 + 84.99	**27.** 20,842 + 15,077	**28.** 47,618 + 35,687	**29.** 54,967 + 27,095
30. 5 4 + 3	**31.** 29 5 + 7	**32.** 44 73 + 48	**33.** 181 397 + 716	**34.** $ 51.10 6.79 + 15.78
35. 3,740 567 + 296	**36.** 3,261 1,859 + 3,144	**37.** 34,026 49 + 1,271	**38.** $ 113,50 25.31 + 13.82	**39.** 21,936 381 + 5,770
40. 42,607 9,583 + 7,619	**41.** 16,535 22,846 + 715	**42.** 34,653 6,902 + 40,429	**43.** 23,278 24,711 + 8,064	**44.** 58,371 10,050 + 12,849

Solve.

45. The Robinsons traveled 457 km on Monday, 376 km on Tuesday, and 232 km on Wednesday. What was the total distance they traveled?

46. The Robinsons spent $52.48 for food and $24.95 for gas. How much did they spend in all?

Problem Solving

At the stationery store, James sold a calendar that cost $3.95. The customer gave him $5.00. What change should he give back?

Start with $3.95.

Say: Give back:

$4.00

$5.00

Practice

Name the coins and bills needed to make the change.

1. Newspaper for 25¢
   Given $1 bill

2. Pencils for 75¢
   Given $5 bill

3. Notebook for $1.89
   Given $2.00

4. Pens for $3.65
   Given $5 bill

5. Cards for $4.89
   Given $10 bill

6. Posters for $8.56
   Given $10 bill

7. Stationery for $9.89
   Given $20 bill

8. Books for $12.49
   Given $20 bill

★ **9.** Calculator for $56.72
   Given $50 bill and $20 bill

★ **10.** Notebook for $1.32
   Given $5 bill and two pennies

Subtract.

1. 57
(51) − 23

2. 68
(51) − 29

3. 75
(51) − 48

4. 476
(51) − 295

5. 624
(52) − 539

6. $ 4.85
(52) − 1.96

7. 986
(52) − 99

8. $ 8.04
(54) − 0.68

9. 700
(54) − 598

10. 7,372
(52) − 185

11. 9,153
(52) − 2,667

12. 9,700
(54) − 693

13. $ 71.69
(52) − 43.14

14. 8,765
(52) − 7,002

15. 8,000
(54) − 1,973

16. 42,139
(56) − 16,624

17. 65,892
(56) − 46,076

18. 72,007
(56) − 8,962

19. $ 5,826.72
(56) − 3,986.58

20. 532,514
(56) − 348,768

Estimate the answers. *(60)*

21. 674
− 230

22. 4,412
− 1,936

23. $ 7.86
− 5.23

24. $ 9.92
− 4.05

Complete. *(59)*

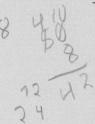

25. 21, 26, 31, 36, __?__, __?__, __?__, __?__

26. 58, 50, 42, 34, __?__, __?__, __?__, __?__

27. 2, 4, 3, 5, 4, __?__, __?__, __?__, __?__

Solve. *(62)*

28. $13 + 5 = n$

29. $56 - 21 = n$

30. $n = 72 \div 9$

31. $3 + 5 + 7 = n$

32. A first class ticket costs
(64) $105. A coach ticket costs
$81. How much more does the
first class ticket cost?

33. A magazine cost $1.25. Janice
(68) gave the clerk a $5 bill. Name
the coins and bills needed to
make the change.

Subtract.

1. 91
(51) − 57

2. 80
(51) − 56

3. 48
(51) − 29

4. 526
(51) − 218

5. 434
(52) − 76

6. $ 5.03
(54) − 1.76

7. 700
(54) − 238

8. 824
(52) − 398

9. 651
(52) − 487

10. 6,293
(52) − 2,536

11. $ 82.61
(52) − 43.95

12. 6,000
(54) − 5,762

13. 7,200
(54) − 980

14. 9,010
(54) − 7,218

15. 8,256
(52) − 3,747

16. 63,149
(56) − 25,629

17. 72,507
(56) − 37,892

18. $ 635.72
(56) − 46.05

19. 322,675
(56) − 254,283

20. 676,507
(56) − 29,870

Estimate the answers. *(60)*

21. 659
− 527

22. $ 9.97
− 3.32

23. 4,165
− 2,769

24. 5,930
− 2,100

Complete. *(59)*

25. 21, 29, 37, 45, __?__ , __?__ , __?__ , __?__

26. 98, 88, 98, 68, __?__ , __?__ , __?__ , __?__

27. 35, 40, 41, 46, 47, __?__ , __?__ , __?__ , __?__

Solve. *(62)*

28. $16 - 7 = n$

29. $n = 69 + 5$

30. $28 + 16 + 41 = n$

31. $n = 7 \times 9$

32. A baggage handler worked 9 hours
(64) a day for 7 days. How many
hours did he work in all?

33. A calculator costs $7.95. Sandy
(68) gave the clerk a $10 bill. Name
the coins and bills needed to
make the change.

1. Round 858 to the nearest hundred.

   A 600

   B 700

   C 800

   D 900

---

2. Compare:

$$\frac{3}{7} \equiv 2$$

   E <

   F >

   G =

   H ≠

---

3. How many pounds are in 48 oz?

   A 16

   B 14

   C 3

   D 2

---

4. Which is not a radius of the circle?

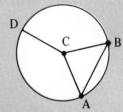

   E $\overline{AC}$

   F $\overline{CB}$

   G $\overline{DC}$

   H $\overline{AB}$

---

5. Which figure is shown?

   A sphere

   B circle

   C cone

   D cylinder

---

6. Which of the following numbers is the smallest?

   E 7,789

   F 7,790

   G 7,792

   H 7,830

---

7. What part is shaded?

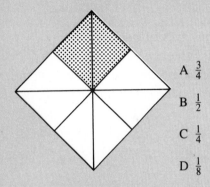

   A $\frac{3}{4}$

   B $\frac{1}{2}$

   C $\frac{1}{4}$

   D $\frac{1}{8}$

---

8. What is the value of 8 in 8,924?

   E 80

   F 800

   G 8,000

   H 80,000

---

9. Compare:

$$\frac{6}{6} \equiv 1$$

   A <

   B >

   C =

   D ≠

---

10. Simplify:

$$\frac{3}{9} = \underline{\ \ ?\ \ }$$

   E $\frac{1}{9}$

   F $\frac{1}{3}$

   G $\frac{3}{6}$

   H $\frac{2}{3}$

Multiplying

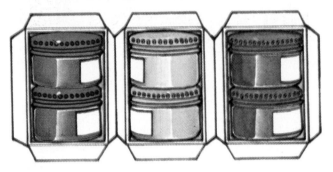

How many jars of paint?
Addition Sentence → $2 + 2 + 2 = 6$
Multiplication Sentence → $3 \times 2 = 6$
There are 6 jars of paint.

Here are 2 rows with 5 flowers in each row.

Multiplication Sentence → $2 \times 5 = 10$
The **factors** are 2 and 5.
The **product** is 10.

Practice

Write a multiplication sentence for each.

1.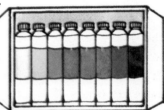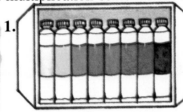

2.

3.

4. $9 + 9 + 9 = 27$

5. $5 + 5 + 5 + 5 = 20$

6. $7 + 7 + 7 + 7 = 28$

7. $4 + 4 + 4 + 4 + 4 = 20$

8. In $9 \times 6 = 54$, what are the factors? What is the product?

More Properties

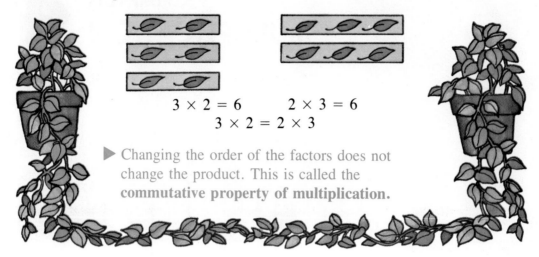

$$3 \times 2 = 6 \qquad 2 \times 3 = 6$$
$$3 \times 2 = 2 \times 3$$

▶ Changing the order of the factors does not change the product. This is called the **commutative property of multiplication.**

A. Solve.

1. $4 \times 3 = n \times 4$ **2.** $6 \times 5 = 5 \times n$ **3.** $23 \times 7 = n \times 23$

Look at the following.

$(3 \times 2) \times 4$

$= 6 \times 4$

$= 24$

$3 \times (2 \times 4)$

$= 3 \times 8$

$= 24$

$$(3 \times 2) \times 4 = 3 \times (2 \times 4)$$

▶ Changing the grouping of the factors does not change the product. This is called the **associative property of multiplication.**

B. Solve.

4. $(8 \times 2) \times 3 = 8 \times (n \times 3)$ **5.** $(4 \times 2) \times 5 = n \times (2 \times 5)$

▶ When multiplying a number by 1, the product is that number. This is called the **property of one for multiplication.**

C. Solve.

6. $1 \times 5 = n$ **7.** $24 \times 1 = n$ **8.** $n \times 6 = 6$

▶ When multiplying a number by 0, the product is always 0.

D. Solve.

9. $0 \times 8 = n$ **10.** $12 \times 0 = n$ **11.** $n \times 7 = 0$

Look at the following.

$3 \times (2 + 1)$
$= 3 \times 3$
$= 9$

$(3 \times 2) + (3 \times 1)$
$= 6 + 3$
$= 9$

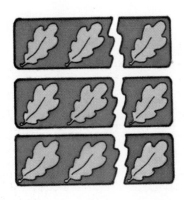
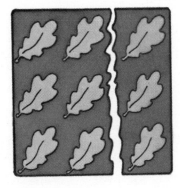

In both cases, there are 9 leaves.
$3 \times (2 + 1) = (3 \times 2) + (3 \times 1)$
This is called the **distributive property.**

E. Solve.

12. $3 \times (5 + 2) = (3 \times 5) + (n \times 2)$ **13.** $4 \times (6 + 3) = (4 \times 6) + (4 \times n)$

14. $2 \times (3 + n) = (2 \times 3) + (2 \times 5)$ **15.** $n \times (5 + 6) = (4 \times 5) + (4 \times 6)$

Using Patterns

Look at these patterns.

$4 \times 1 \qquad = 4$
$4 \times 10 \qquad = 40$
$4 \times 100 \qquad = 400$
$4 \times 1,000 \quad = 4,000$
$4 \times 10,000 = 40,000$

A. Look for a pattern. Complete.

1. $5 \times 1 \qquad = 5$
$5 \times 10 \qquad = 50$
$5 \times 100 \qquad = 500$
$5 \times 1,000 = 5,000$
$5 \times 10,000 = \underline{}?$

2. $6 \times 1 \qquad = 6$
$6 \times 10 \qquad = 60$
$6 \times 100 \qquad = 600$
$6 \times 1,000 \quad = \underline{}?$
$6 \times 10,000 = \underline{}?$

3. $1 \times 9 \qquad = 9$
$10 \times 9 \qquad = 90$
$100 \times 9 \qquad = \underline{}?$
$1,000 \times 9 \quad = \underline{}?$
$10,000 \times 9 = \underline{}?$

B. Complete.

4. $\begin{array}{r} 10 \\ \times 3 \\ \hline 0 \end{array}$

5. $\begin{array}{r} 100 \\ \times 3 \\ \hline 00 \end{array}$

6. $\begin{array}{r} 1,000 \\ \times 3 \\ \hline ,000 \end{array}$

7. $\begin{array}{r} 10,000 \\ \times 3 \\ \hline \end{array}$

C. Look for a pattern. Complete.

8. $4 \times 6 \qquad = 24$
$4 \times 60 \qquad = 240$
$4 \times 600 \qquad = 2,400$
$4 \times 6,000 \quad = 24,000$
$4 \times 60,000 = \underline{}?$

9. $5 \times 3 \qquad = 15$
$5 \times 30 \qquad = 150$
$5 \times 300 \qquad = 1,500$
$5 \times 3,000 \quad = \underline{}?$
$5 \times 30,000 = \underline{}?$

10. $7 \times 8 \qquad = 56$
$7 \times 80 \qquad = 560$
$7 \times 800 \qquad = \underline{}?$
$7 \times 8,000 \quad = \underline{}?$
$7 \times 80,000 = \underline{}?$

D. Complete.

11. $\begin{array}{r} 20 \\ \times 3 \\ \hline 0 \end{array}$

12. $\begin{array}{r} 200 \\ \times 3 \\ \hline 00 \end{array}$

13. $\begin{array}{r} 2,000 \\ \times 3 \\ \hline ,000 \end{array}$

14. $\begin{array}{r} 20,000 \\ \times 3 \\ \hline \end{array}$

E. Multiply.

15. $\begin{array}{r} 10 \\ \times 3 \\ \hline \end{array}$

16. $\begin{array}{r} 30 \\ \times 6 \\ \hline \end{array}$

17. $\begin{array}{r} 100 \\ \times 4 \\ \hline \end{array}$

18. $\begin{array}{r} \$2,000 \\ \times 9 \\ \hline \end{array}$

19. $\begin{array}{r} 40,000 \\ \times 7 \\ \hline \end{array}$

Multiply.

1. 10
    × 9

2. 30
    × 9

3. 50
    × 9

4. 40
    × 3

5. $50
    × 4

6. 100
    × 6

7. 300
    × 7

8. 600
    × 4

9. 800
    × 7

10. 500
    × 6

11. 1,000
    × 3

12. 3,000
    × 4

13. $6,000
    × 8

14. 90,000
    × 9

15. 80,000
    × 2

16. 800
    × 4

17. 10
    × 3

18. 4,000
    × 8

19. 700
    × 2

20. $70,000
    × 5

21. 300
    × 9

22. 1,000
    × 5

23. 20,000
    × 7

24. 40,000
    × 5

25. 40
    × 7

Solve.

26. There were 20 teams in the playoffs. There were 9 players on each team. How many players were there in all?

27. There were 400 tickets sold for each game. There were 9 games. How many tickets were sold?

Multiply.

1. 3 $\times$9	**2.** 7 $\times$1	**3.** 2 $\times$0	**4.** 9 $\times$6	**5.** 3 $\times$2	**6.** 5 $\times$3	**7.** 6 $\times$7
8. 5 $\times$6	**9.** 4 $\times$7	**10.** 3 $\times$4	**11.** 6 $\times$2	**12.** 4 $\times$2	**13.** 5 $\times$7	**14.** 0 $\times$3
15. 0 $\times$8	**16.** 1 $\times$6	**17.** 9 $\times$4	**18.** 7 $\times$0	**19.** 3 $\times$8	**20.** 2 $\times$6	**21.** 1 $\times$8
22. 6 $\times$3	**23.** 0 $\times$1	**24.** 9 $\times$9	**25.** 2 $\times$7	**26.** 5 $\times$8	**27.** 4 $\times$9	**28.** 5 $\times$1
29. 8 $\times$6	**30.** 4 $\times$0	**31.** 7 $\times$6	**32.** 3 $\times$6	**33.** 8 $\times$3	**34.** 2 $\times$5	**35.** 9 $\times$8
36. 0 $\times$0	**37.** 9 $\times$5	**38.** 4 $\times$3	**39.** 6 $\times$0	**40.** 0 $\times$9	**41.** 3 $\times$3	**42.** 7 $\times$4
43. 2 $\times$1	**44.** 9 $\times$7	**45.** 4 $\times$8	**46.** 4 $\times$4	**47.** 8 $\times$5	**48.** 3 $\times$7	**49.** 1 $\times$4
50. 6 $\times$9	**51.** 6 $\times$4	**52.** 8 $\times$8	**53.** 6 $\times$5	**54.** 8 $\times$2	**55.** 4 $\times$6	**56.** 1 $\times$9
57. 3 $\times$1	**58.** 8 $\times$9	**59.** 5 $\times$0	**60.** 6 $\times$1	**61.** 8 $\times$7	**62.** 1 $\times$1	**63.** 7 $\times$2
64. 2 $\times$9	**65.** 7 $\times$3	**66.** 8 $\times$1	**67.** 7 $\times$9	**68.** 5 $\times$2	**69.** 9 $\times$3	**70.** 6 $\times$8
71. 2 $\times$8	**72.** 5 $\times$9	**73.** 2 $\times$2	**74.** 2 $\times$3	**75.** 7 $\times$7	**76.** 9 $\times$2	**77.** 4 $\times$5

Keeping Fit

Compare. Use $>$, $<$, and $=$.

1. 81,397 ⫤ 482,013

2. 67,462 ⫤ 959,688

3. 66,642 ⫤ 67,634

4. 318,748 ⫤ 138,784

Add.

5. 6,519
   + 856

6. 8,924
   + 9,654

7. 85,408
   + 75,926

8. 126,037
   + 82,918

9. 363,791
   + 902,528

10. 4,419
    6,895
    + 8,734

11. 264
    489
    + 72

12. 1,495
    676
    + 5,071

13. 91,073
    4,986
    + 52,397

14. 412,605
    30,716
    + 691

Subtract.

15. 73
    − 25

16. 82
    − 8

17. 652
    − 439

18. 800
    − 721

19. 329
    − 52

20. 2,494
    − 205

21. 7,040
    − 3,276

22. 33,521
    − 17,604

23. 52,893
    − 7,196

24. 40,617
    − 20,832

25. 72,470
    − 9,987

26. 108,363
    − 44,659

27. 356,085
    − 8,240

28. 689,402
    − 421,397

Choose the number sentence that fits the problem.

29. Rodney has 12 blue pens and 14 black pens. How many pens does he have in all?

$12 + 14 = n$
$12 \times 14 = n$
$14 - 12 = n$

30. Edna had $13.76. She spent $8.69. How much did she have left?

$13.76 + 8.69 = n$
$13.76 - 8.69 = n$
$13.76 \times 8.69 = n$

Solve.

31. Mike bought a radio for $19.75 and a tape recorder for $35.69. How much did he spend in all?

32. Millie had $15.00. She spent $6.95 on records. How much money did she have left?

33. Mr. Harris repaired 449 telephones one week and 256 telephones the next week. How many phones did he repair during these two weeks?

34. Susan caught 5 bluefish, 20 snappers, 15 cod, and 1 bass. How many fish did she catch in all?

Renaming in Multiplication

Multiply 3 × 26.

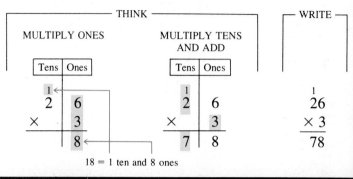

THINK

MULTIPLY ONES

Tens	Ones
2	6
×	3
	8

18 = 1 ten and 8 ones

MULTIPLY TENS AND ADD

Tens	Ones
2	6
×	3
7	8

WRITE

```
  1
 26
× 3
 78
```

A. Find 4 × 23. Complete.

1. Multiply ones. 4 × 3 = ___?___

2. Rename. 12 = ___?___ ten and 2 ones.

3. Multiply tens. 4 × 2 = ___?___ tens.

4. 8 tens + 1 ten = ___?___ tens.

5. What is the product?

WRITE
```
  1
 23
× 4
 92  ← Product
```

Use the steps to multiply 5 × 653.

Step 1	**Step 2**	**Step 3**
MULTIPLY ONES	MULTIPLY TENS	MULTIPLY HUNDREDS
1	2 1	2 1
6 5 3	6 5 3	6 5 3
× 5	× 5	× 5
5	6 5	3,2 6 5

B. Complete.

6.	**7.**	**8.**	**9.**	**10.**
82	¹173	²215	³¹262	$429
× 2	× 2	× 4	× 5	× 6
4	46	60	10	4

Multiply.

1. 34
   × 2

2. 91
   × 6

3. 64
   × 8

4. 78
   × 7

5. $80
   × 4

6. 75
   × 7

7. 39
   × 5

8. 53
   × 6

9. 25
   × 3

10. 90
   × 9

11. 67
   × 8

12. 82
   × 7

13. $76
   × 6

14. 23
   × 9

15. 50
   × 5

16. 221
   × 4

17. 513
   × 3

18. 113
   × 7

19. 611
   × 5

20. 308
   × 9

21. 261
   × 6

22. 272
   × 4

23. 651
   × 7

24. $188
   × 5

25. 102
   × 8

26. 735
   × 4

27. 432
   × 9

28. 676
   × 8

29. 255
   × 3

30. 350
   × 6

31. $336
   × 7

32. 61
   × 9

33. 84
   × 6

34. 12
   × 8

35. 112
   × 4

36. 24
   × 9

37. 238
   × 8

38. 66
   × 4

39. 243
   × 3

40. 424
   × 6

41. 87
   × 6

42. 729
   × 7

43. $344
   × 5

44. 46
   × 8

45. 562
   × 9

★ Complete.

46. ?5
   × 7
   ———
   665

47. ?4?
   × 6
   ———
  4,488

48. 6?
   × 4
   ———
  268

49. 4??
   × 8
   ———
  3,672

50. 5??
   × 7
   ———
  3,892

Solve.

51. There are 34 students in each class. 8 classes eat lunch at noon. How many students eat at noon?

52. Each day 672 cartons of milk are sold. How many cartons are sold in 5 days?

Multiplying Larger Numbers

There are 2,342 seats available for each game. How many seats are available for 6 games?

Multiply 6 × 2,342.

Step 1
ONES

$$\begin{array}{r} \overset{1}{2,3\,4\,2} \\ \times\,6 \\ \hline 2 \end{array}$$

Step 2
TENS

$$\begin{array}{r} \overset{2\,1}{2,3\,4\,2} \\ \times\,6 \\ \hline 5\,2 \end{array}$$

Step 3
HUNDREDS

$$\begin{array}{r} \overset{2\,2\,1}{2,3\,4\,2} \\ \times\,6 \\ \hline 0\,5\,2 \end{array}$$

Step 4
THOUSANDS

$$\begin{array}{r} \overset{2\,2\,1}{2,3\,4\,2} \\ \times\,6 \\ \hline 1\,4,0\,5\,2 \end{array}$$

There were 14,052 seats available for 6 games.

A. Complete.

1.
$$\begin{array}{r} \overset{3\;\;1\,2}{1,925} \\ \times\,4 \\ \hline ,700 \end{array}$$

2.
$$\begin{array}{r} \overset{1\;3\,2}{3,243} \\ \times\,7 \\ \hline ,701 \end{array}$$

3.
$$\begin{array}{r} \overset{1}{28,325} \\ \times\,3 \\ \hline ,975 \end{array}$$

4.
$$\begin{array}{r} \overset{3\,4}{14,968} \\ \times\,5 \\ \hline 40 \end{array}$$

5.
$$\begin{array}{r} \overset{1\,3}{45,629} \\ \times\,4 \\ \hline 16 \end{array}$$

B. Multiply.

6.
$$\begin{array}{r} 7,341 \\ \times\,2 \\ \hline \end{array}$$

7.
$$\begin{array}{r} 4,108 \\ \times\,6 \\ \hline \end{array}$$

8.
$$\begin{array}{r} 25,051 \\ \times\,7 \\ \hline \end{array}$$

9.
$$\begin{array}{r} 63,205 \\ \times\,6 \\ \hline \end{array}$$

10.
$$\begin{array}{r} 19,455 \\ \times\,3 \\ \hline \end{array}$$

C. Multiply dollars and cents.

Example Multiply 7 × $26.50.

MULTIPLY

$$\begin{array}{r} \overset{4\,3}{\$26.50} \\ \times\,7 \\ \hline 18550 \end{array}$$

PLACE MONEY NOTATION

$$\begin{array}{r} \overset{4\,3}{\$26.50} \\ \times\,7 \\ \hline \$185.50 \end{array}$$

11.
$$\begin{array}{r} \$7.24 \\ \times\,8 \\ \hline \end{array}$$

12.
$$\begin{array}{r} \$0.59 \\ \times\,7 \\ \hline \end{array}$$

13.
$$\begin{array}{r} \$81.65 \\ \times\,6 \\ \hline \end{array}$$

14.
$$\begin{array}{r} \$73.94 \\ \times\,9 \\ \hline \end{array}$$

15.
$$\begin{array}{r} \$468.21 \\ \times\,5 \\ \hline \end{array}$$

Multiply.

1. 3,102
    × 2

2. 1,015
    × 6

3. 5,111
    × 5

4. $1,476
    × 2

5. 2,530
    × 4

6. 1,535
    × 6

7. $4,308
    × 5

8. 2,764
    × 8

9. 9,877
    × 4

10. 7,536
    × 5

11. 15,042
    × 3

12. 78,192
    × 5

13. 37,950
    × 6

14. 57,213
    × 7

15. $89,526
    × 8

16. $42.16
    × 7

17. $12.32
    × 4

18. $70.95
    × 8

19. $217.13
    × 9

20. $105.03
    × 8

21. 2,378
    × 3

22. $50.45
    × 7

23. 32,552
    × 5

24. 85,348
    × 6

25. 3,122
    × 4

★ **26.** 12,345,679
        × 9

★ **27.** 12,345,679
        × 8

★ **28.** 12,345,679
        × 3

Solve.

29. The team earned $134.50 each month selling juice. How much was earned in 6 months?

30. New uniforms cost $57.95. How much will 9 new uniforms cost?

Cross-Number Puzzle

ACROSS

1. 1,593 + 2,696

4. 4 × 216

6. four thousand, two hundred six

7. 600 + 30 + 0

9. 205 + 67 + 269

12. 637 + 48 + 105

13. 823 − 767

14. 4,879 + 277

16. 96 × 9

17. 2,136 − 2,051

DOWN

1. 13,811 − 8,936

2. 670 − 586

3. 409 + 516

4. 24,380 + 39,176 + 23,135

5. Round 356 to the nearest hundred.

8. 3,000 + 50 + 8

10. 10,362 − 9,906

11. 100 + 60 + 4

12. 600 + 75 + 75

15. (6 × 10) + (5 × 1)

Multiply.

1. 40
(76) × 4

2. 900
× 4

3. 800
× 9

4. 2,000
× 3

5. $50,000
× 7

6. 51
(80) × 2

7. 24
× 8

8. 41
× 5

9. $2.83
× 9

10. 917
× 6

11. 804
× 5

12. $906
× 8

13. 3,456
(82) × 2

14. 7,089
× 7

15. $76.76
× 3

16. 6,089
× 7

17. 49,208
× 5

18. 55,625
× 7

19. $372.15
× 8

20. 50,006
× 7

Solve. *(80)*

21. Envelopes cost $0.40 each. What is the cost of 8 envelopes?

Find Out!
Aids to Memory

The distributive property can make mental multiplication easier.

Multiply 4×12.

Think: $4 \times 12 = 4 \times (10 + 2)$
$= (4 \times 10) + (4 \times 2)$
$= 40 + 8$
$= 48$

Write: $4 \times 12 = 48$

Complete.

1. $3 \times 17 = 3 \times (10 + 7)$
$= (3 \times 10) + (3 \times 7)$
$= \underline{\ ?\ } + \underline{\ ?\ }$
$= \underline{\ ?\ }$

2. $2 \times 34 = 2 \times (30 + 4)$
$= (2 \times \underline{\ ?\ }) + (2 \times \underline{\ ?\ })$
$= \underline{\ ?\ } + \underline{\ ?\ }$
$= \underline{\ ?\ }$

Multiply mentally. Write only the answer.

3. 4×15

4. 6×18

5. 3×45

6. 2×58

7. 5×31

Problem Solving

Oscar bought 2 bags of topsoil for $1.25 each and a plant for $2.75. How much money did he spend in all?

READ   How many bags of topsoil? 2
How much did each bag cost? $1.25
How much did the plant cost? $2.75

PLAN   Step 1
Find the cost of the topsoil.

Step 2
Find how much Oscar spent in all.

SOLVE   Step 1
$2 \times \$1.25 = \$2.50$

Step 2
$\$2.50 + \$2.75 = \$5.25$

Oscar spent $5.25 altogether.

Mrs. Coleman bought an arrangement of dried flowers for $7.95 and a candle holder for $8.95. She paid with a $20 bill. How much change did she receive?

READ   1. How much was the arrangement of dried flowers?

2. How much was the candle holder?

3. How much money did she have in all?

PLAN   4. Step 1 is to find how much she spent in all. What is step 2?

SOLVE   Step 1
5. $\$7.95 + \$8.95 = \underline{\quad?\quad}$

Step 2
6. $\$20.00 - \$16.90 = \underline{\quad?\quad}$

7. How much change did Mrs. Coleman receive?

Practice

Solve.

1. At a sale, Mr. Johnson bought a fern for $2.95 and a flower pot for $1.25. How much change did he receive from $10.00?

2. Sam bought a watering can for $3.50 and a sprinkler for $5.95. How much change did he receive from $20.00?

3. At the sale, roses cost $1.25 each and orchids cost $3.95 each. How much will 2 roses and 1 orchid cost?

4. Sandra bought some fertilizer. She bought 8 bags for $8.49 each and 1 bag for $10.99. How much did she pay in all?

5. Mrs. Seeth bought 9 vases for $0.95 each and 4 water hoses for $6.50 each. How much did she pay for the supplies?

6. Bernice sold 3 lilac bushes for $7.95 each and 6 rose bushes for $15.95 each. How much money did she collect in all?

7. Charlie bought 5 packages of seeds. The cost of the seeds was 7 packages for 84¢. How much did he pay for 5 packages? [HINT: First find the cost of 1 package.]

8. Andy bought 8 tomato plants. The cost was 6 plants for 96¢. How much did he pay for 8 plants? [HINT: First find the cost of 1 plant.]

Multiples

×	1	2	3	4	5	6	7	8	9	
1	1	2	3	4	5	6	7	8	9	
2	2	4	6	8	10	12	14	16	18	
3	3	6	9	12	15	18	21	24	27	← Multiples of 3
4	4	8	12	16	20	24	28	32	36	
5	5	10	15	20	25	30	35	40	45	← Multiples of 5
6	6	12	18	24	30	36	42	48	54	
7	7	14	21	28	35	42	49	56	63	
8	8	16	24	32	40	48	56	64	72	
9	9	18	27	36	45	54	63	72	81	

A. Use the multiplication table to find these products:

   1. $3 \times 1 =$ ___?___ 3 is a **multiple** of 3.

   2. $3 \times 2 =$ ___?___ 6 is a **multiple** of 3.

   3. $3 \times 3 =$ ___?___ 9 is a **multiple** of 3.

B. The table shows the multiples of a number. Some multiples
of 3 are 3, 6, 9, 12, 15, 18, 21, 24, and 27.
Complete.

   4. Some multiples of 2 are 2, 4, __?__, 8, __?__, and 12.

   5. Some multiples of 6 are 6, __?__, __?__, 24, __?__, and __?__.

   6. Some multiples of 8 are __?__, __?__, __?__, __?__, __?__, and __?__.

C. Some multiples of 3 are 3, 6, 9, 12, 15, 18, 21, and 24.
Some multiples of 4 are 4, 8, 12, 16, 20, 24, 28, and 32.
12 and 24 are multiples of both 3 and 4.

12 and 24 are **common multiples** of 3 and 4.

Find the first three common multiples for each.

7. 3 and 6   **8.** 2 and 3   **9.** 4 and 6

Practice

Name the first five multiples for each.

1. 1	**2.** 9	**3.** 8	**4.** 5	**5.** 7	**6.** 4
7. 10	**8.** 11	**9.** 12	**10.** 13	**11.** 15	**12.** 20
13. 21	**14.** 22	**15.** 23	★ **16.** 32	★ **17.** 59	★ **18.** 87

Find the first three common multiples for each.

19. 2 and 4	**20.** 3 and 5	**21.** 2 and 5
22. 5 and 10	**23.** 4 and 10	**24.** 2 and 7
25. 6 and 10	**26.** 3 and 7	**27.** 5 and 6
28. 4 and 9	★ **29.** 28 and 30	★ **30.** 17 and 23

31. Make a multiplication table that includes the multiples of 10, 11, and 12.

Find Out!
Calculator Activity

Make up 2 problems using one digit three times so that each answer is 30. Use addition, subtraction, or multiplication.

Example $6 \times 6 - 6 = 30$

More Patterning

Look at these patterns in multiplication.

$23 \times 1 = 23$	$30 \times 2 = 60$
$23 \times 10 = 230$	$30 \times 20 = 600$
$23 \times 100 = 2,300$	$30 \times 200 = 6,000$

A. Look for a pattern. Complete.

1. $47 \times 1 = 47$
$47 \times 10 = 470$
$47 \times 100 = \underline{\ ?\ }$

2. $50 \times 3 = 150$
$50 \times 30 = 1,500$
$50 \times 300 = \underline{\ ?\ }$

3. $4 \times 36 = 144$
$40 \times 36 = 1,440$
$400 \times 36 = \underline{\ ?\ }$

B. Complete.

4. $\begin{array}{r} 20 \\ \times\ 3 \\ \hline 0 \end{array}$

5. $\begin{array}{r} 200 \\ \times\ 3 \\ \hline 0\ 0 \end{array}$

6. $\begin{array}{r} 2,000 \\ \times\ 3 \\ \hline ,000 \end{array}$

C. Look for a pattern. Complete.

7. $236 \times 1 = 236$
$236 \times 10 = 2,360$
$236 \times 100 = \underline{\ ?\ }$

8. $1 \times 800 = 800$
$10 \times 800 = 8,000$
$100 \times 800 = \underline{\ ?\ }$

9. $361 \times 2 = 722$
$361 \times 20 = 7,220$
$361 \times 200 = \underline{\ ?\ }$

D. Complete.

10. $\begin{array}{r} 600 \\ \times\ 3 \\ \hline 00 \end{array}$

11. $\begin{array}{r} 600 \\ \times\ 30 \\ \hline ,000 \end{array}$

12. $\begin{array}{r} 600 \\ \times\ 300 \\ \hline 0,000 \end{array}$

E. Multiply.

13. $\begin{array}{r} 21 \\ \times\ 10 \\ \hline \end{array}$

14. $\begin{array}{r} 76 \\ \times\ 10 \\ \hline \end{array}$

15. $\begin{array}{r} 40 \\ \times\ 20 \\ \hline \end{array}$

16. $\begin{array}{r} 500 \\ \times\ 10 \\ \hline \end{array}$

17. $\begin{array}{r} 200 \\ \times\ 30 \\ \hline \end{array}$

18. $\begin{array}{r} 600 \\ \times\ 20 \\ \hline \end{array}$

19. $\begin{array}{r} 300 \\ \times\ 100 \\ \hline \end{array}$

20. $\begin{array}{r} 700 \\ \times\ 400 \\ \hline \end{array}$

21. $\begin{array}{r} 500 \\ \times\ 500 \\ \hline \end{array}$

22. $\begin{array}{r} 900 \\ \times\ 700 \\ \hline \end{array}$

Multiply.

1.	77	2.	77	3.	53	4.	53	5.	70	6.	70
	× 1		× 10		× 1		× 10		× 1		× 10

7.	80	8.	80	9.	46	10.	46	11.	59	12.	59
	× 1		× 10		× 3		× 30		× 4		× 40

13.	422	14.	422	15.	422	16.	600	17.	600
	× 1		× 10		× 100		× 10		× 100

18.	900	19.	900	20.	822	21.	822	22.	822
	× 10		× 100		× 2		× 20		× 200

Solve.

23. Alligators lay about 50 eggs at one time. About how many eggs would 500 alligators lay?

★ **24.** Alligators lay about 50 eggs at one time. About how many eggs would 25,000 alligators lay?

Find Out!
Brainteaser

Take 10 coins and arrange them as shown. Now, move only 3 coins and change the triangle so that it points downward.

Multiplying by Tens

548 peanuts are in each box. How many peanuts are in 24 boxes?

Step 1	Step 2	Step 3
MULTIPLY BY ONES	MULTIPLY BY TENS	ADD

Step 1
MULTIPLY BY ONES
```
   548
 × 24
  2192
```

Step 2
MULTIPLY BY TENS
```
   548
 × 24
  2192
 10960
```

Step 3
ADD
```
    548
  × 24
   2192
  10960
  13,152
```

There are 13,152 peanuts in 24 boxes.

A. Complete. It is not necessary to write the zero when multiplying by tens.

1.	2.	3.	4.	5.
45	29	101	877	425
× 17	× 64	× 44	× 63	× 35
315	116	404	2631	2125
45	174	404	5262	1275

B. Solve. First write the factors in vertical form. Be sure to line up the numbers correctly.

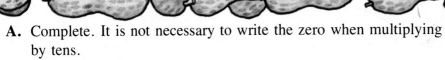

Example $37 \times 214 = n$

```
    214
  × 37
  1 498
  6 42
  7,918        n = 7,918
```

6. $93 \times 86 = n$

7. $52 \times 407 = n$

8. $75 \times 398 = n$

C. Multiply.

9.	10.	11.	12.	13.
32	43	59	36	384
× 45	× 62	× 33	× 58	× 62

14.	15.	16.	17.	18.
613	291	108	$0.68	$1.87
× 24	× 37	× 29	× 49	× 74

Multiply.

1. 32 × 14	**2.** 40 × 17	**3.** 56 × 17	**4.** 92 × 45	**5.** 43 × 24	**6.** 67 × 81
7. 58 × 91	**8.** 44 × 62	**9.** 84 × 39	**10.** $93 × 68	**11.** 82 × 77	**12.** 65 × 56
13. 456 × 18	**14.** $989 × 91	**15.** 101 × 47	**16.** 754 × 29	**17.** 327 × 63	**18.** 672 × 52
19. $4.62 × 94	**20.** $4.07 × 36	**21.** $5.76 × 89	**22.** $2.07 × 75	**23.** $0.25 × 87	**24.** $0.98 × 82
25. $6.64 × 28	**26.** 63 × 12	**27.** 304 × 67	**28.** 42 × 34	**29.** $702 × 47	**30.** 28 × 14
31. 73 × 73	**32.** $1.39 × 51	**33.** 487 × 63	**34.** 908 × 12	**35.** 488 × 94	**36.** $8.37 × 66

Solve.

37. $34 \times 92 = n$ **38.** $67 \times 125 = n$ **39.** $83 \times 746 = n$

40. There are 15 oranges in each bag. How many oranges are in 48 bags?

41. The owner spends $9.50 a day on part-time help. How much does he spend in 75 days?

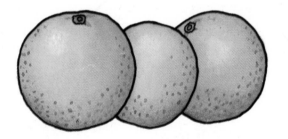

Find Out!
Brainteaser

Complete.

A, 12, B, 24, C, 36, ___?___ , ___?___ , ___?___

A, A, 2, B, B, 6, C, C, 18, ___?___ , ___?___ , ___?___

Multiplying by Hundreds

The radio station plays 325 records each day. How many records are played in 127 days?

Step 1	Step 2	Step 3	Step 4
ONES	TENS	HUNDREDS	ADD

Step 1
ONES
```
   325
 × 127
  2275
```

Step 2
TENS
```
   325
 × 127
  2275
  6500
```

Step 3
HUNDREDS
```
   325
 × 127
  2275
  6500
 32500
```

Step 4
ADD
```
    325
  × 127
   2275
   6500
  32500
  41,275
```

41,275 records are played.

A. Complete. It is not necessary to write the zeros.

1.
```
   341
 × 526
  2046
   682
  1705
```

2.
```
   878
 × 163
  2634
  5268
```

3.
```
   409
 × 733
  1227
  1227
```

4.
```
   558
 × 237
  3906
```

5.
```
   629
 × 455
  3145
```

B. Here are two ways to multiply when there is a zero in the multiplier.

```
   862
 × 305
  4 310
  0 00
  258 6
 262,910
```

```
   862
 × 305
  4 310          ← NO ZEROS
  258 6
 262,910
```

Multiply.

6.
```
   413
 × 309
```

7.
```
  $658
 × 403
```

8.
```
   249
 × 702
```

9.
```
   947
 × 508
```

10.
```
 $4.97
 × 606
```

Multiply.

1.	314 × 192	**2.**	$246 × 153	**3.**	538 × 537	**4.**	349 × 216	**5.**	784 × 618
6.	628 × 343	**7.**	$9.26 × 354	**8.**	532 × 948	**9.**	678 × 396	**10.**	$8.93 × 547
11.	$2.50 × 102	**12.**	627 × 205	**13.**	799 × 603	**14.**	401 × 303	**15.**	$8.75 × 408
16.	578 × 309	**17.**	$7.82 × 505	**18.**	643 × 208	**19.**	$808 × 709	**20.**	207 × 604
21.	976 × 357	**22.**	284 × 209	**23.**	975 × 801	**24.**	$3.92 × 222	**25.**	161 × 837
26.	498 × 475	**27.**	$139 × 505	**28.**	764 × 482	**29.**	602 × 846	**30.**	$1.32 × 401

Solve.

★ **31.** $a \times b = b \times \square$

★ **32.** $a \times (b + c) = (a \times b) + (a \times \square)$

33. A popular disc jockey receives 218 fan letters each day. How many letters are received in 365 days?

Estimating Products

An apartment building has 37 stories.
There are 23 apartments on each
floor. Donna estimated the number of
apartments. Then she multiplied to
find the exact answer.

ESTIMATE	40	EXACT	37
	× 20		× 23
	800		111
			74
			851

Since the products are close, the exact
product is reasonable.

A. Look at the example, then complete.

ESTIMATE	400	EXACT	384
	× 400		× 415
	160,000		1 920
			3 84
			153 6
			159,360

1. 384 is rounded to __?__ .

2. 415 is rounded to __?__ .

3. The estimated product is __?__ .

4. Is the exact product reasonable?

B. It costs $2.80 to wash each window. Mr. Gavin wants 5 windows
washed. He estimated the cost.
  Step 1 Round the money to the nearest dollar.
          $2.80 is rounded to $3.00.

  Step 2 Multiply the rounded numbers. $3.00 × 5

  5. The cost is about __?__ .

C. Estimate the products.

	6. 384	**7.** 5,861	**8.** 37	**9.** 67	**10.** 296
	× 2	× 3	× 49	× 85	× 301

Multiply. Then check by estimating.

1. 39
× 2

2. 312
× 9

3. 876
× 2

4. 314
× 7

5.   76
× 24

6.   335
× 704

Estimate the product.

7. 45
× 9

8. 23
× 6

9.   39
× 77

10. 412
× 5

11. 1,452
× 8

12.   322
× 497

Estimate the cost.

13. $2.95
× 8

14. $4.50
× 4

15. $3.17
× 7

Solve.

16. The building has 3 elevators. Each elevator holds 19 people. About how many people will the 3 elevators hold?

17. On each of the 46 floors, 11 apartments have a terrace. About how many apartments have a terrace?

18. Peter did 45 × 61 on his calculator. The display read 305. Is the answer reasonable?

19. Jane did 389 × 406 on her calculator. The display read 157,934. Is the answer reasonable?

Problem Solving

1. Mr. Walker has a class of 30 students. Each student sold 10 tickets for the band concert. How many tickets did the class sell in all?

2. Mrs. Meeks ordered box lunches for the band members. She ordered 50 box lunches. Each box lunch cost $1.25. What was the total cost of the lunches?

3. Posters were made for the concert. The posters cost twenty-three dollars and seventy-five cents. Write this as a standard numeral.

4. Carole practiced 25 hours one week, 30 hours the next week, and 62 hours the next week. How many hours did she practice in all?

5. Mr. Mahoney spent $3.75 on tickets. How much change did he receive from a $20 bill?

6. The school bought 70 new band outfits. Each outfit cost $87.75. What was the total cost?

7. Mrs. Meeks took 40 band members to a city music festival. The cost for each student ticket was $0.85. The bus cost $75. How much money was paid in all?

Multiply.

1. 30
(76) × 4

2. 500
(76) × 5

3. 7,000
(76) × 2

4. 60,000
(76) × 8

5. 92
(80) × 7

6. 817
(80) × 9

7. $23.56
(82) × 3

8. 50,192
(82) × 6

9. 12
(90) × 10

10. 82
(90) × 50

11. 504
(90) × 100

12. 789
(90) × 700

13. 46
(92) × 15

14. $45
(92) × 79

15. $8.94
(92) × 73

16. 572
(92) × 21

17. 335
(94) × 401

18. 843
(94) × 767

19. $6.20
(94) × 412

Estimate the products. *(96)*

20. 614
× 8

21. 57
× 19

22. Name the first five multiples of 7. *(88)*

23. Find the first three common multiples of 2 and 5. *(88)*

Solve. *(86, 98)*

24. One parakeet costs $3.75. How much will 5 parakeets cost?

25. Ella sold 15 bird cages on Monday and 10 on Tuesday. Each bird cage cost $10. How much did she make in all?

Multiply.

1. 50
(76) × 7

2. 600
(76) × 4

3. 3,000
(76) × 9

4. 80,000
(76) × 5

5. 65
(80) × 8

6. 434
(80) × 6

7. 7,809
(82) × 3

8. $514.28
(82) × 2

9. 39
(90) × 10

10. 76
(90) × 50

11. 864
(90) × 100

12. 284
(90) × 600

13. 37
(92) × 28

14. $55
(92) × 77

15. 605
(92) × 93

16. $7.36
(92) × 48

17. 784
(94) × 606

18. $9.29
(94) × 211

19. 540
(94) × 723

Estimate the products. *(96)*

20. 5,751
× 9

21. 62
× 49

22. Name the first five multiples of 13. *(88)*

23. Find the first three common multiples of 4 and 5. *(88)*

Solve. *(86, 98)*

24. There are 29 students in each class. How many students are in 23 classes?

25. Harry bought 2 notebooks for $1.35 each. He also bought a pen for $2.50. How much did he spend in all?

1. Mike bought two baseball bats at a sporting goods store. Each bat cost $5.21. How much did he spend?

   A $10.42

   B $10.62

   C $11.24

   D $11.42

---

2. What is the temperature?

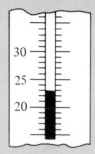

   E 30°F

   F 28°F

   G 25°F

   H 23°F

---

3. Myra bought a shirt for $5.95. She gave the clerk a $20 bill. What change should she receive?

   A A $10 bill, a $5 bill, and a nickel

   B A $10 bill, four $1 bills, and a nickel

   C A $10 bill, four dimes, and a nickel

   D Four $1 bills and a nickel

4. Jim worked 20 minutes on Monday and 25 minutes on Tuesday. How long did he work in all?

   E 1 hour

   F 50 minutes

   G 45 minutes

   H 35 minutes

---

5. What time is indicated?

   A 7:50

   B 8:10

   C 10:20

   D 10:40

---

6. Maria received the following grades on her report card. What is her average?

Subject	Grade
Math	95
Social Studies	90
Science	85
Penmanship	90

   E 95

   F 90

   G 85

   H 80

Division

How many 5's are there in 15?

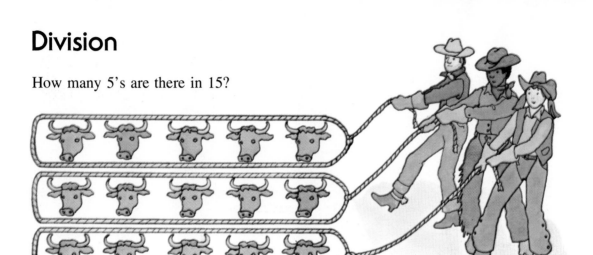

$$15 \div 5 = 3 \text{ or } 5\overline{)15}^{3}$$

The *divisor* is 5.
The *dividend* is 15.
The *quotient* is 3.

How many 4's are there in 22?

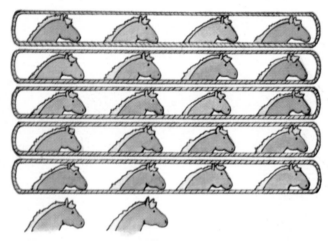

$$22 \div 4 = 5\,r\,2 \text{ or } 4\overline{)22}^{5\,r\,2}$$
$$\begin{array}{r} -20 \\ \hline 2 \end{array}$$

The *quotient* is 5.
The *remainder* is 2.

Practice

Name the divisor, dividend, quotient, and remainder.

$$
\begin{array}{r} 4 \\ \textbf{1. } 3\overline{)12} \\ -12 \\ \hline \end{array}
\qquad
\begin{array}{r} 2 \\ \textbf{2. } 9\overline{)18} \\ -18 \\ \hline \end{array}
\qquad
\begin{array}{r} 3\,r\,2 \\ \textbf{3. } 7\overline{)23} \\ -21 \\ \hline 2 \end{array}
\qquad
\begin{array}{r} 6 \\ \textbf{4. } 5\overline{)30} \\ -30 \\ \hline \end{array}
\qquad
\begin{array}{r} 7\,r\,1 \\ \textbf{5. } 4\overline{)29} \\ -28 \\ \hline 1 \end{array}
$$

6. $15 \div 5 = 3$ **7.** $20 \div 9 = 2\,r\,2$ **8.** $25 \div 4 = 6\,r\,1$ **9.** $14 \div 7 = 2$ **10.** $30 \div 6 = 5$

Divide.

11. $54 \div 9$ **12.** $36 \div 4$ **13.** $44 \div 7$ **14.** $64 \div 8$ **15.** $50 \div 8$

$9\overline{)54}$ $4\overline{)36}$ $7\overline{)44}$ $8\overline{)64}$ $8\overline{)50}$

RACE TIME

Divide.

1. $1\overline{)9}$ **2.** $2\overline{)14}$ **3.** $6\overline{)36}$ **4.** $4\overline{)36}$ **5.** $5\overline{)5}$ **6.** $4\overline{)16}$

7. $4\overline{)12}$ **8.** $9\overline{)54}$ **9.** $7\overline{)42}$ **10.** $2\overline{)8}$ **11.** $5\overline{)45}$ **12.** $2\overline{)12}$

13. $8\overline{)72}$ **14.** $6\overline{)30}$ **15.** $1\overline{)5}$ **16.** $3\overline{)3}$ **17.** $7\overline{)28}$ **18.** $5\overline{)15}$

19. $8\overline{)40}$ **20.** $3\overline{)18}$ **21.** $5\overline{)20}$ **22.** $2\overline{)16}$ **23.** $9\overline{)9}$ **24.** $6\overline{)24}$

25. $3\overline{)21}$ **26.** $7\overline{)49}$ **27.** $3\overline{)24}$ **28.** $1\overline{)2}$ **29.** $7\overline{)35}$ **30.** $3\overline{)12}$

31. $4\overline{)24}$ **32.** $9\overline{)45}$ **33.** $6\overline{)12}$ **34.** $7\overline{)14}$ **35.** $5\overline{)25}$ **36.** $6\overline{)6}$

37. $1\overline{)8}$ **38.** $9\overline{)27}$ **39.** $2\overline{)18}$ **40.** $7\overline{)63}$ **41.** $5\overline{)30}$ **42.** $1\overline{)3}$

43. $9\overline{)81}$ **44.** $8\overline{)64}$ **45.** $3\overline{)27}$ **46.** $8\overline{)32}$ **47.** $5\overline{)10}$ **48.** $4\overline{)28}$

49. $3\overline{)6}$ **50.** $6\overline{)54}$ **51.** $2\overline{)10}$ **52.** $6\overline{)48}$ **53.** $2\overline{)2}$ **54.** $1\overline{)7}$

55. $9\overline{)36}$ **56.** $1\overline{)4}$ **57.** $2\overline{)0}$ **58.** $9\overline{)18}$ **59.** $2\overline{)6}$ **60.** $8\overline{)48}$

61. $4\overline{)0}$ **62.** $9\overline{)63}$ **63.** $3\overline{)9}$ **64.** $7\overline{)7}$ **65.** $8\overline{)8}$ **66.** $6\overline{)0}$

67. $8\overline{)16}$ **68.** $1\overline{)0}$ **69.** $4\overline{)32}$ **70.** $7\overline{)21}$ **71.** $3\overline{)0}$ **72.** $8\overline{)56}$

73. $5\overline{)40}$ **74.** $8\overline{)24}$ **75.** $2\overline{)4}$ **76.** $6\overline{)18}$ **77.** $5\overline{)35}$ **78.** $3\overline{)15}$

79. $9\overline{)0}$ **80.** $4\overline{)8}$ **81.** $1\overline{)1}$ **82.** $7\overline{)56}$ **83.** $4\overline{)4}$ **84.** $7\overline{)0}$

85. $9\overline{)72}$ **86.** $4\overline{)20}$ **87.** $8\overline{)0}$ **88.** $1\overline{)7}$ **89.** $1\overline{)6}$ **90.** $6\overline{)42}$

0 and 1 in Division

The quotient of any number divided by 1 is that number.

$$12 \div 1 = 12 \qquad 1\overline{)8}\;^{8}$$

When 0 is divided by any non-zero number, the quotient is 0.

$$0 \div 12 = 0 \qquad 8\overline{)0}\;^{0}$$

When a number is divided by itself, the quotient is 1.

$$12 \div 12 = 1 \qquad 8\overline{)8}\;^{1}$$

A. Divide.

1. $8 \div 1$ **2.** $25 \div 1$ **3.** $1\overline{)39}$ **4.** $0 \div 4$ **5.** $0 \div 7$

6. $18\overline{)0}$ **7.** $44\overline{)0}$ **8.** $11 \div 11$ **9.** $8\overline{)8}$ **10.** $72\overline{)72}$

Practice

Divide.

1. $7 \div 1$ **2.** $32 \div 1$ **3.** $1\overline{)13}$ **4.** $1\overline{)49}$ **5.** $1\overline{)64}$

6. $0 \div 9$ **7.** $0 \div 56$ **8.** $24\overline{)0}$ **9.** $39\overline{)0}$ **10.** $48\overline{)0}$

11. $4 \div 4$ **12.** $16 \div 16$ **13.** $30\overline{)30}$ **14.** $52\overline{)52}$ **15.** $88\overline{)88}$

16. $81 \div 81$ **17.** $1\overline{)64}$ **18.** $12\overline{)0}$ **19.** $0 \div 56$ **20.** $1\overline{)32}$

21. $1\overline{)20}$ **22.** $32\overline{)32}$ **23.** $15 \div 15$ **24.** $29 \div 1$ **25.** $5\overline{)0}$

★ Complete.

26. $36 \div \underline{\ ?\ } = 1$ **27.** $\underline{\ ?\ }\overline{)19}\;^{19}$ **28.** $\underline{\ ?\ } \div 68 = 0$

Patterns in Division

Look at this pattern.

$$8 \div 8 = 1$$
$$80 \div 8 = 10$$
$$800 \div 8 = 100$$
$$8,000 \div 8 = 1,000$$
$$80,000 \div 8 = 10,000$$

A. Complete.

1. $7 \div 7 = \underline{\ ?\ }$ $7\overline{)7}^{\,?}$

2. $70 \div 7 = \underline{\ ?\ }$ $7\overline{)70}^{\,?}$

3. $700 \div 7 = \underline{\ ?\ }$ $7\overline{)700}^{\,?}$

4. $7,000 \div 7 = \underline{\ ?\ }$ $7\overline{)7,000}^{\,?}$

B. Complete.

5. $21 \div 3 = \underline{\ ?\ }$ $3\overline{)21}^{\,?}$

6. $210 \div 3 = \underline{\ ?\ }$ $3\overline{)210}^{\,?}$

7. $2,100 \div 3 = \underline{\ ?\ }$ $3\overline{)2,100}^{\,?}$

8. $21,000 \div 3 = \underline{\ ?\ }$ $3\overline{)21,000}^{\,?}$

C. Divide.

9. $6\overline{)60}$ 10. $6\overline{)600}$ 11. $6\overline{)6,000}$ 12. $6\overline{)60,000}$

13. $9\overline{)72}$ 14. $9\overline{)720}$ 15. $9\overline{)7,200}$ 16. $9\overline{)72,000}$

17. $4\overline{)2,800}$ 18. $5\overline{)25,000}$ 19. $2\overline{)40}$ 20. $3\overline{)240}$

Divide.

1. $2\overline{)40}$ 2. $3\overline{)60}$ 3. $9\overline{)90}$ 4. $4\overline{)80}$ 5. $5\overline{)50}$

6. $3\overline{)30}$ 7. $3\overline{)90}$ 8. $2\overline{)60}$ 9. $4\overline{)40}$ 10. $2\overline{)80}$

11. $4\overline{)800}$ 12. $3\overline{)900}$ 13. $2\overline{)600}$ 14. $6\overline{)540}$ 15. $5\overline{)350}$

16. $3\overline{)150}$ 17. $5\overline{)450}$ 18. $7\overline{)490}$ 19. $8\overline{)320}$ 20. $9\overline{)630}$

21. $7\overline{)7,000}$ 22. $4\overline{)8,000}$ 23. $3\overline{)2,700}$ 24. $6\overline{)3,600}$ 25. $5\overline{)5,000}$

26. $6\overline{)4,200}$ 27. $7\overline{)5,600}$ 28. $8\overline{)6,400}$ 29. $9\overline{)7,200}$ 30. $8\overline{)4,000}$

31. $5\overline{)50,000}$ 32. $4\overline{)80,000}$ 33. $3\overline{)90,000}$ 34. $3\overline{)24,000}$

35. $2\overline{)16,000}$ 36. $7\overline{)42,000}$ 37. $6\overline{)54,000}$ 38. $8\overline{)32,000}$

39. $3\overline{)2,100}$ 40. $6\overline{)60}$ 41. $9\overline{)900}$ 42. $4\overline{)28,000}$

43. $7\overline{)630}$ 44. $5\overline{)30,000}$

45. $6\overline{)4,800}$ 46. $9\overline{)810}$

★ 47. $8\overline{)8,000,000}$

★ 48. $6\overline{)42,000,000}$

Solve.

49. 600 bottles of juice are needed for the school picnic. There are 6 bottles in each pack. How many packs are needed?

50. There are 1,400 sandwiches to be packed in 7 boxes. Each box holds the same number of sandwiches. How many sandwiches will be in each box?

Dividing 2- and 3-Digit Numbers

The pet shop had 168 fish in 4 large tanks.
Each tank had the same number of fish.
How many fish were in each tank?

$4\overline{)168}$ ESTIMATE.
How many 4's in 1? none

$4\overline{)168}$ How many 4's in 16? 4
Write 4 in the tens place.

$\begin{array}{r} 4 \\ 4\overline{)168} \\ 16\downarrow \\ \hline 8 \end{array}$ MULTIPLY. $4 \times 4 = 16$
SUBTRACT.
Bring down the 8.

$\begin{array}{r} 42 \\ 4\overline{)168} \\ 16\downarrow \\ \hline 8 \\ 8 \\ \hline 0 \end{array}$ ESTIMATE. How many 4's in 8? 2
Write 2 in the ones place.
MULTIPLY and SUBTRACT.
The quotient is 42.

42 fish were in each tank.

A. Divide $7\overline{)294}$. Complete.

   1. $29 \div 7$ is about ___?___

   2. Write 4 in the ___?___ place.

   3. Complete.

$\begin{array}{r} 4 \\ 7\overline{)294} \\ 28 \\ \hline 14 \end{array}$

B. Divide.

   4. $3\overline{)96}$ **5.** $2\overline{)264}$ **6.** $6\overline{)732}$ **7.** $4\overline{)\$128}$ **8.** $6\overline{)438}$

Divide.

1. 2)$\overline{46}$ **2.** 3)$\overline{69}$ **3.** 5)$\overline{55}$ **4.** 2)$\overline{86}$ **5.** 4)$\overline{88}$

6. 4)$\overline{48}$ **7.** 3)$\overline{36}$ **8.** 2)$\overline{64}$ **9.** 2)$\overline{48}$ **10.** 3)$\overline{93}$

11. 3)$\overline{42}$ **12.** 2)$\overline{56}$ **13.** 5)$\overline{65}$ **14.** 7)$\overline{\$91}$ **15.** 4)$\overline{68}$

16. 8)$\overline{96}$ **17.** 3)$\overline{87}$ **18.** 6)$\overline{78}$ **19.** 5)$\overline{80}$ **20.** 7)$\overline{84}$

21. 2)$\overline{268}$ **22.** 7)$\overline{777}$ **23.** 3)$\overline{696}$ **24.** 2)$\overline{684}$ **25.** 3)$\overline{396}$

26. 4)$\overline{484}$ **27.** 3)$\overline{369}$ **28.** 4)$\overline{884}$ **29.** 2)$\overline{446}$ **30.** 3)$\overline{993}$

31. 2)$\overline{528}$ **32.** 3)$\overline{672}$ **33.** 8)$\overline{\$896}$ **34.** 2)$\overline{936}$ **35.** 6)$\overline{852}$

36. 7)$\overline{854}$ **37.** 4)$\overline{676}$ **38.** 5)$\overline{665}$ **39.** 7)$\overline{994}$ **40.** 5)$\overline{960}$

41. 2)$\overline{126}$ **42.** 3)$\overline{276}$ **43.** 7)$\overline{427}$ **44.** 9)$\overline{369}$ **45.** 5)$\overline{255}$

46. 8)$\overline{648}$ **47.** 6)$\overline{246}$ **48.** 4)$\overline{328}$ **49.** 9)$\overline{549}$ **50.** 3)$\overline{189}$

51. 5)$\overline{315}$ **52.** 2)$\overline{\$134}$ **53.** 6)$\overline{162}$ **54.** 3)$\overline{147}$ **55.** 7)$\overline{266}$

56. 6)$\overline{402}$ **57.** 5)$\overline{380}$ **58.** 4)$\overline{192}$ **59.** 8)$\overline{432}$ **60.** 9)$\overline{\$738}$

61. 4)$\overline{948}$ **62.** 2)$\overline{28}$ **63.** 9)$\overline{225}$ **64.** 3)$\overline{363}$ **65.** 4)$\overline{76}$

★ Complete.

66. 4)$\overline{\ ?}$ = 42   **67.** 7)$\overline{\ ?}$ = 51   **68.** 6)$\overline{\ ?}$ = 24   **69.** ?)$\overline{219}$ = 73   **70.** ?)$\overline{976}$ = 122

Solve.

71. The pet shop had 135 cans of cat food on 5 shelves. The same number of cans was on each shelf. How many cans were on each shelf?

72. The pet shop had 45 birds in 3 large cages. The same number of birds was in each cage. How many birds were in each cage?

Dividing With Remainders

At Paumonok School, 189 books were shared by 6 classes. How many books did each class get? How many books were left over?

$6)\overline{189}$ ESTIMATE.
How many 6's in 1? none

$\dfrac{3}{6)\overline{189}}$ How many 6's in 18? 3
Write 3 in the tens place.

$\begin{array}{r} 3 \\ 6)\overline{189} \\ 18\downarrow \\ \hline 9 \end{array}$ MULTIPLY. $3 \times 6 = 18$
SUBTRACT.
Bring down the 9.

$\begin{array}{r} 31 \\ 6)\overline{189} \\ 18 \\ \hline 9 \end{array}$ ESTIMATE.
How many 6's in 9? about 1
Write 1 in the ones place.

$\begin{array}{r} 31\,r3 \\ 6)\overline{189} \\ 18 \\ \hline 9 \\ 6 \\ \hline 3 \end{array}$ MULTIPLY and SUBTRACT.

The quotient is 31.
The remainder is 3.

CHECK
$\begin{array}{r} 31 \\ \times\ 6 \\ \hline 186 \\ +\ \ 3 \\ \hline 189 \end{array}$

There were 31 books for each class. There were 3 books left over.

A. Complete.

1. $\begin{array}{r} 1 \\ 6)\overline{75} \\ 6 \\ \hline \end{array}$
2. $\begin{array}{r} 5 \\ 5)\overline{29} \\ 25 \\ \hline \end{array}$
3. $\begin{array}{r} 1 \\ 3)\overline{367} \\ 3 \\ \hline \end{array}$
4. $\begin{array}{r} 1 \\ 4)\overline{657} \\ 4 \\ \hline \end{array}$
5. $\begin{array}{r} 6 \\ 4)\overline{273} \\ 24 \\ \hline \end{array}$

B. Divide and check.

6. $3)\overline{67}$
7. $2)\overline{39}$
8. $8)\overline{95}$
9. $6)\overline{45}$
10. $7)\overline{52}$

11. $4)\overline{847}$
12. $5)\overline{726}$
13. $8)\overline{943}$
14. $7)\overline{359}$
15. $5)\overline{362}$

Divide and check.

1. $2\overline{)45}$ 2. $8\overline{)89}$ 3. $4\overline{)89}$ 4. $5\overline{)57}$ 5. $3\overline{)94}$

6. $5\overline{)96}$ 7. $4\overline{)55}$ 8. $6\overline{)74}$ 9. $8\overline{)92}$ 10. $3\overline{)52}$

11. $6\overline{)41}$ 12. $4\overline{)15}$ 13. $7\overline{)65}$ 14. $5\overline{)28}$ 15. $9\overline{)74}$

16. $8\overline{)50}$ 17. $2\overline{)19}$ 18. $3\overline{)25}$ 19. $6\overline{)57}$ 20. $7\overline{)40}$

21. $4\overline{)447}$ 22. $2\overline{)685}$ 23. $3\overline{)694}$ 24. $7\overline{)778}$ 25. $3\overline{)368}$

26. $2\overline{)573}$ 27. $6\overline{)792}$ 28. $4\overline{)695}$ 29. $5\overline{)931}$ 30. $7\overline{)958}$

31. $3\overline{)682}$ 32. $8\overline{)925}$ 33. $2\overline{)659}$ 34. $7\overline{)866}$ 35. $4\overline{)533}$

36. $8\overline{)249}$ 37. $5\overline{)459}$ 38. $6\overline{)307}$ 39. $3\overline{)127}$ 40. $4\overline{)247}$

41. $7\overline{)359}$ 42. $2\overline{)145}$ 43. $3\overline{)275}$ 44. $5\overline{)206}$ 45. $8\overline{)409}$

46. $4\overline{)315}$ 47. $6\overline{)455}$ 48. $9\overline{)411}$ 49. $3\overline{)113}$ 50. $7\overline{)527}$

51. $6\overline{)145}$ 52. $8\overline{)334}$ 53. $2\overline{)157}$ 54. $5\overline{)426}$ 55. $3\overline{)257}$

56. $5\overline{)82}$ 57. $7\overline{)288}$ 58. $3\overline{)67}$ 59. $6\overline{)823}$ 60. $5\overline{)173}$

61. $8\overline{)95}$ 62. $3\overline{)934}$ 63. $4\overline{)511}$ 64. $6\overline{)52}$ 65. $7\overline{)86}$

★ Complete.

66. $\overset{8\,r\,1}{?\overline{)25}}$ 67. $\overset{21\,r\,2}{4\overline{)\,?}}$ 68. $\overset{136\,r\,2}{?\overline{)682}}$ 69. $\overset{232\,r\,1}{2\overline{)\,?}}$

Solve.

70. How many rows of 6 chairs can be formed from 35 chairs? How many chairs will be left over?

71. David's book has 109 pages. He has 9 days to read it. How many pages should he read each day? How many extra pages are there?

Divide.

1. $27\overline{)0}$ **2.** $55\overline{)55}$ **3.** $1\overline{)92}$ **4.** $65\overline{)0}$ **5.** $1\overline{)32}$
(105)   *(105)*   *(105)*   *(105)*   *(105)*

6. $8\overline{)5,600}$ **7.** $4\overline{)3,600}$ **8.** $2\overline{)120}$ **9.** $9\overline{)810}$ **10.** $6\overline{)24,000}$
(106)   *(106)*   *(106)*   *(106)*   *(106)*

11. $6\overline{)60}$ **12.** $5\overline{)250}$ **13.** $3\overline{)90}$ **14.** $7\overline{)3,500}$ **15.** $4\overline{)16,000}$
(106)   *(106)*   *(106)*   *(106)*   *(106)*

16. $4\overline{)88}$ **17.** $7\overline{)847}$ **18.** $5\overline{)455}$ **19.** $8\overline{)272}$ **20.** $6\overline{)84}$
(108)   *(108)*   *(108)*   *(108)*   *(108)*

21. $3\overline{)458}$ **22.** $9\overline{)98}$ **23.** $7\overline{)734}$ **24.** $5\overline{)96}$ **25.** $3\overline{)133}$
(110)   *(110)*   *(110)*   *(110)*   *(110)*

Solve. *(108)*

26. There are 968 new tires. How many cars can get 4 new tires? How many tires will be left over?

27. A car dealer has 132 cars in stock. There are 6 salespersons. Each must sell the same number of cars. How many cars must each salesperson sell?

Find Out!
Brainteaser

Use these digits: 1   2   3   4   5   6   7   8 and 9.
Place $+$, $-$, and $\times$ between them so that the answer is 100.
Do not change the order of the digits.

Example $1 \times 2 + 34 + 56 + 7 - 8 + 9 = 100$

1. Complete. Use $+$, $-$, and $\times$.
$123 + 4 - 5 \quad 67 \quad 89 = 100$

2. There are several solutions.
Try to find at least one more solution.

Keeping Fit

Add.

1.   4
     2
     3
  + 8

2.   3
     5
     2
     9
  + 6

3.   8
     5
     6
     9
  + 7

4.   36
  + 62

5.   74
  + 16

6.   93
  + 27

7.   79
  + 87

8.   309
  + 511

9.   634
  + 272

10.   723
  + 331

11.   553
  + 547

12. $ 6.06
  + 7.05

13. $ 3.34
  + 6.52

14.   1,125
  + 3,652

15.   5,634
  + 1,206

16.   7,842
  + 1,058

17.   9,356
  +   144

18. $ 23.54
  + 11.14

19. $ 52.59
  + 10.11

20.   66,394
  + 22,715

21.   27,433
  + 39,189

22.   87,643
  + 92,899

23. $ 512.35
  +   61.42

24.   49
     85
  + 76

25.   63
     21
  + 47

26.   97
     53
  + 24

27.   32
     5
  + 53

28.   362
     106
  + 503

29.   474
     95
  + 206

30.   501
     632
  + 541

31.   694
     36
  + 322

32.   9,346
     1,079
  +   453

33.   69,892
     7,431
  +   804

34.   84,593
     1,607
  + 53,819

35.   64,902
     76,326
  +   2,989

36.   409,764
  + 280,809

37.   704,301
  + 293,422

38. $ 905,511
  + 147,933

39. $ 820,490
  +   62,419

40.   11,123,451
     9,184,931
  +   6,327,422

41.   911,424,634
     82,433,523
  +   43,216,416

42.   722,332,809
     634,557,223
  +   29,694,120

43.   844,796,321
     355,325,436
  + 269,436,852

44. 36,894 + 26,504 + 2,384

45. 61,542,809 + 365 + 4,324,101

46. 202,897,342 + 631,946 + 1,126,998

47. 406,582,340 + 1,116 + 84

Problem Solving

There are 9,800 tickets available for a concert. 3,575 tickets were sold. How many tickets were not sold?

Using smaller numbers in place of larger numbers will help you decide what operation to use.

PLAN: Which operation should we use?
        Think: 10 tickets
              5 tickets were sold

$$\begin{array}{r} {\scriptstyle 7\ 9\ 10} \\ 9,8\cancel{0}\cancel{0} \\ -\ 3,575 \\ \hline 6,225 \end{array}$$

Use subtraction.

There are 6,225 tickets left.

A. Each ticket cost $9.75. 895 tickets were sold the first week. How much money was collected?

  1. PLAN: $2 a ticket   Use ___?___ .
            5 tickets sold

  2. How much money was collected?

B. Solve.

  3. One rock group made $5,875 in one night. There are 5 people in the group. Each person makes the same amount. How much did each person make?

Tell which operation to use ($+$, $-$, $\times$, $\div$). Solve.

1. Ushers sold 125 souvenir programs for $2.25 each. How much did they collect?

2. Antonio made $224 in 8 nights. How much did he make each night?

3. Carolyn spent $16.75 for posters of rock groups. She paid with a $20 bill. What was her change?

4. Fred parked 200 cars for a rock concert. The cost for each car was $2.75. How much did he collect?

5. There were 786 tickets sold on Monday, 586 on Tuesday, and 323 on Wednesday. How many tickets were sold in all?

6. Mrs. Kennedy rents costumes to rock groups. She made $1,375 each week. How much did she make in 4 weeks?

Dividing 4- and 5-Digit Numbers

The amusement park had 6,835 tickets
to sell. There were 3 ticket booths.
Each booth had the same number
of tickets. How many tickets did
each booth have?

$$
\begin{array}{r}
2\ 278\,r1,\ \text{or}\ 2{,}278\,r1 \\
3\overline{)6{,}835} \\
6\phantom{{,}835} \\
\hline
8\phantom{{,}35} \\
6\phantom{{,}35} \\
\hline
23 \\
21 \\
\hline
25 \\
24 \\
\hline
1
\end{array}
$$

Each booth had 2,278 tickets.
1 ticket was left over.

A. Complete.

1.
$$
\begin{array}{r}
2\ 84 \\
3\overline{)8{,}523} \\
6\phantom{{,}523} \\
\hline
2\ 5 \\
2\ 4 \\
\hline
12
\end{array}
$$

2.
$$
\begin{array}{r}
1\ 52 \\
5\overline{)7{,}642} \\
5\phantom{{,}642} \\
\hline
2\ 6 \\
2\ 5 \\
\hline
14
\end{array}
$$

3.
$$
\begin{array}{r}
24\ 1 \\
4\overline{)96{,}540} \\
8\phantom{6{,}540} \\
\hline
16 \\
16 \\
\hline
5
\end{array}
$$

4.
$$
\begin{array}{r}
1\ 8 \\
4\overline{)7{,}511} \\
4\phantom{{,}511} \\
\hline
3\ 5
\end{array}
$$

5.
$$
\begin{array}{r}
1{,}2 \\
7\overline{)8{,}736} \\
7\phantom{{,}736} \\
\hline
1\ 7
\end{array}
$$

6.
$$
\begin{array}{r}
12 \\
5\overline{)62{,}331} \\
5\phantom{2{,}331} \\
\hline
12
\end{array}
$$

B. Divide.

7. $5\overline{)5{,}720}$ 8. $8\overline{)8{,}969}$ 9. $4\overline{)9{,}957}$ 10. $7\overline{)8{,}067}$

11. $2\overline{)84{,}314}$ 12. $6\overline{)93{,}252}$ 13. $7\overline{)92{,}139}$ 14. $3\overline{)78{,}953}$

Divide.

1. $2\overline{)5{,}242}$ **2.** $3\overline{)9{,}933}$ **3.** $8\overline{)9{,}256}$ **4.** $5\overline{)7{,}125}$ **5.** $3\overline{)3{,}396}$

6. $2\overline{)2{,}644}$ **7.** $4\overline{)9{,}848}$ **8.** $7\overline{)9{,}359}$ **9.** $6\overline{)6{,}798}$ **10.** $5\overline{)8{,}490}$

11. $3\overline{)6{,}964}$ **12.** $4\overline{)6{,}505}$ **13.** $6\overline{)7{,}639}$ **14.** $7\overline{)8{,}847}$ **15.** $5\overline{)9{,}361}$

16. $4\overline{)8{,}458}$ **17.** $5\overline{)7{,}567}$ **18.** $6\overline{)8{,}174}$ **19.** $8\overline{)9{,}397}$ **20.** $2\overline{)6{,}563}$

21. $2\overline{)56{,}442}$ **22.** $3\overline{)45{,}639}$ **23.** $7\overline{)85{,}974}$ **24.** $4\overline{)48{,}848}$

25. $5\overline{)89{,}285}$ **26.** $3\overline{)39{,}963}$ **27.** $5\overline{)65{,}985}$ **28.** $6\overline{)74{,}274}$

29. $4\overline{)46{,}385}$ **30.** $5\overline{)71{,}863}$ **31.** $3\overline{)76{,}838}$ **32.** $8\overline{)89{,}235}$

33. $7\overline{)87{,}987}$ **34.** $2\overline{)84{,}821}$ **35.** $6\overline{)72{,}875}$ **36.** $5\overline{)62{,}322}$

37. $5\overline{)84{,}625}$ **38.** $4\overline{)8{,}727}$

39. $7\overline{)8{,}878}$ **40.** $7\overline{)84{,}829}$

41. $4\overline{)9{,}279}$ **42.** $8\overline{)8{,}976}$

43. $2\overline{)31{,}294}$ **44.** $5\overline{)57{,}584}$

★ **45.** $4\overline{)493{,}824}$ ★ **46.** $2\overline{)987{,}654}$

★ **47.** $3\overline{)6{,}345{,}678}$ ★ **48.** $5\overline{)4{,}278{,}695}$

Solve.

49. In 7 days, 7,847 people rode the roller coaster. The same number rode each day. How many people rode it each day?

50. In 3 months, 67,458 people visited the park. The same number visited the park each month. How many people came each month?

Smaller Quotients

The art museum has 1,275 paintings.
They are equally divided among 5 exhibits.
How many paintings are in each exhibit?

$$5\overline{)1,275}$$

ESTIMATE.
How many 5's in 1? none

$$\begin{array}{r} 2 \\ 5\overline{)1,275} \end{array}$$

How many 5's in 12? about 2
Write 2 in the hundreds place.

$$\begin{array}{r} 25 \\ 5\overline{)1,275} \\ 10\downarrow \\ \hline 27 \end{array}$$

MULTIPLY and SUBTRACT.
Bring down the 7.
ESTIMATE. How many 5's in 27? about 5
Write 5 in the tens place.

$$\begin{array}{r} 255 \\ 5\overline{)1,275} \\ 10 \\ \hline 27 \\ 25\downarrow \\ \hline 25 \\ 25 \\ \hline 0 \end{array}$$

MULTIPLY and SUBTRACT.
Bring down the 5.
ESTIMATE. How many 5's in 25? 5
Write 5 in the ones place.
MULTIPLY and SUBTRACT.
The quotient is 255.

255 paintings are in each exhibit.

A. Complete.

1. $$\begin{array}{r} 59 \\ 4\overline{)2,377} \\ 20 \\ \hline 37 \\ 36 \\ \hline 1 \end{array}$$

2. $$\begin{array}{r} 34 \\ 7\overline{)2,443} \\ 21 \\ \hline 34 \end{array}$$

3. $$\begin{array}{r} 9 \\ 6\overline{)56,209} \\ 54 \\ \hline 22 \end{array}$$

4. $$\begin{array}{r} 5 \\ 4\overline{)20,592} \\ 20 \end{array}$$

B. Divide.

5. $6\overline{)3,528}$

6. $5\overline{)\$2,915}$

7. $9\overline{)5,076}$

8. $7\overline{)1,669}$

9. $4\overline{)34,252}$

10. $9\overline{)37,125}$

11. $3\overline{)\$15,411}$

12. $8\overline{)53,132}$

Divide.

1. $2\overline{)1,794}$ **2.** $3\overline{)2,349}$ **3.** $5\overline{)1,195}$ **4.** $4\overline{)2,628}$ **5.** $7\overline{)6,293}$

6. $4\overline{)1,260}$ **7.** $5\overline{)4,225}$ **8.** $3\overline{)2,559}$ **9.** $6\overline{)2,832}$ **10.** $9\overline{)6,165}$

11. $3\overline{)2,785}$ **12.** $7\overline{)1,728}$ **13.** $6\overline{)3,527}$ **14.** $7\overline{)5,409}$ **15.** $8\overline{)4,098}$

16. $6\overline{)4,112}$ **17.** $8\overline{)2,794}$ **18.** $9\overline{)8,445}$ **19.** $4\overline{)3,342}$ **20.** $7\overline{)3,746}$

21. $8\overline{)15,976}$ **22.** $3\overline{)24,861}$ **23.** $5\overline{)20,885}$ **24.** $9\overline{)21,186}$

25. $7\overline{)32,669}$ **26.** $6\overline{)34,392}$ **27.** $5\overline{)19,935}$ **28.** $7\overline{)64,813}$

29. $5\overline{)21,146}$ **30.** $3\overline{)11,527}$ **31.** $8\overline{)45,542}$ **32.** $4\overline{)26,851}$

33. $6\overline{)16,653}$ **34.** $5\overline{)23,882}$ **35.** $7\overline{)25,838}$ **36.** $8\overline{)15,898}$

37. $7\overline{)2,737}$ **38.** $4\overline{)1,536}$ **39.** $9\overline{)7,416}$ **40.** $2\overline{)1,372}$

41. $3\overline{)\$24,534}$ **42.** $8\overline{)69,552}$ **43.** $5\overline{)\$43,170}$ **44.** $6\overline{)52,926}$

45. $4\overline{)2,392}$ **46.** $5\overline{)19,840}$ **47.** $7\overline{)26,432}$ **48.** $9\overline{)74,295}$

49. $2\overline{)16,571}$ **50.** $3\overline{)17,325}$ **51.** $3\overline{)2,889}$ **52.** $7\overline{)4,774}$

53. $4\overline{)2,573}$ **54.** $3\overline{)\$19,326}$ **55.** $7\overline{)65,324}$ **56.** $6\overline{)\$4,344}$

★ **57.** $6\overline{)592,590}$ ★ **58.** $9\overline{)111,111}$ ★ **59.** $5\overline{)487,655}$ ★ **60.** $4\overline{)674,628}$

★ **61.** $9\overline{)1,010,101}$ ★ **62.** $8\overline{)3,653,232}$ ★ **63.** $5\overline{)4,090,913}$ ★ **64.** $7\overline{)9,552,151}$

Solve.

65. The museum sold 12,762 gifts in 6 days. The same number were sold each day. How many gifts were sold each day?

66. The museum has 2,943 items not on display. The same number are stored in each of 9 rooms. How many items are in each room?

Zeros in the Quotient

Divide $2\overline{)6,126}$

$$
\begin{array}{r}
3 \\
2\overline{)6,126}
\end{array}
$$
ESTIMATE. How many 2's in 6? 3
Write 3 in the thousands place.

$$
\begin{array}{r}
306 \\
2\overline{)6,126} \\
6\downarrow\downarrow \\
\hline
12
\end{array}
$$
MULTIPLY and SUBTRACT. Bring down the 1.
How many 2's in 1? Write 0 in the hundreds place.
Bring down the 2.
How many 2's in 12? 6
Write 6 in the tens place.

$$
\begin{array}{r}
3063 \\
2\overline{)6,126} \\
6 \\
\hline
12 \\
12\downarrow \\
\hline
06 \\
6 \\
\hline
0
\end{array}
$$
MULTIPLY and SUBTRACT.
Bring down the 6.
How many 2's in 6? 3
Write 3 in the ones place.
The quotient is 3063, or 3,063.

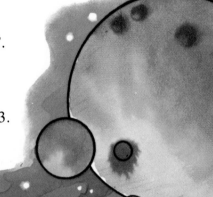

A. Complete.

1.
$$
\begin{array}{r}
\$10 \\
4\overline{)\$404} \\
4 \\
\hline
04
\end{array}
$$

2.
$$
\begin{array}{r}
10 \\
9\overline{)9,234} \\
9 \\
\hline
2
\end{array}
$$

3.
$$
\begin{array}{r}
90 \\
2\overline{)1,812} \\
18 \\
\hline
\end{array}
$$

4.
$$
\begin{array}{r}
3 \\
3\overline{)92,612} \\
9 \\
\hline
\end{array}
$$

B. Divide.

5. $6\overline{)619}$

6. $7\overline{)\$8,435}$

7. $3\overline{)39,200}$

8. $5\overline{)12,003}$

Practice

Divide.

1. $3\overline{)612}$

2. $2\overline{)520}$

3. $4\overline{)\$4,128}$

4. $6\overline{)2,043}$

5. $4\overline{)83,601}$

6. $6\overline{)\$61,812}$

7. $7\overline{)79,156}$

8. $5\overline{)25,000}$

9. $8\overline{)402}$

10. $5\overline{)5,600}$

11. $7\overline{)56,192}$

12. $8\overline{)9,664}$

Divisibility

Divide to find out if one number is divisible by another.

$$\begin{array}{r} 8 \\ 8\overline{)64} \\ 64 \\ \hline 0 \end{array}$$ There is no remainder.
64 is divisible by 8.

$$\begin{array}{r} 7\,r\,1 \\ 9\overline{)64} \\ 63 \\ \hline 1 \end{array}$$ There is a remainder.
64 is not divisible by 9.

A. Look at these examples.

$$\begin{array}{r} 10 \\ 2\overline{)20} \end{array}\qquad \begin{array}{r} 6\,r\,2 \\ 3\overline{)20} \end{array}\qquad \begin{array}{r} 5 \\ 4\overline{)20} \end{array}\qquad \begin{array}{r} 4 \\ 5\overline{)20} \end{array}\qquad \begin{array}{r} 3\,r\,2 \\ 6\overline{)20} \end{array}$$

1. Name 3 numbers that 20 is divisible by.

2. Name 2 numbers that 20 is not divisible by.

B. **Even numbers** are divisible by 2.
Odd numbers are not divisible by 2.
Are the numbers even or odd?

  3. 5   **4.** 10   **5.** 25   **6.** 34   **7.** 53   **8.** 448

C. Is the first number divisible by the second?

  9. 30; 6   **10.** 37; 5   **11.** 44; 2   **12.** 54; 6   **13.** 108; 8

Practice

Are the numbers even or odd?

  1. 14   **2.** 47   **3.** 66   **4.** 83   **5.** 321   **6.** 948

Is the first number divisible by the second?

  7. 16; 3   **8.** 24; 6   **9.** 33; 5   **10.** 36; 9   **11.** 42; 4

12. 45; 4   **13.** 56; 2   **14.** 76; 4   **15.** 84; 3   **16.** 95; 5

17. 110; 8   **18.** 112; 2   **19.** 144; 7   **20.** 150; 6   **21.** 189; 3

22. 200; 2   **23.** 230; 7   **24.** 243; 8   **25.** 344; 7   **26.** 350; 5

Factors

$1 \times 8 = 8$ $2 \times 4 = 8$

factors   factors

The **factors** of 8 are 1, 2, 4, and 8.

8

2

4

A. Complete.

1. $1 \times \underline{\ ?\ } = 18$ **2.** $2 \times \underline{\ ?\ } = 18$ **3.** $3 \times \underline{\ ?\ } = 18$

4. The factors of 18 are 1, 2, $\underline{\ ?\ }$, $\underline{\ ?\ }$, $\underline{\ ?\ }$, and $\underline{\ ?\ }$.

B. Division can also be used to find the factors of a number.

$1\overline{)12}$ → 12 $2\overline{)12}$ → 6 $3\overline{)12}$ → 4 ← These show the same factors. → $4\overline{)12}$ → 3

5. The factors of 12 are 1, 2, $\underline{\ ?\ }$, $\underline{\ ?\ }$, $\underline{\ ?\ }$, and $\underline{\ ?\ }$.

6. Use division to find the factors of 20.

C. Find all the factors of each number.

7. 16   **8.** 12   **9.** 25   **10.** 22   **11.** 35

D. What are the common factors of 6 and 12?

Factors of 6:   1, 2, 3, 6
Factors of 12:   1, 2, 3, 4, 6, 12

The **common factors** of 6 and 12 are 1, 2, 3, and 6.

Find the common factors.

12. 10 and 20   **13.** 14 and 35   **14.** 15 and 20   **15.** 8 and 40

Find all the factors.

1. 4	**2.** 10	**3.** 16	**4.** 6	**5.** 12
6. 18	**7.** 15	**8.** 38	**9.** 24	**10.** 9
11. 22	**12.** 33	**13.** 21	**14.** 14	**15.** 48
16. 39	**17.** 34	**18.** 25	**19.** 44	**20.** 35
21. 42	**22.** 27	**23.** 45	**24.** 36	**25.** 49
★**26.** 41	★**27.** 13	★**28.** 89	★**29.** 100	★**30.** 144

Find the common factors.

31. 8 and 20	**32.** 10 and 18	**33.** 15 and 20	**34.** 12 and 15
35. 16 and 24	**36.** 9 and 18	**37.** 33 and 27	**38.** 32 and 16
39. 12 and 36	**40.** 6 and 24	**41.** 30 and 42	**42.** 21 and 49
43. 24 and 40	**44.** 30 and 40	**45.** 6 and 15	**46.** 15 and 35
★**47.** 50 and 75	★**48.** 60 and 72		★**49.** 80 and 100

Find Out!
Brainteaser

These are some consecutive even numbers: 2, 4, 6, 8, 10.
These are other consecutive even numbers: 36, 38, 40, 42, 44.

1. Find 3 consecutive even numbers whose sum is 78.

$$\underline{\quad ? \quad} + \underline{\quad ? \quad} + \underline{\quad ? \quad} = 78$$

2. Find 3 consecutive even numbers whose sum is 216.

★ **3.** Find 5 consecutive even numbers whose sum is 1,000.

Factor Trees

Some numbers have many factors.

The factors of 20 are
1, 2, 4, 5, 10, and 20.

20 is called a **composite number**
since it has many factors.

Some numbers have only 2 factors.

The factors of 3 are
1 and 3.

3 is called a **prime number**
since it has only 2 factors.

A. **1.** What are the factors of 13?

2. Is 13 prime or composite?

B. Factor trees show the prime factorization of a number.
Here is how to make a factor tree for 8.

3. What 2 factors of 8 were used first?

4. Factor these numbers until you have
all prime factors. What is the
prime factorization of 8?

$$8$$
$$2 \times 4$$
$$2 \times 2 \times 2$$

C. The prime factorization of a number will always be
the same, even if the first factors used are different.
Complete these factor trees.

5.
$$18$$
$$2 \times 9$$
$$2 \times 3 \times \underline{?}$$

6.
$$18$$
$$3 \times 6$$
$$3 \times \underline{?} \times \underline{?}$$

D. Draw factor trees to find prime factorizations.

7. 30   **8.** 28   **9.** 24   **10.** 45   **11.** 16

Complete these factor trees.

1.
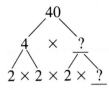

2.

3.

4.

5.

6.
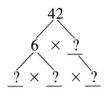

7.
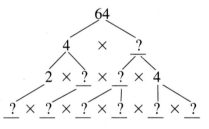

8.
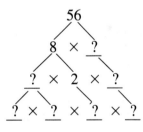

Draw factor trees to find prime factorizations.

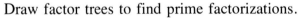

9. 36	**10.** 25	**11.** 54	**12.** 41	**13.** 48
14. 60	**15.** 32	**16.** 78	**17.** 46	**18.** 80
19. 15	**20.** 53	**21.** 75	**22.** 52	**23.** 72
24. 51	**25.** 81	★ **26.** 144	★ **27.** 200	★ **28.** 312

★ **29.** Make the factor tree for 60 in five different ways.

Problem Solving

Find the amount of change for each purchase.

1. Mrs. Ramirez spent $15.65 for model airplanes. She gave the clerk $20.00

2. Jan spent $4.28 for a kite and $19.89 for a paint set. She gave the clerk $30.00

3. Charles spent $4.79 on poster board and $4.55 for paints. He gave the clerk $10.00

4. Mr. Lee spent $9.56 for puzzles and $12.78 for a chess set. He gave the clerk $30.00

5. Mr. McConnell spent $5.95 for a domino set, $6.89 for a model car, and $14.98 for a game. He gave the clerk $50.00.

6. Mrs. Chan spent $19.99 for one game, $23.45 for another game, and $18.88 for a model ship. She gave the clerk $70.00.

7. Emma spent $4.35 for balloons and $8.96 for yarn. She gave the clerk $20.00.

8. Mr. Ortiz spent $36.71 for a racing car set. He gave the clerk $40.00.

9. Bert spent $8.82 for a model truck and $3.52 for model trains. He gave the clerk $20.00.

10. Juanita spent $9.25 for a paper flower kit and $2.95 for an art book. She gave the clerk $15.00.

11. Roberto spent $10.50 on hobby books. He gave the clerk $15.00.

12. Kim spent $23.99 for a football game. She gave the clerk $25.00.

Divide.

1. $16\overline{)0}$
(105)

2. $32\overline{)32}$
(105)

3. $1\overline{)25}$
(105)

4. $63\overline{)63}$
(105)

5. $7\overline{)2,100}$
(106)

6. $5\overline{)350}$
(106)

7. $8\overline{)72,000}$
(106)

8. $6\overline{)36,000}$
(106)

9. $4\overline{)64}$
(108)

10. $6\overline{)672}$
(108)

11. $5\overline{)94}$
(110)

12. $8\overline{)915}$
(110)

13. $7\overline{)7,826}$
(116)

14. $5\overline{)61,240}$
(116)

15. $3\overline{)1,714}$
(118)

16. $4\overline{)\$349.72}$
(118)

17. $7\overline{)704}$
(120)

18. $9\overline{)12,000}$
(116)

19. $4\overline{)1,206}$
(120)

Is the first number divisible by the second? *(121)*

20. 15; 5

21. 24; 3

Find the common factors. *(122)*

22. 10 and 12

23. 6 and 15

Solve. *(114, 126)*

24. There were 23 shelves. On each shelf there were 51 glasses. How many glasses were there in all?

25. There were 120 plates in all. There were 8 plates on each table. How many tables were there?

Divide.

1. $1\overline{)42}$
(105)

2. $5\overline{)0}$
(105)

3. $19\overline{)19}$
(105)

4. $46\overline{)0}$
(105)

5. $3\overline{)90}$
(106)

6. $8\overline{)6,400}$
(106)

7. $6\overline{)360}$
(106)

8. $7\overline{)5,600}$
(106)

9. $3\overline{)96}$
(108)

10. $4\overline{)128}$
(108)

11. $7\overline{)82}$
(110)

12. $6\overline{)143}$
(110)

13. $6\overline{)8,243}$
(116)

14. $8\overline{)92,632}$
(116)

15. $5\overline{)\$32.45}$
(118)

16. $7\overline{)24,456}$
(118)

17. $4\overline{)30,010}$
(120)

18. $5\overline{)5,012}$
(120)

19. $6\overline{)4,923}$
(120)

Is the first number divisible by the second? *(121)*

20. 22; 2

21. 30; 4

Find the common factors. *(122)*

22. 7 and 14

23. 9 and 21

Solve. *(114, 126)*

24. Mr. Johnson planted 312 rows of tomato plants with 26 plants in each row. How many plants were there?

25. At a farm, 8 people picked 2,112 tomatoes. Each person picked the same number of tomatoes. How many tomatoes did each pick?

Basic Skills Check

1.

$$\begin{array}{r} 462 \\ 214 \\ + 603 \end{array}$$

A 1,216
B 1,279
C 1,389
D 1,481

2.

$$\begin{array}{r} 1,534 \\ \times 2 \end{array}$$

E 3,068
F 3,056
G 2,756
H 2,058

3.

$$\begin{array}{r} \$0.56 \\ \times 2 \end{array}$$

A $2.56
B $2.12
C $1.12
D $0.58

4.

$$\begin{array}{r} 9,491 \\ - 7,267 \end{array}$$

E 2,244
F 2,224
G 1,224
H 224

5.

$72 \div 8 = \square$

A 7
B 8
C 9
D 12

6.

$$\begin{array}{r} \frac{6}{10} \\ - \frac{5}{10} \end{array}$$

E $\frac{1}{10}$
F $\frac{1}{6}$
G $\frac{1}{5}$
H $\frac{5}{10}$

7.

$4\overline{)832}$

A 20 r 8
B 28
C 208
D 280

8.

$\frac{3}{9} + \frac{5}{9} = \square$

E $\frac{9}{8}$
F $\frac{8}{9}$
G $\frac{3}{5}$
H $\frac{15}{81}$

9.

$6\overline{)\$2.40}$

A $4.00
B $0.40
C $0.04
D $0.004

10.

$374 - 23 = \square$

E 853
F 851
G 358
H 351

11.

$$\begin{array}{r} \$ 43.67 \\ + 63.54 \end{array}$$

A $19.87
B $20.13
C $107.21
D $117.21

12.

$2\overline{)3,002}$

E 1,510
F 1,501
G 151
H 15 r 2

13.

$$\begin{array}{r} \frac{3}{7} \\ + \frac{2}{7} \end{array}$$

A $\frac{7}{5}$
B $\frac{6}{7}$
C $\frac{5}{7}$
D $\frac{3}{9}$

14.

$36 + 62 + 41 = \square$

E 239
F 139
G 136
H 39

15.

$$\begin{array}{r} \$ 28.19 \\ - 19.28 \end{array}$$

A $8.91
B $9.91
C $11.11
D $47.47

Patterns in Division

Here is an easy way to think of division.

$$20\overline{)60}$$

THINK
$6 \div 2 = 3$

So, $20\overline{)60}^{\,3}$ Check. $3 \times 20 = 60$

$$30\overline{)120}$$

THINK
$12 \div 3 = 4$

So, $30\overline{)120}^{\,4}$ Check. $4 \times 30 = 120$

Now, look at these patterns.

$$20\overline{)60}^{\,3} \longrightarrow 20\overline{)600}^{\,30} \longrightarrow 20\overline{)6,000}^{\,300} \longrightarrow 20\overline{)60,000}^{\,3,000}$$

$$30\overline{)120}^{\,4} \longrightarrow 30\overline{)1,200}^{\,40} \longrightarrow 30\overline{)12,000}^{\,400}$$

CHAPTER 6
MORE DIVISION

Divide.

1. $40\overline{)80}$ 2. $40\overline{)800}$ 3. $40\overline{)8,000}$ 4. $40\overline{)80,000}$

5. $20\overline{)40}$ 6. $20\overline{)400}$ 7. $20\overline{)4,000}$ 8. $20\overline{)40,000}$

9. $30\overline{)900}$ 10. $20\overline{)1,400}$ 11. $50\overline{)3,500}$ 12. $20\overline{)80}$

13. $70\overline{)2,800}$ 14. $30\overline{)210}$ 15. $30\overline{)1,800}$ 16. $60\overline{)48,000}$

17. $60\overline{)54,000}$ 18. $40\overline{)3,600}$ 19. $70\overline{)560}$ 20. $80\overline{)3,200}$

21. $90\overline{)270}$ 22. $50\overline{)400}$ 23. $90\overline{)4,500}$ 24. $70\overline{)28,000}$

Dividing by Multiples of 10

Find 876 ÷ 20.

ESTIMATE.

$20\overline{)876}$

How many 20's in 8? none
How many 2 0's in 8 7?
Think: How many 2's in 8?
Try 4 in the tens place.

$$\begin{array}{r} 4 \\ 20\overline{)876} \end{array}$$

$$\begin{array}{r} 4 \\ 20\overline{)876} \\ \underline{80} \\ 7 \end{array}$$

MULTIPLY and SUBTRACT.
7 is less than 20.
The estimate is correct.

$$\begin{array}{r} 4 \\ 20\overline{)876} \\ \underline{80\downarrow} \\ 76 \end{array}$$

Bring down the 6.
ESTIMATE. How many 2 0's in 7 6?
Think: How many 2's in 7?
Try 3 in the ones place.

$$\begin{array}{r} 43r16 \\ 20\overline{)876} \\ \underline{80} \\ 76 \\ \underline{60} \\ 16 \end{array}$$

MULTIPLY and SUBTRACT.
The remainder is less than 20.

The quotient is 43.
The remainder is 16.

A. Find 1,697 ÷ 40.

1. 169 ÷ 40 = ___?___

16 ÷ 4 = ___?___

$$\begin{array}{r} 4 \\ 40\overline{)1,697} \\ \underline{1\ 60\downarrow} \\ 97 \end{array}$$

2. Complete to find the quotient.

B. Divide.

3. $40\overline{)89}$ **4.** $30\overline{)248}$ **5.** $20\overline{)623}$ **6.** $40\overline{)1,240}$ **7.** $50\overline{)1,635}$

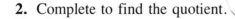

Divide.

1. $50\overline{)65}$ 2. $20\overline{)43}$ 3. $30\overline{)67}$ 4. $40\overline{)91}$ 5. $60\overline{)63}$

6. $20\overline{)480}$ 7. $20\overline{)620}$ 8. $40\overline{)285}$ 9. $50\overline{)219}$ 10. $30\overline{)182}$

11. $50\overline{)231}$ 12. $70\overline{)294}$ 13. $80\overline{)405}$ 14. $70\overline{)421}$ 15. $60\overline{)366}$

16. $30\overline{)6,480}$ 17. $40\overline{)9,240}$ 18. $20\overline{)6,380}$ 19. $30\overline{)4,260}$

20. $20\overline{)7,848}$ 21. $40\overline{)5,326}$ 22. $70\overline{)8,334}$ 23. $30\overline{)7,532}$

24. $30\overline{)2,760}$ 25. $50\overline{)3,550}$ 26. $40\overline{)2,960}$ 27. $60\overline{)5,920}$

28. $60\overline{)5,544}$ 29. $70\overline{)3,886}$ 30. $40\overline{)3,108}$ 31. $90\overline{)5,494}$

32. $20\overline{)166}$ 33. $80\overline{)6,240}$ 34. $30\overline{)84}$ 35. $60\overline{)244}$

36. $60\overline{)88}$ 37. $30\overline{)390}$ 38. $90\overline{)5,454}$ 39. $30\overline{)6,435}$

Solve.

40. The librarian put 160 filmstrips in 20 boxes. She put the same number in each box. How many filmstrips were in each box?

41. Each slide tray holds 30 slides. How many slide trays were needed for 1,234 slides? How many slides were left over?

Dividing by Tens and Ones

Smith's Store had 729 sweaters. There were 34 sweaters in each drawer. How many drawers were used?

$$34\overline{)729}$$

ESTIMATE.
How many 34's in 7? none
How many 34's in 72?
Think: How many 3's in 7?
Try 2.

$$\begin{array}{r} 2 \\ 34\overline{)729} \end{array}$$

$$\begin{array}{r} 2 \\ 34\overline{)729} \\ 68\downarrow \\ \hline 49 \end{array}$$

MULTIPLY and SUBTRACT. Bring down the 9.

ESTIMATE. How many 34's in 49?
Think: How many 3's in 4?
Try 1.

$$\begin{array}{r} 21r15 \\ 34\overline{)729} \\ 68 \\ \hline 49 \\ 34 \\ \hline 15 \end{array}$$

MULTIPLY and SUBTRACT.

The quotient is 21.
The remainder is 15.

CHECK:
$$\begin{array}{r} 21 \\ \times\ 34 \\ \hline 84 \\ 63 \\ \hline 714 \\ +\ 15 \\ \hline 729 \end{array}$$

21 drawers were used. 15 sweaters were left over.

A. Find $4,715 \div 23$.

1. $47 \div 23$ is about ___?___ .

2. Why is a 0 in the tens place?

3. Complete to find the quotient.

$$\begin{array}{r} 20 \\ 23\overline{)4,715} \\ 46\downarrow \\ \hline 11 \end{array}$$

B. Divide and check.

4. $35\overline{)78}$ 5. $53\overline{)589}$ 6. $32\overline{)331}$ 7. $72\overline{)216}$ 8. $44\overline{)7,505}$

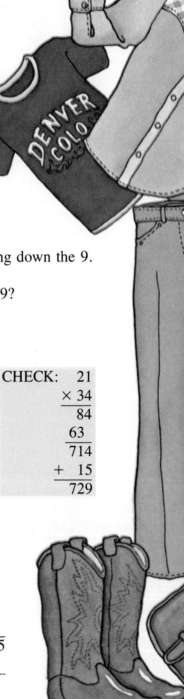

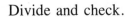

Divide and check.

1. $21\overline{)84}$ 2. $44\overline{)88}$ 3. $31\overline{)93}$ 4. $14\overline{)28}$ 5. $29\overline{)58}$

6. $32\overline{)75}$ 7. $21\overline{)36}$ 8. $24\overline{)33}$ 9. $22\overline{)47}$ 10. $32\overline{)89}$

11. $51\overline{)714}$ 12. $31\overline{)961}$ 13. $42\overline{)756}$ 14. $32\overline{)544}$ 15. $40\overline{)920}$

16. $41\overline{)945}$ 17. $61\overline{)860}$ 18. $11\overline{)689}$ 19. $51\overline{)769}$ 20. $42\overline{)937}$

21. $55\overline{)6,765}$ 22. $23\overline{)4,669}$ 23. $31\overline{)9,672}$ 24. $37\overline{)4,144}$

25. $12\overline{)3,756}$ 26. $42\overline{)6,132}$ 27. $63\overline{)7,308}$ 28. $42\overline{)9,954}$

29. $24\overline{)2,511}$ 30. $41\overline{)6,384}$ 31. $23\overline{)9,734}$ 32. $13\overline{)2,879}$

33. $62\overline{)8,499}$ 34. $32\overline{)6,819}$

35. $51\overline{)5,530}$ 36. $21\overline{)8,758}$

37. $24\overline{)768}$ 38. $20\overline{)91}$

39. $54\overline{)7,745}$ 40. $45\overline{)967}$

41. $72\overline{)958}$ 42. $11\overline{)3,322}$

43. $32\overline{)69}$ 44. $24\overline{)96}$

45. $36\overline{)516}$ 46. $42\overline{)896}$

Solve.

47. 1,243 belts
11 per box
How many boxes?

48. 372 hats
12 per crate
How many crates?

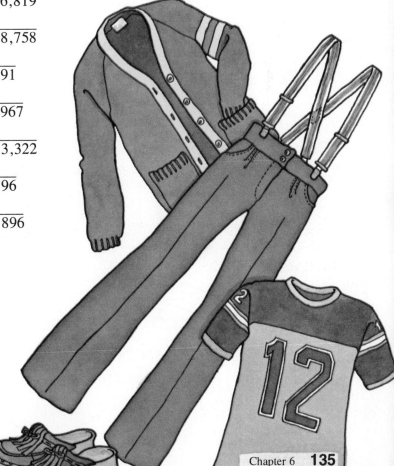

Smaller Quotients

1,809 chairs were bought for the auditorium. There will be 43 rows with the same number of chairs in each row. How many seats will be in each row?

$$43\overline{)1,809}$$

ESTIMATE.
How many 4 3's in 1 8 0?
Think: How many 4's in 18?

$$\begin{array}{r} 4 \\ 43\overline{)1,809} \end{array}$$

Try 4.

$$\begin{array}{r} 4 \\ 43\overline{)1,809} \\ \underline{1\,7\,2\downarrow} \\ 8\,9 \end{array}$$

MULTIPLY and SUBTRACT.
Bring down the 9.
ESTIMATE. How many 4 3's in 8 9?
Think: How many 4's in 8? Try 2.

$$\begin{array}{r} 4\,2\,r3 \\ 43\overline{)1,809} \\ \underline{1\,7\,2} \\ 8\,9 \\ \underline{8\,6} \\ 3 \end{array}$$

MULTIPLY and SUBTRACT.

The quotient is 42.
The remainder is 3.

There will be 42 chairs in each row with 3 extra chairs.

A. Complete.

1. $34\overline{)173}$ (5)

2. $57\overline{)342}$ (6)

3. $31\overline{)1,023}$ (3)

4. $53\overline{)2,760}$ (5)

B. Divide.

5. $33\overline{)297}$

6. $41\overline{)250}$

7. $53\overline{)2,870}$

8. $54\overline{)2,734}$

Divide.

1. $89\overline{)534}$ 2. $72\overline{)576}$ 3. $61\overline{)305}$

4. $52\overline{)364}$ 5. $43\overline{)344}$ 6. $39\overline{)117}$

7. $41\overline{)390}$ 8. $32\overline{)163}$ 9. $31\overline{)285}$

10. $61\overline{)504}$ 11. $73\overline{)521}$ 12. $83\overline{)350}$

13. $82\overline{)760}$ 14. $67\overline{)278}$ 15. $52\overline{)348}$

16. $65\overline{)2,210}$ 17. $88\overline{)5,456}$ 18. $21\overline{)1,890}$

19. $61\overline{)4,758}$ 20. $71\overline{)2,485}$ 21. $58\overline{)1,740}$

22. $54\overline{)1,248}$ 23. $62\overline{)2,115}$ 24. $72\overline{)2,740}$

25. $45\overline{)1,502}$ 26. $45\overline{)1,542}$ 27. $64\overline{)3,426}$

28. $53\overline{)1,624}$ 29. $51\overline{)2,044}$ 30. $32\overline{)2,052}$

31. $79\overline{)165}$ 32. $44\overline{)352}$ 33. $32\overline{)1,290}$

34. $72\overline{)4,824}$ 35. $53\overline{)224}$ 36. $68\overline{)3,536}$

★ Complete.

37. $\underline{\quad?\quad} \div 52 = 8\,r\,12$

38. $\underline{\quad?\quad} \div 62 = 57\,r\,3$

Dividing 5-Digit Numbers

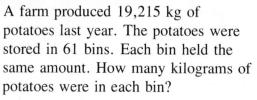

A farm produced 19,215 kg of potatoes last year. The potatoes were stored in 61 bins. Each bin held the same amount. How many kilograms of potatoes were in each bin?

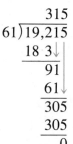

$$
\begin{array}{r}
315 \\
61)\overline{19,215} \\
18\ 3 \\
\hline
91 \\
61 \\
\hline
305 \\
305 \\
\hline
0
\end{array}
$$

There were 315 kg in each bin.

A. Find 35,312 ÷ 33.

    1. ESTIMATE. How many 3 3's in 2 3 1?
        Think: How many 3's in 23? Try 7.
        Is the estimate correct?

$$
\begin{array}{r}
1\ 0 \\
33)\overline{3\ 5,3\ 1\ 2} \\
3\ 3\downarrow\downarrow \\
\hline
2\ 3\ 1
\end{array}
$$

    2. Complete to find the quotient.

B. Complete.

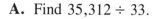

         3 1   8   8   1

3. 23)71,852   **4.** 30)25,410   **5.** 33)26,632   **6.** 72)84,297

         69↓   24 0   26 4

         2 8

C. Divide.

    7. 50)35,006   **8.** 35)73,601   **9.** 21)95,179   **10.** 41)25,666

Divide.

1. $20\overline{)22,000}$ **2.** $40\overline{)48,080}$

3. $60\overline{)95,880}$ **4.** $30\overline{)63,000}$

5. $30\overline{)98,499}$ **6.** $40\overline{)86,092}$

7. $20\overline{)60,110}$ **8.** $80\overline{)88,895}$

9. $27\overline{)54,081}$ **10.** $32\overline{)71,552}$

11. $61\overline{)66,795}$ **12.** $45\overline{)48,195}$

13. $41\overline{)44,009}$ **14.** $31\overline{)65,819}$

15. $64\overline{)73,688}$ **16.** $36\overline{)86,840}$

17. $40\overline{)24,480}$ **18.** $70\overline{)73,680}$

19. $80\overline{)70,400}$ **20.** $30\overline{)13,250}$

21. $32\overline{)20,512}$ **22.** $31\overline{)25,730}$ **23.** $91\overline{)36,400}$ **24.** $72\overline{)17,640}$

25. $75\overline{)38,506}$ **26.** $62\overline{)24,959}$ **27.** $42\overline{)13,175}$ **28.** $84\overline{)17,819}$

29. $92\overline{)46,010}$ **30.** $42\overline{)29,531}$ **31.** $53\overline{)37,690}$ **32.** $21\overline{)10,693}$

33. $20\overline{)50,000}$ **34.** $65\overline{)46,280}$ **35.** $51\overline{)81,753}$ **36.** $22\overline{)15,934}$

37. $51\overline{)51,016}$ **38.** $70\overline{)27,443}$ **39.** $77\overline{)38,962}$ **40.** $32\overline{)68,674}$

★ **41.** $40\overline{)683,760}$ ★ **42.** $23\overline{)556,651}$ ★ **43.** $74\overline{)160,141}$

Solve.

44. A trucker put 10,689 boxes of fruit on 21 trucks. How many boxes were there per truck?

45. There are 25,584 cartons of eggs. Each truck can hold 82 cartons. How many trucks are needed?

Estimates That Are Too Large

Find 1,785 ÷ 25.

$$25\overline{)1{,}785}$$

Estimate.
How many 2 5's in 1 7 8?
Think: How many 2's in 17?
Try 8.

$$\begin{array}{r} 8 \\ 25\overline{)1{,}785} \end{array}$$

$$\begin{array}{r} 8 \\ 25\overline{)1{,}785} \\ 200 \end{array}$$

Multiply.
Can't subtract. 200 > 178.

$$\begin{array}{r} 7 \\ 25\overline{)1{,}785} \\ 175\downarrow \\ \hline 35 \end{array}$$

Try 7.
Multiply and subtract.
Bring down the 5.

$$\begin{array}{r} 7\,1\,r\,10 \\ 25\overline{)1{,}785} \\ 175 \\ \hline 35 \\ 25 \\ \hline 10 \end{array}$$

Estimate.
How many 2 5's in 3 5?
Think: How many 2's in 3? Try 1.
Multiply and subtract.
The quotient is 71.
The remainder is 10.

A. Find 82,344 ÷ 47.

$$\begin{array}{r} 2 \\ 47\overline{)82{,}344} \\ 94 \end{array}$$

1. Is the estimate 2 correct?

2. Try ___?___ .

3. Complete to find the quotient.

B. Complete.

4. $\begin{array}{r} 7 \\ 20\overline{)142} \end{array}$ **5.** $\begin{array}{r} 1 \\ 38\overline{)604} \end{array}$ **6.** $\begin{array}{r} 6 \\ 37\overline{)2{,}576} \end{array}$ **7.** $\begin{array}{r} 8 \\ 78\overline{)63{,}545} \end{array}$

C. Divide.

8. $45\overline{)836}$ **9.** $33\overline{)610}$ **10.** $27\overline{)1{,}652}$ **11.** $34\overline{)92{,}463}$

Divide.

1. 12)306   **2.** 49)823   **3.** 15)225   **4.** 27)863   **5.** 36)658

6. 22)183   **7.** 39)225   **8.** 42)284   **9.** 69)483   **10.** 48)351

11. 66)437   **12.** 51)405   **13.** 78)215   **14.** 26)182   **15.** 57)260

16. 18)3,240   **17.** 34)6,537   **18.** 24)8,493   **19.** 46)8,243

20. 24)1,992   **21.** 34)1,884   **22.** 58)3,872   **23.** 79)3,606

24. 67)3,015   **25.** 88)4,088   **26.** 37)1,776   **27.** 57)4,674

28. 27)51,382   **29.** 32)92,494   **30.** 37)90,872   **31.** 28)94,602

32. 84)73,082   **33.** 49)35,704   **34.** 51)35,196   **35.** 56)50,064

36. 39)5,234   **37.** 14)2,493   **38.** 29)42,144   **39.** 49)3,577

40. 47)91,556   **41.** 59)413   **42.** 38)16,800   **43.** 28)827

★ **44.** 39)100,000   ★ **45.** 45)200,000   ★ **46.** 65)300,000

Solve.

47. 2,926 nails are put in 38 bags. The same number is put in each bag. How many nails are in each bag?

48. Mrs. Diaz has 164 tools. She puts 36 tools in each kit. How many kits will she have? How many tools will be left over?

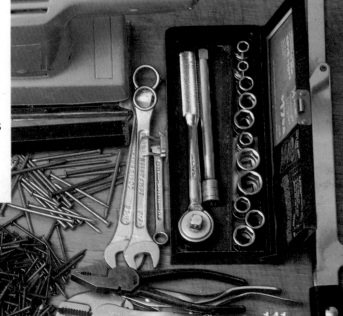

Divide.

1. $60\overline{)3,600}$
(130)

2. $40\overline{)280}$
(130)

3. $50\overline{)35,000}$
(130)

4. $30\overline{)60}$
(130)

5. $80\overline{)48,000}$
(130)

6. $20\overline{)80}$
(130)

7. $7\overline{)210}$
(130)

8. $9\overline{)5,400}$
(130)

9. $70\overline{)693}$
(132)

10. $40\overline{)52}$
(132)

11. $70\overline{)3,670}$
(132)

12. $90\overline{)4,055}$
(132)

13. $40\overline{)9,727}$
(132)

14. $40\overline{)853}$
(132)

15. $60\overline{)2,640}$
(132)

16. $30\overline{)76}$
(132)

17. $76\overline{)844}$
(134)

18. $32\overline{)66}$
(134)

19. $53\overline{)6,943}$
(134)

20. $21\overline{)714}$
(134)

21. $43\overline{)86}$
(134)

22. $64\overline{)9,295}$
(134)

23. $57\overline{)84}$
(134)

24. $45\overline{)624}$
(134)

25. $73\overline{)442}$
(136)

26. $94\overline{)7,898}$
(136)

27. $84\overline{)6,048}$
(136)

28. $53\overline{)325}$
(136)

29. $45\overline{)315}$
(136)

30. $94\overline{)768}$
(136)

31. $62\overline{)1,319}$
(136)

32. $62\overline{)310}$
(136)

33. $40\overline{)16,259}$
(138)

34. $52\overline{)31,876}$
(138)

35. $20\overline{)85,893}$
(138)

36. $32\overline{)46,528}$
(138)

37. $21\overline{)68,250}$
(138)

38. $70\overline{)44,380}$
(138)

39. $40\overline{)49,360}$
(138)

40. $73\overline{)54,392}$
(138)

41. $51\overline{)3,525}$
(140)

42. $35\overline{)630}$
(140)

43. $45\overline{)12,345}$
(140)

44. $52\overline{)361}$
(140)

45. $49\overline{)343}$
(140)

46. $14\overline{)25,620}$
(140)

47. $69\overline{)3,816}$
(140)

48. $29\overline{)5,674}$
(140)

Solve.

49. There are 252 cars in the garage.
(136) On each floor there are 42 cars. How many floors are there?

50. In 31 days, 8,432 cars used the
(134) parking garage. How many cars used it per day?

Find Out!

Calculator Activity

9 9 7 6 5 4 3 2 1

Place addition or subtraction signs between some digits to make a number sentence that has an answer of 100. Do not change the order of the digits.

Keeping Fit

Write standard numerals.

1. 600,000 + 40,000 + 7,000 + 40 + 3

2. 70,000 + 9,000 + 600 + 30 + 1

3. 900,000 + 8,000 + 500 + 70 + 4

Round to the nearest ten.

4. 71   5. 46   6. 85   7. 32   8. 18

Round to the nearest hundred.

9. 675   10. 910   11. 234   12. 694   13. 183

Add.

14.
```
   62
   34
 + 79
```

15.
```
 6,452
+3,987
```

16.
```
  709
  324
+ 357
```

17.
```
 5,204
   977
+6,241
```

18.
```
 452,321
+963,482
```

19.
```
  390
   45
+  75
```

20.
```
 4,317
+6,249
```

21.
```
 97,845
+ 1,567
```

22.
```
  455
  370
+ 926
```

23.
```
 39,254
    624
+ 1,572
```

Subtract.

24.
```
 5,072
-3,191
```

25.
```
  614
-  59
```

26.
```
 62,135
-43,240
```

27.
```
 5,296
-  378
```

28.
```
 29,154
-   365
```

29.
```
  725
- 145
```

30.
```
 6,450
-1,234
```

31.
```
 33,561
- 4,923
```

32.
```
 7,004
-6,205
```

33.
```
  983
-  58
```

Multiply.

34.
```
  375
× 82
```

35.
```
   17
× 74
```

36.
```
  604
× 39
```

37.
```
 1,456
×   6
```

38.
```
  543
×232
```

39.
```
 7,352
×    6
```

40.
```
  529
× 63
```

41.
```
   78
× 23
```

42.
```
  881
×205
```

43.
```
  325
× 50
```

Dividing Money

A fifth grade class sold 21 boxes of cards. They collected $57.75. Each box was the same price. What was the cost of each box of cards?

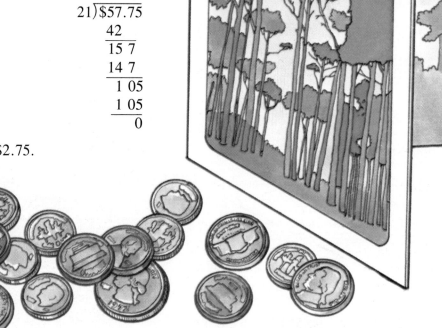

Step 1 DIVIDE	**Step 2** PLACE MONEY NOTATION
$$\begin{array}{r} 2\ 75 \\ 21\overline{)\$57.75} \\ 42 \\ \hline 15\ 7 \\ 14\ 7 \\ \hline 1\ 05 \\ 1\ 05 \\ \hline 0 \end{array}$$	$$\begin{array}{r} \$\ 2.75 \\ 21\overline{)\$57.75} \\ 42 \\ \hline 15\ 7 \\ 14\ 7 \\ \hline 1\ 05 \\ 1\ 05 \\ \hline 0 \end{array}$$

Each box cost $2.75.

A. Complete.

1. $\overset{0\ 3}{3\overline{)\$1.17}}$

2. $\overset{8}{5\overline{)\$42.50}}$

3. $\overset{1}{5\overline{)\$734.55}}$

4. $\overset{5}{16\overline{)\$8.32}}$

5. $\overset{7}{12\overline{)\$89.04}}$

6. $\overset{7}{26\overline{)\$190.84}}$

B. Divide.

7. $4\overline{)\$4.16}$

8. $6\overline{)\$44.46}$

9. $7\overline{)\$932.61}$

10. $57\overline{)\$4.56}$

11. $63\overline{)\$47.25}$

12. $40\overline{)\$236.00}$

Divide.

1. 3)$2.61   **2.** 2)$7.42   **3.** 4)$3.76   **4.** 9)$2.16

5. 7)$29.61   **6.** 5)$16.95   **7.** 2)$35.04   **8.** 6)$26.52

9. 6)$725.46   **10.** 8)$193.76   **11.** 6)$265.98   **12.** 4)$853.68

13. 12)$3.84   **14.** 37)$8.14   **15.** 79)$3.95   **16.** 40)$2.40

17. 41)$71.34   **18.** 77)$89.32   **19.** 31)$16.43   **20.** 58)$33.64

21. 65)$802.10   **22.** 35)$858.55 **23.** 43)$105.78 **24.** 88)$548.24

25. 4)$52.96   **26.** 52)$6.24   **27.** 43)$700.04 **28.** 5)$632.25

29. 16)$35.52   **30.** 3)$1.29   **31.** 74)$65.86   **32.** 8)$35.60

★ **33.** 6)$1,436.28   ★ **34.** 11)$7,562.06   ★ **35.** 35)$8,386.70

Solve.

36. Marilyn sold 15 boxes of cards and received $48.00. Each box cost the same. How much did each box cost?

37. Michael received $15.75 for selling 75 cards. Each card cost the same. How much did each card cost?

Averages

Rudy's bowling scores for three games were 110, 125, and 89. What was his average?

▶ To find the average of a group of numbers:
 1. Find the sum of the numbers.

 2. Divide the sum by the number of addends. The quotient is the average.

Rudy found his average this way.

sum of scores ÷ number of scores = average
$$324 \quad ÷ \quad 3 \quad = \quad 108$$

Rudy's average was 108.

A. Complete to find the average of 26, 28, 27, 29, and 30.

 1. $26 + 28 + 27 + 29 + 30 =$ ___?___

 2. ___?___ $÷ 5 =$ _28_

B. Find the averages.

3. 80	**4.** 65¢	**5.** 7	**6.** 300	**7.** $3.50
84	40¢	9	600	$2.19
76	60¢	3	600	$6.37
		4	100	
		7		

Find the averages.

1. 6
     9
   12

2. 7
   7
   7
   7

3. $17
   $28
   $20
   $15

4. 20
   30
   40

5. 30
   42
   24
   36
   13

6. 500
   400
   500
   600

7. 124
   175
    25

8. $4.58
   $3.36
   $4.20
   $5.26

9. 540
    75
   440
   500
   600

10. $265
    $252
    $160
    $ 83

Solve.

11. Rudy spent $5.75 on bowling one week, $4.20 the next week, and $4.33 the next week. What was the average per week he spent for bowling?

12. Annette's scores for 4 games were 92, 105, 73, and 94. What was her average?

★ **13.** The bowling alley recorded the number of people bowling each day. What was the average?

Monday – 82	Tuesday – 134
Wednesday – 126	Thursday – 175
Friday – 226	Saturday – 310
Sunday – 221	

Problem Solving

Mr. Costello pays $3,900 for 12 months rent for his flower shop. He has rented the shop for 3 years. How much rent does he pay per month?

$$\begin{array}{r} \$\ \ 325 \\ 12\overline{)\$3,900} \end{array}$$

He pays $325 per month for rent.

There is **too much** information in the problem. It is not necessary to know how long he has rented the shop.

A. Mr. Costello pays $0.75 for each rose. He sells each for $1.25. How much does he make on each rose that he sells?

   PLAN: **1.** What must you know in order to solve the problem?

   2. Is there too much information given to solve the problem?

B. Write too much or enough. Solve.

1. Ms. Baker bought a vase for $4.50. She owns 10 vases. She gave the sales clerk $10.00. How much change did she receive?

2. Mr. Costello bought 24 vases at $2.50 each. How much did he pay in all?

Write **too much** or **enough.** Solve.

1. Mr. Costello has 130 carnations and 150 tulips. How many more tulips does he have?

2. Mrs. Lee bought violets for $2.35. She gave the clerk $10. What change did she get?

3. There were 7 baskets in the window. Each basket had 15 flowers. How many flowers were there in the window?

4. Michelle is 12 years old. She earned $3.75 on Thursday, $3.25 on Friday, and $7.50 on Saturday. How much did she earn in all?

5. Sam bought 12 yellow tulips for $4.80. He gave the clerk $5. How much change did he receive?

6. Michelle put flowers in 3 vases. She used 16 carnations and 8 roses. How many more carnations did she use?

7. Mr. Lee bought roses for $6.75, vases for $10.95, and lilies for $5.30. How much did he pay for the flowers?

8. Michelle has 75 vases. She puts 15 in each box. Each vase cost $10.95. How many boxes does she need?

9. Mr. Costello pays each worker $120 a week. There are 10 workers. How much does he pay in all?

10. Flower pots are on sale for $1.30 each. How much will 5 flower pots cost?

More Number Sentences

Multiplication and division are related. Look at these pairs of related sentences.

$$3 \times 4 = 12 \qquad 10 \div 5 = 2$$
$$12 \div 4 = 3 \qquad 2 \times 5 = 10$$

Addition and subtraction are also related. Look at these pairs of related sentences.

$$9 + 6 = 15 \qquad 12 - 5 = 7$$
$$15 - 6 = 9 \qquad 7 + 5 = 12$$

A. Write a related sentence for each. Complete.

1. $9 \times 7 = 63$
  $63 \div \underline{} = 9$

2. $40 \div 5 = 8$
  $\underline{} \times 5 = 40$

3. $6 + 7 = 13$
  $13 - 7 = \underline{}$

B. Complete. Use related sentences.

Examples

$$\square \times 7 = 56$$
Think: $56 \div 7 = 8$
So, $\square = 8$

$$n \div 9 = 7$$
Think: $7 \times 9 = 63$
So, $n = 63$

4. $\square \times 3 = 45$
Think: $45 \div 3 = 15$
So, $\square = \underline{}$

5. $\square \div 2 = 12$
Think: $12 \times 2 = 24$
So, $\square = \underline{}$

6. $n + 9 = 17$
Think: $17 - 9 = 8$
So, $n = \underline{}$

7. $n - 5 = 14$
Think: $14 + 5 = 19$
So, $n = \underline{}$

C. Solve.

8. $\square \times 8 = 72$

9. $\square + 6 = 14$

10. $\square \div 4 = 8$

11. $n \div 5 = 9$

12. $n + 8 = 16$

13. $n - 4 = 9$

Solve.

1. $\square + 3 = 21$

2. $\square - 5 = 0$

3. $\square + 8 = 14$

4. $\square - 2 = 14$

5. $\square - 5 = 6$

6. $\square - 6 = 9$

7. $\square \times 6 = 36$

8. $\square \times 13 = 78$

9. $\square \times 9 = 189$

10. $\square \div 2 = 8$

11. $\square \div 9 = 4$

12. $\square \div 6 = 4$

13. $n + 10 = 85$

14. $n \div 40 = 12$

15. $n - 9 = 50$

16. $n + 12 = 49$

17. $n \div 42 = 18$

18. $n \times 7 = 105$

19. $n \times 4 = 96$

20. $n \div 3 = 90$

21. $h + 14 = 28$

22. $n \div 7 = 5$

23. $n \times 7 = 154$

24. $n - 43 = 128$

25. $n \div 12 = 23$

26. $n - 32 = 113$

27. $n \times 44 = 836$

28. $n + 14 = 168$

29. $n \div 27 = 43$

30. $n - 86 = 41$

Find Out!
Brainteaser

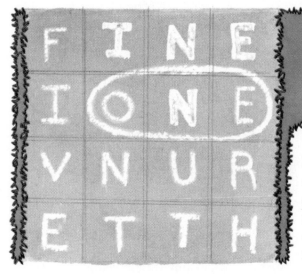

Find as many words for numbers as you can. Start in any square and move in any direction. Do not enter the same square twice while spelling a word. The sum of all numbers is 63. One word is done for you.

Problem Solving: Estimating Answers

Estimate the answers.

1. Lynn bought 4 guppies. They cost
   $0.79 each. About how much did
   they cost in all?

2. She spent $2.23 at the fish store.
   She gave the clerk $5. About how
   much change did she get?

3. One fish tank holds 12 L of water.
   Another holds 32 L. About how
   many more liters does the larger
   tank hold?

4. Lynn bought a fish bowl for
   $1.19, plants for $1.75, and
   gravel for $1.10. About how
   much did she spend in all?

5. One tank had 18 fish and another
   had 27 fish. About how many
   fish were there in all?

6. Shells cost $0.69 each. Lynn
   bought 7 shells. About how much
   did they cost?

7. One book about fish cost $2.89.
   Another book cost $1.65. About
   how much was the difference?

8. A tank sells for $7.50. It is on
   sale for $5.89. About how much
   could be saved by buying it on
   sale?

9. The fish store had 72 goldfish, 46
   tetras, and 108 guppies. About
   how many fish were there?

10. There are 6 shells in each tank.
    The fish store has 31 tanks.
    About how many shells are there
    in all?

Divide.

1. $60\overline{)420}$ **2.** $50\overline{)35,000}$ **3.** $30\overline{)153}$ **4.** $50\overline{)3,450}$
(130)   *(130)*   *(132)*   *(132)*

5. $34\overline{)83}$ **6.** $23\overline{)483}$ **7.** $72\overline{)432}$ **8.** $61\overline{)5,130}$
(134)   *(134)*   *(136)*   *(136)*

9. $44\overline{)63,392}$ **10.** $41\overline{)16,482}$ **11.** $54\overline{)43,916}$ **12.** $32\overline{)80,320}$
(138)   *(138)*   *(138)*   *(138)*

13. $23\overline{)8,099}$ **14.** $57\overline{)21,537}$ **15.** $68\overline{)48,385}$ **16.** $28\overline{)980}$
(140)   *(140)*   *(140)*   *(140)*

17. $24\overline{)\$19.92}$ **18.** $93\overline{)\$72.54}$ **19.** $41\overline{)\$9.43}$ **20.** $40\overline{)\$180.00}$
(144)   *(144)*   *(144)*   *(144)*

Find the averages. *(146)*

21.	**22.**	**23.**
$9.31	87	24
$9.18	30	29
$9.20	74	25
	57	37
		5

Write **too much** or **enough.** Solve. *(148)*

24. The scores on Jon's science tests were 88, 96, 87, and 89. He made $4.55 mowing lawns. What was his average on all the science tests?

Estimate the answers. *(152)*

25. The science test had 28 questions on each page. The test was 2 pages long. Estimate how many questions were on the test.

Divide.

1. $40\overline{)80}$
(130)

2. $60\overline{)4,200}$
(130)

3. $30\overline{)270}$
(132)

4. $80\overline{)3,294}$
(132)

5. $41\overline{)82}$
(134)

6. $22\overline{)3,586}$
(134)

7. $81\overline{)735}$
(136)

8. $62\overline{)3,596}$
(136)

9. $81\overline{)57,105}$
(138)

10. $51\overline{)89,913}$
(138)

11. $21\overline{)58,874}$
(138)

12. $32\overline{)23,056}$
(138)

13. $51\overline{)3,519}$
(140)

14. $24\overline{)1,995}$
(140)

15. $77\overline{)14,250}$
(140)

16. $42\overline{)289}$
(140)

17. $12\overline{)\$4.08}$
(144)

18. $27\overline{)\$41.31}$
(144)

19. $78\overline{)\$971.10}$
(144)

20. $51\overline{)\$32.13}$
(144)

Find the averages. *(146)*

21. 9
    11
    16
    21
    23

22. 100
    120
    115
    117

23. $4.44
    $5.55
    $6.66

Write **too much** or **enough.** Solve. *(148)*

24. The baseball team scored 6, 9, 1, and 4 home runs in 4 games. There are 15 people on the team. What was the team's average score?

Estimate the answers. *(152)*

25. On Monday, 271 people went to the baseball game. On Wednesday, 215 went to the game. Estimate how many people went to the games on the two days.

Basic Skills Check

1. What is the value of 5 in 7,562?

    A 5,000

    B 500

    C 50

    D 5

---

2. What part is shaded?

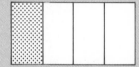

    E $\frac{3}{4}$

    F $\frac{1}{2}$

    G $\frac{1}{4}$

    H $\frac{1}{8}$

---

3. Round 48 to the nearest ten.

    A 80

    B 60

    C 50

    D 40

---

4. Which of the numbers is the largest?

    E 896

    F 869

    G 698

    H 689

---

5. Which figure is shown?

    A square

    B triangle

    C rectangle

    D cube

---

6. How many pints are in 3 qt?

    E 15 pt

    F 12 pt

    G 6 pt

    H $4\frac{1}{2}$ pt

---

7. Compare:

$$\frac{5}{6} \equiv \frac{3}{6}$$

    A >

    B <

    C =

    D ≠

---

8. Name the diameter of the circle.

    E $\overline{EG}$

    F $\overline{EF}$

    G $\overline{EH}$

    H none of the above

---

9. What time does the clock show?

    A 3:06

    B 3:30

    C 6:30

    D 9:30

---

10. How many centimeters are in 3 m?

    E 13 cm

    F 30 cm

    G 130 cm

    H 300 cm

Measuring in Centimeters

A **centimeter** (cm) is a metric unit of length.

This model car is 5 cm long.

This model is 5 cm long, to the nearest centimeter.

A. Find the length of each. Use your ruler.

1.

2.

B. Find the length of each to the nearest centimeter.

3.

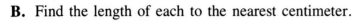

4.

C. Find the length of each to the nearest centimeter.

5. ├──────────────────────┤   **6.** ├──────────┤

7. ├─────────────────────────────────┤

8. ├──────────┤   **9.** ├────────────────┤

10. ├────────────────────────────────┤

D. Use your ruler to draw lines of these lengths.

11. 4 cm   **12.** 11 cm   **13.** 15 cm   **14.** 9 cm

Measuring with String

Sometimes you can't measure with a ruler. Try to measure the distance around your arm with your ruler!

Try this way of measuring.
You will need a partner to help you.

A. Stretch out your arm. Have your partner wrap a piece of string around your elbow.

B. Be sure your partner marks the measurement of your elbow on the string in some way.

C. Now place the string on a flat surface and measure it with a ruler. What is the distance around your elbow to the nearest centimeter?

D. Bend your arm. Now what is the distance around your elbow?

E. Have your partner help you measure each of these. Use string and a ruler.

    1. Your ankle   **2.** Your knee

    3. Your wrist   **4.** Your head

Materials: string
centimeter ruler

1. Measure to the nearest centimeter.
(156)

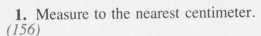

2. Measure to the nearest millimeter.
(161)

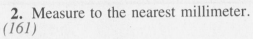

Complete.

3. 5 m = ___?___ cm
(159)

4. 700 cm = ___?___ m
(159)

5. 6 km = ___?___ m
(159)

6. 8,000 m = ___?___ km
(159)

7. 3 cm = ___?___ mm
(162)

8. 40 mm = ___?___ cm
(162)

9. 2 m = ___?___ mm
(162)

10. 4,000 mL = ___?___ L
(165)

11. 3 t = ___?___ kg
(168)

12. 2,000 g = ___?___ kg
(168)

Tell which unit you would use to measure each of the following. Use km, m, cm, mm, L, mL, t, kg, or g. *(170)*

13. Capacity of a cup

14. Mass of a pear

15. Length of a bus

16. Capacity of a barrel

17. Mass of a person

18. Thickness of a key

Find Out!
Brainteaser

In each row there is one picture that is the opposite of the first picture. Find it and copy its letter.

1.   **a.**   **b.**   **c.**   **d.**

2.   **a.**   **b.**   **c.**   **d.**

Problem Solving

A piglet on Mr. McCabe's farm is 40 kg. One of the hogs is heavier than the piglet. How much more is the hog?

A. Read the problem above.

1. How much is the piglet?

2. How much is the hog?

3. What does the problem ask?

4. Can you solve the problem? Why or why not?

> Some problems do not have enough information to solve them.

B. Charlie the chicken was born in Cleveland, Ohio. Harriet the hen is 5 years younger than Charlie. How old is Harriet?

5. How much younger is Harriet than Charlie?

6. How old is Charlie?

7. What does the problem ask?

8. Can you solve the problem? Why or why not?

C. Tell if there is **enough** or **not enough** information. Solve the problem if you can.

9. The farm rooster began crowing at 6:15 am. He crowed until 7:45 am. How long did he crow?

10. Farmer McCabe's silo is 15 meters high. How much corn does it hold?

Tell if there is **enough** or **not enough** information. Solve the problem if you can.

1. Henrietta the hen lays an egg every day. How many eggs will she lay in two weeks?

2. One of the goats is 3 years old. Her father is 4 times as old as she is. How old is her father?

3. Billy the goat is 5 years old. His sister is 3 years old. His father is 4 times as old as his sister. How old is his mother?

4. Fido can run 1 kilometer in 5 minutes. How long will it take him to run from the farmhouse to the barn?

5. Terry the toad jumped 25 centimeters. Fred the frog jumped farther. How much farther did Fred the frog jump?

6. Farmer McCabe's cow gives 4 liters of milk twice a day. How many liters of milk will she give in a week?

7. Cliff the cat's tail is 3 times as long as Rob the rat's tail. How long is Cliff the cat's tail?

8. When Helga the horse runs around the track 5 times, she has run 1 kilometer. How many times must she run around the track to run 3 kilometers?

Temperature

Temperature is measured in degrees Celsius (° C).

A. Water boils at 100° C.
   1. At what temperature does
      water freeze?

B. Average room temperature is 20° C.
   2. Is 15° C hot or cool?

C. The temperature outside is 12° C.
   3. Is it cool or very cold?

D. The temperature was 28° C. It fell
14 degrees. Find the temperature now.

   4. Find 28° C on the thermometer.

   5. Count down 14 degrees.

   6. What is the temperature now?

E. The temperature was −4° C. It
rose 16 degrees. Find the
temperature now.

   7. Find −4° C on the thermometer.

   8. Count up 16 degrees.

   9. What is the temperature now?

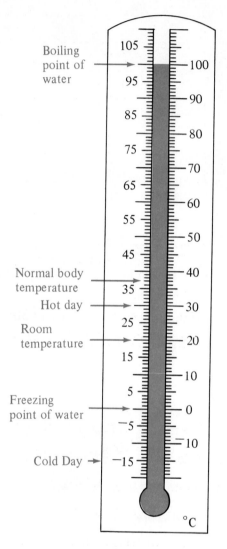

F. Complete.

	Temperature before	Change	Temperature after
10.	32° C	fall of 17° C	
11.	−2° C	rise of 7° C	
12.	12° C	fall of 20° C	

Complete.

	Temperature before	Change	Temperature after
1.	18° C	rise of 11° C	
2.	32° C	fall of 8° C	
3.	−7° C	rise of 10° C	
4.	2° C	rise of 9° C	
5.	15° C	fall of 20° C	
6.	−3° C	fall of 7° C	

Solve.

7. The temperature outside is 10° C. Will the skating pond freeze?

8. The temperature of a bowl of soup is 100° C. Is it cool enough to eat?

9. The temperature outside is 30° C. Is it summer or winter?

10. The temperature of a room is 25° C. Do you need a sweater?

Find Out!
Calculator Activity

1. Add the digits in 597. [HINT: 5 + 9 + 7 = ?]

2. Subtract the answer from 597.

3. Divide that answer by 9.

4. Is the answer to step 3 a whole number?

5. Repeat steps 1–4 for several other 3-digit numbers. Is the answer to step 3 always a whole number?

Hours, Minutes, and Seconds

A day is divided into 24 hours.

> 1 day (d) = 24 hours (h)
>
> 1 hour = 60 minutes (min)
>
> 1 minute = 60 seconds (s)

A. Complete.

1. 1 d = 24 h
2 d = __?__ h

2. 1 min = 60 s
3 min = __?__ s

3. 1 h = 60 min
$1\frac{1}{2}$ h = __?__ min

4. 1 min = 60 s
$2\frac{1}{2}$ min = __?__ s

B. We use am and pm to label time.

> am—from midnight to noon
>
> pm—from noon to midnight

5. What time will it be 3 hours after 4:20 am?

6. What time was it 7 hours before 6:45 pm?

C. Hours and minutes can be added. Complete.

7.   3 h 20 min
  + 4 h 14 min
  _____
    __?__ h __?__ min

8.   7 h 50 min
  + 1 h 30 min
  _____
    8 h 80 min, or 9 h __?__ min

D. Hours and minutes can be subtracted. Complete.

9.   5 h 40 min
  − 3 h 15 min
  _____
    __?__ h __?__ min

10.   ⁵ϐ h ⁷⁵1̶5̶ min   (THINK 60 min + 15 min)
  − 2 h 40 min
  _____
    __?__ h __?__ min

How many hours are there in each?

1. 3 days   **2.** 4 days   **3.** 7 days

How many minutes are there in each?

4. 2 hours   **5.** 3 hours   **6.** 12 hours

How many seconds are there in each?

7. 4 minutes   **8.** 2 minutes   **9.** 5 minutes

What time will it be 6 hours later?

10. 11:20 am   **11.** 7:00 pm   **12.** 1:15 pm

What time was it 4 hours earlier?

13. 6:30 am   **14.** 5:40 pm   **15.** 10:20 am

Add.

16.   3 h 20 min
     + 1 h 10 min

17.   6 h 45 min
     + 3 h 15 min

18.   5 h 40 min
     + 2 h 50 min

19.   4 h 35 min
     + 2 h 45 min

20.   6 h 55 min
     + 3 h 20 min

21.   7 h 15 min
     + 8 h 45 min

Subtract.

22.   7 h 50 min
     − 3 h 10 min

23.   7 h 10 min
     − 3 h 45 min

24.   8 h
     − 3 h 25 min

Solve.

25. Carlos left school at 11:30 am. He returned at 12:45 pm. How long was he away?

26. Anna started her homework at 4:15 pm. She worked for 2 hours and 40 minutes. When did she finish?

27. Tim started hiking at 8:40 am. He hiked for 3 hours and 20 minutes. When did he stop?

28. Betsy went to sleep at 9:30 pm. She heard a dog bark at 1:15 am. How long had she been asleep?

Calendar

January

S	M	T	W	T	F	S
		1	2	3	4	5
6	7	8	9	10	11	12
13	14	15	16	17	18	19
20	21	22	23	24	25	26
27	28	29	30	31		

A. Today is Thursday. The date is January 10.

1. What day will it be in 4 days?

2. What will be the date?

3. What day was it 3 days ago?

B. There are 4 days between Tuesday, January 15, and Sunday, January 20. Complete.

4. There are __?__ days between Monday, January 21, and Tuesday, January 29.

5. There are __?__ days between Thursday, January 17, and Wednesday, January 30.

C. There are 12 months in a year.

6. What month will it be in 6 months?

7. What month was it 11 months ago?

D.

| 1 decade = 10 years |
| 1 century = 100 years |

8. What year will it be 6 years from now?

9. What year was it a decade ago?

10. What year will it be a century from now?

MONTHS OF THE YEAR

January	July
February	August
March	September
April	October
May	November
June	December

Today is Sunday, September 26. What day and date will it be:

1. 2 days from now?   **2.** 5 days from now?   **3.** 7 days from now?

Today is Wednesday, June 25. What day and date was it?

4. 3 days ago?   **5.** 6 days ago?   **6.** 8 days ago?

It is now May. What month will it be:

7. 4 months from now?   **8.** 12 months from now?   **9.** 7 months from now?

It is now August. What month was it:

10. 6 months ago?   **11.** 9 months ago?   **12.** 14 months ago?

It is now 1982. What year will it be:

13. 7 years from now?   **14.** 12 years from now?

15. 1 decade from now?   **16.** 2 centuries from now?

It is now 1985. What year was it:

17. 8 years ago?   **18.** 14 years ago?

19. How many days are between Wednesday, February 2, and Friday, February 11?

Find Out!

Brainteaser

Mrs. Pick has 3 bags. One has 2 apples, one has 2 lemons, and the third has 1 apple and 1 lemon. The bags should be labeled AA, LL, and AL according to their contents. However, all the labels were put on wrong. How can she draw just one thing from one bag and tell what is in all the bags?

Length in the Customary System

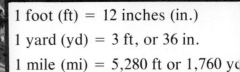

1 foot (ft) = 12 inches (in.)
1 yard (yd) = 3 ft, or 36 in.
1 mile (mi) = 5,280 ft or 1,760 yd

A. Complete.

1. 4 ft = __?__ in.

2. 3 mi = __?__ ft

3. 2 yd = __?__ in.

4. 9 ft = __?__ yd

5. 24 in. = __?__ ft

6. 108 in. = __?__ yd

7. 4 yd = __?__ ft

8. 2 mi = __?__ yd

When we add measures, sometimes we must simplify the answer.

$$\begin{array}{r} 3 \text{ ft} \quad 9 \text{ in.} \\ + 4 \text{ ft} \quad 8 \text{ in.} \\ \hline 7 \text{ ft} \quad 17 \text{ in.} \end{array}$$ 17 in. = 1 ft + 5 in., so the sum is 8 ft 5 in.

B. Complete.

9.
$$\begin{array}{r} 9 \text{ ft} \quad 8 \text{ in.} \\ + 3 \text{ ft} \quad 6 \text{ in.} \\ \hline 12 \text{ ft} \quad 14 \text{ in.} \end{array} = 13 \text{ ft } \underline{} \text{ in.}$$

10.
$$\begin{array}{r} 8 \text{ ft} \quad 8 \text{ in.} \\ + 7 \text{ ft} \quad 4 \text{ in.} \\ \hline 15 \text{ ft} \quad 12 \text{ in.} \end{array} = \underline{} \text{ ft}$$

C. Sometimes we have to rename in order to subtract.

Example
$$\begin{array}{r} \overset{2}{\cancel{3}} \text{ ft} \quad \overset{16}{\cancel{4}} \text{ in.} \\ - 1 \text{ ft} \quad 6 \text{ in.} \\ \hline 1 \text{ ft} \quad 10 \text{ in.} \end{array}$$ (THINK: 1 ft = 12 in. and 4 in. + 12 in. = 16 in.)

Subtract.

11.
$$\begin{array}{r} 8 \text{ ft} \quad 5 \text{ in.} \\ - 2 \text{ ft} \quad 1 \text{ in.} \\ \hline \end{array}$$

12.
$$\begin{array}{r} 9 \text{ ft} \quad 2 \text{ in.} \\ - 5 \text{ ft} \quad 6 \text{ in.} \\ \hline \end{array}$$

Complete.

1. 2 ft = ___?___ in.

2. 5 ft = ___?___ in.

3. 2 yd = ___?___ in.

4. 36 in. = ___?___ ft

5. 48 in. = ___?___ ft

6. 5 yd = ___?___ ft

7. 7 yd = ___?___ ft

8. 4 mi = ___?___ ft

9. 5 mi = ___?___ ft

10. 15 ft = ___?___ yd

11. 18 ft = ___?___ yd

12. 4 mi = ___?___ yd

13. 3 mi = ___?___ yd

14. 72 in. = ___?___ yd

15. 144 in. = ___?___ yd

Add.

16.   4 ft 8 in.
    + 3 ft 2 in.

17.   6 ft 7 in.
    + 4 ft 1 in.

18.   8 ft 3 in.
    + 10 ft 4 in.

19.   9 ft 9 in.
    + 2 ft 5 in.

20.   8 ft 7 in.
    + 2 ft 8 in.

21.   9 ft 8 in.
    + 3 ft 4 in.

Subtract.

22.   8 ft 6 in.
    − 2 ft 4 in.

23.   6 ft 9 in.
    − 4 ft 8 in.

24.   12 ft 5 in.
    − 6 ft 5 in.

25.   3 ft 4 in.
    − 2 ft 6 in.

26.   6 ft 6 in.
    − 3 ft 8 in.

27.   8 ft
    − 2 ft 4 in.

Find Out!
Brainteaser

Some clocks are 24 hour clocks.
1:00 means 1:00 am; 13:00 means 1:00 pm;
20:00 means 8:00 pm.

What do these mean?

1. 15:00

2. 18:00

3. 4:00

4. 23:00

5. 11:00

6. 14:00

Liquid Measure

1 cup = $\frac{1}{2}$ pint (pt)
2 cups = 1 pt
2 pt = 1 quart (qt)
4 qt = 1 gallon (gal)

A. Complete.

1. 8 cups = __?__ pt

2. 2 qt = __?__ pt

3. 4 qt = __?__ gal

4. 7 pt = __?__ qt

B. A cup contains 8 fluid ounces (fl oz).
How many fluid ounces are in 3 cups?

C. How many cups are there in 24 fl oz? 40 fl oz?

_____ Practice

Complete.

1. 3 cups = __?__ fl oz

2. 4 cups = __?__ pt

3. 3 gal = __?__ qt

4. 16 fl oz = __?__ cups

5. 5 pt = __?__ cups

6. 4 qt = __?__ pt

7. 8 pt = __?__ qt

8. 4 gal = __?__ qt

9. 12 qt = __?__ gal

10. 3 pt = __?__ qt

11. 6 qt = __?__ gal

12. 5 cups = __?__ pt

Solve.

13. A recipe for iced tea for 25 people calls for 4 quarts 2 cups of
boiling water. How many cups of boiling water is this?

Weight

16 ounces (oz) = 1 pound (lb)
2,000 lb = 1 ton

A. Complete.

1. 2 lb = ___?___ oz

2. 32 oz = ___?___ lb

3. 3 tons = ___?___ lb

4. 10,000 lb = ___?___ tons

5. 18 oz = ___?___ lb ___?___ oz

6. 2 lb 4 oz = ___?___ oz

B. Complete.

1. $\frac{1}{2}$ lb = ___?___ oz   THINK: $\frac{1}{2}$ of 16 oz = ___?___ oz

2. $\frac{1}{2}$ ton = ___?___ lb   THINK: $\frac{1}{2}$ of 2,000 lbs = ___?___ lb

Practice

Complete.

1. 5 lb = ___?___ oz

2. 64 oz = ___?___ lb

3. $\frac{1}{2}$ lb = ___?___ oz

4. 4 tons = ___?___ lb

5. 8,000 lb = ___?___ tons

6. $\frac{1}{5}$ ton = ___?___ lb

7. 22 oz = ___?___ lb ___?___ oz

8. 5 lb 6 oz = ___?___ oz

Solve.

9. How much does 32 ounces of meat cost at $1.10 a pound?

10. How many ounces of cheese are in 2 pounds 7 ounces?

Fahrenheit Scale

In the customary system
the **Fahrenheit** (F) scale
is used to measure temperature.

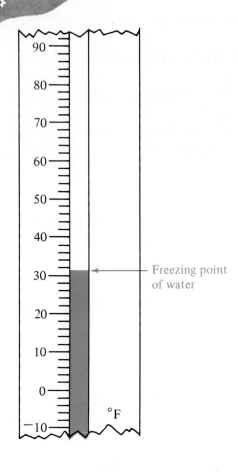

A. Look at the thermometer.

1. Water boils at 212° F
   on the Fahrenheit scale.
   At what temperature does
   it freeze?

2. The temperature was
   64° F. It rose 14°.
   What is it now?

3. The temperature was
   8° F. It fell 12°.
   What is it now?

4. Room temperature is
   68° F. Is 80° hot or
   cold?

B. Complete.

	Temperature before	Change	Temperature after
5.	26° F	Rise of 12°	
6.	68° F	Fall of 18°	
7.		Rise of 6°	84° F
8.	−4° F		18° F

C. Solve.

9. The temperature is 65° F. Is it warm or very hot?

10. The temperature is 20° F. Could you go swimming in a pond?

Solve.

1. Oxygen turns into liquid at −119° F. Is this warm or cold?

2. The temperature was 30° F. It rose 24°. What is it now?

3. The temperature was 62° F. It fell 28°. What is it now?

4. Normal body temperature is about 99° F. If you have a temperature of 102° F, are you warm or cool?

Complete.

	Temperature before	Change	Temperature after
5.	35° F	Rise of 21°	
6.	10° F	Fall of 12°	
7.	70° F		80° F
8.	50° F		30° F
9.		Rise of 46°	86° F
10.		Fall of 16°	62° F

Solve.

11. The temperature is −20° F. Is it cool or very cold?

12. The temperature is 50° F. Can it snow or rain?

Problem Solving • Physical Therapists

Physical therapists help with disabilities that were caused by disease or accidents.

1. Mary hurt her leg and must learn to walk again. Each day she walks 10 meters holding a walker. How far will she walk in 3 weeks of treatment?

2. Mrs. Hoffman must receive 9 hours of treatment each month for arthritis. How many hours of treatment will she receive in a year?

3. Jay injured his knee and went to Ms. Petersen for treatment. She prescribed a whirlpool bath for 30 minutes a day. How many hours of treatment did Jay receive in 10 days?

4. Carlos lifts weights to strengthen his injured arm muscles. He started lifting a 2 kg mass. Every week he adds 1 more kilogram. How many kilograms will he lift at the end of 10 weeks?

5. Mr. Klein keeps a record of his patients. One month he helped 147 patients, the second month 158 patients, and the third month 172 patients. What was the average number of patients he helped per month?

6. Each day Ms. Dawson spends from 8:30 am to noon with patients, from 1:00 pm to 2:30 pm in a meeting, and from 2:30 pm to 5:00 pm writing up records. How many hours does she work each day?

1. Measure to the nearest centimeter.
(156)

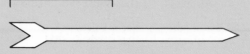

2. Measure to the nearest millimeter.
(161)

Complete.

3. 4 m = __?__ cm   **4.** 6 L = __?__ mL   **5.** 6,000 m = __?__ km
(159)   *(165)*   *(159)*

6. 9 L = __?__ mL   **7.** 8 t = __?__ kg   **8.** 7,000 g = __?__ kg
(165)   *(168)*   *(168)*

Tell which unit you would use to measure each: km, m, cm, mm, L, mL, t, kg, or g. *(170)*

9. Capacity of a bucket   **10.** Length of a book

11. Height of a tree   **12.** Mass of a dog

Complete. *(174)*

	Temperature before	Change	Temperature after
13.	21° C	rise of 8°	
14.	9° C	fall of 12° C	

Add or subtract. *(176)*

15.   4 h 40 min   **16.**   6 h 25 min
      − 3 h 10 min   + 2 h 35 min

Tell if there is **enough** or **not enough** information. Solve the problem if you can. *(172)*

17. Sara earned $1.25 an hour. Last week she worked 7 hours. How much did she earn this week?

Solve.

18. At what Celsius temperature does water boil?
(174)

19. Today is Tuesday. What day will it be 5 days from now?
(178)

20. John went to the bank at 10:30 am. He worked until 1:30 pm.
(186) How long did he work?

1. Measure to the nearest centimeter.
(156)

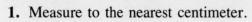

2. Measure to the nearest millimeter.
(161)

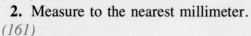

Complete.

3. 500 cm = __?__ m   **4.** 3 km = __?__ m   **5.** 20 mm = __?__ cm
(159)   *(159)*   *(162)*

6. 4 L = __?__ mL   **7.** 8 kg = __?__ g   **8.** 6,000 kg = __?__ t
(165)   *(168)*   *(168)*

Tell which unit you would use to measure each: km, m, cm, mm, L, mL, t, kg, or g. *(170)*

9. Height of a giraffe   **10.** Capacity of a glass

11. Mass of a locomotive   **12.** Capacity of a wading pool

Complete. *(174)*

	Temperature before	Change	Temperature after
13.	14° C	fall of 9°	
14.	−8° C	rise of 15°	

Add or subtract. *(176)*

15.   9 h 40 min
       − 5 h 30 min

16.   4 h 45 min
       + 5 h 25 min

Tell if there is **enough** or **not enough** information. Solve the problem if you can. *(172)*

17. Kevin needed 3 pillowcases and 6 sheets for camp. How much did he spend on pillowcases and sheets?

Solve.

18. At what Celsius temperature does water freeze?
(174)

19. Today is Wednesday. What day was it 6 days ago?
(178)

20. Liz returned from her vacation on Thursday, September 26. She
(178) left 5 days ago. What day and date was it?

1. Mrs. White goes to the supermarket and spends $7.56 for 6 lbs of hamburger meat. How much does 1 lb of meat cost?

   A $1.11   B $1.23

   C $1.26   D $1.31

2. What unit would you use to measure the distance between 2 towns?

   E Kilometers   F Meters

   G Centimeters   H Millimeters

3. Mrs. Diaz's kitchen is a square. The room measures 4 m on each side. How many square meters of tile will she need to cover the floor?

   A 8 m²   B 12 m²

   C 16 m²   D 20 m²

4. What is the temperature?

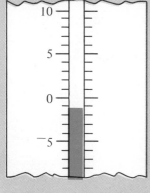

   E 5°C   F 0°C

   G −1°C   H −5°C

5. Joe wants to find out his mass. He stands on a scale and it reads 27 kg. How many grams is this?

   A 27 g   B 270 g

   C 2,700 g   D 27,000 g

6. Jean earns $6.50 a week doing odd jobs for the McNeils. How much will she earn in 4 weeks?

   E $2.60   F $24.00

   G $26.00   H $260.00

7. Mr. Gray's sports car gets 12 miles per gallon. How much gas would he need if he wanted to go 96 mi?

   A 5 gal   B 6 gal

   C 8 gal   D 9 gal

8. What is the best price for pens?

   E 1 for $0.39   F 2 for $0.72

   G 3 for $1.00   H 4 for $1.50

9. While on vacation, Amy spent $0.75 for post cards, $0.50 for stamps, and $0.39 for a pen. How much did she spend in all?

   A $1.30   B $1.64

   C $1.89   D $1.99

Fractions

1. On a piece of paper, draw a rectangle 10 cm by 15 cm.

2. Mark each side into parts which are 5 cm long.

3. Draw lines as shown. Now the rectangle is divided into how many squares?

4. On a piece of colored paper, draw another rectangle 10 cm by 15 cm. Divide it the same way. Cut out the 6 squares.

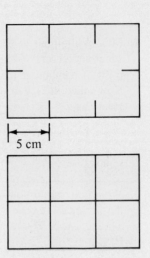

5 cm

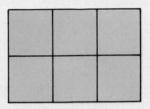

5. Place one of the colored squares in a corner of the rectangle. Now 1 square out of 6 is covered. The fraction $\frac{1}{6}$ means 1 out of 6.

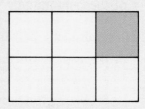

$\dfrac{1}{6}$ ⟵ Numerator
⟵ Denominator

6. Place another square in another corner of the rectangle. Now 2 out of 6 squares are covered. Write a fraction for 2 out of 6.

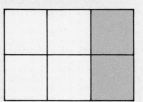

7. Cover 3 squares. Write the fraction.

8. Cover 4 squares. Write the fraction.

9. Cover 5 squares. Write the fraction.

10. Cover 6 squares. Write the fraction.

How Fractions Are Used

Fractions are used to name parts of things.

They can name part of a set.
$\frac{3}{5}$ of the fish are gold.

They can name part of a whole.
$\frac{3}{4}$ of the tank is filled.

▶ When fractions name parts of a whole, the parts must be the same size. With sets, the parts need not be the same.

A. Look at the set. Complete.

    1. __?__ of the set is snails.

    2. __?__ of the set is fish.

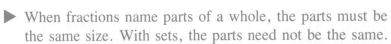

B. Jill mixed gravel for the tank.

    3. What part is blue?

    4. What part is green?

C. What part is shaded?

5.   **6.**   **7.**   **8.**

D. Look at this number line.

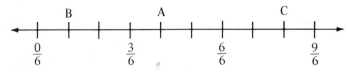

Name the fraction for each of these points.

    9. *A*   **10.** *B*   **11.** *C*

What part is shaded?

1.

2.

3.

4.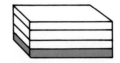

5.

6.

7.

8.

9.

10.

11.

12.

Look at these number lines.

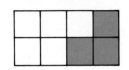

Name the fraction for each of these points.

13. *A*   **14.** *B*   **15.** *C*   **16.** *D*   **17.** *E*   **18.** *F*

Solve.

19. 7 fish
3 are guppies.
What fraction are guppies?

20. 10 shells
7 are white.
What fraction are white?

Equal Fractions

$\frac{1}{2}$ of Jan's garden has tomatoes

or, $\frac{2}{4}$ of Jan's garden has tomatoes.

$\frac{1}{2} = \frac{2}{4}$ These are equal fractions.

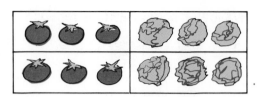

$\frac{2}{3}$ of the tomatoes are red

or, $\frac{4}{6}$ of the tomatoes are red.

$\frac{2}{3} = \frac{4}{6}$ These are equal fractions.

A. $\frac{6}{10}$ of Jim's garden has flowers.

    1. Give another name for $\frac{6}{10}$.

    2. Complete. $\frac{6}{10} = \underline{}$.

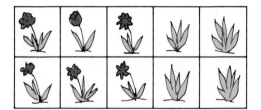

B. $\frac{1}{4}$ of the plants have flowers.

    3. Complete. $\frac{1}{4} = \underline{}$.

C. Look at the number line. Complete.

    4. $\frac{1}{4} = \frac{?}{8}$

    5. $\frac{3}{4} = \frac{?}{8}$

D. Write three equal fractions for the shaded part of each.

Example:

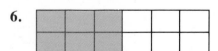 $\frac{4}{8}$

 $\frac{2}{4}$

 $\frac{1}{2}$

    6.

    7.

Write two equal fractions for each shaded part.

1.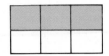
2.
3.

4.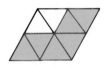
5.
6.

7.
8.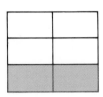
9.

Write three equal fractions for the shaded part of each.

10.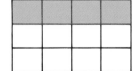
11.
12.

Find Out!

Brainteaser

Barbara has to deliver a paper at each house on her route. The houses are represented by circles. Start at circle A and find a route for Barbara that will go by each circle only once and end up back at circle A.

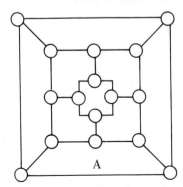

Equal Fractions

1. Fold a piece of paper
   into three equal parts.
   Shade 2 parts.

   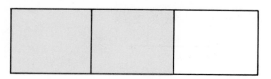

   $\frac{2}{3}$ of the paper is shaded.

   The numerator is 2.
   The denominator is 3.

2. Fold each part in half.
   Now there are 6 parts.
   4 parts are shaded.

   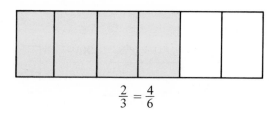

   New numerator $\longrightarrow$ $2 \times 2 = 4$
   New denominator $\longrightarrow$ $\overline{3 \times 2 = 6}$

   $\frac{2}{3}$ and $\frac{4}{6}$ are **equal fractions.**

   $\frac{2}{3} = \frac{4}{6}$

   ▶ To get an equal fraction, multiply the numerator
   and the denominator by the same number.

3. Fold a piece of paper into fourths. Shade $\frac{3}{4}$.

   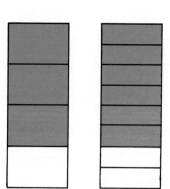

4. Fold each part in half. Now there are 8 parts.
   How many parts are shaded?

5. Complete. $\frac{3}{4} = \frac{?}{8}$

★ 6. Fold a piece of paper in half.
   Fold each part in half.
   Fold each part in half again.
   Fold each part in half again.

   Complete: $\frac{1}{2} = \frac{?}{4} = \frac{?}{8} = \frac{?}{16}$

Building Equal Fractions

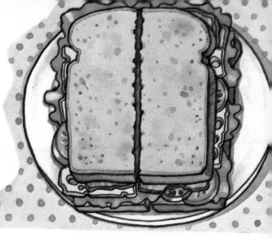

Many equal fractions can be built from $\frac{1}{2}$.

$\frac{1 \times 2}{2 \times 2} = \frac{2}{4}$ $\frac{1 \times 3}{2 \times 3} = \frac{3}{6}$ $\frac{1 \times 4}{2 \times 4} = \frac{4}{8}$ $\frac{1 \times 5}{2 \times 5} = \frac{5}{10}$

$\frac{1}{2}, \frac{2}{4}, \frac{3}{6}, \frac{4}{8}, \frac{5}{10}, \ldots$ are equal fractions.

A. List the first 5 equal fractions for each.

1. $\frac{1}{3}$
2. $\frac{2}{5}$
3. $\frac{3}{4}$
4. $\frac{2}{7}$
5. $\frac{5}{8}$
6. $\frac{1}{10}$

B. Equal fractions can be found with a given denominator or numerator.

Examples	**Think**	**Answers**
$\frac{2}{3} = \frac{?}{12}$	$12 \div 3 = 4$ so, $\frac{2 \times 4}{3 \times 4} = \frac{8}{12}$	$\frac{2}{3} = \frac{8}{12}$
$\frac{5}{6} = \frac{15}{?}$	$15 \div 5 = 3$ so $\frac{5 \times 3}{6 \times 3} = \frac{15}{18}$	$\frac{5}{6} = \frac{15}{18}$

Solve.

7. $\frac{1}{4} = \frac{?}{12}$
8. $\frac{4}{5} = \frac{?}{15}$
9. $\frac{3}{4} = \frac{6}{?}$
10. $\frac{2}{5} = \frac{4}{?}$

Practice

List the first 5 equal fractions for each.

1. $\frac{1}{4}$
2. $\frac{5}{6}$
3. $\frac{1}{5}$
4. $\frac{3}{8}$
5. $\frac{1}{8}$
6. $\frac{1}{7}$
7. $\frac{3}{5}$

8. $\frac{5}{7}$
9. $\frac{1}{6}$
10. $\frac{2}{9}$
11. $\frac{4}{5}$
12. $\frac{1}{9}$
13. $\frac{3}{10}$
14. $\frac{7}{8}$

Solve.

15. $\frac{1}{2} = \frac{?}{8}$
16. $\frac{1}{4} = \frac{?}{20}$
17. $\frac{2}{3} = \frac{?}{15}$
18. $\frac{2}{5} = \frac{?}{20}$

19. $\frac{1}{5} = \frac{2}{?}$
20. $\frac{1}{6} = \frac{3}{?}$
21. $\frac{5}{6} = \frac{25}{?}$
22. $\frac{3}{4} = \frac{9}{?}$

Checking for Equal Fractions

Does $\frac{1}{3}$ equal $\frac{2}{6}$?
Cross multiply and check.

$\frac{1}{3} \diagtimes \frac{2}{6}$ $1 \times 6 = 6$

$3 \times 2 = 6$

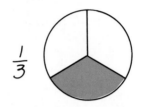 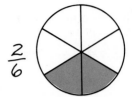

The products are the same. So, $\frac{1}{3} = \frac{2}{6}$.

A. Does $\frac{3}{5}$ equal $\frac{5}{8}$. Cross multiply.

Complete. $\frac{3}{5} \diagtimes \frac{5}{8}$ **1.** $3 \times 8 =$ ___?___

2. $5 \times 5 =$ ___?___

3. Does $\frac{3}{5} = \frac{5}{8}$?

B. True or false?

   4. $\frac{2}{4} = \frac{3}{6}$ **5.** $\frac{2}{3} = \frac{3}{4}$ **6.** $\frac{6}{8} = \frac{9}{12}$ **7.** $\frac{2}{8} = \frac{3}{12}$

Practice

True or false?

1. $\frac{3}{9} = \frac{1}{3}$ **2.** $\frac{1}{4} = \frac{2}{5}$ **3.** $\frac{2}{8} = \frac{1}{4}$ **4.** $\frac{1}{2} = \frac{4}{8}$

5. $\frac{2}{5} = \frac{4}{10}$ **6.** $\frac{4}{6} = \frac{2}{3}$ **7.** $\frac{5}{8} = \frac{1}{2}$ **8.** $\frac{5}{8} = \frac{3}{4}$

9. $\frac{2}{10} = \frac{3}{15}$ **10.** $\frac{9}{15} = \frac{6}{10}$ **11.** $\frac{6}{8} = \frac{9}{10}$ **12.** $\frac{8}{10} = \frac{7}{8}$

13. $\frac{3}{7} = \frac{4}{10}$ **14.** $\frac{5}{6} = \frac{6}{7}$ **15.** $\frac{6}{7} = \frac{8}{9}$ **16.** $\frac{5}{8} = \frac{15}{18}$

17. $\frac{3}{5} = \frac{4}{7}$ **18.** $\frac{7}{10} = \frac{6}{9}$ ★ **19.** $\frac{14}{16} = \frac{21}{24}$ ★ **20.** $\frac{45}{90} = \frac{34}{68}$

Keeping Fit

Subtract.

1. 85
  − 8

2. 33
  − 6

3. 72
  − 29

4. 56
  − 18

5. 92
  − 34

6. 64
  − 47

7. 256
  − 39

8. 687
  − 58

9. 786
  − 259

10. 841
  − 312

11. 936
  − 818

12. 582
  − 224

13. 716
  − 241

14. 428
  − 156

15. 944
  − 365

16. 726
  − 457

17. 412
  − 236

18. 817
  − 555

19. 5,487
  − 218

20. 6,874
  − 449

21. 3,576
  − 1,238

22. 5,872
  − 2,426

23. 9,463
  − 3,177

24. 8,636
  − 2,459

25. 7,249
  − 2,356

26. 6,544
  − 3,652

27. 8,235
  − 4,546

28. 7,368
  − 5,499

29. $ 35.74
  − 16.85

30. $ 87.56
  − 29.79

31. 806
  − 45

32. 408
  − 27

33. 605
  − 321

34. 908
  − 254

35. 700
  − 238

36. 600
  − 431

37. 8,007
  − 2,645

38. 9,009
  − 2,456

39. 6,000
  − 2,327

40. 8,000
  − 1,456

41. $ 30.00
  − 17.56

42. $ 50.00
  − 19.99

43. 45,286
  − 3,159

44. 68,726
  − 5,284

45. 75,342
  − 43,721

46. 89,429
  − 36,247

47. 276,845
  − 54,718

48. 672,928
  − 41,543

49. 824,369
  − 757,268

50. 777,656
  − 321,288

51. 387,212
  − 199,544

52. 622,354
  − 253,565

53. $ 2,726.05
  − 1,345.96

54. $ 5,281.17
  − 3,176.89

Least Common Multiples

What are the common multiples of 2 and 3?

Multiples of 2: 2, 4, 6, 8, 10, 12, 14, 16, 18, . . .

Multiples of 3: 3, 6, 9, 12, 15, 18, 21, . . .

Common multiples of 2 and 3 are 6, 12, 18, . . .

A. Find the first three common multiples of each pair.

   1. 4 and 6   **2.** 3 and 4   **3.** 5 and 10

B. Find the LCM.

   Example   Multiples of 4: 4, 8, 12, 16, 20, 24, . . .

                   Multiples of 6: 6, 12, 18, 24, 30, . . .

                   Common multiples of 4 and 6: 12, 24, . . .

                   12 is the least common multiple (LCM) of 4 and 6.

   4. 3 and 6   **5.** 2 and 8   **6.** 4 and 9

Here is a quick way to find the LCM of 4 and 5.

Step 1: List some multiples of the larger number in order.

Step 2: List some multiples of the smaller number in order until one matches.

Multiples of 5: 5, 10, 15, 20, 25, 30, . . .

Multiples of 4: 4, 8, 12, 16, 20

20 is the LCM of 4 and 5.

C. Find the LCM.

   7. 2 and 7   **8.** 4 and 10   **9.** 2 and 6

   10. 8 and 16   **11.** 3 and 11   **12.** 6 and 9

Find the LCM.

1. 3 and 5   **2.** 2 and 5   **3.** 3 and 7   **4.** 3 and 10

5. 5 and 8   **6.** 2 and 11   **7.** 5 and 6   **8.** 3 and 8

9. 4 and 8   **10.** 3 and 9   **11.** 5 and 15   **12.** 4 and 16

13. 6 and 12   **14.** 2 and 4   **15.** 3 and 12   **16.** 5 and 10

17. 10 and 15   **18.** 6 and 10   **19.** 6 and 15   **20.** 9 and 12

21. 10 and 12   **22.** 6 and 8   **23.** 8 and 10   **24.** 8 and 12

25. 6 and 18   **26.** 8 and 9   **27.** 6 and 16   **28.** 7 and 14

29. 9 and 15   **30.** 6 and 7   **31.** 4 and 12   **32.** 5 and 7

★ **33.** 2, 3, and 4   ★ **34.** 3, 4, and 5   ★ **35.** 2, 4, and 6

★ **36.** 2, 3, and 9   ★ **37.** 3, 6, and 8   ★ **38.** 3, 5, and 6

Find Out!

Activity

How Did You Get to School Today?

Take a survey. Find out what fraction of your class comes to school by walking, by bus, by bike, or by car. First, count the number of students in class today. This will be the denominator of each fraction. Then, complete the chart.

Method	Fraction
Walk	
Bus	
Bike	
Car	

Comparing Fractions

You can use the numberline to compare $\frac{4}{9}$ and $\frac{7}{9}$.

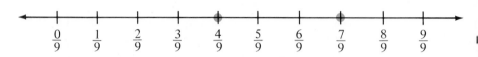

Say: $\frac{4}{9}$ is less than $\frac{7}{9}$ or $\frac{7}{9}$ is greater than $\frac{4}{9}$

Write: $\frac{4}{9} < \frac{7}{9}$ or $\frac{7}{9} > \frac{4}{9}$

A. To compare fractions with different denominators, first find a common denominator.

Example   Compare $\frac{1}{3}$ and $\frac{1}{4}$

$$\frac{1}{3} = \frac{4}{12} \quad\quad \frac{1}{4} = \frac{3}{12}$$

$$\frac{4}{12} > \frac{3}{12} \quad\quad \text{So, } \frac{1}{3} > \frac{1}{4}$$

Compare $\frac{2}{3} \equiv \frac{3}{5}$. Use >, <, or =.

1. Complete. $\frac{2}{3} = \frac{?}{15}$ $\frac{3}{5} = \frac{?}{15}$

2. So, $\frac{2}{3} \equiv \frac{3}{5}$

B. Compare. Use >, <, and =.

3. $\frac{5}{8} \equiv \frac{7}{8}$ **4.** $\frac{2}{3} \equiv \frac{5}{6}$ **5.** $\frac{3}{10} \equiv \frac{2}{5}$ **6.** $\frac{2}{3} \equiv \frac{3}{4}$

Practice

Compare. Use >, <, and =.

1. $\frac{4}{9} \equiv \frac{2}{9}$ **2.** $\frac{3}{10} \equiv \frac{7}{10}$ **3.** $\frac{5}{7} \equiv \frac{6}{7}$ **4.** $\frac{9}{12} \equiv \frac{6}{12}$

5. $\frac{3}{8} \equiv \frac{1}{6}$ **6.** $\frac{3}{4} \equiv \frac{4}{5}$ **7.** $\frac{5}{8} \equiv \frac{3}{4}$ **8.** $\frac{3}{4} \equiv \frac{5}{6}$

Write two equal fractions for the shaded part of each. *(194)*

1.

2.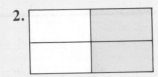

3.

Solve. *(197)*

4. $\frac{2}{5} = \frac{?}{10}$

5. $\frac{3}{4} = \frac{9}{?}$

6. $\frac{5}{6} = \frac{?}{12}$

True or false? *(198)*

7. $\frac{7}{8} = \frac{3}{4}$

8. $\frac{1}{3} = \frac{3}{9}$

9. $\frac{5}{8} = \frac{15}{18}$

Find the LCM. *(200)*

10. 9 and 12

11. 3 and 4

12. 5 and 7

Compare. Use >, <, and =. *(202)*

13. $\frac{3}{7} \equiv \frac{5}{7}$

14. $\frac{2}{3} \equiv \frac{3}{8}$

15. $\frac{3}{8} \equiv \frac{5}{6}$

Find Out!

Brainteaser

In each row, the first picture is related to the second. In the same way, the third picture is related to one of the four choices to the right. Choose the correct picture.

1. | **a.** **b.** **c.** **d.**

2. | **a.** **b.** **c.** **d.**

3. 3 | 6 | 4 | **a.** 5 **b.** 6 **c.** 8 **d.** 9

Greatest Common Factor

What is the greatest common factor (GCF) of 24 and 32?

Factors of 24: 1, 2, 3, 4, 6, 8, 12, 24

Factors of 32: 1, 2, 4, 8, 16, 32

The GCF of 24 and 32 is 8.

A. **1.** What are the factors of 12 and 36?

    2. What are the common factors of 12 and 36?

    3. What is the GCF of 12 and 36?

B. Here is a quick way to find the GCF of 12 and 18.

    4. List the factors of the smaller number, 12.

    5. Which is the largest factor that 18 is divisible by? That number is the GCF.

C. Find the GCF.

    6. 18 and 24   **7.** 3 and 9   **8.** 15 and 12   **9.** 12 and 20

Practice

Find the GCF.

1. 6 and 8	**2.** 4 and 7	**3.** 2 and 8	**4.** 5 and 11
5. 3 and 12	**6.** 8 and 10	**7.** 8 and 12	**8.** 6 and 15
9. 18 and 27	**10.** 10 and 15	**11.** 12 and 16	**12.** 15 and 20
13. 16 and 20	**14.** 18 and 21	**15.** 12 and 30	**16.** 15 and 30
17. 15 and 45	**18.** 24 and 36	**19.** 40 and 48	**20.** 21 and 35

Simplest Form

Look at $\frac{6}{8}$.

$2 \times 3 = 6$. 2 is a factor of 6.
$2 \times 4 = 8$. 2 is a factor of 8.
2 is a **common** factor of 6 and 8.

Look at $\frac{3}{4}$.

$1 \times 3 = 3$. 1 is a factor of 3.
$1 \times 4 = 4$. 1 is a factor of 4.
1 is the **only** common factor of 3 and 4.

So, $\frac{6}{8}$ is not in simplest form. $\frac{3}{4}$ is in simplest form.

▶ A fraction is in simplest form when 1 is the only common factor of the numerator and denominator.

A. These fractions are **not** in simplest form. Find as many common factors of the numerator and denominator as you can.

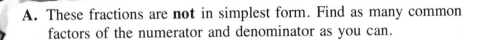

Factors   Common factors

Example $\dfrac{12}{20}$ ⟶ 1, 2, 3, 4, 6, 12   1, 2, 4
                        ⟶ 1, 2, 4, 5, 10, 20

1. $\frac{3}{9}$ 2. $\frac{6}{10}$ 3. $\frac{6}{18}$ 4. $\frac{8}{12}$ 5. $\frac{12}{15}$

B. Which are in simplest form?

6. $\frac{2}{5}$ 7. $\frac{8}{10}$ 8. $\frac{5}{8}$ 9. $\frac{7}{10}$ 10. $\frac{6}{15}$

Practice

Which are in simplest form?

1. $\frac{1}{4}$ 2. $\frac{5}{10}$ 3. $\frac{2}{3}$ 4. $\frac{2}{8}$ 5. $\frac{1}{3}$ 6. $\frac{3}{15}$

7. $\frac{4}{5}$ 8. $\frac{12}{16}$ 9. $\frac{4}{9}$ 10. $\frac{15}{25}$ 11. $\frac{8}{9}$ 12. $\frac{6}{7}$

13. $\frac{7}{14}$ 14. $\frac{9}{10}$ 15. $\frac{9}{21}$ 16. $\frac{21}{24}$ 17. $\frac{5}{18}$ ★18. $\frac{55}{121}$

19. $\frac{16}{55}$ of the vacation days were spent hiking. Is this fraction in simplest form?

Simplifying Fractions

To simplify a fraction, divide the numerator
and denominator by the greatest common factor.

Fraction	GCF	Divide	Simplest form
$\frac{2}{8}$	2	$\frac{2 \div 2}{8 \div 2} = \frac{1}{4}$	$\frac{1}{4}$
$\frac{10}{15}$	5	$\frac{10 \div 5}{15 \div 5} = \frac{2}{3}$	$\frac{2}{3}$

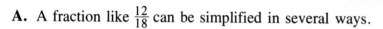

A. A fraction like $\frac{12}{18}$ can be simplified in several ways.

   1. Divide 12 and 18 by several common factors until
   the only common factor is 1.

   Complete. $\frac{12}{18} = \frac{12 \div 2}{18 \div 2} = \frac{6}{9}$

   Then, $\frac{6}{9} = \frac{6 \div 3}{9 \div 3} = $ ___?___

   2. Divide by the greatest common factor of 12 and 18.
   Complete. $\frac{12}{18} = \frac{12 \div 6}{18 \div 6} = $ ___?___

B. Complete.

   3. $\frac{10}{20} = \frac{10 \div 10}{20 \div 10} = $ ___?___

   4. $\frac{18}{27} = \frac{18 \div 9}{27 \div 9} = $ ___?___

C. Simplify. Use any way you wish.

   5. $\frac{8}{14}$ **6.** $\frac{18}{24}$ **7.** $\frac{9}{15}$

   8. $\frac{12}{20}$ **9.** $\frac{15}{24}$ **10.** $\frac{21}{28}$

   11. $\frac{6}{18}$ **12.** $\frac{15}{20}$ **13.** $\frac{16}{42}$

Simplify.

1. $\frac{2}{8}$ 2. $\frac{3}{6}$ 3. $\frac{3}{9}$ 4. $\frac{5}{10}$ 5. $\frac{7}{21}$ 6. $\frac{3}{15}$

7. $\frac{9}{12}$ 8. $\frac{10}{15}$ 9. $\frac{10}{16}$ 10. $\frac{15}{18}$ 11. $\frac{9}{21}$ 12. $\frac{12}{15}$

13. $\frac{15}{20}$ 14. $\frac{14}{21}$ 15. $\frac{8}{22}$ 16. $\frac{6}{15}$ 17. $\frac{8}{14}$ 18. $\frac{10}{25}$

19. $\frac{8}{36}$ 20. $\frac{18}{30}$ 21. $\frac{16}{24}$ 22. $\frac{24}{40}$ 23. $\frac{12}{28}$ 24. $\frac{12}{30}$

25. $\frac{16}{48}$ 26. $\frac{15}{45}$ 27. $\frac{18}{45}$ 28. $\frac{12}{32}$ 29. $\frac{18}{48}$ 30. $\frac{30}{60}$

31. $\frac{12}{21}$ 32. $\frac{17}{34}$ 33. $\frac{25}{30}$ 34. $\frac{8}{40}$ 35. $\frac{16}{44}$ 36. $\frac{40}{72}$

37. $\frac{15}{35}$ 38. $\frac{9}{18}$ 39. $\frac{9}{15}$

40. $\frac{18}{42}$ 41. $\frac{8}{12}$ 42. $\frac{5}{60}$

★ 43. $\frac{175}{875}$ ★ 44. $\frac{192}{288}$ ★ 45. $\frac{150}{450}$

Solve.

46. There are 32 students in Pam's class. 24 students have brown hair. Write and simplify the fraction of students with brown hair.

47. There are 30 students in Juan's class. 10 students have blue eyes. Write and simplify the fraction of students with blue eyes.

Problem Solving

There were 31 fifth graders and 18 sixth graders on a field trip. There were 8 adults. How many people went on the trip?

Answer 57 people

CHECK Is the answer reasonable?
Estimate the answer.

Estimate
$$
\begin{array}{r}
30 \\
20 \\
+\ 10 \\
\hline
60
\end{array}
$$

So, 60 people is near 57 people. The answer is reasonable.

> To check if an answer is reasonable, estimate the answer. Then, check the label on the answer.

Estimate the answers. Write **reasonable** or **unreasonable.** Correct the unreasonable answers.

1. The bus went 19 km to the museum, 22 km to the zoo, and 38 km back to the school. How far did it go in all?

   Answer 79 km

2. The field trip took 5 hours. The bus left at 8:30 am. At what time did it return?

   Answer 1:30 am

Estimate the answers. Write **reasonable** or **unreasonable.** Correct the unreasonable answers.

1. The bus stopped after going 20 km. The museum is 83 km from the school. How much further does the bus have to go?
Answer   63 km

2. The museum opens at 9:30 am. It closes at 5:00 pm. How long is it open?
Answer   24 hours

3. On a trip, Simon had $2.00. He spent $1.19 for lunch. How much money did he have left?
Answer $3.19

4. It took 1 hour 15 minutes to get to the museum. It took twice as long to return. How long did it take to return?
Answer   2 hours 30 minutes

5. In one day, 7 classes visited the park. Each class had 32 students. How many students visited the park that day?
Answer   650 students

★ **6.** There are 68 students going on a field trip. Each van holds 9 students. How many vans are needed for the trip?
Answer   8 vans

Ratio

Numbers can be compared by **ratio.**
The ratio of riders to horses is 6 to 8.
The ratio of horses to riders is 8 to 6.

A. The ratio of clowns to balloons is 2 to 3.

    1. What is the ratio of balloons to clowns?

B. Look at these pictures.

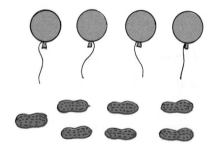

    Name the ratio to compare.

    2. Balloons to elephants   **3.** Elephants to balloons

    4. Peanuts to tents   **5.** Tents to peanuts

C. Prices can be thought of as ratios.
Name the price ratios.

    Example: 75¢   Ratio 2 for 75¢

6. 80¢   **7.**   25¢

Look at these pictures.

Name the ratio to compare.

1. Tickets to dogs

2. Tigers to jugglers

3. Tigers to horses

4. Horses to lions

5. Tickets to lions

6. Horses to jugglers

Name the price ratios.

7. 4 apples for 60¢

8. 3 hats for 50¢

9. 2 posters for 95¢

10. 12 peanuts for 15¢

11. 3 pretzels for 35¢

12. 6 whistles for 80¢

Find Out!
Calculator Activity

Multiply 142,857 by 1, by 2, and by 3. What do you notice about the digits in each answer?

By what other numbers can you multiply 142,857 and get the same digits in the answer?

142,857

Ratios as Fractions

Barry has 2 cats and 3 hamsters.

The ratio of cats to hamsters is 2 to 3. This can also be written as a fraction. The ratio of cats to hamsters is $\frac{2}{3}$.

The ratio of hamsters to cats is 3 to 2 or $\frac{3}{2}$.

A. Write fractions.

1. 6 to 5   **2.** 3 to 8   **3.** 1 to 7   **4.** 5 to 2

B. Write ratios.

5. $\frac{1}{8}$ **6.** $\frac{4}{3}$ **7.** $\frac{7}{10}$ **8.** $\frac{3}{5}$

C. Ratios and fractions can be used to compare. Look at the chart.

PETS

Cats	Hamsters	Dogs	Fish
9	4	12	5

The ratio of dogs to fish is 12 to 5.
12 to 5 can be written as $\frac{12}{5}$.

Compare. Use both ratios and fractions.

9. Hamsters to dogs   **10.** Fish to cats

11. Cats to hamsters   **12.** Dogs to hamsters

Write fractions.

1. 1 to 2   **2.** 5 to 3   **3.** 4 to 3   **4.** 6 to 2

5. 5 to 6   **6.** 2 to 9   **7.** 8 to 7   **8.** 1 to 10

9. 3 to 7   **10.** 8 to 11   **11.** 16 to 4   **12.** 20 to 5

13. Rover's and Fido's weights are in the ratio of 3 to 4.

Write ratios.

14. $\frac{1}{5}$ **15.** $\frac{2}{9}$ **16.** $\frac{5}{8}$ **17.** $\frac{3}{10}$ **18.** $\frac{7}{4}$ **19.** $\frac{2}{5}$

20. $\frac{4}{5}$ **21.** $\frac{8}{3}$ **22.** $\frac{3}{7}$ **23.** $\frac{5}{4}$ **24.** $\frac{5}{10}$ **25.** $\frac{9}{8}$

26. Tom the cat eats $\frac{2}{5}$ as much as Alley the cat.

Compare. Use both ratios and fractions.

27. Cost of a rabbit to the cost of a hamster

28. Cost of a guinea pig to the cost of a rabbit

29. Cost of a hamster to the cost of a guinea pig

COST OF PETS

Rabbit	Hamster	Guinea Pig
$8	$4	$9

30. Hours asleep to hours awake

31. Hours awake to hours asleep

★ **32.** Hours awake to hours in a day

★ **33.** Hours in a day to hours asleep

★ **34.** Hours asleep to hours in a day

PUPPY'S SLEEPING HABITS

Hours Awake	Hours Asleep
9	15

Problem Solving: Better Buys

Smart shoppers compare prices to find the better buy.

Which is the better buy?
Pens   3 for 39¢, or 4 for 48?

$$3 \text{ for } 39¢ \text{ or } 3\overline{)39¢} \quad \text{13¢ for each pen}$$

$$4 \text{ for } 48¢ \text{ or } 4\overline{)48¢} \quad \text{12¢ for each pen}$$

12¢ for each pen is less than 13¢ for each pen.

So, 4 for 48¢ is a better buy.

Practice

Which is the better buy?

1. *Baseballs*   1 for $6, or
3 for $14

2. *Pads*   1 for 42¢, or
2 for 90¢

3. *Pencils*   6 for 50¢, or
9 for 80¢

4. *Posters*   1 for $2.50, or
3 for $8.00

5. *Cheese*   3 for $1.40, or
6 for $2.50

6. *Model planes*   2 for $7, or
3 for $9

7. *Juice*   1 can for $0.29, or
3 cans for $0.82

8. *Puzzles*   2 for $1.80, or
5 for $4.90

What part is shaded? *(190, 192)*

1.

2.

3.

Write two equivalent fractions for the shaded part of each. *(194)*

4.

5.

6.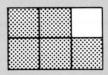

Solve. *(197)*

7. $\frac{3}{4} = \frac{?}{12}$ **8.** $\frac{2}{5} = \frac{?}{20}$ **9.** $\frac{4}{7} = \frac{8}{?}$ **10.** $\frac{3}{5} = \frac{9}{?}$

Find the LCM. *(200)*

11. 4 and 6   **12.** 7 and 12   **13.** 8 and 9   **14.** 11 and 13

Compare. Use >, <, and =. *(202)*

15. $\frac{3}{8} \equiv \frac{4}{9}$ **16.** $\frac{7}{11} \equiv \frac{3}{5}$ **17.** $\frac{6}{8} \equiv \frac{4}{10}$ **18.** $\frac{5}{12} \equiv \frac{8}{14}$

Find the GCF. *(204)*

19. 27 and 36   **20.** 15 and 45   **21.** 16 and 32   **22.** 20 and 42

Simplify. *(206)*

23. $\frac{5}{10}$ **24.** $\frac{4}{12}$ **25.** $\frac{6}{14}$ **26.** $\frac{8}{26}$ **27.** $\frac{16}{40}$ **28.** $\frac{54}{78}$

Write the ratio in fraction form. *(212)*

29. 4 to 6   **30.** 12 for 10   **31.** 8 to 20

Solve. *(214)*

32. Needles 3 for 18¢ or
            1 for 9¢
   Which is the better buy?

33. Rings 2 for $14 or
          3 for $15
   Which is the better buy?

Chapter Test

What part is shaded? *(190, 192)*

1.   2.   3.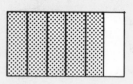

Write two equivalent fractions for the shaded part of each. *(194)*

    5.   6.

Solve. *(197)*

7. $\frac{1}{6} = \frac{?}{18}$ **8.** $\frac{2}{9} = \frac{?}{18}$ **9.** $\frac{3}{8} = \frac{9}{?}$ **10.** $\frac{1}{2} = \frac{6}{?}$

Find the LCM. *(200)*

11. 3 and 5   **12.** 4 and 7   **13.** 9 and 6   **14.** 14 and 21

Compare. Use >, <, and =. *(202)*

15. $\frac{11}{12} \equiv \frac{4}{5}$ **16.** $\frac{6}{7} \equiv \frac{13}{15}$ **17.** $\frac{4}{12} \equiv \frac{6}{9}$ **18.** $\frac{3}{4} \equiv \frac{24}{30}$

Find the GCF. *(204)*

19. 32 and 48   **20.** 63 and 35   **21.** 49 and 70   **22.** 76 and 12

Simplify. *(206)*

23. $\frac{4}{16}$ $\frac{3}{8}$ $\frac{1}{4}$ **24.** $\frac{7}{14}$ $\frac{1}{7}$ **25.** $\frac{8}{14}$ $\frac{4}{7}$ **26.** $\frac{6}{28}$ $\frac{2}{9}$ **27.** $\frac{18}{12}$ $\frac{9}{6}$ **28.** $\frac{39}{63}$

Write the ratio in fraction form. *(212)*

29. 6 to 8   **30.** 5 for 15   **31.** 6 for 10

Solve. *(214)*

32. Soda   1 case for $6 or
4 cases for $20
Which is the better buy?

33. Erasers   3 for 24¢ or
5 for 45¢
Which is the better buy?

1.

$$540$$
$$324$$
$$+ 135$$
$$\overline{999}$$

A 889
B 899
C 998
D 999

6.

$$9{,}348$$
$$- 5{,}237$$

E 14,585
F 4,111
G 4,101
H 3,101

11.

$$6{,}394$$
$$1{,}202$$
$$+ 1{,}703$$

A 9,299
B 8,299
C 7,298
D 7,289

2.

$$962$$
$$- 478$$
$$\overline{484}$$

E 1,440
F 484
G 448
H 428

7.

$$\frac{7}{8}$$
$$- \frac{1}{4}$$

A $\frac{3}{8}$
B $\frac{5}{8}$
C $\frac{3}{4}$
D $\frac{6}{4}$

12.

$$36$$
$$\times 12$$

E 362
F 372
G 402
H 432

3.

$$10\overline{)880}$$
$$\frac{80}{80}$$

A 8
B 48
C 84
D 88

8.

$$\frac{5}{12}$$
$$+ \frac{1}{6}$$

E $\frac{7}{12}$
F $\frac{8}{12}$
G $\frac{9}{6}$
H $\frac{11}{12}$

13.

$$6\overline{)3.66}$$

A $0.62
B $0.61
C $0.32
D $0.30

4.

$$\frac{1}{2}$$
$$- \frac{1}{3}$$

E $\frac{1}{6}$
F $\frac{1}{3}$
G $\frac{2}{3}$
H $\frac{5}{6}$

9.

$$\$0.96$$
$$\times 8$$

A $6.68
B $7.68
C $8.72
D $8.76

14.

$$\frac{5}{9}$$
$$+ \frac{1}{3}$$

E $\frac{8}{9}$
F $\frac{2}{3}$
G $\frac{4}{9}$
H $\frac{1}{9}$

5.

$$60\overline{)720}$$
$$\frac{60}{120}$$

A 12
B 60
C 80
D 120

10.

$$84$$
$$\times 14$$

E 70
F 98
G 1,166
H 1,176

15.

$$33{,}642$$
$$- 12{,}231$$

A 43,573
B 45,873
C 11,811
D 21,411

Adding Fractions

$$\frac{1}{5} + \frac{3}{5} = \frac{4}{5}$$

$$\frac{1}{5} + \frac{3}{5}$$

It is easy to add fractions with the same denominator.

$$\begin{array}{r} \frac{1}{5} \\ + \frac{3}{5} \\ \hline \frac{4}{5} \end{array}$$

To add fractions with the same denominator:

1. Add the numerators.
2. Use the same denominator.

A. Complete.

1. $\begin{array}{r} \frac{5}{7} \\ + \frac{1}{7} \\ \hline \frac{?}{7} \end{array}$

2. $\begin{array}{r} \frac{3}{10} \\ + \frac{4}{10} \\ \hline \frac{7}{?} \end{array}$

3. $\begin{array}{r} \frac{4}{12} \\ \frac{1}{12} \\ + \frac{2}{12} \\ \hline \frac{?}{12} \end{array}$

4. $\frac{1}{9} + \frac{4}{9} = \frac{?}{9}$

5. $\frac{3}{15} + \frac{2}{15} + \frac{6}{15} = \frac{11}{?}$

B. Add.

6. $\begin{array}{r} \frac{3}{9} \\ + \frac{1}{9} \\ \hline \end{array}$

7. $\begin{array}{r} \frac{3}{7} \\ + \frac{2}{7} \\ \hline \end{array}$

8. $\begin{array}{r} \frac{3}{13} \\ \frac{4}{13} \\ + \frac{5}{13} \\ \hline \end{array}$

9. $\frac{1}{6} + \frac{4}{6}$

10. $\frac{2}{11} + \frac{4}{11} + \frac{3}{11}$

Practice

Add.

1. $\begin{array}{r} \frac{1}{5} \\ + \frac{1}{5} \\ \hline \end{array}$

2. $\begin{array}{r} \frac{4}{9} \\ + \frac{3}{9} \\ \hline \end{array}$

3. $\begin{array}{r} \frac{1}{12} \\ + \frac{4}{12} \\ \hline \end{array}$

4. $\begin{array}{r} \frac{1}{10} \\ + \frac{2}{10} \\ \hline \end{array}$

5. $\begin{array}{r} \frac{3}{11} \\ + \frac{2}{11} \\ \hline \end{array}$

6. $\frac{3}{10} + \frac{1}{10} + \frac{3}{10}$

7. $\frac{2}{12} + \frac{3}{12} + \frac{2}{12}$

8. $\frac{1}{9} + \frac{3}{9} + \frac{4}{9}$

Adding and Simplifying

The class decorated $\frac{2}{6}$ of the gym in the morning. They decorated $\frac{1}{6}$ of the gym in the afternoon. What part of the gym did they decorate in all?

$$\begin{array}{r} \frac{2}{6} \\ + \frac{1}{6} \\ \hline \frac{3}{6} \end{array} = \frac{3 \div 3}{6 \div 3} = \frac{1}{2} \quad \text{They decorated } \frac{1}{2} \text{ of the gym.}$$

A. Sometimes the answer can be simplified. Complete.

1. $\begin{array}{r} \frac{1}{6} \\ + \frac{3}{6} \\ \hline \frac{4}{6} \end{array} = \frac{4 \div 2}{6 \div 2} = \frac{?}{3}$

2. $\begin{array}{r} \frac{1}{4} \\ + \frac{1}{4} \\ \hline \frac{2}{4} \end{array} = \frac{2 \div ?}{4 \div ?} = \frac{1}{2}$

3. $\begin{array}{r} \frac{2}{8} \\ + \frac{2}{8} \\ \hline \frac{4}{8} \end{array} = \frac{4 \div ?}{8 \div ?} = \frac{?}{2}$

4. $\begin{array}{r} \frac{1}{10} \\ \frac{2}{10} \\ + \frac{2}{10} \\ \hline \frac{5}{10} \end{array} = \frac{?}{2}$

5. $\frac{4}{9} + \frac{2}{9} = \frac{6}{9} = \frac{?}{3}$

6. $\frac{1}{12} + \frac{2}{12} + \frac{3}{12} = \frac{6}{12} = \frac{?}{2}$

B. Add and simplify.

7. $\begin{array}{r} \frac{1}{6} \\ + \frac{1}{6} \\ \hline \end{array}$

8. $\begin{array}{r} \frac{1}{9} \\ + \frac{2}{9} \\ \hline \end{array}$

9. $\begin{array}{r} \frac{1}{8} \\ + \frac{5}{8} \\ \hline \end{array}$

10. $\begin{array}{r} \frac{1}{10} \\ + \frac{3}{10} \\ \hline \end{array}$

11. $\begin{array}{r} \frac{1}{18} \\ + \frac{2}{18} \\ \hline \end{array}$

12. $\begin{array}{r} \frac{1}{12} \\ + \frac{5}{12} \\ \hline \end{array}$

13. $\begin{array}{r} \frac{1}{9} \\ \frac{2}{9} \\ + \frac{3}{9} \\ \hline \end{array}$

14. $\begin{array}{r} \frac{3}{12} \\ \frac{2}{12} \\ + \frac{3}{12} \\ \hline \end{array}$

15. $\begin{array}{r} \frac{1}{15} \\ \frac{2}{15} \\ + \frac{2}{15} \\ \hline \end{array}$

16. $\frac{2}{12} + \frac{4}{12}$

17. $\frac{1}{6} + \frac{1}{6} + \frac{2}{6}$

Add and simplify.

1. $\frac{2}{10}$
$+ \frac{3}{10}$

2. $\frac{1}{8}$
$+ \frac{5}{8}$

3. $\frac{3}{15}$
$+ \frac{2}{15}$

4. $\frac{1}{9}$
$\frac{4}{9}$
$+ \frac{1}{9}$

5. $\frac{3}{12}$
$\frac{5}{12}$
$+ \frac{2}{12}$

6. $\frac{2}{15}$
$\frac{6}{15}$
$+ \frac{4}{15}$

7. $\frac{2}{10} + \frac{4}{10}$

8. $\frac{4}{14} + \frac{3}{14}$

9. $\frac{2}{18} + \frac{4}{18} + \frac{3}{18}$

10. $\frac{5}{20} + \frac{7}{20} + \frac{3}{20}$

★ 11. $\frac{25}{150} + \frac{15}{150}$

★ 12. $\frac{50}{250} + \frac{4}{250}$

Solve. Simplify the answer.

13. Sara worked $\frac{2}{6}$ hour making decorations and $\frac{1}{6}$ hour making punch. What fraction of an hour did she work in all?

14. At the dance, Anton ate $\frac{2}{8}$ of a pizza. Susan also ate $\frac{2}{8}$. How much did they eat in all?

Keeping Fit

Find the LCM.

1. 4 and 8

2. 3 and 9

3. 5 and 15

4. 2 and 5

5. 3 and 7

6. 4 and 9

7. 4 and 10

8. 8 and 12

9. 6 and 10

10. 5 and 6

11. 2 and 8

12. 8 and 10

13. 5 and 10

14. 3 and 5

15. 4 and 12

16. 6 and 7

17. 9 and 6

18. 10 and 12

Adding Different Denominators

Adam planted $\frac{2}{3}$ of his garden with
vegetables and $\frac{1}{4}$ with sunflowers.
What part of the garden did he use?

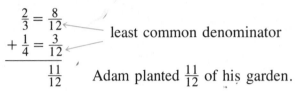

$$\frac{2}{3} = \frac{8}{12}$$

least common denominator

$$+\frac{1}{4} = \frac{3}{12}$$

$$\frac{11}{12}$$ Adam planted $\frac{11}{12}$ of his garden.

▶ To add fractions with different denominators:
   Step 1 Find equal fractions with the same denominator.
   Step 2 Add.

A. To find equal fractions, first find the least common denominator,
   or LCD.

   Add: $\frac{1}{4} + \frac{3}{8} + \frac{3}{12}$. Complete.

   1. Multiples of 4: _?_ , _?_ , _?_ , _?_ , _?_ , _?_

   2. Multiples of 8: _?_ , _?_ , _?_

   3. Multiples of 12: _?_ , _?_

   4. Use _?_ as the LCD.

   5. $\frac{1}{4} = \frac{6}{24}$

   $\frac{3}{8} = \frac{?}{24}$

   $+\frac{3}{12} = \frac{?}{24}$

   $\frac{21}{24} = \frac{?}{?}$

B. Add

   6. $\frac{3}{4}$
   $+\frac{1}{8}$

   7. $\frac{1}{4}$
   $+\frac{2}{5}$

   8. $\frac{3}{9}$
   $+\frac{1}{6}$

   9. $\frac{1}{3}$
   $\frac{1}{9}$
   $+\frac{1}{6}$

   10. $\frac{1}{2} + \frac{1}{8} + \frac{1}{4}$

   11. $\frac{1}{3} + \frac{1}{9} + \frac{2}{12}$

Add ~~and simplify.~~

1. $\frac{1}{2}$ $\frac{3}{6}$
    $+\frac{2}{6}$ $\frac{2}{6}$

2. $\frac{1}{4}$ $\frac{2}{8}$
    $+\frac{3}{8}$ $\frac{3}{8}$

3. $\frac{2}{3}$ $\frac{4}{6}$
    $+\frac{1}{6}$ $\frac{1}{6}$

4. $\frac{5}{6}$ $\frac{25}{30}$
    $+\frac{1}{15}$ $\frac{2}{30}$

5. $\frac{2}{4}$ $\frac{10}{20}$
    $+\frac{2}{5}$ $\frac{8}{20}$

6. $\frac{3}{6}$ $\frac{6}{12}$
    $+\frac{1}{4}$ $\frac{3}{12}$

7. $\frac{1}{4} + \frac{1}{7} + \frac{1}{2}$
    $\frac{7}{28}$ $\frac{4}{28}$ $\frac{14}{28}$

8. $\frac{1}{4} + \frac{1}{3} + \frac{1}{6}$
    $\frac{6}{24}$ $\frac{8}{24}$ $\frac{4}{24}$ =

9. $\frac{1}{3} + \frac{1}{6} + \frac{2}{4}$
    $\frac{4}{12}$ $\frac{2}{12}$ $\frac{6}{12}$: 12

10. $\frac{1}{5} + \frac{1}{10} + \frac{1}{2}$
    $\frac{2}{10}$ $\frac{1}{10}$ $\frac{5}{10}$

11. $\frac{2}{3}$ $\frac{16}{24}$
    $+\frac{1}{8}$ $\frac{3}{24}$

12. $\frac{1}{2}$ $\frac{5}{10}$
    $+\frac{1}{5}$ $\frac{2}{10}$

13. $\frac{5}{100}$ $\frac{5}{100}$
    $+\frac{3}{20}$ $\frac{15}{100}$

14. $\frac{2}{6}$ $\frac{8}{24}$
    $\frac{1}{8}$ $\frac{3}{24}$
    $+\frac{1}{4}$ $\frac{6}{24}$

15. $\frac{4}{10} + \frac{2}{20} + \frac{6}{100}$
    $\frac{40}{100}$ $\frac{10}{100}$ $\frac{6}{100}$

16. $\frac{1}{6}$ $\frac{2}{12}$
    $+\frac{3}{4}$ $\frac{9}{12}$

17. $\frac{1}{8}$ $\frac{5}{40}$
    $\frac{3}{5}$ $\frac{24}{40}$
    $+\frac{2}{10}$ $\frac{8}{40}$

18. $\frac{1}{2}$
    $+\frac{3}{10}$

19. $\frac{10}{1000}$
    $+\frac{5}{100}$

20. $\frac{1}{5} + \frac{3}{10} + \frac{2}{15}$

★ 21. $\frac{2}{18}$
      $+\frac{9}{30}$

★ 22. $\frac{8}{26}$
      $+\frac{13}{39}$

★ 23. $\frac{10}{24}$
      $+\frac{17}{36}$

★ 24. $\frac{3}{42}$
      $\frac{1}{12}$
      $+\frac{2}{7}$

★ 25. $\frac{3}{24} + \frac{4}{32} + \frac{1}{16}$

Solve. Simplify the answer.

26. Kitty picked $\frac{1}{2}$ basket of corn on Monday. She picked $\frac{3}{10}$ basket on Tuesday. What fraction of a basket of corn did she pick in all?

27. What fraction of the field is corn if $\frac{3}{5}$ is planted with feed corn and $\frac{1}{8}$ is planted with sweet corn?

Mixed Numbers as Fractions

2 wholes $\quad + \quad \dfrac{3}{4} \quad = \quad 2\dfrac{3}{4}$

$2 + \dfrac{3}{4} = 2\dfrac{3}{4} \longleftarrow$ Mixed Number

$\dfrac{8}{4} + \dfrac{3}{4} = \dfrac{11}{4} \longleftarrow$ Fraction

So, $2\dfrac{3}{4} = \dfrac{11}{4}$

A. Here is a short cut for writing $2\dfrac{3}{5}$ as a fraction. Complete.

$2\overset{+}{\underset{\times}{\dfrac{3}{5}}} = \dfrac{13}{5}$

    1. Multiply: $5 \times 2 = \underline{\ ?\ }$

    2. Add: $10 + 3 = \underline{\ ?\ }$

    3. Write $\underline{\ ?\ }$ as the numerator.

    4. Write $\underline{\ ?\ }$ as the denominator.

B. Write fractions.

  5. $5\dfrac{1}{6}$ **6.** $2\dfrac{3}{5}$ **7.** $4\dfrac{2}{3}$ **8.** $11\dfrac{3}{7}$ **9.** $13\dfrac{1}{4}$ **10.** $18\dfrac{1}{3}$

Practice

Write fractions.

  1. $3\dfrac{1}{8}$ **2.** $2\dfrac{5}{6}$ **3.** $4\dfrac{2}{5}$ **4.** $6\dfrac{1}{3}$ **5.** $7\dfrac{2}{9}$

  6. $1\dfrac{7}{12}$ **7.** $3\dfrac{5}{8}$ **8.** $2\dfrac{4}{9}$ **9.** $6\dfrac{4}{7}$ **10.** $5\dfrac{2}{3}$

  11. $4\dfrac{3}{8}$ **12.** $1\dfrac{3}{20}$ **13.** $8\dfrac{3}{5}$ ★**14.** $125\dfrac{5}{8}$ ★**15.** $261\dfrac{3}{5}$

Fractions as Mixed Numbers

The fraction $\frac{7}{3}$ can be written as a mixed number.

Jack's way

$\frac{7}{3} = \frac{6}{3} + \frac{1}{3}$

$\frac{7}{3} = 2 + \frac{1}{3}$

So, $\frac{7}{3} = 2\frac{1}{3}$

Gina's way

$\frac{7}{3}$ means 7 divided by 3

$$3\overline{)7} = 2\frac{1}{3} \quad \longleftarrow \text{Remainder}$$
$$\underset{1}{\underline{6}} \qquad \uparrow 3 \quad \longleftarrow \text{Divisor}$$
$$\qquad \text{Quotient}$$

So, $\frac{7}{3} = 2\frac{1}{3}$

A. Write mixed numbers. Complete.

1. $\frac{35}{8}$

$8\overline{)35} = 4\frac{?}{8}$
$\underline{32}$
$\quad 3$

2. $\frac{45}{6}$

$6\overline{)45} = 7\frac{3}{6} = 7\frac{?}{?}$
$\underline{42}$
$\quad 3$

B. Write mixed numbers.

3. $\frac{9}{5}$ 　　 4. $\frac{19}{4}$ 　　 5. $\frac{14}{3}$ 　　 6. $\frac{24}{7}$ 　　 7. $\frac{17}{8}$

8. $\frac{18}{4}$ 　　 9. $\frac{25}{10}$ 　　 10. $\frac{57}{6}$ 　　 11. $\frac{44}{8}$ 　　 12. $\frac{39}{9}$

Practice

Write mixed numbers.

1. $\frac{7}{2}$ 　　 2. $\frac{9}{4}$ 　　 3. $\frac{8}{3}$ 　　 4. $\frac{7}{4}$ 　　 5. $\frac{8}{5}$ 　　 6. $\frac{9}{7}$

7. $\frac{11}{2}$ 　　 8. $\frac{13}{5}$ 　　 9. $\frac{13}{6}$ 　　 10. $\frac{17}{5}$ 　　 11. $\frac{19}{3}$ 　　 12. $\frac{12}{4}$

13. $\frac{30}{4}$ 　　 14. $\frac{27}{6}$ 　　 15. $\frac{26}{8}$ 　　 16. $\frac{59}{9}$ 　　 17. $\frac{40}{6}$ 　　 18. $\frac{60}{8}$

19. $\frac{58}{4}$ 　　 20. $\frac{82}{6}$ 　　 21. $\frac{99}{5}$ 　　 22. $\frac{45}{10}$ 　　 23. $\frac{21}{7}$ 　　 24. $\frac{42}{6}$

Sums as Mixed Numbers

When the sum of two fractions is 1 or greater, rename the sum as a whole number or mixed number. Look at these examples.

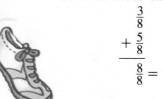

$$\begin{array}{r} \frac{3}{8} \\ +\frac{5}{8} \\ \hline \frac{8}{8}=1 \end{array}$$

$$\begin{array}{r} \frac{3}{5} \\ \frac{4}{5} \\ +\frac{7}{5} \\ \hline \frac{14}{5}=2\frac{4}{5} \end{array}$$

$$\begin{array}{r} \frac{7}{9} \\ +\frac{8}{9} \\ \hline \frac{15}{9}=1\frac{6}{9}, \text{ or } 1\frac{2}{3} \end{array}$$

A. Complete.

1. $\begin{array}{r} \frac{1}{4} \\ +\frac{3}{4} \\ \hline \frac{4}{4}=\underline{\ ?\ } \end{array}$

2. $\begin{array}{r} \frac{3}{6} \\ +\frac{5}{6} \\ \hline \frac{8}{6}=1\frac{2}{6}, \text{ or } 1\frac{?}{3} \end{array}$

3. $\begin{array}{r} \frac{3}{7} \\ \frac{5}{7} \\ +\frac{2}{7} \\ \hline \frac{10}{7}=\underline{\ ?\ } \end{array}$

4. $\begin{array}{r} \frac{4}{8} \\ \frac{7}{8} \\ +\frac{3}{8} \\ \hline \frac{14}{8}=1\frac{6}{8}, \text{ or } 1\frac{?}{4} \end{array}$

B. Add and simplify.

5. $\begin{array}{r} \frac{2}{3} \\ +\frac{1}{3} \\ \hline \end{array}$

6. $\begin{array}{r} \frac{3}{6} \\ +\frac{5}{6} \\ \hline \end{array}$

7. $\begin{array}{r} \frac{7}{8} \\ \frac{7}{8} \\ +\frac{3}{8} \\ \hline \end{array}$

8. $\begin{array}{r} \frac{7}{12} \\ \frac{11}{12} \\ +\frac{9}{12} \\ \hline \end{array}$

C. Add and simplify.

Example The LCD of 6 and 8 is 24.

$$\begin{array}{r} \frac{5}{6}=\frac{20}{24} \\ +\frac{7}{8}=\frac{21}{24} \\ \hline \frac{41}{24}=1\frac{17}{24} \end{array}$$

9. $\begin{array}{r} \frac{5}{6} \\ +\frac{3}{8} \\ \hline \end{array}$

10. $\begin{array}{r} \frac{3}{5} \\ +\frac{5}{6} \\ \hline \end{array}$

11. $\begin{array}{r} \frac{6}{8} \\ +\frac{5}{10} \\ \hline \end{array}$

12. $\begin{array}{r} \frac{10}{15} \\ +\frac{5}{6} \\ \hline \end{array}$

Add and simplify.

1. $\dfrac{3}{5}$
$+\dfrac{4}{5}$

2. $\dfrac{7}{8}$
$+\dfrac{3}{4}$

3. $\dfrac{3}{4}$
$+\dfrac{2}{8}$

4. $\dfrac{4}{7}$
$+\dfrac{5}{7}$

5. $\dfrac{2}{3}$
$+\dfrac{4}{6}$

6. $\dfrac{3}{4}$
$+\dfrac{3}{4}$

7. $\dfrac{5}{8}$
$+\dfrac{7}{8}$

8. $\dfrac{3}{5}$
$+\dfrac{8}{10}$

9. $\dfrac{3}{6}$
$\dfrac{3}{4}$
$+\dfrac{1}{2}$

10. $\dfrac{3}{9}$
$\dfrac{4}{6}$
$+\dfrac{2}{3}$

11. $\dfrac{3}{4}$
$+\dfrac{6}{10}$

12. $\dfrac{4}{5}$
$+\dfrac{4}{6}$

13. $\dfrac{2}{3}$
$+\dfrac{3}{4}$

14. $\dfrac{1}{2}$
$+\dfrac{4}{5}$

15. $\dfrac{8}{9}$
$+\dfrac{2}{6}$

16. $\dfrac{7}{8}$
$\dfrac{5}{8}$
$+\dfrac{6}{8}$

17. $\dfrac{5}{6}$
$+\dfrac{3}{4}$

18. $\dfrac{6}{9}$
$\dfrac{2}{3}$
$+\dfrac{4}{6}$

19. $\dfrac{4}{5}$
$+\dfrac{2}{3}$

20. $\dfrac{6}{8}$
$+\dfrac{5}{6}$

★ **21.** $\dfrac{31}{52}$
$+\dfrac{11}{13}$

★ **22.** $\dfrac{43}{76}$
$+\dfrac{4}{19}$

★ **23.** $\dfrac{23}{27}$
$+\dfrac{15}{45}$

Solve.

24. Gary jogged $\dfrac{4}{10}$ of the distance around the track on Monday and $\dfrac{6}{10}$ of the distance on Tuesday. How many times did he go around the track in all?

25. Marge jogged for $\dfrac{2}{3}$ hour on Saturday and $\dfrac{2}{3}$ hour on Sunday. How long did she jog in the two days?

Adding Mixed Numbers

Andy spent $2\frac{3}{10}$ hours mowing the lawn and $1\frac{2}{10}$ hours raking leaves. How much time did he spend doing yard work?

Step 1	Step 2	Step 3
$2\frac{3}{10}$ $+\ 1\frac{2}{10}$ $\overline{\frac{5}{10}}$	$2\frac{3}{10}$ $+\ 1\frac{2}{10}$ $\overline{3\frac{5}{10}}$	$2\frac{3}{10}$ $+\ 1\frac{2}{10}$ $\overline{3\frac{5}{10}}$, or $3\frac{1}{2}$

Andy spent $3\frac{1}{2}$ hours doing yard work.

A. Add and simplify.

1. $3\frac{1}{3}$
   $+\ 2\frac{1}{3}$

2. $4\frac{1}{5}$
   $+\ 2\frac{3}{5}$

3. $1\frac{3}{8}$
   $+\ 3$

4. $5\frac{1}{6}$
   $+\ 7\frac{1}{6}$

5. $8\frac{3}{12}$
   $+\ 6\frac{5}{12}$

B. To add mixed numbers with different denominators, first find the LCD. Complete.

6. $1\frac{2}{3} = 1\frac{8}{12}$
   $+\ 3\frac{1}{4} = 3\frac{?}{12}$
   $\overline{4\frac{?}{12}}$

7. $4\frac{1}{5} = 4\frac{?}{10}$
   $+\ 2\frac{3}{10} = 2\frac{3}{10}$
   $\overline{6\frac{5}{10}} = \underline{\ ?\ }$

8. $3\frac{1}{6} = 3\frac{2}{12}$
   $+\ 4\frac{2}{3} = 4\frac{?}{12}$
   $\overline{7\frac{?}{12}} = \underline{\ ?\ }$

C. Add and simplify.

9. $4\frac{2}{7}$
   $+\ 6\frac{3}{7}$

10. $3\frac{3}{8}$
    $+\ 4\frac{1}{4}$

11. $2\frac{1}{4}$
    $+\ 6\frac{2}{5}$

12. $23\frac{1}{10}$
    $+\ 36\frac{5}{6}$

13. $3\frac{2}{6}$
    $+\ 5\frac{2}{3}$

14. $12\frac{10}{100}$
    $+\ 14\frac{5}{20}$

15. $10\frac{2}{6}$
    $+\ 14\frac{1}{3}$

16. $1\frac{2}{15}$
    $+\ 7\frac{4}{45}$

Add and simplify.

1. 5
$+ 2\frac{1}{3}$

2. $4\frac{5}{6}$
$+ 8$

3. $5\frac{3}{7}$
$+ 1\frac{3}{7}$

4. $1\frac{3}{8}$
$+ 3\frac{2}{8}$

5. $4\frac{1}{5}$
$+ 2\frac{3}{5}$

6. $3\frac{1}{6}$
$+ 4\frac{1}{6}$

7. $6\frac{3}{10}$
$+ 4\frac{5}{10}$

8. $6\frac{4}{9}$
$+ 1\frac{2}{9}$

9. $2\frac{3}{8}$
$+ 4\frac{1}{8}$

10. $3\frac{7}{12}$
$+ 6\frac{1}{12}$

11. $7\frac{4}{12}$
$+ 1\frac{1}{2}$

12. $5\frac{1}{6}$
$+ 3\frac{1}{2}$

13. $2\frac{2}{8}$
$+ 6\frac{2}{4}$

14. $15\frac{4}{6}$
$+ 10\frac{2}{9}$

15. $11\frac{2}{18}$
$+ 7\frac{2}{4}$

16. $3\frac{5}{12}$
$+ 6\frac{1}{3}$

17. $14\frac{4}{100}$
$+ 2\frac{16}{100}$

18. $5\frac{3}{5}$
$+ 6\frac{3}{20}$

19. $12\frac{3}{14}$
$+ 5\frac{2}{7}$

20. $14\frac{3}{8}$
$+ 6\frac{1}{3}$

21. $16\frac{7}{10}$
$+ 23\frac{1}{10}$

22. $23\frac{1}{2}$
$6\frac{1}{3}$
$+ 11\frac{1}{5}$

23. $14\frac{1}{3}$
$19\frac{1}{4}$
$+ 11\frac{1}{6}$

24. $15\frac{1}{10}$
$7\frac{1}{6}$
$+ 18\frac{3}{5}$

25. $78\frac{7}{24}$
$+ 89\frac{13}{36}$

Keeping Fit

Add.

1. 32
$+ 45$

2. 60
$+ 19$

3. 246
$+ 741$

4. 21
75
$+ 92$

5. 814
307
$+ 692$

6. $2,475$
$8,698$
$+ 8,485$

Subtract.

7. 61
$- 46$

8. 125
$- 92$

9. $1,942$
$- 319$

10. $27,835$
$- 16,829$

11. $42,683$
$- 11,807$

12. 174
$- 87$

13. 524
$- 199$

14. $6,518$
$- 2,989$

15. $37,180$
$- 2,714$

16. $75,254$
$- 1,938$

Renaming Mixed Numbers

Mary Beth used $1\frac{4}{5}$ jars of brown paint and $2\frac{3}{5}$ jars of green paint to paint scenery for the class play. How many jars did she use in all?

$$1\frac{4}{5}$$
$$+\ 2\frac{3}{5}$$
$$\overline{}$$

$$3\frac{7}{5} = 3 + 1\frac{2}{5} = 4\frac{2}{5}$$

She used $4\frac{2}{5}$ jars of paint in all.

▶ You need to rename when the sum of the fractions is greater than 1.

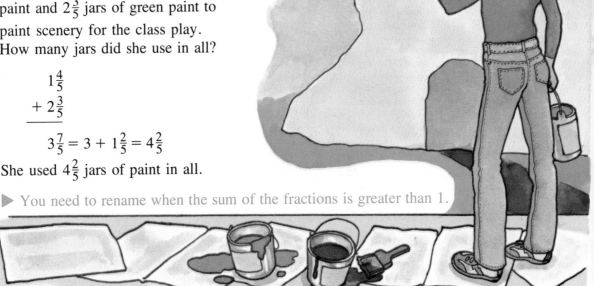

A. Add and simplify.

1. $\quad 3\frac{5}{9}$
$\quad +\ 2\frac{8}{9}$
$\quad \overline{}$

2. $\quad 2\frac{4}{5}$
$\quad +\ 3\frac{5}{6}$
$\quad \overline{}$

3. $\quad 3\frac{5}{8}$
$\quad +\ 5\frac{7}{8}$
$\quad \overline{}$

B. Sometimes we must find a common denominator. Complete.

4. $\quad 3\frac{5}{6} = 3\frac{15}{18}$
$\quad +\ 2\frac{2}{9} = 2\frac{4}{18}$
$\quad \overline{}$
$\quad\quad 5\frac{?}{18} = 6\frac{?}{18}$

5. $\quad 5\frac{9}{10} = 5\frac{9}{10}$
$\quad +\ 4\frac{3}{5} = 4\frac{6}{10}$
$\quad \overline{}$
$\quad\quad 9\frac{?}{10} = 10\frac{?}{10},$ or $\underline{\ \ ?\ \ }$

C. Add and simplify.

6. $\quad 4\frac{2}{3}$
$\quad +\ 3\frac{5}{6}$
$\quad \overline{}$

7. $\quad 7\frac{3}{4}$
$\quad +\ 2\frac{5}{8}$
$\quad \overline{}$

8. $\quad 6\frac{3}{5}$
$\quad +\ 1\frac{2}{3}$
$\quad \overline{}$

9. $\quad 16\frac{7}{10}$
$\quad +\ 28\frac{5}{6}$
$\quad \overline{}$

10. $\quad 21\frac{7}{8}$
$\quad +\ 13\frac{1}{3}$
$\quad \overline{}$

11. $\quad 10\frac{4}{5}$
$\quad +\ 3\frac{12}{20}$
$\quad \overline{}$

12. $\quad 17\frac{5}{6}$
$\quad +\ 4\frac{3}{4}$
$\quad \overline{}$

13. $\quad 11\frac{8}{16}$
$\quad +\ 9\frac{9}{12}$
$\quad \overline{}$

14. $\quad 15\frac{75}{100}$
$\quad +\ 7\frac{1}{2}$
$\quad \overline{}$

15. $\quad 21\frac{3}{7}$
$\quad +\ 39\frac{5}{6}$
$\quad \overline{}$

Add and simplify.

1. $7\frac{4}{5}$
   $+ 2\frac{2}{5}$

2. $5\frac{2}{3}$
   $+ 4\frac{2}{3}$

3. $5\frac{6}{7}$
   $+ 1\frac{5}{7}$

4. $9\frac{3}{5}$
   $+ 4\frac{2}{5}$

5. $7\frac{8}{9}$
   $+ 2\frac{4}{9}$

6. $4\frac{7}{8}$
   $+ 9\frac{3}{8}$

7. $6\frac{3}{4}$
   $+ 8\frac{3}{4}$

8. $2\frac{3}{5}$
   $+ 9\frac{4}{5}$

9. $11\frac{2}{5}$
   $+ 6\frac{4}{5}$

10. $18\frac{5}{8}$
    $+ 9\frac{7}{8}$

11. $10\frac{7}{16}$
    $+ 17\frac{5}{8}$

12. $19\frac{6}{10}$
    $+ 28\frac{75}{100}$

13. $41\frac{3}{4}$
    $+ 27\frac{5}{12}$

14. $28\frac{3}{4}$
    $+ 17\frac{6}{8}$

15. $4\frac{2}{3}$
    $+ 8\frac{11}{12}$

16. $7\frac{4}{5}$
    $+ 6\frac{7}{10}$

17. $18\frac{3}{5}$
    $+ 5\frac{5}{12}$

18. $15\frac{4}{5}$
    $+ 9\frac{7}{10}$

19. $18\frac{2}{3}$
    $+ 26\frac{7}{12}$

20. $6\frac{3}{4}$
    $+ 9\frac{1}{2}$

21. $4\frac{3}{7}$
    $+ 2\frac{6}{7}$

22. $38\frac{2}{3}$
    $+ 29\frac{4}{5}$

23. $9\frac{7}{9}$
    $+ 6\frac{2}{9}$

24. $13\frac{750}{1000}$
    $+ 10\frac{50}{100}$

25. $2\frac{3}{4}$
    $+ 1\frac{3}{4}$

26. $17 + 13\frac{5}{6}$

27. $2\frac{3}{7} + 4\frac{5}{7}$

★ 28. $7\frac{8}{15} + 5\frac{4}{5} + 6\frac{2}{3}$

Solve.

29. Megan used $1\frac{7}{10}$ pieces of cardboard to build a fence and $3\frac{9}{10}$ pieces for a house. How many pieces did she use in all?

30. Dan used $2\frac{1}{2}$ pieces of fabric to make one costume and $3\frac{6}{10}$ pieces to make another. How many pieces did he use for both?

Write fractions. *(224)*

1. $5\frac{1}{2}$ **2.** $4\frac{2}{3}$ **3.** $3\frac{5}{8}$ **4.** $4\frac{5}{6}$ **5.** $7\frac{3}{10}$ **6.** $8\frac{3}{4}$

Write mixed numbers. *(225)*

7. $\frac{4}{3}$ **8.** $\frac{11}{8}$ **9.** $\frac{38}{5}$ **10.** $\frac{25}{6}$ **11.** $\frac{66}{9}$ **12.** $\frac{22}{4}$

Add.

13. $\begin{array}{r} \frac{2}{8} \\ + \frac{3}{8} \\ \hline \end{array}$ *(218)*
14. $\begin{array}{r} \frac{2}{3} \\ + \frac{1}{4} \\ \hline \end{array}$ *(222)*
15. $\begin{array}{r} \frac{1}{8} \\ \frac{1}{4} \\ + \frac{1}{6} \\ \hline \end{array}$ *(222)*
16. $\begin{array}{r} 4\frac{2}{6} \\ + 3\frac{3}{6} \\ \hline \end{array}$ *(228)*
17. $\begin{array}{r} 2\frac{3}{5} \\ + 4\frac{1}{10} \\ \hline \end{array}$ *(228)*

Add and simplify.

18. $\begin{array}{r} \frac{4}{8} \\ + \frac{2}{8} \\ \hline \end{array}$ *(220)*
19. $\begin{array}{r} \frac{2}{6} \\ + \frac{2}{9} \\ \hline \end{array}$ *(222)*
20. $\begin{array}{r} \frac{3}{5} \\ \frac{3}{10} \\ + \frac{1}{4} \\ \hline \end{array}$ *(222)*
21. $\begin{array}{r} 4\frac{3}{6} \\ + 3\frac{5}{6} \\ \hline \end{array}$ *(228)*
22. $\begin{array}{r} 6\frac{2}{3} \\ + 4\frac{7}{8} \\ \hline \end{array}$ *(230)*

Find Out!
Brainteaser

In each row, the first four figures form a pattern. Which figure,
a, b, c, or **d,** is the next figure in the pattern?

1. △ ▽ △ ▽   **a.** ▽   **b.** ▷   **c.** △   **d.** ◁

2. ◯ ○ ∘ ◯   **a.** ○   **b.** ◯   **c.** ◯   **d.** ∘

3. ⌣ 𝄔 ⌢ 𝄕   **a.** 𝄕   **b.** 𝄔   **c.** ⌢   **d.** ⌣

232   Review

Rounding Mixed Numbers

We can round a mixed number to the nearest whole number.
Round $3\frac{5}{8}$ to the nearest whole number.

$3\frac{5}{8}$ is closer to 4
than to 3.

Round $3\frac{5}{8}$ to 4.

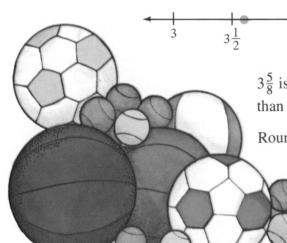

A. Round to the nearest whole number. Complete.

1. $5\frac{1}{3}$ is closer to __?__ than to 6.

Round $5\frac{1}{3}$ to __?__ .

2. $4\frac{1}{2}$ is halfway between 4 and 5.

Round $4\frac{1}{2}$ to __?__ .

B. Round to the nearest whole number.

3. $8\frac{2}{3}$ **4.** $9\frac{1}{5}$ **5.** $16\frac{1}{2}$ **6.** $2\frac{1}{6}$ **7.** $12\frac{8}{9}$

Practice

Round to the nearest whole number.

1. $4\frac{2}{5}$ **2.** $3\frac{1}{4}$ **3.** $10\frac{5}{7}$ **4.** $8\frac{2}{4}$ **5.** $25\frac{2}{3}$

6. $36\frac{1}{10}$ **7.** $18\frac{75}{100}$ **8.** $13\frac{10}{20}$ **9.** $4\frac{1}{3}$ **10.** $16\frac{7}{8}$

11. $14\frac{2}{3}$ **12.** $23\frac{11}{19}$ **13.** $45\frac{2}{5}$ **14.** $17\frac{7}{10}$ **15.** $51\frac{1}{2}$

16. $61\frac{4}{5}$ **17.** $43\frac{8}{9}$ **18.** $77\frac{2}{7}$ ★ **19.** $\frac{3}{4}$ ★ **20.** $\frac{1}{10}$

Subtracting Fractions

Naomi spent $\frac{4}{5}$ hour painting a chair.

She spent $\frac{3}{5}$ hour painting a shelf.

How much longer did it take her to paint the chair?

$$\begin{array}{r} \frac{4}{5} \\ -\frac{3}{5} \\ \hline \frac{1}{5} \end{array}$$

▶ To subtract fractions with the same denominator:
  Step 1: Subtract the numerators.
  Step 2: Use the same denominator.

A. Complete.

1.
$$\begin{array}{r} \frac{7}{10} \\ -\frac{4}{10} \\ \hline \frac{?}{10} \end{array}$$

2.
$$\begin{array}{r} \frac{5}{8} \\ -\frac{3}{8} \\ \hline \frac{2}{8} = \frac{?}{4} \end{array}$$

3.
$$\begin{array}{r} \frac{8}{9} \\ -\frac{5}{9} \\ \hline \frac{?}{9} = \frac{?}{3} \end{array}$$

4. $\frac{4}{5} - \frac{2}{5} = \frac{?}{5}$

5. $\frac{9}{15} - \frac{6}{15} = \frac{?}{15} = \frac{?}{5}$

B. To subtract fractions with different denominators, first find the LCD. Complete.

6.
$$\begin{array}{r} \frac{5}{8} = \frac{5}{8} \\ -\frac{1}{2} = \frac{4}{8} \\ \hline \frac{?}{8} \end{array}$$

7.
$$\begin{array}{r} \frac{7}{10} = \frac{7}{10} \\ -\frac{1}{2} = \frac{5}{10} \\ \hline \frac{?}{10} = \frac{?}{5} \end{array}$$

8.
$$\begin{array}{r} \frac{7}{10} = \frac{21}{30} \\ -\frac{1}{6} = \frac{5}{30} \\ \hline \frac{?}{30} = \frac{?}{15} \end{array}$$

C. Subtract and simplify.

9.
$$\begin{array}{r} \frac{5}{8} \\ -\frac{1}{8} \\ \hline \end{array}$$

10.
$$\begin{array}{r} \frac{9}{10} \\ -\frac{7}{10} \\ \hline \end{array}$$

11.
$$\begin{array}{r} \frac{11}{12} \\ -\frac{2}{3} \\ \hline \end{array}$$

12.
$$\begin{array}{r} \frac{4}{5} \\ -\frac{3}{10} \\ \hline \end{array}$$

13.
$$\begin{array}{r} \frac{3}{10} \\ -\frac{1}{6} \\ \hline \end{array}$$

Subtract and simplify.

1. $\frac{7}{9}$
   $-\frac{2}{9}$

2. $\frac{4}{5}$
   $-\frac{1}{5}$

3. $\frac{8}{10}$
   $-\frac{1}{10}$

4. $\frac{5}{8}$
   $-\frac{3}{8}$

5. $\frac{5}{6}$
   $-\frac{3}{6}$

6. $\frac{11}{12}$
   $-\frac{5}{12}$

7. $\frac{7}{10}$
   $-\frac{1}{10}$

8. $\frac{5}{6}$
   $-\frac{2}{3}$

9. $\frac{7}{8}$
   $-\frac{3}{4}$

10. $\frac{61}{100}$
    $-\frac{3}{10}$

11. $\frac{3}{4}$
    $-\frac{1}{3}$

12. $\frac{4}{8}$
    $-\frac{4}{10}$

13. $\frac{3}{6}$
    $-\frac{3}{8}$

14. $\frac{10}{12}$
    $-\frac{1}{2}$

15. $\frac{55}{100}$
    $-\frac{5}{20}$

16. $\frac{5}{6}$
    $-\frac{1}{6}$

17. $\frac{9}{10}$
    $-\frac{2}{5}$

18. $\frac{5}{16}$
    $-\frac{3}{12}$

19. $\frac{13}{15}$
    $-\frac{7}{10}$

20. $\frac{9}{10}$
    $-\frac{2}{10}$

21. $\frac{2}{5}$
    $-\frac{1}{3}$

22. $\frac{75}{100}$
    $-\frac{4}{50}$

23. $\frac{7}{20}$
    $-\frac{2}{20}$

24. $\frac{7}{9}$
    $-\frac{1}{9}$

25. $\frac{5}{6}$
    $-\frac{1}{9}$

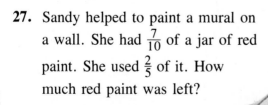

Solve.

26. Carlos worked for $\frac{3}{4}$ hour on Monday and $\frac{1}{2}$ hour on Tuesday. How much longer did he work on Monday than on Tuesday?

27. Sandy helped to paint a mural on a wall. She had $\frac{7}{10}$ of a jar of red paint. She used $\frac{2}{5}$ of it. How much red paint was left?

Subtracting Mixed Numbers

Here is how to subtract mixed numbers.

Step 1   **Step 2**   **Step 3**

$$6\frac{7}{8}$$
$$-2\frac{3}{8}$$
$$\overline{\quad\frac{4}{8}\quad}$$

$$6\frac{7}{8}$$
$$-2\frac{3}{8}$$
$$\overline{\quad4\frac{4}{8}\quad}$$

$$6\frac{7}{8}$$
$$-2\frac{3}{8}$$
$$\overline{\quad4\frac{4}{8}\text{, or }4\frac{1}{2}\quad}$$

A. To subtract mixed numbers with different denominators, first find the LCD. Complete.

1. $8\frac{3}{4} = 8\frac{9}{12}$ **2.** $6\frac{3}{5} = 6\frac{6}{10}$ **3.** $11\frac{3}{4} = 11\frac{9}{12}$

     $-3\frac{1}{3} = 3\frac{4}{12}$ $-2\frac{1}{10} = 2\frac{1}{10}$ $-\;6\frac{3}{6} = \;6\frac{6}{12}$

         $5\frac{?}{12}$ $4\frac{5}{10}$, or $4\frac{?}{2}$ $5\frac{?}{12}$, or $5\frac{?}{4}$

B. Subtract and simplify.

4. $7\frac{2}{3}$ **5.** $8\frac{7}{8}$ **6.** $8\frac{1}{2}$ **7.** $5\frac{7}{9}$ **8.** $17\frac{5}{12}$

    $-4\frac{1}{3}$ $-2\frac{3}{8}$ $-\;6$ $-3\frac{1}{3}$ $-\;9\frac{1}{6}$

Practice

Subtract and simplify.

1. $9\frac{4}{5}$ **2.** $10\frac{7}{8}$ **3.** $4\frac{7}{10}$ **4.** $8\frac{5}{6}$ **5.** $6\frac{17}{24}$

   $-6\frac{3}{5}$ $-\;7$ $-2\frac{1}{10}$ $-3\frac{1}{6}$ $-5\frac{9}{24}$

6. $8\frac{1}{3}$ **7.** $16\frac{2}{3}$ **8.** $18\frac{3}{5}$ **9.** $4\frac{5}{6}$ **10.** $20\frac{3}{10}$

   $-3\frac{1}{9}$ $-\;9\frac{1}{4}$ $-12\frac{1}{3}$ $-4\frac{1}{2}$ $-15\frac{1}{6}$

11. $8\frac{60}{100}$ **12.** $7\frac{3}{5}$ ★ **13.** $66\frac{18}{42}$ ★ **14.** $15\frac{25}{51}$ ★ **15.** $18\frac{66}{96}$

   $-4\frac{2}{5}$ $-2\frac{1}{5}$ $-51\frac{5}{12}$ $-\;7\frac{3}{17}$ $-\;7\frac{5}{12}$

Renaming Mixed Numbers

Look at the picture.
One whole is divided
into 4 equal parts.
So, $3 = 2\frac{4}{4}$

2 $+$ $\frac{4}{4}$

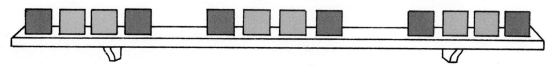

A. Complete.

1. $4 = 3\frac{?}{5}$ **2.** $7 = 6\frac{?}{4}$ **3.** $5 = 4\frac{?}{2}$ **4.** $13 = 12\frac{?}{8}$

B. A mixed number can be written in different ways.

Examples
$$7\frac{3}{5} = 7 + \frac{3}{5}$$
$$= 6 + \frac{5}{5} + \frac{3}{5}$$
$$= 6\frac{8}{5}$$

$$5\frac{3}{8} = 5 + \frac{3}{8}$$
$$= 4 + \frac{8}{8} + \frac{3}{8}$$
$$= 4\frac{11}{8}$$

Complete.

5. $6\frac{1}{3} = 5 + \frac{3}{3} + \frac{1}{3} = 5\frac{?}{3}$ **6.** $4\frac{7}{10} = 3 + \frac{10}{10} + \frac{7}{10} = 3\frac{?}{10}$

C. Rename in one step. Complete.

7. $5\frac{2}{5} = 4\frac{?}{5}$ **8.** $8\frac{5}{9} = 7\frac{?}{9}$ **9.** $12\frac{7}{8} = 11\frac{?}{8}$ **10.** $17\frac{5}{11} = 16\frac{?}{11}$

Practice

Complete.

1. $6\frac{2}{3} = 5\frac{?}{3}$ **2.** $5\frac{1}{8} = 4\frac{?}{8}$ **3.** $9\frac{1}{3} = 8\frac{?}{3}$

4. $4\frac{7}{9} = 3\frac{?}{9}$ **5.** $7\frac{3}{10} = 6\frac{?}{10}$ **6.** $3\frac{1}{4} = 2\frac{?}{4}$

7. $7\frac{2}{15} = 6\frac{?}{15}$ **8.** $6\frac{7}{100} = 5\frac{?}{100}$ **9.** $18\frac{5}{6} = 17\frac{?}{6}$

10. $12\frac{6}{25} = 11\frac{?}{25}$ ★ **11.** $16\frac{7}{33} = 14\frac{?}{33}$ ★ **12.** $25\frac{6}{17} = 23\frac{?}{17}$

Renaming in Subtraction

Scott bought 2 bags of potting soil. He used $\frac{3}{4}$ of a bag. How much soil was left?

$$2 = 1\frac{4}{4}$$
$$-\frac{3}{4} = \frac{3}{4}$$
$$\overline{\qquad 1\frac{1}{4}}$$

$1\frac{1}{4}$ bags were left.

A. Complete.

1.
$$3 = 2\frac{5}{5}$$
$$-\frac{1}{5} = \frac{1}{5}$$
$$\overline{\qquad ?}$$

2.
$$4 = 3\frac{?}{8}$$
$$-1\frac{5}{8} = 1\frac{5}{8}$$
$$\overline{\qquad ?}$$

B. Sometimes a mixed number must be renamed.

Example

Can't subtract

$$7\frac{1}{5}$$
$$-2\frac{3}{5}$$
$$\overline{\qquad}$$

Rename

$$7\frac{1}{5} = 6\frac{6}{5}$$
$$-2\frac{3}{5} = 2\frac{3}{5}$$
$$\overline{\qquad 4\frac{3}{5}}$$

Complete.

3.
$$6\frac{1}{3} = 5\frac{?}{3}$$
$$-3\frac{2}{3} = 3\frac{2}{3}$$
$$\overline{\qquad ?}$$

4.
$$7\frac{3}{8} = 6\frac{?}{8}$$
$$-2\frac{7}{8} = 2\frac{7}{8}$$
$$\overline{\qquad 4\frac{4}{8}, \text{ or } \underline{\ ?\ }}$$

5.
$$5\frac{1}{6} = 4\frac{?}{6}$$
$$-3\frac{5}{6} = 3\frac{5}{6}$$
$$\overline{\qquad 1\frac{?}{6}, \text{ or } \underline{\ ?\ }}$$

C. Subtract and simplify.

6.
$$6\frac{3}{7}$$
$$-1\frac{5}{7}$$
$$\overline{\qquad}$$

7.
$$4\frac{2}{5}$$
$$-3\frac{4}{5}$$
$$\overline{\qquad}$$

8.
$$7\frac{5}{8}$$
$$-4\frac{7}{8}$$
$$\overline{\qquad}$$

9.
$$18\frac{1}{6}$$
$$-9\frac{5}{6}$$
$$\overline{\qquad}$$

10.
$$10\frac{3}{15}$$
$$-6\frac{9}{15}$$
$$\overline{\qquad}$$

Subtract and simplify.

1. $\begin{array}{r} 7 \\ -\ \frac{2}{3} \\ \hline \end{array}$ **2.** $\begin{array}{r} 2 \\ -\ \frac{7}{10} \\ \hline \end{array}$ **3.** $\begin{array}{r} 8 \\ -\ \frac{4}{7} \\ \hline \end{array}$

4. $\begin{array}{r} 3 \\ -\ 2\frac{3}{8} \\ \hline \end{array}$ **5.** $\begin{array}{r} 6 \\ -\ 3\frac{5}{6} \\ \hline \end{array}$ **6.** $\begin{array}{r} 9 \\ -\ 3\frac{5}{12} \\ \hline \end{array}$

7. $\begin{array}{r} 5\frac{75}{100} \\ -\ 4\frac{80}{100} \\ \hline \end{array}$ **8.** $\begin{array}{r} 12\frac{1}{3} \\ -\ 7\frac{2}{3} \\ \hline \end{array}$ **9.** $\begin{array}{r} 19\frac{2}{5} \\ -\ 12\frac{4}{5} \\ \hline \end{array}$

10. $\begin{array}{r} 4\frac{1}{11} \\ -\ 2\frac{5}{11} \\ \hline \end{array}$ **11.** $\begin{array}{r} 18\frac{1}{9} \\ -\ 9\frac{2}{9} \\ \hline \end{array}$ **12.** $\begin{array}{r} 20\frac{3}{8} \\ -\ 7\frac{5}{8} \\ \hline \end{array}$

13. $\begin{array}{r} 6\frac{1}{4} \\ -\ 2\frac{3}{4} \\ \hline \end{array}$ **14.** $\begin{array}{r} 16\frac{3}{10} \\ -\ 4\frac{8}{10} \\ \hline \end{array}$ **15.** $\begin{array}{r} 18\frac{1}{16} \\ -\ 5\frac{5}{16} \\ \hline \end{array}$

16. $\begin{array}{r} 28\frac{3}{8} \\ -\ 17\frac{5}{8} \\ \hline \end{array}$ **17.** $\begin{array}{r} 32 \\ -\ 26\frac{73}{100} \\ \hline \end{array}$ **18.** $\begin{array}{r} 18\frac{5}{100} \\ -\ 12\frac{7}{100} \\ \hline \end{array}$ **19.** $\begin{array}{r} 52\frac{13}{18} \\ -\ 31\frac{17}{18} \\ \hline \end{array}$ **20.** $\begin{array}{r} 17\frac{3}{10} \\ -\ 8\frac{7}{10} \\ \hline \end{array}$

★ **21.** $\begin{array}{r} 3\frac{7}{41} \\ -\ \frac{9}{41} \\ \hline \end{array}$ ★ **22.** $\begin{array}{r} 18 \\ -\ 9\frac{6}{65} \\ \hline \end{array}$ ★ **23.** $\begin{array}{r} 48\frac{32}{60} \\ -\ 27\frac{55}{60} \\ \hline \end{array}$ ★ **24.** $\begin{array}{r} 29\frac{15}{26} \\ -\ 14\frac{17}{26} \\ \hline \end{array}$ ★ **25.** $\begin{array}{r} 38\frac{150}{1,000} \\ -\ 29\frac{900}{1,000} \\ \hline \end{array}$

Solve.

26. Sheila bought 3 packages of parsley seeds. She planted $1\frac{3}{4}$ packages. How many packages did she have left?

27. Richard needs $4\frac{1}{4}$ bags of soil to fill a window box. He only has $3\frac{3}{4}$ bags. How much more soil does he need?

Renaming Twice

Sometimes we must rename twice before subtracting.

Step 1: Find the LCD.

Step 2: Rename the mixed number.

$$5\frac{1}{3} = 5\frac{2}{6} = 4\frac{8}{6}$$
$$-\,2\frac{5}{6} = 2\frac{5}{6} = 2\frac{5}{6}$$
$$2\frac{3}{6} = 2\frac{1}{2}$$

A. Complete.

1.
$$6\frac{1}{2} = 6\frac{5}{10} = 5\frac{?}{10}$$
$$-\,4\frac{3}{5} = 4\frac{6}{10} = 4\frac{6}{10}$$

2.
$$4\frac{1}{2} = 4\frac{3}{6} = 3\frac{?}{6}$$
$$1\frac{5}{6} = 1\frac{5}{6} = 1\frac{5}{6}$$
$$2\frac{4}{6} = \underline{\quad?\quad}$$

B. Subtract and simplify.

3.
$$9\frac{2}{3}$$
$$-\,4\frac{5}{6}$$

4.
$$17\frac{1}{2}$$
$$-\;9\frac{3}{4}$$

5.
$$5\frac{1}{3}$$
$$-\,3\frac{1}{2}$$

6.
$$7\frac{3}{10}$$
$$-\,2\frac{4}{5}$$

Practice

Subtract and simplify.

1.
$$7\frac{1}{3}$$
$$-\,4\frac{5}{9}$$

2.
$$9\frac{1}{10}$$
$$-\,2\frac{4}{5}$$

3.
$$6\frac{1}{8}$$
$$-\,4\frac{3}{4}$$

4.
$$7\frac{1}{2}$$
$$-\,5\frac{7}{8}$$

5.
$$5\frac{2}{3}$$
$$-\,4\frac{5}{6}$$

6.
$$6\frac{1}{2}$$
$$-\,2\frac{3}{5}$$

7.
$$9\frac{5}{6}$$
$$-\,3\frac{8}{9}$$

8.
$$17\frac{1}{6}$$
$$-\;9\frac{3}{4}$$

9.
$$18\frac{1}{12}$$
$$-\,13\frac{3}{4}$$

10.
$$20\frac{1}{10}$$
$$-\;6\frac{3}{5}$$

11.
$$6\frac{3}{8}$$
$$-\,2\frac{1}{2}$$

12.
$$9\frac{2}{3}$$
$$-\,4\frac{4}{5}$$

★ 13.
$$18\frac{1}{36}$$
$$-\,14\frac{3}{18}$$

★ 14.
$$29\frac{5}{100}$$
$$-\,16\frac{33}{50}$$

★ 15.
$$32\frac{400}{1,000}$$
$$-\,28\frac{75}{100}$$

Using Properties

Properties of Addition

Commutative Property

$$\frac{1}{5} + \frac{3}{5} = \frac{4}{5} \qquad \frac{3}{5} + \frac{1}{5} = \frac{4}{5}$$

$$\text{So } \frac{1}{5} + \frac{3}{5} = \frac{3}{5} + \frac{1}{5}$$

Associative Property

$$\left(\frac{1}{9} + \frac{4}{9}\right) + \frac{2}{9} = \frac{7}{9} \qquad \frac{1}{9} + \left(\frac{4}{9} + \frac{2}{9}\right) = \frac{7}{9}$$

$$\text{So } \left(\frac{1}{9} + \frac{4}{9}\right) + \frac{2}{9} = \frac{1}{9} + \left(\frac{4}{9} + \frac{2}{9}\right)$$

A. Check the properties by finding these sums.

1. $\frac{3}{6} + \frac{1}{6}$ and $\frac{1}{6} + \frac{3}{6}$

2. $\left(\frac{3}{7} + \frac{1}{7}\right) + \frac{2}{7}$ and $\frac{3}{7} + \left(\frac{1}{7} + \frac{2}{7}\right)$

3. $\frac{5}{100} + \frac{8}{100}$ and $\frac{8}{100} + \frac{5}{100}$

4. $\left(\frac{3}{12} + \frac{4}{12}\right) + \frac{4}{12}$ and $\frac{3}{12} + \left(\frac{4}{12} + \frac{4}{12}\right)$

B. Solve without computing.

5. $\frac{4}{7} + \frac{2}{7} = \frac{2}{7} + n$

6. $\left(\frac{1}{8} + \frac{3}{8}\right) + \frac{2}{8} = \frac{1}{8} + \left(\frac{3}{8} + n\right)$

7. $\frac{6}{10} + \frac{3}{10} = n + \frac{6}{10}$

8. $\left(\frac{2}{15} + \frac{1}{15}\right) + \frac{4}{15} = n + \left(\frac{1}{15} + \frac{4}{15}\right)$

Practice

Solve without computing.

1. $\frac{1}{9} + \frac{5}{9} = \frac{5}{9} + n$

2. $\left(\frac{3}{9} + \frac{1}{9}\right) + \frac{4}{9} = \frac{3}{9} + \left(n + \frac{4}{9}\right)$

3. $\frac{4}{8} + \frac{2}{8} = n + \frac{2}{8}$

4. $\left(\frac{2}{7} + \frac{3}{7}\right) + \frac{1}{7} = \frac{2}{7} + \left(\frac{3}{7} + n\right)$

5. $\frac{2}{5} + \frac{1}{5} = \frac{1}{5} + n$

6. $\left(\frac{1}{12} + \frac{5}{12}\right) + \frac{3}{12} = n + \left(\frac{5}{12} + \frac{3}{12}\right)$

7. $\frac{5}{12} + \frac{7}{12} = n + \frac{7}{12}$

8. $\left(\frac{4}{10} + \frac{1}{10}\right) + \frac{2}{10} = \frac{4}{10} + \left(n + \frac{2}{10}\right)$

9. $\frac{4}{20} + n = \frac{3}{20} + \frac{4}{20}$

10. $\left(\frac{50}{100} + \frac{10}{100}\right) + n = \frac{50}{100} + \left(\frac{10}{100} + \frac{3}{100}\right)$

11. $n + \frac{2}{35} = \frac{2}{35} + \frac{6}{35}$

12. $\left(\frac{7}{24} + n\right) + \frac{6}{24} = \left(\frac{7}{24} + \frac{4}{24}\right) + \frac{6}{24}$

Problem Solving

Marcy had $4\frac{1}{2}$ balls of rope. She used $2\frac{3}{4}$ balls of rope to macrame a wall hanging. How much rope did she have left?

Using whole numbers in place of fractions or mixed numbers will help you decide what operation to use.

THINK 5 balls of rope.
  3 are used.

$4\frac{1}{2} = 4\frac{2}{4} = 3\frac{6}{4}$

Which operation should we use?
Use subtraction.

$-2\frac{3}{4} = 2\frac{3}{4} = 2\frac{3}{4}$

$1\frac{3}{4}$

Marcy had $1\frac{3}{4}$ balls of rope left.

A. Kevin needs $2\frac{3}{10}$ strips of brown leather and $3\frac{8}{10}$ strips of tan leather to make a whistle holder. How much leather does he need in all?

1. Replace the mixed numbers with whole numbers.
$2\frac{3}{10}$ rounds to ___?___. $3\frac{8}{10}$ rounds to ___?___.

2. Which operation should you use?

3. Complete. $2\frac{3}{10} + 3\frac{8}{10} = 5\frac{?}{10} = $ ___?___

B. Solve.

4. Jane Ellen used $15\frac{2}{3}$ skeins of yarn to knit a sweater and $1\frac{1}{2}$ skeins to knit a cap. How many skeins did she use in all?
[HINT: Use whole numbers in place of the mixed numbers.]

Solve.

1. Lisa had 3 cans of paint. She used $1\frac{3}{4}$ cans to paint a play house. How much was left?

2. Dan had $\frac{2}{3}$ dozen eggs. He used $\frac{1}{4}$ dozen for an omelette. What fraction of a dozen was left?

3. Jack spent $1\frac{1}{4}$ hours making a cup and saucer out of clay. It took $\frac{3}{4}$ h to make the cup. How long did it take to make the saucer?

4. Cleo mixed $2\frac{1}{2}$ cans of yellow paint and $1\frac{3}{4}$ cans of blue paint to make green paint. How many cans of paint did she use in all?

5. Reggie needs $\frac{3}{4}$ of a package of potting soil to make a small terrarium. He needs $1\frac{1}{2}$ packages to make a large terrarium. How much soil does he need for the two terrariums?

★6. Janet gave $\frac{1}{3}$ of her stamp collection to Mike and $\frac{3}{8}$ of the collection to Melba. What fraction of her collection did Janet keep?

Multiplying Fractions

David's parents gave him $\frac{1}{3}$ of their garden to use.

He planted $\frac{1}{2}$ of his share of the garden with vegetables.

What part of the whole garden did David plant with vegetables?

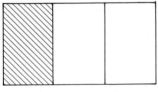

$\frac{1}{3}$

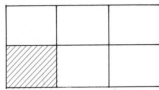

$\frac{1}{2}$ of $\frac{1}{3}$

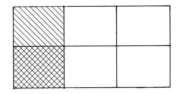

$\frac{1}{6}$

David planted $\frac{1}{6}$ of the garden with vegetables.

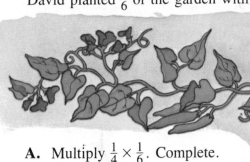

A. Multiply $\frac{1}{4} \times \frac{1}{6}$. Complete.

   1. Multiply the numerators. $1 \times 1 = $ ___?___

   2. Multiply the denominators. $4 \times 6 = $ ___?___

   3. $\frac{1}{4} \times \frac{1}{6} = \frac{1 \times 1}{4 \times 6} = $ ___?___

▶ To multiply two or more fractions:

  Step 1: Multiply the numerators.
  Step 2: Multiply the denominators.

B. Multiply.

   4. $\frac{1}{5} \times \frac{1}{2}$ **5.** $\frac{1}{3} \times \frac{1}{4}$ **6.** $\frac{1}{6} \times \frac{1}{8}$ **7.** $\frac{1}{7} \times \frac{1}{5}$

   8. $\frac{1}{9} \times \frac{1}{7}$ **9.** $\frac{1}{100} \times \frac{1}{10}$ **10.** $\frac{1}{4} \times \frac{1}{5} \times \frac{1}{3}$ **11.** $\frac{1}{2} \times \frac{1}{3} \times \frac{1}{7}$

Multiply.

1. $\frac{1}{2} \times \frac{1}{6}$ **2.** $\frac{1}{3} \times \frac{1}{8}$ **3.** $\frac{1}{6} \times \frac{1}{4}$ **4.** $\frac{1}{9} \times \frac{1}{2}$ **5.** $\frac{1}{5} \times \frac{1}{8}$

6. $\frac{1}{4} \times \frac{1}{5}$ **7.** $\frac{1}{7} \times \frac{1}{3}$ **8.** $\frac{1}{8} \times \frac{1}{4}$ **9.** $\frac{1}{6} \times \frac{1}{5}$ **10.** $\frac{1}{9} \times \frac{1}{8}$

11. $\frac{1}{2} \times \frac{1}{3} \times \frac{1}{4}$ **12.** $\frac{1}{4} \times \frac{1}{5} \times \frac{1}{3}$ **13.** $\frac{1}{7} \times \frac{1}{2} \times \frac{1}{3}$ **14.** $\frac{1}{2} \times \frac{1}{9} \times \frac{1}{2}$

15. $\frac{1}{3} \times \frac{1}{6} \times \frac{1}{2}$ **16.** $\frac{1}{4} \times \frac{1}{4} \times \frac{1}{2}$ **17.** $\frac{1}{3} \times \frac{1}{5} \times \frac{1}{2}$ **18.** $\frac{1}{6} \times \frac{1}{5} \times \frac{1}{3}$

19. $\frac{1}{3} \times \frac{1}{4} \times \frac{1}{5}$ **20.** $\frac{1}{3} \times \frac{1}{6}$ **21.** $\frac{1}{8} \times \frac{1}{6}$ **22.** $\frac{1}{7} \times \frac{1}{7} \times \frac{1}{2}$

23. $\frac{1}{4} \times \frac{1}{2}$ **24.** $\frac{1}{6} \times \frac{1}{7} \times \frac{1}{3}$ **25.** $\frac{1}{4} \times \frac{1}{7}$ **26.** $\frac{1}{9} \times \frac{1}{2} \times \frac{1}{3}$

 Solve without computing. Use the properties for multiplication.

27. $\frac{3}{5} \times \frac{4}{6} = \frac{4}{6} \times n$

28. $4 \times \left(\frac{1}{3} \times \frac{3}{4}\right) = \left(4 \times \frac{1}{3}\right) \times n$

29. $\frac{2}{3} \times \frac{1}{3} = n \times \frac{2}{3}$

30. $\left(\frac{6}{15} \times n\right) \times \frac{1}{2} = \frac{6}{15} \times \left(\frac{1}{3} \times \frac{1}{2}\right)$

31. $\frac{5}{9} \times n = \frac{3}{8} \times \frac{5}{9}$

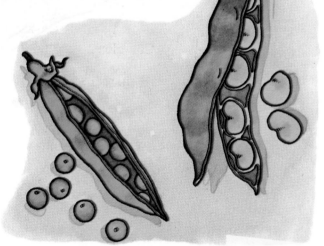

Solve.

32. $\frac{1}{4}$ of a garden is used for flowers. $\frac{1}{3}$ of this is for daisies. How much of the garden is for daisies?

33. $\frac{1}{2}$ of a field is used for vegetables. $\frac{1}{4}$ of this is for beans. How much of the field will be for beans?

More Multiplying

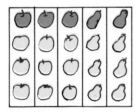

$\frac{3}{5}$ of the fruit
are apples.

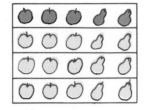

$\frac{3}{4}$ of the fruit
are yellow.

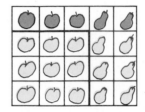

$\frac{9}{20}$ of the fruit
are yellow apples.

$$\frac{3}{5} \times \frac{3}{4} = \frac{9}{20}$$

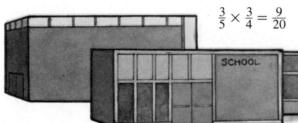

A. Complete.

$\frac{5}{6} \times \frac{1}{8}$

1. Multiply the numerators. $5 \times 1 = \underline{\quad?\quad}$

2. Multiply the denominators. $6 \times 8 = \underline{\quad?\quad}$

3. $\frac{5}{6} \times \frac{1}{8} = \underline{\quad?\quad}$

B. Multiply.

4. $\frac{2}{5} \times \frac{3}{7}$ 5. $\frac{1}{8} \times \frac{3}{4}$ 6. $\frac{3}{4} \times \frac{5}{8}$ 7. $\frac{2}{3} \times \frac{5}{7}$

C. Sometimes the answer must be simplified.

Examples $\frac{2}{3} \times \frac{5}{6} = \frac{10}{18}$ $\frac{3}{4} \times \frac{2}{6} = \frac{6}{24}$

$\phantom{Examples \quad \frac{2}{3} \times \frac{5}{6} } = \frac{10 \div 2}{18 \div 2}$ $\phantom{\frac{3}{4} \times \frac{2}{6} } = \frac{6 \div 6}{24 \div 6}$

$\phantom{Examples \quad \frac{2}{3} \times \frac{5}{6} } = \frac{5}{9}$ $\phantom{\frac{3}{4} \times \frac{2}{6} } = \frac{1}{4}$

Multiply and simplify.

8. $\frac{3}{4} \times \frac{5}{9}$ 9. $\frac{3}{8} \times \frac{4}{5}$ 10. $\frac{5}{12} \times \frac{3}{10}$ 11. $\frac{2}{3} \times \frac{3}{4}$

12. $\frac{9}{10} \times \frac{2}{3}$ 13. $\frac{1}{2} \times \frac{4}{5} \times \frac{1}{3}$ 14. $\frac{5}{6} \times \frac{3}{4} \times \frac{2}{3}$ 15. $\frac{1}{3} \times \frac{2}{5} \times \frac{3}{4}$

Multiply and simplify.

1. $\frac{3}{4} \times \frac{7}{8}$ **2.** $\frac{1}{2} \times \frac{3}{7}$ **3.** $\frac{2}{3} \times \frac{5}{7}$ **4.** $\frac{4}{9} \times \frac{1}{3}$ **5.** $\frac{3}{8} \times \frac{5}{7}$

6. $\frac{4}{5} \times \frac{1}{2}$ **7.** $\frac{5}{6} \times \frac{3}{8}$ **8.** $\frac{6}{7} \times \frac{2}{3}$ **9.** $\frac{3}{8} \times \frac{4}{7}$ **10.** $\frac{4}{9} \times \frac{3}{5}$

11. $\frac{4}{5} \times \frac{5}{6}$ **12.** $\frac{3}{4} \times \frac{8}{9}$ **13.** $\frac{3}{4} \times \frac{2}{9}$ **14.** $\frac{2}{5} \times \frac{5}{8}$ **15.** $\frac{4}{9} \times \frac{3}{2}$

16. $\frac{7}{10} \times \frac{3}{10}$ **17.** $\frac{1}{6} \times \frac{5}{7}$ **18.** $\frac{4}{5} \times \frac{3}{8}$ **19.** $\frac{3}{8} \times \frac{4}{3}$ **20.** $\frac{5}{16} \times \frac{4}{15}$

21. $\frac{2}{3} \times \frac{5}{8} \times \frac{1}{10}$ **22.** $\frac{3}{4} \times \frac{1}{5} \times \frac{2}{3}$ **23.** $\frac{2}{3} \times \frac{3}{5} \times \frac{4}{7}$

24. $\frac{1}{6} \times \frac{2}{3} \times \frac{3}{7}$ **25.** $\frac{1}{8} \times \frac{2}{5} \times \frac{5}{7}$ **26.** $\frac{5}{12} \times \frac{3}{10} \times \frac{4}{7}$

Solve. Simplify the answer.

27. It took Barney $\frac{3}{4}$ hour to walk to school. It took Bob $\frac{1}{2}$ as long as Barney. What part of an hour did it take Bob?

28. Jill had $\frac{1}{2}$ carton of milk. She drank $\frac{2}{3}$ of it. What part of the carton did she drink?

Find Out!
Calculator Activity

Compute. Write down your answers.

1. $1 + 2$ **2.** $(2 \times 3) \div 2$

3. $1 + 2 + 3$ **4.** $(3 \times 4) \div 2$

5. $1 + 2 + 3 + 4$ **6.** $(4 \times 5) \div 2$

7. $1 + 2 + 3 + 4 + 5$ **8.** $(5 \times 6) \div 2$

9. What is the sum of the whole numbers from 1 through 20? Use the methods shown in both columns.

Multiplying a Fraction and a Whole Number

Barbara spent 5 hours working in her garden. Valerie spent $\frac{3}{4}$ as much time working in her garden. How much time did Valerie spend?

A whole number can be renamed as a fraction.

$$5 = \frac{5}{1} \qquad 2 = \frac{2}{1} \qquad 12 = \frac{12}{1}$$

To multiply $\frac{3}{4} \times 5$, rename 5 as $\frac{5}{1}$.

$$\frac{3}{4} \times \frac{5}{1} = \frac{3 \times 5}{4 \times 1} = \frac{15}{4} = 3\frac{3}{4}$$

Valerie spent $3\frac{3}{4}$ hours working in her garden.

A. Complete.

$\frac{1}{8} \times 7$

    1. Rename the whole number. $7 = \underline{\quad ? \quad}$

    2. Multiply the numerators. $1 \times 7 = \underline{\quad ? \quad}$

    3. Multiply the denominators. $8 \times 1 = \underline{\quad ? \quad}$

    4. $\frac{1}{8} \times \frac{7}{1} = \underline{\quad ? \quad}$

B. Multiply.

5. $\frac{1}{5} \times 4$ **6.** $\frac{1}{8} \times 3$ **7.** $4 \times \frac{3}{11}$ **8.** $5 \times \frac{2}{11}$

C. Multiply and simplify.

Examples
$$3 \times \frac{5}{6} = \frac{3}{1} \times \frac{5}{6}$$
$$= \frac{15}{6}$$
$$= \frac{15 \div 3}{6 \div 3}$$
$$= \frac{5}{2}, \text{ or } 2\frac{1}{2}$$

$$\frac{1}{6} \times 4 = \frac{1}{6} \times \frac{4}{1}$$
$$= \frac{4}{6}$$
$$= \frac{4 \div 2}{6 \div 2}$$
$$= \frac{2}{3}$$

9. $\frac{2}{3} \times 6$ **10.** $8 \times \frac{3}{4}$ **11.** $\frac{3}{8} \times 2$ **12.** $5 \times \frac{3}{10}$

13. $\frac{4}{15} \times 3$ **14.** $6 \times \frac{3}{4}$ **15.** $\frac{11}{20} \times 2$ **16.** $7 \times \frac{1}{14}$

Multiply and simplify.

1. $\frac{1}{6} \times 5$ 2. $3 \times \frac{1}{8}$ 3. $4 \times \frac{1}{7}$ 4. $\frac{1}{8} \times 7$ 5. $\frac{2}{5} \times 2$

6. $\frac{2}{7} \times 3$ 7. $8 \times \frac{2}{19}$ 8. $\frac{5}{6} \times 5$ 9. $3 \times \frac{3}{8}$ 10. $\frac{1}{7} \times 9$

11. $2 \times \frac{5}{8}$ 12. $\frac{5}{8} \times 4$ 13. $16 \times \frac{1}{4}$ 14. $\frac{2}{3} \times 9$ 15. $\frac{3}{5} \times 6$

16. $\frac{4}{9} \times 3$ 17. $12 \times \frac{5}{6}$ 18. $\frac{3}{4} \times 20$ 19. $\frac{5}{12} \times 3$ 20. $7 \times \frac{2}{17}$

21. $\frac{5}{6} \times 9$ 22. $14 \times \frac{3}{4}$ 23. $\frac{3}{10} \times 6$ 24. $6 \times \frac{3}{19}$ 25. $\frac{33}{100} \times 2$

26. $25 \times \frac{2}{6}$ 27. $\frac{2}{3} \times 15$ 28. $3 \times \frac{11}{7}$ 29. $\frac{5}{6} \times 3$ 30. $6 \times \frac{1}{9}$

Complete.

★ 31. $\underline{\quad?\quad} \times \frac{3}{5} = \frac{12}{5}$ ★ 32. $2 \times \frac{?}{7} = \frac{6}{7}$ ★ 33. $\frac{3}{8} \times \underline{\quad?\quad} = \frac{3}{4}$ ★ 34. $\underline{\quad?\quad} \times \frac{1}{14} = \frac{1}{2}$

Solve.

35. Jean earned 2 dollars mowing a lawn. She spent $\frac{3}{4}$ of it. How much did she spend?

36. It took John 3 hours to trim the hedges. It took Jason $\frac{1}{2}$ as long. How many hours did it take Jason?

Find Out!
Brainteaser

Give the next four fractions in each pattern.

1. $\frac{1}{2}, \frac{3}{4}, \frac{5}{6}, \frac{7}{8}, \cdots$

2. $\frac{1}{2}, \frac{2}{3}, \frac{3}{4}, \frac{4}{5}, \cdots$

3. $\frac{1}{2}, \frac{1}{4}, \frac{1}{8}, \frac{1}{16}, \cdots$

4. $\frac{1}{2}, \frac{2}{3}, \frac{3}{5}, \frac{5}{8}, \cdots$

Multiplying Mixed Numbers

Carla's stamp collection filled $7\frac{3}{4}$ books. $\frac{2}{3}$ of the stamps were from European countries. How many books were filled with European stamps?

$$\frac{2}{3} \times 7\frac{3}{4} = \frac{2}{3} \times \frac{31}{4}$$
$$= \frac{62}{12}$$
$$= 5\frac{2}{12}, \text{ or } 5\frac{1}{6}$$

Step 1 Rename each mixed number as a fraction.

Step 2 Multiply. Follow the rules for multiplying fractions.

Step 3 Simplify.

$5\frac{1}{6}$ books were filled with European stamps.

A. Complete.

1. $\frac{3}{8} \times 2\frac{1}{3}$

$2\frac{1}{3} = \underline{\ ?\ }$

$\frac{3}{8} \times \frac{7}{3} = \underline{\ ?\ }$

$\frac{21}{24} = \underline{\ ?\ }$

2. $1\frac{3}{4} \times \frac{5}{8}$

$1\frac{3}{4} = \underline{\ ?\ }$

$\frac{7}{4} \times \frac{5}{8} = \underline{\ ?\ }$

$\frac{35}{32} = \underline{\ ?\ }$

B. Multiply and simplify.

3. $2\frac{2}{5} \times \frac{1}{3}$ **4.** $\frac{3}{10} \times 4\frac{1}{2}$ **5.** $6\frac{5}{8} \times \frac{1}{4}$ **6.** $\frac{2}{3} \times 4\frac{1}{9}$

C. To multiply two mixed numbers, first rename both mixed numbers as fractions.

Example $3\frac{1}{3} \times 2\frac{2}{5} = \frac{10}{3} \times \frac{12}{5}$
$$= \frac{120}{15} = 8$$

Complete.

7. $4\frac{1}{4} \times 1\frac{2}{5} = \frac{17}{4} \times \frac{7}{5}$
$$= \frac{?}{20}$$
$$= 5\frac{?}{20}$$

8. $2\frac{3}{8} \times 5\frac{3}{4} = \frac{19}{8} \times \frac{23}{4}$
$$= \frac{437}{?}$$
$$= 13\frac{?}{32}$$

D. Multiply and simplify.

9. $2\frac{1}{7} \times 1\frac{1}{2}$ **10.** $3\frac{2}{3} \times 1\frac{1}{12}$ **11.** $5\frac{1}{10} \times 6\frac{2}{5}$ **12.** $4\frac{2}{9} \times 3\frac{2}{3}$

Multiply and simplify.

1. $1\frac{2}{3} \times \frac{1}{6}$ **2.** $4\frac{1}{2} \times \frac{1}{3}$ **3.** $\frac{2}{7} \times 3\frac{5}{6}$ **4.** $\frac{2}{9} \times 3\frac{1}{5}$

5. $5\frac{1}{4} \times \frac{1}{2}$ **6.** $8\frac{2}{3} \times \frac{1}{2}$ **7.** $\frac{1}{10} \times 9\frac{1}{2}$ **8.** $\frac{2}{6} \times 4\frac{1}{7}$

9. $1\frac{3}{4} \times 2\frac{1}{5}$ **10.** $3\frac{7}{10} \times 1\frac{4}{9}$ **11.** $2\frac{2}{11} \times 1\frac{3}{10}$ **12.** $6\frac{1}{3} \times 2\frac{7}{8}$

13. $3\frac{1}{10} \times 2\frac{3}{10}$ **14.** $3\frac{2}{15} \times 2\frac{1}{5}$ **15.** $1\frac{11}{12} \times 2\frac{1}{2}$ **16.** $6\frac{4}{9} \times 3\frac{1}{3}$

17. $\frac{1}{8} \times 2\frac{1}{4}$ **18.** $3\frac{9}{14} \times 1\frac{1}{2}$ **19.** $2\frac{7}{10} \times 1\frac{1}{5}$ **20.** $\frac{1}{8} \times 1\frac{4}{5}$

21. $\frac{2}{11} \times 3\frac{1}{3}$ **22.** $6\frac{3}{7} \times 2\frac{1}{10}$ **23.** $5\frac{1}{4} \times \frac{1}{5}$ **24.** $10\frac{1}{5} \times 11\frac{2}{6}$

25. $\frac{1}{10} \times 6\frac{2}{15}$ **26.** $4\frac{7}{11} \times \frac{7}{9}$ **27.** $17\frac{3}{10} \times \frac{7}{10}$ **28.** $14\frac{1}{12} \times 8\frac{5}{8}$

Solve. Simplify the answer.

29. Andrew had $7\frac{1}{2}$ boxes of shells. He collected $\frac{3}{4}$ of these on vacation. How many boxes did he collect on vacation?

30. John had $11\frac{1}{2}$ boxes of baseball cards. $\frac{1}{5}$ of these were duplicates. How many boxes were filled with duplicates?

Find Out!
Brainteaser

Mr. Johnson has a bag with less than 80 marbles.

When he divides the marbles into groups of 3, there is 1 marble left over. When he divides them into groups of 4, there is 1 marble left over. When he divides them into groups of 5, there is also 1 marble left over. How many marbles does he have?

Problem Solving • Floor-Covering Installers

Solve.

1. Joy Stuart needs 315 tiles to cover the office floor. One box contains 5 tiles. How many boxes does she need? [HINT: Divide]

2. Joy worked from 8:00 am to 10:15 am to take the tile from the warehouse to the office. How long did it take her to do this?

3. Bill Ferrara had to tell a client the cost of new floor tiles. He knew that 20 cartons were needed. One carton cost $25.95. What was the total cost of the tiles?

4. Bill knew that he needed 1,585 tiles for one job. 790 of them were for the kitchen. The rest were for the den. How many tiles were for the den?

5. Bill and Joy started work with their company on September 1, 1976. They worked as apprentices until March 1, 1979. How many months were they apprentices?

6. Joy hired a helper so she could complete a job on time. The helper worked 32 hours. Joy paid him $4.20 an hour. How much did he earn?

Write fractions. *(224)*

1. $3\frac{1}{4}$ **2.** $2\frac{3}{7}$ **3.** $5\frac{1}{10}$ **4.** $3\frac{1}{6}$ **5.** $7\frac{5}{8}$

Write mixed numbers. *(225)*

6. $\frac{5}{2}$ **7.** $\frac{7}{4}$ **8.** $\frac{13}{3}$ **9.** $\frac{25}{4}$ **10.** $\frac{59}{8}$

Add and simplify.

11. $\begin{array}{r} \frac{1}{6} \\ + \frac{4}{6} \\ \hline \end{array}$ *(218)* **12.** $\begin{array}{r} \frac{1}{4} \\ + \frac{2}{5} \\ \hline \end{array}$ *(222)* **13.** $\begin{array}{r} \frac{1}{3} \\ + \frac{2}{12} \\ \hline \end{array}$ *(222)* **14.** $\frac{1}{4} + \frac{1}{3} + \frac{1}{6}$ *(222)*

15. $\begin{array}{r} \frac{2}{3} \\ + \frac{5}{6} \\ \hline \end{array}$ *(226)* **16.** $\begin{array}{r} 4\frac{5}{8} \\ + 2\frac{1}{8} \\ \hline \end{array}$ *(228)* **17.** $\begin{array}{r} 3\frac{5}{6} \\ + 6\frac{2}{3} \\ \hline \end{array}$ *(230)* **18.** $\begin{array}{r} 10\frac{3}{4} \\ + 7\frac{5}{6} \\ \hline \end{array}$ *(230)*

Subtract and simplify.

19. $\begin{array}{r} \frac{8}{9} \\ - \frac{4}{9} \\ \hline \end{array}$ *(234)* **20.** $\begin{array}{r} \frac{7}{12} \\ - \frac{1}{3} \\ \hline \end{array}$ *(234)* **21.** $\begin{array}{r} \frac{2}{3} \\ - \frac{2}{5} \\ \hline \end{array}$ *(234)* **22.** $\begin{array}{r} \frac{5}{6} \\ - \frac{1}{3} \\ \hline \end{array}$ *(234)*

23. $\begin{array}{r} 4\frac{3}{4} \\ - 1\frac{1}{4} \\ \hline \end{array}$ *(236)* **24.** $\begin{array}{r} 8\frac{2}{3} \\ - 3\frac{1}{2} \\ \hline \end{array}$ *(236)* **25.** $\begin{array}{r} 17\frac{5}{8} \\ - 11 \\ \hline \end{array}$ *(236)* **26.** $\begin{array}{r} 6 \\ - 4\frac{2}{3} \\ \hline \end{array}$ *(238)* **27.** $\begin{array}{r} 8\frac{2}{3} \\ - 2\frac{3}{4} \\ \hline \end{array}$ *(240)*

Multiply and simplify.

28. $\frac{1}{5} \times \frac{1}{10}$
(244)

29. $\frac{3}{4} \times \frac{2}{3}$
(246)

30. $\frac{3}{5} \times \frac{1}{2} \times \frac{1}{8}$
(246)

31. $\frac{4}{9} \times 4$
(248)

Solve. *(242, 252)*

32. Jill spent $2\frac{1}{2}$ hours doing homework. Math took $\frac{3}{4}$ hour. How long did she spend on other subjects?

33. Sally spent 35 hours babysitting in one month. She was paid $1.25 an hour. How much did she earn?

Write fractions. *(224)*

1. $4\frac{1}{2}$ **2.** $5\frac{3}{8}$ **3.** $9\frac{5}{6}$ **4.** $8\frac{7}{10}$ **5.** $3\frac{9}{100}$

Write mixed numbers. *(225)*

6. $\frac{5}{3}$ **7.** $\frac{9}{7}$ **8.** $\frac{12}{5}$ **9.** $\frac{15}{10}$ **10.** $\frac{43}{8}$

Add and simplify.

11. $\begin{array}{r} \frac{3}{8} \\ + \frac{2}{8} \\ \hline \end{array}$ *(218)*   **12.** $\begin{array}{r} \frac{1}{3} \\ + \frac{4}{15} \\ \hline \end{array}$ *(222)*   **13.** $\begin{array}{r} \frac{3}{10} \\ + \frac{1}{2} \\ \hline \end{array}$ *(222)*   **14.** $\frac{1}{6} + \frac{1}{5} + \frac{1}{3}$ *(222)*

15. $\begin{array}{r} \frac{3}{4} \\ + \frac{3}{10} \\ \hline \end{array}$ *(226)*   **16.** $\begin{array}{r} 6\frac{3}{4} \\ + 4\frac{1}{5} \\ \hline \end{array}$ *(228)*   **17.** $\begin{array}{r} 8\frac{3}{10} \\ + 7\frac{7}{10} \\ \hline \end{array}$ *(230)*   **18.** $\begin{array}{r} 5\frac{1}{2} \\ + 3\frac{1}{3} \\ \hline \end{array}$ *(230)*

Subtract and simplify.

19. $\begin{array}{r} \frac{5}{6} \\ - \frac{1}{6} \\ \hline \end{array}$ *(234)*   **20.** $\begin{array}{r} \frac{5}{12} \\ - \frac{1}{4} \\ \hline \end{array}$ *(234)*   **21.** $\begin{array}{r} \frac{7}{8} \\ - \frac{1}{6} \\ \hline \end{array}$ *(234)*   **22.** $\begin{array}{r} \frac{5}{6} \\ - \frac{1}{2} \\ \hline \end{array}$ *(234)*

23. $\begin{array}{r} 7\frac{5}{8} \\ - 4\frac{3}{8} \\ \hline \end{array}$ *(236)*   **24.** $\begin{array}{r} 8\frac{1}{2} \\ - 4\frac{2}{5} \\ \hline \end{array}$ *(236)*   **25.** $\begin{array}{r} 17\frac{3}{10} \\ - 4 \\ \hline \end{array}$ *(236)*   **26.** $\begin{array}{r} 6 \\ - 4\frac{2}{3} \\ \hline \end{array}$ *(238)*   **27.** $\begin{array}{r} 9\frac{2}{5} \\ - 6\frac{2}{3} \\ \hline \end{array}$ *(240)*

Multiply and simplify.

28. $\frac{1}{3} \times \frac{1}{8}$ *(244)*   **29.** $\frac{2}{5} \times \frac{3}{4}$ *(246)*   **30.** $\frac{1}{3} \times \frac{2}{5} \times \frac{3}{7}$ *(246)*   **31.** $6 \times \frac{5}{8}$ *(248)*

Solve. *(242, 252)*

32. Jason mixed $6\frac{1}{2}$ cans of orange juice with $4\frac{3}{4}$ cans of pineapple juice. How many cans of juice were used in all?

33. Marian worked from 8:45 AM until 11:15 AM on her history report. How long did she work?

1. Round 5,811 to the nearest thousand.

A 5,000

B 5,500

C 6,000

D 7,000

2. What is the value of 7 in the number 76,593?

E 700,000

F 70,000

G 7,000

H 700

3. What part is shaded?

A $\frac{1}{5}$

B $\frac{2}{5}$

C $\frac{3}{5}$

D $\frac{4}{5}$

4. Which of the numbers is the largest?

E 69,999

F 68,799

G 68,981

H 69,374

5. What is the length of line segment $\overline{AB}$ to the nearest centimeter?

A 7 cm

B 6 cm

C 2 cm

D 3 cm

6. How many yards are there in 72 ft?

E 24 yd

F 12 yd

G 8 yd

H 6 yd

7. How many grams are there in 6 kg?

A 30 g

B 60 g

C 600 g

D 6,000 g

8. Which is a vertex of the triangle?

E I

F J

G K

H L

9. Compare:
$\frac{2}{3} \equiv \frac{1}{3}$

A <

B >

C =

D ≠

10. What time does the clock show?

E 12:11

F 12:05

G 11:55

H 11:45

Designs

1. Draw a circle with a compass. Keep the opening of the compass the same for all the steps below.

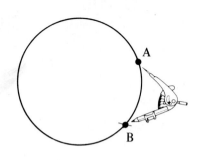

2. Mark any point on the circle. Label it point *A*.

3. Place the compass tip on point *A* and mark point *B*.

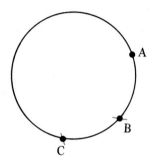

4. Place the compass tip on point *B* and mark point *C*.

5. Repeat step 4 to mark points *D*, *E*, and *F*.

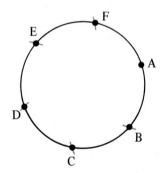

6. Connect the points with line segments as shown.

7. See if you can make some of the other designs shown. Start with steps 1–5 for each design.

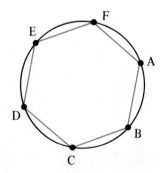

8. Now make up some designs of your own.

Lines, Rays, and Angles

Line segment: $\overline{AB}$ or $\overline{BA}$

Line: $\overleftrightarrow{CD}$ or $\overleftrightarrow{DC}$

Ray: $\overrightarrow{EF}$

Angle: $\angle GHI$ or $\angle IHG$

A. A **line** goes on forever in two directions.
A **line segment** is a part of a line.
Tell which are line segments and which are lines.

1.

2.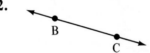

3.

4. Name each line or line segment above in two ways.

B. $\overleftrightarrow{AB}$ and $\overleftrightarrow{CD}$ are intersecting lines.

5. Name a point on both $\overleftrightarrow{AB}$ and $\overleftrightarrow{CD}$.

▶ Two lines or line segments intersect
if they have a common point.

C. A **ray** has one endpoint and goes on forever in one direction.
An **angle** is two rays with a common endpoint. **Name**
each angle or ray in as many ways as possible.

6.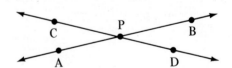

7.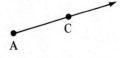

8.

Tell which are line segments, lines, rays, or angles.

1.

2.

3.

4.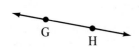

5.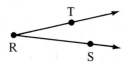

6.

7. Name each figure in Exercises 1–6 in as many ways as possible.

8. Draw $\overline{EF}$ and $\overline{GH}$ so that they intersect at point K.

9. At what point do $\overline{AB}$ and $\overline{AC}$ intersect?

10. At what point do $\overline{AB}$ and $\overline{CD}$ intersect?

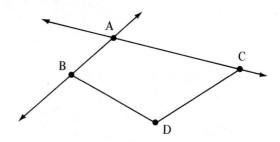

★**11.** Mark two points, C and D. Draw $\overleftrightarrow{CD}$. Can you draw another line through points C and D?

★**12.** Draw a picture of two angles that have a common endpoint but no common sides.

A **plane** is a flat surface.
The figure shows planes b and d.
What is true about their
intersection?

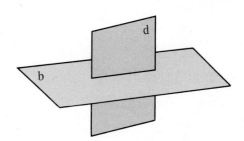

The Protractor

A standard unit of measure of an angle is a **degree.**

A **protractor** is used to measure angles.

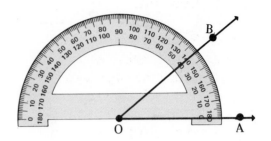

∠*BOA* measures 40°.

A. Here is how a protractor is used to measure ∠*ABC*.

Step 1: Place a protractor so that its center is on point *B*, the vertex of the angle. Place the edge of the protractor on $\overrightarrow{BC}$.

Step 2: Read the measure of the angle where the other ray ($\overrightarrow{BA}$) crosses the scale.

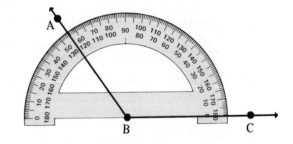

   1. What is the measure of ∠*ABC*?

B. Use a protractor to measure these angles.

   2.

   3.

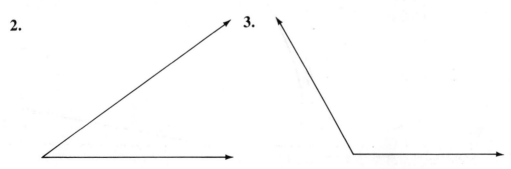

C. Here is how a protractor is used to draw a 60° angle.

Step 1 Draw $\overrightarrow{OA}$.

Step 2 Place the protractor so that the center is on point O and the edge is on $\overrightarrow{OA}$.

Step 3 Find 60° on the scale. Place a dot at 60°. Label it B.

Step 4 Draw a ray from point O through point B. $\angle AOB$ measures 60°.

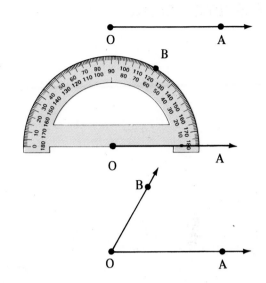

4. Use this method to draw a 100° angle.

Practice

Use a protractor to measure these angles.

1.

2.

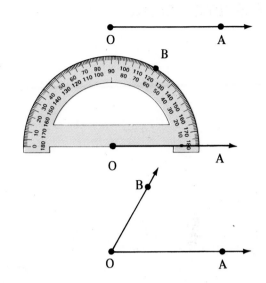

3.

4.

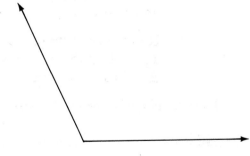

Draw these angles, using a protractor.

5. 20°   **6.** 45°   **7.** 90°   **8.** 110°   **9.** 165°

Angles and Perpendiculars

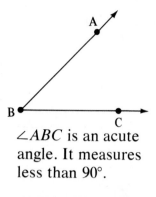

∠*ABC* is an acute angle. It measures less than 90°.

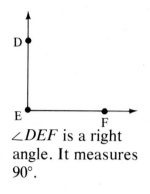

∠*DEF* is a right angle. It measures 90°.

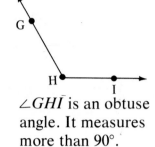

∠*GHI* is an obtuse angle. It measures more than 90°.

A. Measure each angle. Tell if each angle is acute, right, or obtuse.

1.

2.

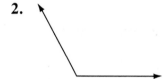

3.

Perpendicular lines or segments form right angles.

Lines AB and *CD* are perpendicular.

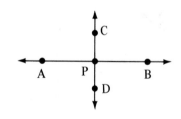

Segments EF and EG are perpendicular.

B. Which lines or segments are perpendicular?

4.

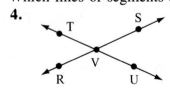

5.

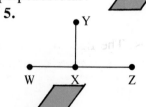

6.

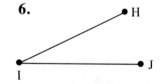

Tell if each angle is acute, right, or obtuse.

1.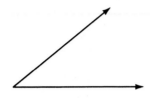

2.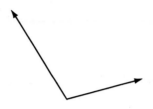

3.

4.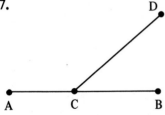

5.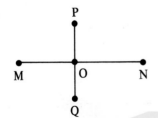

6.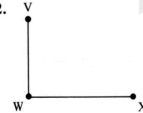

Which lines or segments are perpendicular?

7.

8.

9.

10.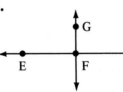

11.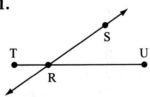

12.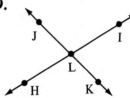

Find Out!
Brainteaser

Lindsay has 2 jars of pennies. The first jar contains 18 more pennies than the second jar. There are 68 pennies in all. How many pennies are in each jar?

Circles

Point *O* is the **center** of the circle.

$\overline{OA}$ and $\overline{OB}$ are **radii** of the circle.

All the points of a circle are the same distance from the center.

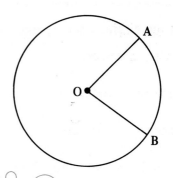

A. 1. Name the radii of the circle with center, *P*.

2. Measure the radii. How do they compare?

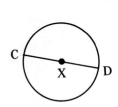

▶ A radius is a line segment from the center of a circle to a point on that circle. All the radii of a circle are the same length.

B. Trace the circle with center, *D*.

3. Draw a line segment with endpoints *E* and *F* on the circle that goes through the center, *D*. This is called a **diameter** of the circle.

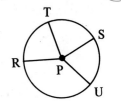

C. Look at the circle with center, *X*.

4. Name a radius and a diameter.

5. Measure the radius.

6. Measure the diameter.

7. Compare the length of the diameter to the length of the radius.

▶ A diameter is twice as long as a radius.

D. Find the length of the radius.

8. Diameter = 16 m

9. Diameter = 5 cm

Look at the circle.

1. Name the center.

2. Name three radii.

3. Name two diameters.

4. *OA* is 3 cm long. How long is
   OB?

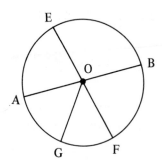

Find the length of the radius.

5. Diameter = 4 m

6. Diameter = 21 m

★7. A **chord** is a line segment whose endpoints are on a
   circle. $\overline{LM}$ is a chord. Draw a longer chord. What is
   the longest chord of the circle?

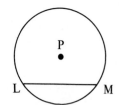

Find Out!

Brainteaser

Trace over the figure shown. You may not lift
your pencil or retrace any line segment or curve.
You may cross over a line segment or curve.

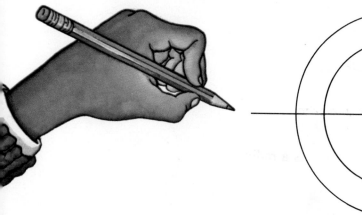

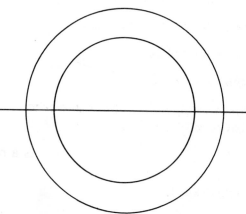

Tell which are lines, line segments, rays, or angles. *(258)*

1.

2.
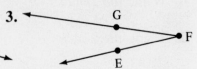

3.
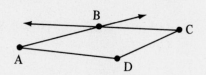

4. At what point do $\overline{AB}$
(258) and $\overline{BC}$ intersect?

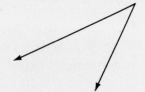

Use a protractor to measure these angles. *(260)*

5.

6.

7.
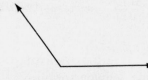

Tell if each angle is acute, right, or obtuse. *(262)*

8.
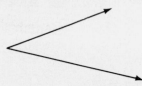

9.
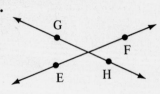

10.
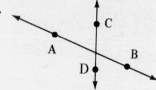

Which lines or segments are perpendicular? *(262)*

11.

12.

13.

Look at the circle. *(264)*

14. Name two radii.

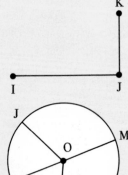

15. Name a diameter.

Keeping Fit

Multiply.

1. 10
   ×8
	2. 40
	   ×6
		3. 100
		   ×5	

4. 300
   ×6
	5. 1,000
	   ×6
		6. 2,000
		   ×7	

7. 20,000
   ×5
	8. 40,000
	   ×9
		9. $4,000
		   ×5
			10. $8,000
			   ×7

11. 72
   ×2
	12. 81
	   ×3
		13. 44
		   ×4
			14. 35
			   ×8

15. 163
   ×2
	16. 142
	   ×4
		17. 216
		   ×6
			18. 225
			   ×2

19. 387
   ×5
	20. 474
	   ×6
		21. $545
		   ×5
			22. $627
			   ×8

23. 5,464
   ×4
	24. 4,728
	   ×6
		25. 5,109
		   ×6
			26. 4,206
			   ×4

27. 27,465
   ×7
	28. 38,247
	   ×9
		29. 19,663
		   ×8
			30. 67,284
			   ×7

31. 35,026
   ×6
	32. 51,097
	   ×4
		33. $78.96
		   ×5
			34. $56.86
			   ×7

35. 57
  ×18
	36. 48
	  ×13
		37. 58
		  ×36
			38. 87
			  ×29

39. 105
  ×22
	40. 206
	  ×31
		41. 565
		  ×35
			42. 763
			  ×56

43. $0.75
  ×27
	44. $0.68
	  ×38
		45. $5.26
		  ×44
			46. $3.65
			  ×52

47. 528
  ×158
	48. 657
	  ×149
		49. 423
		  ×286
			50. 234
			  ×239

51. 746
  ×508
	52. 395
	  ×407
		53. $5.56
		  ×287
			54. $2.79
			  ×368

Problem Solving

On a trip, the Jackson family traveled 5 days in Colorado, 4 days in Idaho, 9 days in Wyoming, and 3 days in Montana. How many weeks did they travel?

PLAN:　　Colorado:　5 days
　　　　　　　Idaho:　4 days
　　　　　Wyoming:　9 days
　　　　　Montana:　3 days

　　Hidden Step:　7 days in a week

SOLVE:　　$5 + 4 + 9 + 3 = 21$ days
　　　　　　　$21 \div 7 = 3$ weeks
So, the Jacksons traveled 3 weeks.

Solve.

1. The Jacksons stopped at a farm. There were 16 hens. Each hen laid 3 eggs. How many dozen eggs is this? (Hidden step: 12 things in a dozen)

2. Joy's last day of work was March 23. She must return on April 24. How many days of vacation did she have? (Hidden step: 31 days in March)

3. Jesse walks about 800 m a day. How many kilometers will he walk in 5 days?

Practice

Find the hidden step in each problem. Solve.

1. Joy drinks 250 mL of milk a day. How many liters does she drink in 4 days?

2. Jim reads about 4 novels each month. How many novels does he read in a year?

3. The length of a radius of Mrs. Jackson's bicycle wheel is 33 cm. What is the length of its diameter?

4. Jesse started building a model airplane on June 16. He finished it on July 12. How many days did it take him?

5. Mr. Jackson eats an apple every day. Each apple has a mass of about 50 g. In how many days will he eat 1 kg of apples?

6. Joy's plant grows about 1 cm each week. Now it is 40 cm tall. In how many weeks will it be 1 m tall?

7. Jesse spent 92 days on his science project. About how many months is this?

8. Jim's last day of school was May 15. He plans to return to school on September 2. How many days of vacation did he have?

Copying Line Segments

We can copy a line segment using a compass and a straightedge.

Copy $\overline{RS}$.

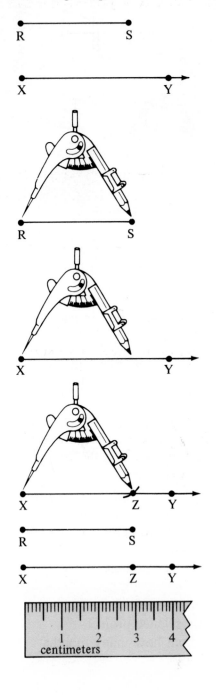

1. Draw $\overrightarrow{XY}$.

2. Put one end of your compass on point R and the other end on point S.

3. Without changing the opening of the compass, put the tip on point X.

4. Draw an arc crossing $\overline{XY}$ at a point. Label it point Z.

5. $\overline{RS}$ is the same length as $\overline{XZ}$. Measure with your ruler to check.

Trace these line segments on your paper. Then copy the line segments. Check your work with a ruler.

1. _____

2. _____

3. _____

4. _____

5. _____

Keeping Fit

Add.

1. $\frac{3}{15} + \frac{5}{15}$

2. $\frac{12}{20} + \frac{7}{20}$

3. $\frac{1}{12} + \frac{5}{12}$

4. $\frac{1}{6} + \frac{3}{8}$

5. $\frac{2}{3} + \frac{1}{9}$

6. $\frac{1}{5} + \frac{1}{15}$

7. $\frac{1}{2} + \frac{1}{8}$

8. $\frac{5}{16} + \frac{1}{8}$

9. $\frac{3}{4} + \frac{1}{12}$

10. $\frac{1}{6} + \frac{1}{12}$

Subtract.

11. $\frac{5}{9} - \frac{4}{9}$

12. $\frac{2}{3} - \frac{1}{3}$

13. $\frac{5}{7} - \frac{1}{7}$

14. $\frac{9}{15} - \frac{2}{15}$

15. $\frac{7}{9} - \frac{4}{9}$

16. $\frac{9}{10} - \frac{7}{10}$

17. $\frac{11}{12} - \frac{7}{12}$

18. $\frac{5}{6} - \frac{1}{6}$

19. $\frac{7}{8} - \frac{1}{4}$

20. $\frac{3}{4} - \frac{2}{3}$

21. $\frac{9}{10} - \frac{1}{5}$

22. $\frac{7}{9} - \frac{1}{3}$

23. $\frac{9}{10} - \frac{1}{2}$

24. $\frac{5}{6} - \frac{1}{4}$

25. $\frac{5}{6} - \frac{3}{4}$

26. $\frac{1}{4} - \frac{1}{6}$

Polygons

A **polygon** is a simple closed curve made up of line segments.

TYPES OF POLYGONS

Triangle	Quadrilateral	Pentagon	Hexagon	Octagon

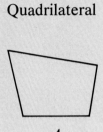  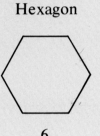 

3 sides	4 sides	5 sides	6 sides	8 sides

A. Which are triangles? quadrilaterals? pentagons? hexagons? octagons?

1.   **2.** 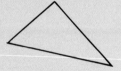 **3.**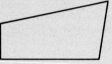

4.   **5.**  **6.**

B. Look at triangle *XYZ*.

7. How many sides does it have? Name them.

8. Point *X* is 1 vertex. Name the other 2 vertices.

9. $\angle X$ is 1 angle. Name the other 2 angles.

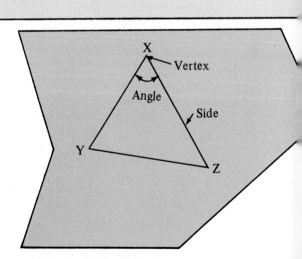

Which are triangles? quadrilaterals? pentagons? hexagons? octagons?

1.

2.

3.

4.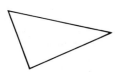

5.

6.

7.

8.

9.

10.

★11.

★12.

Look at triangle *RST*.

13. Name the sides.

14. Name the vertices.

15. Name the angles.

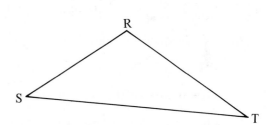

Find Out!
Brainteaser

Take 5 straws of the same length.
Cut 2 of the straws in half. You
now have 3 long straws and 4 straws
half as long. Set aside one of the
short straws. Arrange the 3 long
straws and the 4 shorter straws to
form 5 triangles in which the 3 sides
of each triangle are the same length.
These are called **equilateral** triangles.

Special Quadrilaterals

Parallel lines are lines on a flat surface that do not intersect.
$\overleftrightarrow{AB}$ is parallel to $\overleftrightarrow{CD}$.

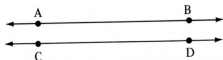

A. Which are parallel?

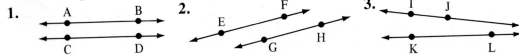

1.   2.   3.

B. Step 1 Draw a 6 cm line segment.
Label it $\overline{AB}$.

Step 2 Draw a 4 cm line segment
parallel to $\overline{AB}$. Label it $\overline{DC}$.
[Hint: Use lined paper to help you.]

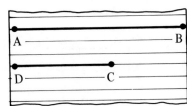

Step 3 Connect the endpoints.

4. How many sides does figure *ABCD* have?

5. What is true of the pair of sides $\overline{AB}$ and $\overline{DC}$?

6. What is true of the pair of sides $\overline{AD}$ and $\overline{BC}$?

▶ A trapezoid is a quadrilateral with one pair of parallel sides.

C. Look at *WXYZ*.

7. What is true of sides $\overline{WX}$ and $\overline{ZY}$?

8. What is true of sides $\overline{WZ}$ and $\overline{XY}$?
Figure *WXYZ* is called a parallelogram.

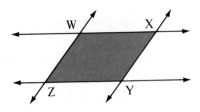

▶ A parallelogram is a quadrilateral with opposite sides parallel.

D. Which are quadrilaterals? trapezoids? parallelograms?

9.   10.   11.

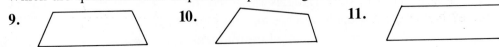

Which are parallel?

1.

2.

3.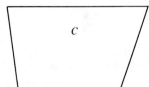

Look at the figures.

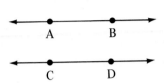

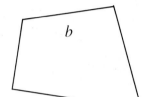

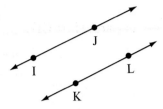

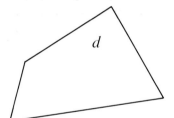

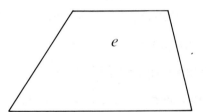

4. Which are quadrilaterals?

5. Which are trapezoids?

6. Which are parallelograms?

Look at figure *JFEA*.

7. How many parallelograms are there? Name them.

8. How many trapezoids are there? Name them.

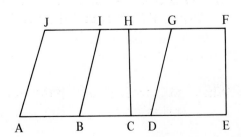

Special Parallelograms

A. Figure *EFGH* is a special parallelogram.

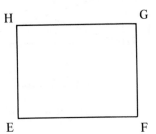

1. Which side is parallel to $\overline{EF}$?

2. Which side is parallel to $\overline{FG}$?

3. What kind of angle is $\angle E$?

4. How many right angles are there?

▶ A rectangle is a parallelogram with four right angles.

B. Figure *ABCD* is a special parallelogram.

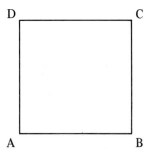

5. Is figure *ABCD* a rectangle?

6. Measure the four sides. What do you find?

▶ A square is a rectangle with all of its sides the same length.

C. Figure *RSTU* is a special parallelogram.

7. Measure the four sides of *RSTU*. What do you find?

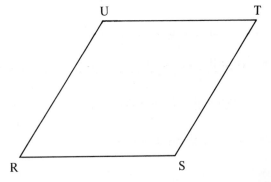

▶ A rhombus is a parallelogram with all of its sides the same length.

D. Look at these parallelograms.

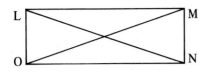

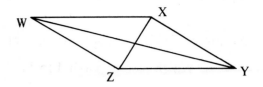

8. In *LMNO*, $\overline{LN}$ is a diagonal. Name the other diagonal.

9. How many diagonals are there in figure *WXYZ*? Name them.

_____ Practice

Look at these figures.

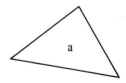

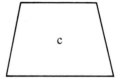

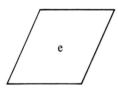

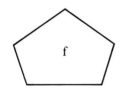

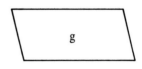

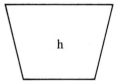

1. Which are quadrilaterals?

2. Which are parallelograms? Which are rhombuses?

3. Which are rectangles? Which are squares?

Name the diagonals in each figure.

4. 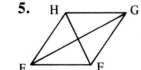 5. 6.   7.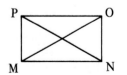

8. Which figures in Exercises 4–7 have diagonals of the same length?

Perimeter

▶ The perimeter of a polygon is the distance around it.

The perimeter of a polygon is found by adding the lengths of its sides.

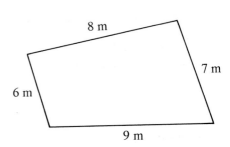

Perimeter = 8 + 7 + 9 + 6

Perimeter = 30 m

A. Complete. Look at the triangle.

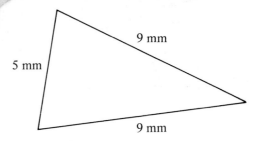

1. Perimeter = 9 + 9 + ___?___

2. Perimeter = ___?___ mm

B. Find the perimeters.

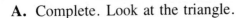

3.

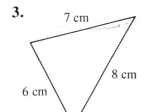
7 cm, 8 cm, 6 cm

4.

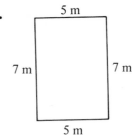
5 m, 7 m, 7 m, 5 m

5.

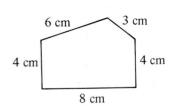
6 cm, 3 cm, 4 cm, 4 cm, 8 cm

C. To find the perimeter of a rectangle, use the rule
Perimeter = $l + w + l + w$.

6. Find the perimeter of rectangle *EFGH*.

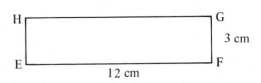

D. Two pupils found the perimeter
of a square.

Phil used $s + s + s + s =$ __?__ cm.
Sarah used $4 \times s =$ __?__ cm.

Complete their work.

7. Phil: $5 + 5 + 5 + 5 =$ __?__ cm.

8. Sarah: $4 \times 5 =$ __?__ cm.

9. Find the perimeter of an
8-cm square in two ways.

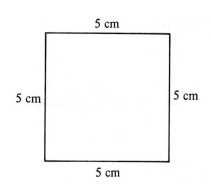

5 cm

5 cm   5 cm

5 cm

Practice

Find the perimeters.

1.

10 m

12 m   4 m

2.

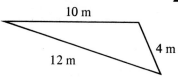

9 cm

4 cm

8 cm

6 cm

3.

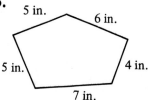

5 in.   6 in.

5 in.   4 in.

7 in.

Find the perimeter of each rectangle.

4.

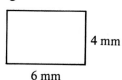

3 cm

10 cm

5.

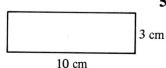

4 mm

6 mm

6.

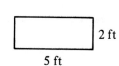

2 ft

5 ft

Find the perimeter of each square.

7.

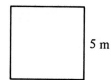

3 cm

8.

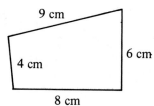

5 m

9.

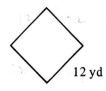

12 yd

Solve.

10. A playground is 90 meters long and 40 meters wide. How much
fencing is needed to fence the playground?

★ **11.** Give the lengths and the widths of three different rectangles,
each with a perimeter of 24 meters.

Slides, Turns, and Flips

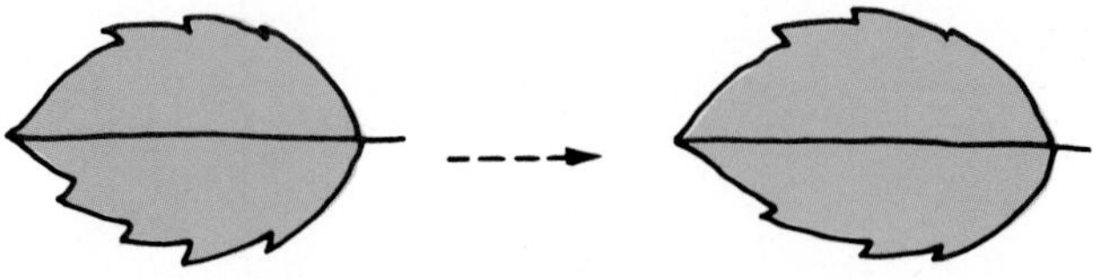

Slide

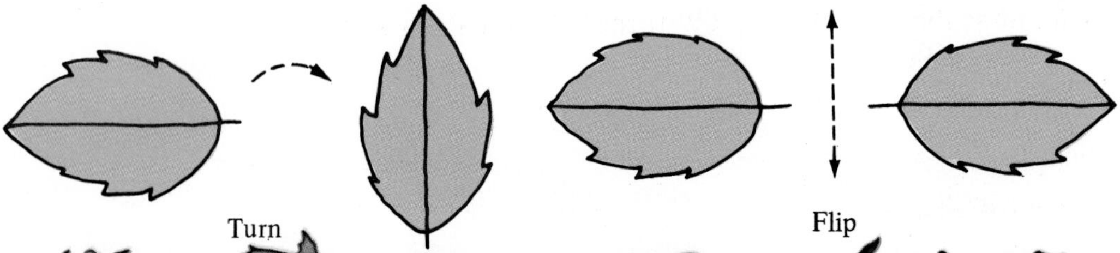

Turn

Flip

A. 1. Cut out a figure like this one.

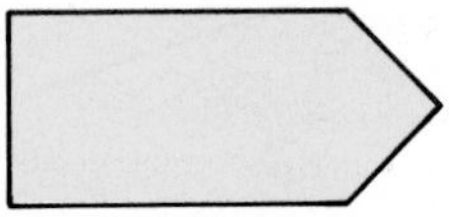

2. Trace the figure on a piece of paper.

3. **Slide** the figure down and trace it again.

4. Did the figure change size or shape?

B. 5. Trace the figure in Item *A* on a piece of paper.

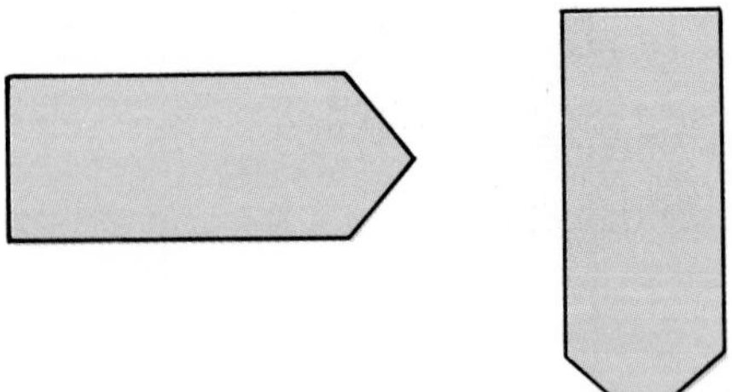

6. **Turn** the figure clockwise. Trace the figure.

7. Did the figure change size or shape?

C. 8. Trace the figure in Item *A* on a piece of paper.

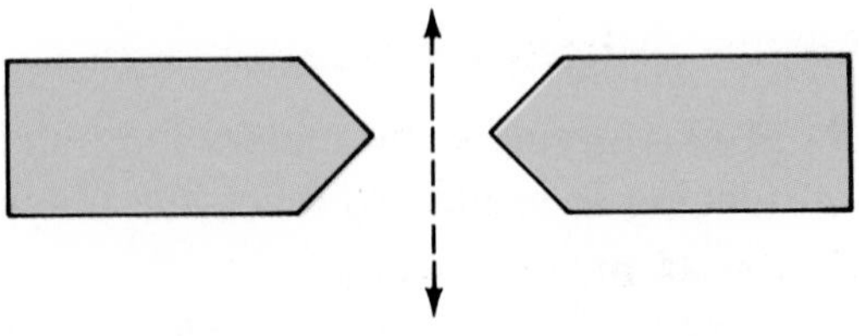

9. **Flip** the figure over. Trace it again.

10. Did the figure change size or shape?

D. Which show slides? Which show turns? Which show flips?

11.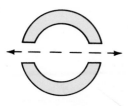

12.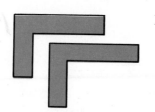

13.

Practice

Which show slides? Which show turns? Which show flips?

1.

2.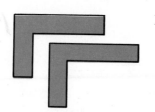

3.

4.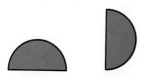

5.

6.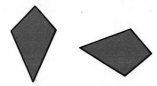

7.

8.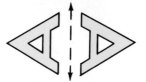

9.

10.

11.

12.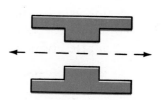

Find Out!
Calculator Activity

Find the perimeter of each rectangle.

1. $l = 67$ cm, $w = 33$ cm

2. $l = 58$ km, $w = 42$ km

3. $l = 84$ m, $w = 16$ m

4. $l = 79$ in., $w = 21$ in.

Symmetry

These figures are **symmetric.** When we fold them in half,
one half matches the other.

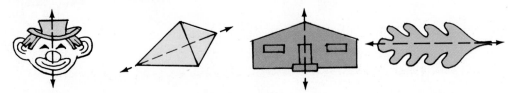

The dotted lines are **lines of symmetry.**

A. Which figures are symmetric?

   1. 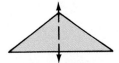   **2.**    **3.**

B. Some figures have more than
   one line of symmetry.

    4. How many lines of symmetry
      are shown in the square?

Practice

Which figures are symmetric?

  1. 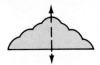   **2.** 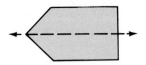   **3.**

  4.   **5.** 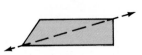   **6.**

Trace each figure. Draw as many lines of symmetry as you can.
How many lines of symmetry does each figure have?

  7.   **8.**   ★**9.**

Congruent Figures

When two figures match each other, they are **congruent.**
Congruent figures are the same size and shape.

A. Which pairs of figures are congruent? Write yes or no.

1.   2.   3.

▶ Line segments with the same measure are congruent.
Angles with the same measure are congruent.

B. Measure to find out which pairs of figures are congruent.

4.   5.   6.

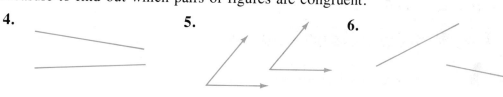

Practice

Which pairs of figures are congruent? Write yes or no.

1.   2.   3.

4.   5.   6.

7.   8.   9.

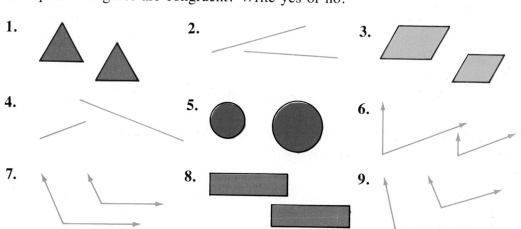

Problem Solving

1. One school earned $476.20 by collecting paper and cans. The school goal is to collect $600 for the library. How much more money must be earned to reach their goal? [HINT: Watch the zeros.]

2. The town council paid $0.16 for every kilogram of litter collected during a "Clean Community Drive." How much money was paid for 375 kg of litter?

3. Each year, about 10,000 pieces of trash are dropped on every kilometer of major U.S. highways. About how many pieces of trash are dropped yearly on a highway 60 km long?

4. Many accidents are caused by litter on roadways. In one year, 864 accidents were caused by litter in one state. Find the average number of these accidents per month.

5. About every 12 minutes a home is damaged by a fire started in trash. About how many of these fires occur in a day?

6. To petition for a trash can for the park, Sarah needs 75 signatures. She has 58 signatures. How many more does she need?

7. One fifth-grade class made anti-litter posters for their school's anti-litter campaign. They spent $2.65 on paper, $2.25 on paints, and $3.75 on decorations. How much money did they spend in all?

8. Hill School organized a "Pick-Up-Litter-In-The-Park" campaign. They expected about 250 people would come. Four times that number of people showed up. How many people came?

Name these figures. *(258)*

1.  **2.**

3. **4.**

Look at triangle *WXY*.

5. Name the vertices. *(272)*

6. Name the sides. *(272)*

7. Find the perimeter. *(278)*

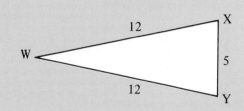

8. Using a protractor, construct an angle of 55°. *(260)*

Match each figure with a name. Use each name once.

9. **10.** **11.**
(262) *(264)* *(262)*

rhombus

parallelogram

trapezoid

12. **13.** **14.**
(274) *(274)* *(274)*

quadrilateral

perpendicular lines

15. **16.** **17.**
(274) *(282)* *(274)*

parallel lines

radius

line of symmetry

right angle

18. A circle has a 6-cm radius. How long is its diameter? *(264)*

Solve. *(268, 284)*

19. Three days ago, there were 3 weeks until vacation. How many days until vacation is it now?

20. How much trash is picked up in 30 days if 96 barrels are picked up each day?

Name these figures. *(258)*

1. **2.** **3.** **4.**

Look at triangle *JKL*.

5. Name the vertices. *(272)*

6. Name the sides. *(272)*

7. Find the perimeter. *(278)*

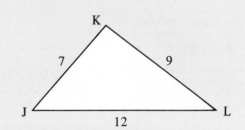

8. Using a protractor, construct an angle of 130°. *(260)*

Match each figure with a name. Use each name once.

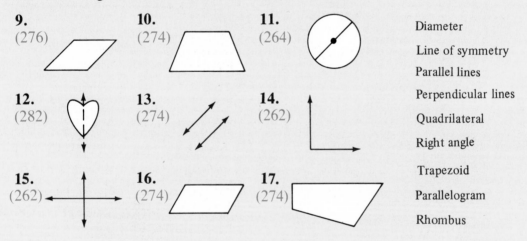

9. *(276)*

10. *(274)*

11. *(264)*

12. *(282)*

13. *(274)*

14. *(262)*

15. *(262)*

16. *(274)*

17. *(274)*

Diameter

Line of symmetry

Parallel lines

Perpendicular lines

Quadrilateral

Right angle

Trapezoid

Parallelogram

Rhombus

18. A circle has an 8-cm diameter. How long is its radius? *(264)*

Solve. *(268, 284)*

19. Mr. Swanson bought a dozen apples. They were priced at $0.35 each. How much did he pay in all?

20. Every hour, 5 trash fires occur in homes in the United States. How many fires occur in a week?

1. Brenda's birthday is exactly 4 months after July 4th. When is her birthday?

   A September 4

   B October 4

   C November 4

   D December 4

2. Which is the best buy for canned corn?

   E 1 can for 42¢

   F 2 cans for 80¢

   G 3 cans for $1.30

   H 4 cans for $2.00

3. The temperature is 7°C. It rises 23°. What is the temperature now?

   A +30°C

   B +29°C

   C +16°C

   D −15°C

4. Barbara wants to buy a belt for $9.58 in the import store. She has $7.25. How much more money does she need?

   E $1.33

   F $2.33

   G $2.83

   H $16.83

5. The bookshelves in Jamie's room are 2 m high. How many centimeters is this?

   A $\frac{1}{2}$ cm

   B 20 cm

   C 200 cm

   D 2,000 cm

6. Which unit would you use to show the mass of an apple?

   E metric ton

   F kilogram

   G meter

   H gram

7. Danny is 29 years old. His father is 30 years older. How old is Danny's father?

   A 32 years

   B 49 years

   C 59 years

   D 95 years

8. Bryan bought 2 tickets to the play for $17.85. How much change did he get from $20.00?

   E $0.15

   F $1.15

   G $2.15

   H $3.15

Butterflies

A centimeter can be divided into 10 equal parts. Each part is called a millimeter. A millimeter is $\frac{1}{10}$ of a centimeter.

Another way to write $\frac{1}{10}$ is 0.1.

The wing span of this monarch butterfly is 83 mm, measured to the nearest millimeter.

It is 8.3 cm measured to the nearest tenth of a centimeter.

Read 8.3 cm as 8 and 3 tenths centimeters.

CHAPTER
DECIMALS **11**

Measure each wingspan to the nearest tenth of a centimeter.

Then measure it to the nearest millimeter.

1.

2.

3.

4.

5.

6.

Tenths

0.5 is a decimal. The dot between the 0 and the 5 is a decimal point.

Picture	Word Name	Fraction	Decimal
	five tenths	$\frac{5}{10}$	0.5

A. How much is shaded? Write a decimal.

1.   **2.**   **3.**

B. Write decimals.

    4. $\frac{8}{10}$ **5.** $\frac{4}{10}$ **6.** $\frac{2}{10}$ **7.** $\frac{1}{10}$

C. Write fractions.

    8. 0.5   **9.** 0.2   **10.** 0.4   **11.** 0.3

D. Decimals can be shown on a place-value chart.

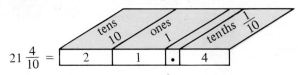

$21\frac{4}{10} =$

Write decimals.

    12. One and six tenths   **13.** Eight and five tenths

    14. $4\frac{2}{10}$ **15.** $6\frac{1}{10}$ **16.** $12\frac{9}{10}$ **17.** $27\frac{3}{10}$

E. Write mixed numbers.

    18. 7.1   **19.** 3.8   **20.** 16.7   **21.** 48.2

How much is shaded? Write a decimal.

1. 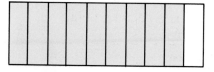 2.

Write decimals.

3. $\frac{2}{10}$ 4. $\frac{5}{10}$ 5. $\frac{9}{10}$ 6. $\frac{6}{10}$ 7. $\frac{8}{10}$

8. $4\frac{1}{10}$ 9. $3\frac{7}{10}$ 10. $16\frac{5}{10}$ 11. $27\frac{8}{10}$ 12. $35\frac{4}{10}$

Write fractions or mixed numbers.

13. 8.4   14. 7.2   15. 10.5   16. 27.6   17. 35.9

18. 47.3   19. 91.1   20. 105.3   21. 150.7   22. 280.6

Write decimals.

23. Nine tenths

24. Four and seven tenths

25. Twenty-six and five tenths

Solve.

26. Bella swam $28\frac{5}{10}$ mi. Write this as a decimal.

27. Josh swam a lap of the pool in $4\frac{6}{10}$ seconds. Write this as a decimal.

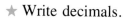 Write decimals.

28. $\frac{17}{10}$ 29. $\frac{21}{10}$ 30. $\frac{38}{10}$ 31. $\frac{56}{10}$ 32. $\frac{98}{10}$

Hundredths

Kevin hiked $\frac{75}{100}$ km up the mountain. We can write $\frac{75}{100}$ as 0.75.

The place-value chart can be extended to hundredths.

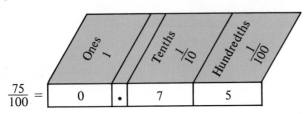

$\frac{75}{100}$ =

Ones 1	.	Tenths $\frac{1}{10}$	Hundredths $\frac{1}{100}$
0	.	7	5

Any fraction with the denominator 100 can be shown as a decimal.

A. Write decimals. Use the place-value chart to help.

1. $\frac{7}{100}$ **2.** $\frac{3}{100}$ **3.** $\frac{15}{100}$ **4.** $\frac{60}{100}$

B. Write fractions.

5. 0.04   **6.** 0.08   **7.** 0.52   **8.** 0.90

C. Read and write these decimals.

Examples   Eight hundredths can be written as 0.08.

Sixteen and ninety-two hundredths can be written as 16.92.

9. Three hundredths   **10.** Eight and sixteen hundredths

D. Write decimals.

Examples $7\frac{78}{100} = 7.78$ $14\frac{21}{100} = 14.21$

11. $6\frac{18}{100}$ **12.** $4\frac{2}{100}$ **13.** $16\frac{25}{100}$ **14.** $72\frac{4}{100}$

E. Write mixed numbers.

Examples $6.93 = 6\frac{93}{100}$ $47.65 = 47\frac{65}{100}$

15. 5.03   **16.** 8.27   **17.** 6.80   **18.** 23.91

Write decimals.

1. $\frac{5}{100}$ **2.** $\frac{7}{100}$ **3.** $\frac{9}{100}$ **4.** $\frac{1}{100}$

5. $\frac{23}{100}$ **6.** $\frac{37}{100}$ **7.** $\frac{82}{100}$ **8.** $\frac{40}{100}$

9. $5\frac{16}{100}$ **10.** $7\frac{32}{100}$ **11.** $13\frac{80}{100}$ **12.** $26\frac{5}{100}$

Write fractions or mixed numbers.

13. 0.01   **14.** 0.07   **15.** 0.06   **16.** 0.03

17. 0.12   **18.** 0.68   **19.** 0.77   **20.** 0.70

21. 6.08   **22.** 7.05   **23.** 8.01   **24.** 12.09

25. 2.41   **26.** 18.29   **27.** 26.40   **28.** 98.60

Write decimals.

29. Five hundredths   **30.** Eight and seven hundredths

31. Four and thirty-two hundredths   **32.** Fifty-three and nine hundredths

Solve.

33. Marcy hiked to an elevation of $2\frac{56}{100}$ km. Write this as a decimal.

Thousandths

The thousandths place is to the right of the hundredths place.

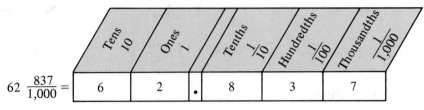

$$62\frac{837}{1,000} = \begin{array}{c|c|c|c|c} \text{Tens} & \text{Ones} & \text{Tenths} & \text{Hundredths} & \text{Thousandths} \\ 10 & 1 & \frac{1}{10} & \frac{1}{100} & \frac{1}{1,000} \\ \hline 6 & 2\ • & 8 & 3 & 7 \end{array}$$

Fractions with the denominator 1,000 can be written as decimals.

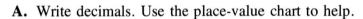

A. Write decimals. Use the place-value chart to help.

1. $\frac{5}{1,000}$ **2.** $\frac{17}{1,000}$ **3.** $\frac{374}{1,000}$ **4.** $\frac{600}{1,000}$

B. Write fractions.

     5. 0.002   **6.** 0.056   **7.** 0.139   **8.** 0.508

C. Read and write these decimals.

     Examples   Eight thousandths can be written as 0.008.

                   Six and thirty-seven thousandths can be written as 6.0037.

   9. One thousandth

10. Seven and two thousandths

11. Five and one hundred four thousandths

12. Twenty-two and six hundred seventy-four thousandths

D. Write decimals.

   13. $6\frac{2}{1,000}$ **14.** $4\frac{32}{1,000}$ **15.** $9\frac{185}{1,000}$ **16.** $18\frac{20}{1,000}$

E. Write mixed numbers.

   17. 10.001   **18.** 3.097   **19.** 17.139   **20.** 16.050

Write decimals.

1. $\frac{7}{1,000}$　　　　　**2.** $\frac{4}{1,000}$　　　　　**3.** $\frac{8}{1,000}$　　　　　**4.** $\frac{16}{1,000}$

5. $\frac{38}{1,000}$　　　　　**6.** $6\frac{80}{1,000}$　　　　　**7.** $7\frac{529}{1,000}$　　　　　**8.** $8\frac{430}{1,000}$

Write fractions or mixed numbers.

9. 0.008　　　　　**10.** 0.001　　　　　**11.** 0.023　　　　　**12.** 0.048

13. 0.413　　　　　**14.** 0.275　　　　　**15.** 0.006　　　　　**16.** 0.092

17. 7.129　　　　　**18.** 8.605　　　　　**19.** 5.040　　　　　**20.** 8.300

Write decimals.

21. Nine thousandths　　　　　**22.** Forty-two thousandths

23. Four and thirty-nine thousandths　　　　　**24.** One and seven hundred thousandths

★ Write decimals.

25. $\frac{4,500}{1,000}$　　　　　**26.** $\frac{3,007}{1,000}$　　　　　**27.** $\frac{5,742}{1,000}$　　　　　**28.** $\frac{9,010}{1,000}$

Find Out!
Calculator Activity

There are 9 numbers below. Place each number in a circle so that the sum of every three numbers in a line is always the same.

1.9	6.4
2.8	7.3
3.7	8.2
4.6	1.9
5.5	

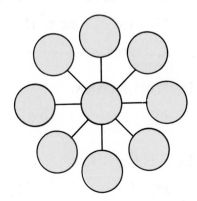

Equal Decimals

$\frac{3}{10}$ or 0.3 of the figure is shaded.

$\frac{30}{100}$ or 0.30 of the figure is shaded.

Look at these fractions.

$$\frac{3}{10} = \frac{3 \times 10}{10 \times 10}$$

$$= \frac{30}{100}$$

So, 0.3 = 0.30.

A. Write as hundredths.

Examples   0.6 = 0.60   0.8 = 0.80

1. 0.2   **2.** 0.7   **3.** 0.9   **4.** 0.4

B. Hundredths can be renamed as thousandths. Complete.

5. $\frac{34}{100} = \frac{34 \times 10}{100 \times 10}$ **6.** $\frac{75}{100} = \frac{75 \times ?}{100 \times ?}$

     $= \frac{?}{1,000}$ $= \frac{?}{}$

     So, 0.34 = ___?___   So, 0.75 = ___?___

C. Write as thousandths.

Examples   0.72 = 0.720   0.04 = 0.040

7. 0.06   **8.** 0.08   **9.** 0.23   **10.** 0.81

Practice

Write as hundredths.

1. 0.1   **2.** 0.6   **3.** 0.8   **4.** 0.4   **5.** 0.2

Write as thousandths.

6. 0.02   **7.** 0.09   **8.** 0.05   **9.** 0.32   **10.** 0.47

11. 0.7 of the beads are round. Write this as hundredths.

Fractions as Decimals

Shelley ran $\frac{1}{2}$ the track. Martin ran 0.5 the track.
Who ran farther?

Change $\frac{1}{2}$ to a decimal.

THINK $2 \times \square = 10$ $\frac{1}{2} = \frac{1 \times 5}{2 \times 5}$

Answer: 5

Multiply numerator $= \frac{5}{10}$
and denominator by 5.

                      $= 0.5$

Since $\frac{1}{2} = 0.5$, they ran the same distance.

A. Write decimals by changing to tenths.

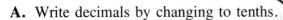

    Example $\frac{3}{5} = \frac{3 \times 2}{5 \times 2}$

                  $= \frac{6}{10}$

                  $= 0.6$

1. $\frac{1}{5}$ **2.** $\frac{4}{5}$ **3.** $\frac{2}{5}$

B. Write decimals by changing to hundredths.

    Example $\frac{3}{4} = \frac{3 \times 25}{4 \times 25}$

                  $= \frac{75}{100}$

                  $= 0.75$

4. $\frac{7}{20}$ **5.** $\frac{2}{25}$ **6.** $\frac{9}{50}$ **7.** $\frac{3}{20}$

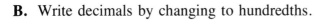

Practice

Write decimals.

1. $\frac{3}{5}$ **2.** $\frac{1}{4}$ **3.** $\frac{3}{25}$ **4.** $\frac{9}{20}$ **5.** $\frac{14}{20}$ **6.** $\frac{11}{25}$

7. $\frac{13}{20}$ **8.** $\frac{9}{25}$ **9.** $\frac{3}{50}$ **10.** $\frac{6}{25}$ ★ **11.** $\frac{1}{250}$ ★ **12.** $\frac{17}{500}$

Write decimals.

1. $\frac{5}{10}$
(290)

2. $7\frac{8}{10}$
(290)

3. $\frac{38}{100}$
(292)

4. $\frac{7}{100}$
(292)

5. $6\frac{3}{100}$
(292)

6. $\frac{42}{1,000}$
(294)

7. $\frac{8}{1,000}$
(294)

8. $16\frac{763}{1,000}$
(294)

Write fractions or mixed numbers.

9. 0.6
(290)

10. 4.5
(290)

11. 0.83
(292)

12. 0.02
(292)

Write decimals.

13. Three and two thousandths
(294)

14. Twelve and thirty-four hundredths
(292)

Write as hundredths. *(296)*

15. 0.4

16. 0.8

17. 0.1

18. 0.2

Write as thousandths. *(296)*

19. 0.03

20. 0.90

21. 0.62

22. 0.08

Compare. Use >, <, or =. *(298)*

23. 0.78 ⬚ 0.87

24. 0.3 ⬚ 0.30

25. 0.74 ⬚ 0.479

26. 0.01 ⬚ 0.010

Find Out!

Brainteaser

Trace over the figure. You
may not lift your pencil
or retrace any line segment.
You may cross over a
line segment.

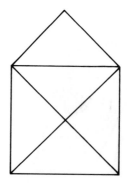

Keeping Fit

Compare. Use >, <, or =.

1. $\frac{1}{4}$ ___ $\frac{3}{8}$ 2. $\frac{3}{6}$ ___ $\frac{5}{10}$ 3. $\frac{2}{5}$ ___ $\frac{3}{8}$

4. $\frac{4}{5}$ ___ $\frac{5}{9}$ 5. $\frac{1}{3}$ ___ $\frac{1}{2}$ 6. $\frac{2}{3}$ ___ $\frac{5}{8}$

7. $\frac{7}{8}$ ___ $\frac{14}{16}$ 8. $\frac{4}{8}$ ___ $\frac{9}{20}$ 9. $\frac{3}{4}$ ___ $\frac{6}{7}$

Add and simplify.

10. $\frac{3}{10}$ $+ \frac{3}{10}$ 11. $\frac{3}{8}$ $+ \frac{1}{4}$ 12. $\frac{1}{2}$ $+ \frac{2}{5}$ 13. $\frac{1}{3}$ $+ \frac{5}{8}$ 14. $\frac{5}{6}$ $+ \frac{5}{8}$

15. $\frac{3}{4}$ $+ \frac{2}{3}$ 16. $\frac{7}{10}$ $+ \frac{3}{5}$ 17. $6\frac{1}{5}$ $+ 6\frac{1}{6}$ 18. $2\frac{3}{4}$ $+ 4$ 19. $3\frac{2}{3}$ $+ 1\frac{2}{3}$

20. $4\frac{1}{2} + 9\frac{4}{5}$ 21. $3\frac{5}{6} + 8\frac{1}{4}$ 22. $6\frac{2}{5} + 3\frac{1}{3}$ 23. $9\frac{3}{4} + 7\frac{1}{2}$

Subtract and simplify.

24. $\frac{5}{8}$ $- \frac{3}{8}$ 25. $\frac{3}{6}$ $- \frac{1}{6}$ 26. $\frac{2}{4}$ $- \frac{1}{2}$ 27. $\frac{7}{8}$ $- \frac{2}{3}$ 28. $\frac{3}{5}$ $- \frac{2}{6}$

29. $4\frac{6}{8}$ $- 2\frac{2}{8}$ 30. $8\frac{5}{6}$ $- 3\frac{1}{2}$ 31. 14 $- 7\frac{3}{10}$ 32. $17\frac{2}{5}$ $- 6\frac{4}{5}$ 33. $9\frac{1}{8}$ $- 5\frac{3}{4}$

34. $12\frac{1}{2} - 4\frac{2}{5}$ 35. $17\frac{1}{3} - 10\frac{4}{10}$ 36. $24\frac{3}{5} - 12\frac{7}{8}$ 37. $6\frac{2}{3} - 5\frac{7}{10}$

38. $8\frac{3}{4} - 2\frac{5}{6}$ 39. $13\frac{4}{7} - 5\frac{2}{3}$ 40. $18\frac{6}{10} - 11\frac{1}{4}$ 41. $28\frac{1}{2} - 13\frac{3}{5}$

Multiply and simplify.

42. $\frac{4}{9} \times \frac{1}{8}$ 43. $\frac{1}{4} \times \frac{5}{6}$ 44. $\frac{3}{8} \times \frac{4}{5}$ 45. $\frac{12}{25} \times \frac{5}{6}$

46. $5 \times \frac{7}{10}$ 47. $\frac{1}{6} \times 4$ 48. $\frac{8}{15} \times 10$ 49. $8 \times \frac{15}{32}$

50. $\frac{3}{7} \times \frac{1}{9}$ 51. $\frac{5}{6} \times \frac{2}{20}$ 52. $\frac{4}{5} \times \frac{5}{8}$ 53. $\frac{13}{21} \times \frac{7}{8}$

Problem Solving

The water level at Lake Geronimo rose 10.2 cm in June. It rose 3.5 cm in July, and 2.4 cm in August. What was the total rise during the three months?

Mini-problems help us find the important information.

Mini-Problem: Rose 10.2 cm in June
Rose 3.5 cm in July
Rose 2.4 cm in August
How far in all?

Answer: 16.1 cm

Write mini-problems. Solve.

1. Bonnie jogged around the lake. She jogged 1.2 km on Monday, 1.3 km on Tuesday, and 0.9 km on Wednesday. How far did she jog in the three days?

2. Richard bought a hamburger for $0.89, a glass of milk for $0.45, and an apple for $0.30. How much did he spend in all?

3. Joe spent $2.58 for a map book, $0.79 for paper, and $0.89 for a pen. How much did he spend in all?

Write mini-problems. Solve.

1. One of Paul's suitcases is 5.7 kg and the other is 8.4 kg. What is the total mass of his suitcases?

2. At breakfast Jan drank 0.25 L of orange juice and 0.25 L of milk. How much liquid did she drink in all?

3. To build a tree house, Pat cut a piece of wood into three pieces. One piece was 1.36 m, the second was 1.42 m, and the third was 1.22 m. How long was the original piece of wood?

4. During the first week of her vacation, Mary hiked 116.5 km. During the second week, she hiked 89.6 km. How much farther did she hike the first week?

5. A rectangular yard is 22.6 yd long and 18.2 yd wide. How much fencing is needed to fence in the yard?

6. Jack wants to frame a picture 15.5 in. long and 30.5 in. wide. How much wood does he need?

7. Barb bought a book for $2.98. She gave the clerk a five-dollar bill. How much change should she get?

8. Bob bought a frank for $0.59, a glass of milk for $0.25, and a pear for $0.30. What was his total bill?

Adding Decimals

Sandy had two parrots. One parrot is 0.65 kg and the other is 0.27 kg. What is their total mass?

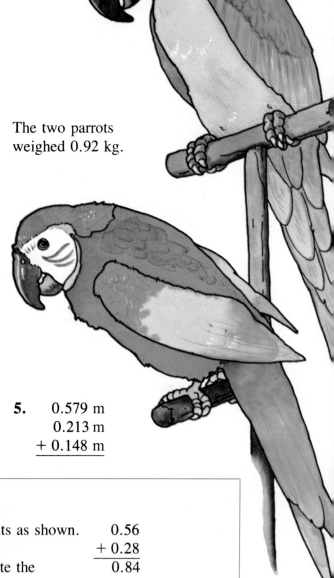

Compare the two forms of addition.

$$\begin{array}{r} \frac{65}{100} \\ + \frac{27}{100} \\ \hline \frac{92}{100} \end{array}$$

$$\begin{array}{r} 0.65 \\ + 0.27 \\ \hline 0.92 \end{array}$$

The two parrots weighed 0.92 kg.

▶ To add decimals, make sure the decimal points line up. Then add as with whole numbers.

A. Add.

1. $\begin{array}{r} 0.5 \\ + 0.2 \\ \hline \end{array}$

2. $\begin{array}{r} 0.17 \\ + 0.49 \\ \hline \end{array}$

3. $\begin{array}{r} 0.381 \\ + 0.476 \\ \hline \end{array}$

4. $\begin{array}{r} 0.247 \\ + 0.358 \\ \hline \end{array}$

5. $\begin{array}{r} 0.579 \text{ m} \\ 0.213 \text{ m} \\ + 0.148 \text{ m} \\ \hline \end{array}$

Add 0.56 + 0.28.

Step 1 Line up the decimal points as shown.

Step 2 Now add. Be sure to write the decimal point in the answer.

$$\begin{array}{r} 0.56 \\ + 0.28 \\ \hline 0.84 \end{array}$$

B. Add.

6. 0.8 + 0.1

7. 0.2 + 0.1 + 0.3

8. 0.67 + 0.19

9. 0.04 + 0.37 + 0.12

10. 0.503 + 0.419

11. 0.601 + 0.213 + 0.149

Add.

1.   0.4
   + 0.2

2.   0.3
   + 0.2

3.   0.1
   + 0.7

4.   0.5
   + 0.3

5.   0.06
   + 0.03

6.   0.28
   + 0.41

7.   0.79
   + 0.11

8.   0.63
   + 0.27

9.   0.007
   + 0.008

10.   0.026
   + 0.035

11.   0.362
   + 0.439

12.   0.123
   + 0.456

13.   0.1
   0.3
   + 0.4

14.   0.3
   0.2
   + 0.4

15.   0.06
   0.32
   + 0.58

16.   0.53
   0.28
   + 0.17

17.   0.43
   0.22
   + 0.17

18.   0.139
   0.278
   + 0.432

19.   0.638 m
   0.129 m
   + 0.174 m

20.   0.239 km
   0.142 km
   + 0.428 km

21. 0.4 + 0.5

22. 0.67 + 0.28

23. 0.407 + 0.239

24. 0.641 + 0.213 + 0.108

★ **25.** 0.438 + 0.27

★ **26.** 0.56 + 0.2 + 0.029 + 0.1

Solve.

27. Priscilla's parakeet ate 0.5 g
of birdseed. Then she ate 0.4 g
more. How much did she eat
in all?

28. Bob's canary is 0.12 kg. In the
spring he gained 0.04 kg. What
was his new mass?

29. One canary is 0.17 kg. A second
canary is 0.16 kg. What is the
total mass?

Sums Greater Than One

Compare the two forms of addition.

$$\begin{array}{r} \frac{8}{10} \\ + \frac{5}{10} \\ \hline \frac{13}{10} \end{array} \qquad \begin{array}{r} 0.8 \\ + 0.5 \\ \hline 1.3 \end{array}$$

▶ When adding decimals, rename the same way as with whole numbers.

A. Add.

1. $\begin{array}{r}0.7 \\ +0.6\end{array}$	**2.** $\begin{array}{r}0.3 \\ +0.9\end{array}$	**3.** $\begin{array}{r}0.8 \\ +0.8\end{array}$	**4.** $\begin{array}{r}4.5 \text{ m} \\ +9.8 \text{ m}\end{array}$
5. $\begin{array}{r}5.67 \\ +8.91\end{array}$	**6.** $\begin{array}{r}4.386 \\ +2.927\end{array}$	**7.** $\begin{array}{r}17.1 \text{ cm} \\ 15.6 \text{ cm} \\ +\ \ 3.7 \text{ cm}\end{array}$	**8.** $\begin{array}{r}4.673 \\ 8.219 \\ +1.536\end{array}$

Add $4.59 + 8.63$.

Step 1 Line up the decimal points as shown.

Step 2 Now add. Be sure to write the decimal point in the answer.

$$\begin{array}{r} 4.59 \\ + 8.63 \\ \hline 13.22 \end{array}$$

B. Add.

9. $0.23 + 0.85$

10. $0.436 + 0.918$

11. $8.45 + 9.79$

12. $14.87 + 6.35 + 7.81$

13. $10.4 + 11.3 + 17.8$

14. $1.413 + 0.726 + 8.209$

Add.

1. 0.2
+ 0.9

2. 5.8
+ 7.3

3. 14.6 cm
+ 12.8 cm

4. 13.7
+ 18.9

5. 0.37
+ 0.84

6. 2.83 m
+ 1.47 m

7. 23.76
+ 14.51

8. 12.58
+ 34.64

9. 0.514
+ 0.728

10. 8.427
+ 1.936

11. 10.781 km
+ 11.235 km

12. 9.384
+ 6.716

13. 3.4
7.2
+ 9.7

14. 12.8
13.6
+ 21.5

15. 1.48
0.26
+ 3.39

16. 5.81 cm
7.23 cm
+ 3.62 cm

17. 6.211
5.436
+ 7.867

18. 6.368
4.871
+ 2.192

19. 0.568
0.239
+ 0.451

20. 10.492
11.387
+ 15.724

21. 0.61 + 0.72

22. 5.48 + 2.96

23. 0.831 + 0.497

★ **24.** 7.2 + 4.83 + 11.043

Solve.

25. Melanie grew 3.6 cm this year and 4.8 cm last year. How much did she grow in the two years?

26. Bill gained 2.8 kg in the fifth grade and 3.1 kg in the sixth grade. How much did he gain in the two years?

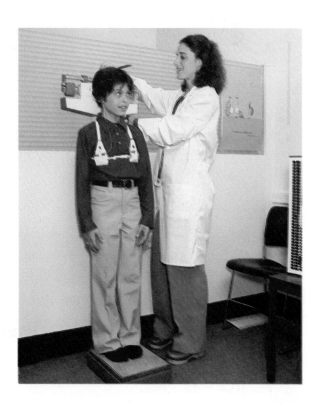

Rounding Decimals

A decimal can be rounded to the nearest whole number.

3.0 3.1 3.2 3.3 3.4 3.5 3.6 3.7 3.8 3.9 4.0

| 3.2 is closer to 3 than to 4. Round 3.2 to 3. | 3.5 is halfway between 3 and 4. Round 3.5 to 4. | 3.9 is closer to 4 than to 3. Round 3.9 to 4. |

▶ To round a decimal to the nearest whole number, look at the tenths digit. If the tenths digit is less than 5, *round down*. If the tenths digit is 5 or greater, *round up*.

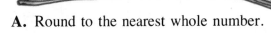

A. Round to the nearest whole number.

    1. 2.8   **2.** 5.1

    3. 4.5   **4.** 36.3

B. Look at the example, then complete.

```
Exact      4.3        Estimate      4
          28.6                     29
        +  9.5                   + 10
        ------                   ----
          42.4                     43
```

    5. 4.3 is rounded to ___?___.

    7. The exact sum is ___?___.

    6. 28.6 is rounded to ___?___.

    8. The estimated sum is ___?___.

    9. Is the exact sum reasonable?

C. Estimate the sums. [HINT: Round each addend to the nearest whole number.]

	10.	**11.**	**12.**	**13.**	**14.**
	8.6	29.5	32.8	38.3	50.5
	+ 3.2	+ 16.8	6.7	41.8	14.2
			+ 21.5	+ 9.1	+ 29.4

Round to the nearest whole number.

1. 3.1   **2.** 8.5   **3.** 9.7   **4.** 10.2   **5.** 12.3

6. 13.6   **7.** 21.8   **8.** 32.5   **9.** 48.9   **10.** 60.4

Estimate the sums. Correct any unreasonable sums.

11.
```
   9.6
 + 3.2
```
Is 27.8 a reasonable sum?

12.
```
   11.3
 +  9.8
```
Is 21.1 a reasonable sum?

Estimate the sums.

13.
```
   7.8
 + 3.2
```
14.
```
   8.2
 + 7.5
```
15.
```
   34.9
 +  4.8
```
16.
```
   29.7
 + 23.9
```
17.
```
   47.1
 + 12.9
```

18.
```
   1.6
   8.1
 + 9.2
```
19.
```
   11.3
    7.2
 + 29.6
```
20.
```
   34.8
    6.7
 + 18.5
```
21.
```
   41.2
   18.9
 + 13.1
```
22.
```
    5.3
   29.6
 + 48.5
```

Solve.

23. Joe needed three pieces of rope to make a macrame belt. The pieces had to be 7.8 m, 8.2 m, and 8.5 m long. Estimate how much rope he needed in all.

24. Sandy added 23.4 + 47.2 + 17.8 on her calculator. The answer was 88.4. What was the estimated sum? Was the calculator answer reasonable?

★ **25.** Joan mixed 1.8 L of blue paint, 2.1 L of yellow paint, and 0.8 L of white paint. Estimate to find how many liters of paint she mixed.

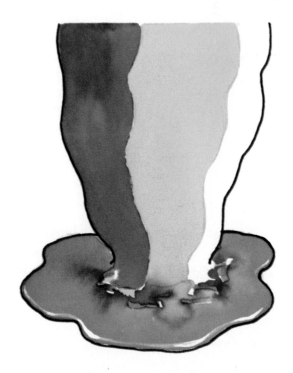

Subtracting Decimals

Valerie had 0.75 m of ribbon.
She used 0.64 m to trim the cover of
a scrapbook. How much ribbon did
she have left?

Compare the two forms of subtraction.

$$\begin{array}{r} \frac{75}{100} \\ -\frac{64}{100} \\ \hline \frac{11}{100} \end{array} \qquad \begin{array}{r} 0.75 \\ -0.64 \\ \hline 0.11 \end{array}$$

Valerie had 0.11 m of ribbon left.

▶ To subtract decimals, make sure the
decimal points line up. Then subtract
as with whole numbers.

A. Subtract.

1.	$\begin{array}{r}0.5\\-0.2\\\hline\end{array}$	**2.**	$\begin{array}{r}0.9\\-0.3\\\hline\end{array}$	**3.**	$\begin{array}{r}0.04\text{ cm}\\-0.01\text{ cm}\\\hline\end{array}$	**4.**	$\begin{array}{r}0.86\\-0.41\\\hline\end{array}$
5.	$\begin{array}{r}0.17\\-0.09\\\hline\end{array}$	**6.**	$\begin{array}{r}0.041\\-0.029\\\hline\end{array}$	**7.**	$\begin{array}{r}0.375\\-0.241\\\hline\end{array}$	**8.**	$\begin{array}{r}0.783\\-0.496\\\hline\end{array}$

Subtract $0.68 - 0.39$.

Step 1 Line up the decimal points as shown.

Step 2 Now subtract. Be sure to write the
decimal point in the answer.

$$\begin{array}{r} \overset{5\ 18}{0.\cancel{6}8} \\ -0.39 \\ \hline 0.29 \end{array}$$

B. Subtract.

9. $0.82 - 0.49$

10. $0.78 - 0.49$

11. $0.673 - 0.587$

12. $0.984 - 0.249$

Practice

Subtract.

1. 0.8
  − 0.7

2. 0.9
  − 0.3

3. 0.2
  − 0.1

4. 0.6
  − 0.2

5. 0.39
  − 0.21

6. 0.96 km
  − 0.87 km

7. 0.98
  − 0.66

8. 0.05
  − 0.02

9. 0.478
  − 0.241

10. 0.792
  − 0.438

11. 0.874 cm
  − 0.797 cm

12. 0.561
  − 0.265

13. 0.9 − 0.4

14. 0.64 − 0.46

15. 0.058 − 0.009

16. 0.372 − 0.184

★ **17.** 0.643 − 0.31

★ **18.** 0.372 − 0.2

★ Write the next decimal in the pattern.

19. 1.1, 1.3, 1.5, __?__ , __?__

20. 3.6, 3.2, 2.8, __?__ , __?__

21. 4.6, 5.1, 5.6, __?__ , __?__

22. 8.9, 8.2, 7.5, __?__ , __?__

Solve.

23. Ron ran 0.95 mi. Then he walked 0.52 mi. How much farther did he run than walk?

24. Jane drank 0.8 qt of juice. Bill drank 0.5 qt. How much more did Jane drink?

Subtracting to Thousandths

Compare the two forms of subtraction.

$$6\frac{3}{10} = 5\frac{13}{10} \qquad \overset{5\ 13}{\cancel{6}.\cancel{3}}$$

$$-2\frac{8}{10} = 2\frac{8}{10} \qquad -2.8$$

$$\overline{\phantom{-2\frac{8}{10} = {}} 3\frac{5}{10}} \qquad \overline{ 3.5}$$

 When subtracting decimals, rename the same way as with whole numbers.

A. Subtract.

1.	1.8	**2.**	3.6	**3.**	2.8 cm	**4.**	6.42
	$-\,0.9$		$-\,1.4$		$-\,1.9$ cm		$-\,0.73$

5.	3.50	**6.**	9.53	**7.**	2.503	**8.**	8.002
	$-\,2.79$		$-\,1.68$		$-\,1.674$		$-\,4.387$

Subtract $9.287 - 5.349$.

Step 1 Line up the decimal points.

Step 2 Now subtract. Be sure to write the decimal point in the answer.

$$\overset{8\ 12\ 7\ 17}{\cancel{9}.\cancel{2}\,\cancel{8}\,\cancel{7}}$$
$$-\,5.3\,4\,9$$
$$\overline{3.9\,3\,8}$$

B. Subtract.

9. $6.8 - 3.9$

10. $4.7 - 2.8$

11. $9.42 - 3.78$

12. $6.3 - 4.5$

13. $7.359 - 4.827$

14. $9.000 - 4.361$

Subtract.

1.   2.8
− 0.7

2.   3.8
− 0.4

3.   6.1
− 0.4

4.   9.2
− 0.6

5.   4.7
− 2.3

6.   7.8
− 5.6

7.   6.2
− 3.7

8.   8.4
− 6.8

9.   5.63
− 2.71

10.   3.47
− 0.15

11.   6.14
− 3.29

12.   4.26
− 1.38

13.   7.31
− 1.47

14.   9.35 cm
− 2.57 cm

15.   6.38
− 4.59

16.   2.75 km
− 1.99 km

17.   1.283
− 0.141

18.   7.358
− 4.226

19.   5.376
− 2.439

20.   8.642
− 4.907

21.   8.406
− 5.439

22.   6.453
− 2.791

23.   5.004
− 2.132

24.   6.000
− 4.387

25. 6.7 − 4.3

26. 8.74 − 5.73

27. 6.5 − 5.9

28. 8.3 − 6.7

29. 8.03 − 5.29

30. 6.572 − 5.395

★**31.** 3.2 − 1.54

★**32.** 6.35 − 5.017

Solve.

33. Durham is 7.1 km away. Kitestown is 4.6 km away. How much farther away is Durham than Kitestown?

★**34.** When the Valdezes left on a trip, the odometer read 5,681.8. When they arrived it read 6,307.3. How far did they travel?

Multiplying Decimals

Look at these multiplication examples.

$\frac{3}{10} \times 2 = \frac{3}{10} \times \frac{2}{1}$ 0.3 $\frac{8}{10} \times 7 = \frac{8}{10} \times \frac{7}{1}$ 0.8

$\quad\quad = \frac{6}{10}$ $\dfrac{\times\ 2}{0.6}$ $\quad\quad = \frac{56}{10}$ $\dfrac{\times\ 7}{5.6}$

$\quad\quad\quad\quad\quad\quad\quad\quad\quad\quad\quad\quad\quad = 5\frac{6}{10}$

▶ To multiply tenths by a whole number, multiply as with whole
numbers. Then place the decimal point in the answer in the tenths
place.

A. Multiply.

1. 0.2   **2.** 0.4   **3.** 0.6   **4.** 0.8
    $\underline{\times\ 2}$ $\underline{\times\ 2}$ $\underline{\times\ 9}$ $\underline{\times\ 5}$

Compare these multiplication examples.

$\frac{2}{10} \times \frac{4}{10} = \frac{2 \times 4}{10 \times 10}$ 0.2 $\frac{4}{10} \times \frac{6}{10} = \frac{4 \times 6}{10 \times 10}$ 0.4

$\quad\quad = \frac{8}{100}$ $\dfrac{\times\ 0.4}{0.08}$ $\quad\quad = \frac{24}{100}$ $\dfrac{\times\ 0.6}{0.24}$

▶ To multiply tenths by tenths, multiply as with whole numbers.
Then place the decimal point in the answer in the hundredths place.

B. Multiply.

5.   0.9   **6.**   0.3   **7.**   0.5   **8.**   0.7
     $\underline{\times\ 0.1}$ $\underline{\times\ 0.2}$ $\underline{\times\ 0.7}$ $\underline{\times\ 0.6}$

C. Multiply.

Examples   4.8   6.5
             $\dfrac{\times\ 3}{14.4}$ $\dfrac{\times\ 0.9}{5.85}$

9. 3.7   **10.** 9.6   **11.**   4.2   **12.**   7.5
    $\underline{\times\ 4}$ $\underline{\times\ 5}$ $\underline{\times\ 0.3}$ $\underline{\times\ 0.8}$

Multiply.

1. 0.1
× 5

2. 0.2
× 4

3. 0.2
× 3

4. 0.1
× 8

5. 0.4
× 9

6. 0.8
× 6

7. 0.7
× 7

8. 0.6
× 5

9. 0.5
× 7

10. 0.3
× 9

11. 0.9
× 8

12. 0.8
× 4

13. 0.8
× 0.1

14. 0.2
× 0.3

15. 0.4
× 0.2

16. 0.1
× 0.7

17. 0.4
× 0.3

18. 0.5
× 0.7

19. 0.3
× 0.9

20. 0.8
× 0.5

21. 5.3
× 3

22. 7.4
× 2

23. 6.7
× 5

24. 8.3
× 7

25. 4.2
× 3

26. 5.7
× 2

27. 8.5
× 9

28. 4.9
× 7

29. 0.3 × 7

30. 0.4 × 8

31. 4.6 × 0.8

32. 8.9 × 0.5

33. 1.4 × 7

34. 3.9 × 0.6

★ Solve without computing.

35. $1.5 + 3.7 = \underline{} + 1.5$
36. $4.2 \times (0.3 + 2.7) = (4.2 \times 0.3) + (4.2 + \underline{})$

37. $3.2 \times 0.8 = 0.8 \times \underline{}$
38. $2.1 + (3.5 + 4.6) = (2.1 + \underline{}) + 4.6$

Solve.

39. Bicycled 2.8 km to the next town.
How far for a round trip?

40. Bicycled 1.5 hours each day.
How many hours in seven days?

Problem Solving

Solve.

1. Klaus Dibiasi of Italy won the Platform Diving Championship at the 1968 Olympics. He scored 53.31 points, 61.27 points, and 48.50 points on his 3 dives. What was his total score? [HINT: Add]

2. Wilma Rudolph was the fastest woman in the 1964 Olympics. She ran 100 meters in 11.1 seconds and 200 meters in 24.0 seconds. How much longer did it take Wilma Rudolph to run 200 meters?

3. In 1964, Don Schollander won the gold medal for the 400-meter freestyle swim. He swam the first 200 meters in 1.970 minutes and the last 200 meters in 2.233 minutes. What was his total time?

4. In the 1976 Olympics, Ed Moses of the U.S.A. ran the 400-meter hurdles in 47.64 seconds. The former world record was 47.82 seconds. How much faster was Ed Moses's time than the previous world record?

5. In the 1976 Olympics the women's 200-meter dash was run in 22.37 seconds. This was a new world record. The previous record was 22.40 seconds. How much faster is the new world record?

6. In 1936, Jesse Owens ran 100 meters in 10.3 seconds. In 1963, Jim Hines ran 100 meters in 9.9 seconds. How much faster did Jim Hines run?

Write decimals.

1. $\frac{4}{10}$
(290)

2. $2\frac{6}{10}$
(290)

3. $\frac{6}{1,000}$
(294)

4. $\frac{9}{100}$
(292)

Write fractions or mixed numbers.

5. 0.8
(290)

6. 5.2
(290)

7. 0.61
(292)

8. 0.082
(294)

Write as hundredths. (296)

9. 0.5

10. 0.1

11. 0.2

12. 0.3

Write as thousandths. (296)

13. 0.01

14. 0.23

15. 0.15

16. 0.08

Compare. Use >, <, or =. (298)

17. 0.46 ≡ 0.64

18. 0.7 ≡ 0.70

19. 0.62 ≡ 0.261

20. 0.02 ≡ 0.020

Add. (304, 306)

21. 0.4
\+ 0.3

22. 1.63
\+ 4.29

23. 0.281
\+ 0.379

24. 3.513
\+ 2.870

Subtract.

25. 0.8 (310)
− 0.3

26. 0.77
(310) − 0.62

27. 8.4
(312) − 2.6

28. 5.730
(312) − 2.973

Multiply. (314)

29. 0.6
× 5

30. 0.3
× 7

31. 0.2
× 0.8

Write a mini-problem. Solve. (302)

32. Sally rode her bicycle 1.4 km to her friend's house and then 3.2 km further to the grocery store. How far did she ride in all?

Solve. (316)

33. In May, there were 96 cm of rain. In April there were 5.3 cm of rain. How much more rain was there in May than in April?

Write decimals.

1. $\frac{7}{10}$
(290)

2. $5\frac{3}{10}$
(290)

3. $\frac{2}{1,000}$
(294)

4. $\frac{8}{100}$
(292)

Write fractions or mixed numbers.

5. 0.3
(290)

6. 8.1
(290)

7. 0.74
(292)

8. 0.06
(292)

Write as hundredths. *(296)*

9. 0.8

10. 0.6

11. 0.9

12. 0.4

Write as thousandths. *(296)*

13. 0.09

14. 0.73

15. 0.99

16. 0.02

Compare. Use >, <, or =. *(298)*

17. 0.39 ≡ 0.93

18. 0.22 ≡ 0.220

19. 0.5 ≡ 0.05

20. 0.090 ≡ 0.90

Add. *(304, 306)*

21.
$$\begin{array}{r} 0.6 \\ + 0.1 \\ \hline \end{array}$$

22.
$$\begin{array}{r} 1.48 \\ + 2.73 \\ \hline \end{array}$$

23.
$$\begin{array}{r} 0.794 \\ + 0.086 \\ \hline \end{array}$$

24.
$$\begin{array}{r} 1.836 \\ + 4.729 \\ \hline \end{array}$$

Subtract.

25.
$$\begin{array}{r} 0.9 \\ - 0.2 \\ \hline \end{array}$$
(310)

26.
$$\begin{array}{r} 0.84 \\ - 0.32 \\ \hline \end{array}$$
(310)

27.
$$\begin{array}{r} 7.8 \\ - 4.9 \\ \hline \end{array}$$
(312)

28.
$$\begin{array}{r} 6.231 \\ - 4.573 \\ \hline \end{array}$$
(312)

Multiply. *(314)*

29.
$$\begin{array}{r} 0.6 \\ \times 8 \\ \hline \end{array}$$

30.
$$\begin{array}{r} 0.9 \\ \times 7 \\ \hline \end{array}$$

31.
$$\begin{array}{r} 0.6 \\ \times 0.5 \\ \hline \end{array}$$

Write a mini-problem. Solve. *(302)*

32. Pedro is filling one bicycle tire with 2.4 L of air. He filled the other tire with 3.1 L of air. How much air will he put in altogether?

Solve. *(316)*

33. Joan jogged 2.3 km on Monday and 1.8 km on Tuesday. How much farther did she jog on Monday?

Basic Skills Check

1.

$$63,432 + 32,564$$

  A 69,596
  B 91,196
  C 95,996
  D 99,596

6.

$$604 - 592$$

  E 12
  F 1,196
  G 18
  H 16

11.

$$13,721 - 2,510$$

  A 15,231
  B 12,111
  C 11,211
  D 16,231

2.

$30)\overline{108}$

  E 6r18
  F 6r6
  G 3r18
  H 3r8

7.

$$221 \times 32$$

  A 253
  B 665
  C 7,072
  D 7,663

12.

$$8\frac{5}{8} - 7\frac{3}{16}$$

  E $2\frac{6}{16}$
  F $1\frac{9}{16}$
  G $1\frac{7}{16}$
  H $1\frac{1}{16}$

3.

$$5\frac{5}{6} + 3\frac{1}{3}$$

  A $8\frac{1}{6}$
  B $9\frac{1}{6}$
  C $9\frac{2}{3}$
  D $9\frac{5}{6}$

8.

$$3\frac{3}{7} - 1\frac{1}{21}$$

  E $1\frac{7}{21}$
  F $1\frac{8}{21}$
  G $2\frac{1}{21}$
  H $2\frac{8}{21}$

13.

$70)\overline{627}$

  A 9r67
  B 9r64
  C 8r67
  D 8r64

4.

$$334 \times 6$$

  E 340
  F 2,004
  G 2,024
  H 3,424

9.

$$800 - 629$$

  A 1,429
  B 271
  C 179
  D 171

14.

$$532 \\ 647 \\ + 102$$

  E 1,482
  F 1,281
  G 1,182
  H 981

5.

$$63 \\ 74 \\ 42 \\ + 56$$

  A 231
  B 234
  C 235
  D 243

10.

$$5,392 + 3,606$$

  E 9,889
  F 8,999
  G 8,998
  H 8,898

15.

$50)\overline{252}$

  A 4r2
  B 4r12
  C 5r2
  D 5r12

Area

This is a square centimeter.
It is used to measure
regions.

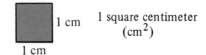

1 cm

1 cm

1 square centimeter
(cm²)

The **area** of a region is the number of unit squares in it.

Count the number of square
centimeters in this region.

The area of this region is 6
square centimeters.
This is written 6 cm².

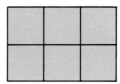

Find the areas in square centimeters.

1.

2.

3.

4.

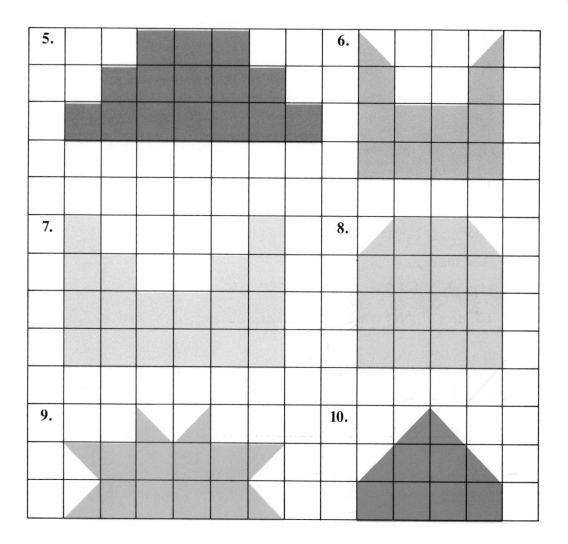

5. **6.**

7. **8.**

9. **10.**

★**11.** Cut 4 pieces of string, each 1 meter long.
Place them on the floor to form a square.
Estimate how many square meters there
are in the area of your classroom floor.

Area of a Rectangle

We can find the area of a rectangle by multiplying.

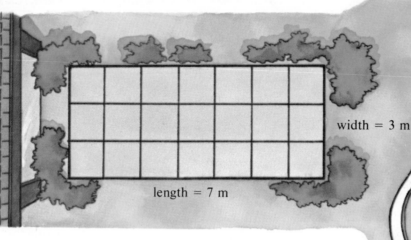

width = 3 m

length = 7 m

A. Look at the diagram.

    1. How many square meters are in each row?

    2. How many rows are there?

    3. Multiply: $3 \times 7 = \underline{\ \ ?\ \ }$

    4. The area of the rectangle is $\underline{\ \ ?\ \ }$ square meters or $\underline{\ \ ?\ \ }$ m².

▶ The area of a rectangle is
the product of the length
and the width. $A = l \times w$

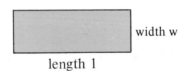

width w

length l

B. Find the areas. Use the formula $A = l \times w$.

5. 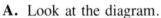 4 cm

    4 cm

6. 3 m

    6 m

7. 5 cm

    4 cm

    8. $l = 5$ m
        $w = 7$ m

    9. $l = 8$ cm
        $w = 4$ cm

    10. $l = 9$ m
         $w = 6$ m

    11. $l = 2$ m
         $w = 12$ m

    12. $l = 4$ cm
         $w = 10$ cm

    13. $l = 7$ m
         $w = 7$ m

Find the areas.

1.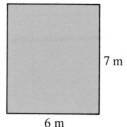
7 m

6 m

2.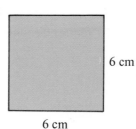
6 cm

6 cm

3.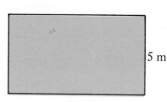
5 m

9 m

4.
4 in.

8 in.

5.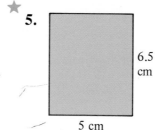
6.5 cm

5 cm

6.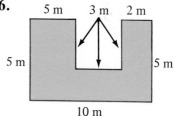
5 m   3 m   2 m

5 m   5 m

10 m

7. $l = 6$ cm
$w = 5$ cm

8. $l = 4$ m
$w = 4$ m

9. $l = 20$ ft
$w = 5$ ft

10. $l = 18$ yd
$w = 3$ yd

Solve.

11. How many square meters of carpet does Sandy need to cover a floor that is 5 m long and 3 m wide?

12. What is the area of a room that is 17 ft long and 5 ft wide?

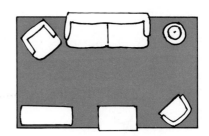

Find Out!
Brainteaser

The figures have the same area, but different perimeters.
Draw 2 figures that have areas of 8 square units but perimeters of 12 units and 14 units.

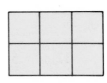

Area of a Right Triangle

Here is a way to find the area of a right triangle.

A. On centimeter graph paper, draw a rectangle 8 cm by 5 cm. Cut it out.

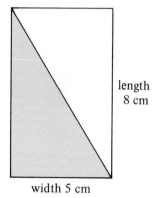

length
8 cm

1. What is the area of the rectangle?

2. Fold along a diagonal of the rectangle. What figures are formed?

3. Is the area of each right triangle half the area of the rectangle?

4. What is the area of each right triangle?

width 5 cm

▶ Use this formula to find the area of a right triangle:
$$A = \frac{1}{2} \times l \times w$$

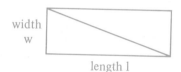

width
w

length l

B. Find the area of each right triangle. Use the formula.

5.

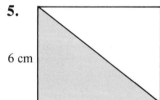

6 cm

8 cm

6.

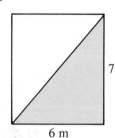

7 m

6 m

7.

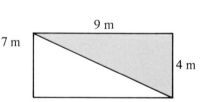

9 m

4 m

8.

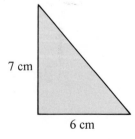

7 cm

6 cm

9.

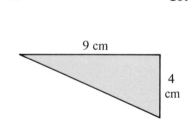

9 cm

4 cm

10.

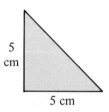

5 cm

5 cm

11. $l = 3$ cm
$w = 4$ cm

12. $l = 5$ cm
$w = 10$ cm

13. $l = 8$ cm
$w = 7$ cm

14. $l = 9$ in.
$w = 6$ in.

Find the area of each right triangle. Use the formula.

1.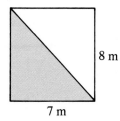

8 m

7 m

2.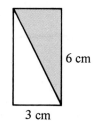

6 cm

3 cm

3.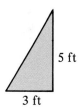

2 yd

9 yd

4.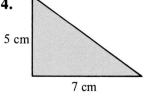

5 cm

7 cm

5.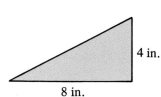

4 in.

8 in.

6.

5 ft

3 ft

7. $l = 2$ cm
$w = 8$ cm

★ **8.** $l = 9.5$ in.
$w = 6$ in.

★ **9.** $l = 4.2$ cm
$w = 4.5$ cm

★ **10.** $l = 6.4$ cm
$w = 4.4$ cm

★ **11.** Find the total area of the kite.

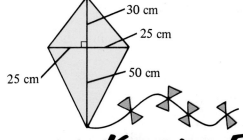

30 cm

25 cm

50 cm

25 cm

Keeping Fit

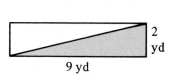

Simplify.

1. $\frac{2}{10}$ **2.** $\frac{8}{16}$ **3.** $\frac{3}{9}$ **4.** $\frac{14}{21}$

5. $\frac{18}{20}$ **6.** $\frac{25}{35}$ **7.** $\frac{24}{36}$ **8.** $\frac{8}{32}$

9. $\frac{16}{20}$ **10.** $\frac{32}{40}$ **11.** $\frac{24}{64}$ **12.** $\frac{46}{50}$ **13.** $\frac{45}{60}$ **14.** $\frac{90}{100}$

15. $\frac{10}{15}$ **16.** $\frac{24}{32}$ **17.** $\frac{35}{50}$ **18.** $\frac{48}{64}$ **19.** $\frac{8}{80}$ **20.** $\frac{75}{100}$

Solid Shapes

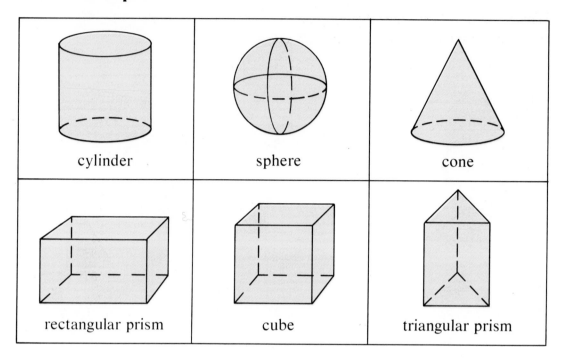

cylinder	sphere	cone
rectangular prism	cube	triangular prism

A. A tin can is a model of a cylinder.

   1. Name a model for each of the solids shown above.

B. Look at the rectangular prism. Match each term with its description.

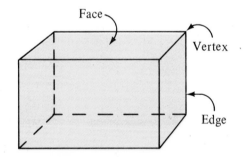

   2. edge   rectangular region

   3. vertex   line segment

   4. face   point

C. Give the number of faces, edges, and vertices for each figure.

   5.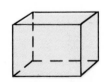

   6.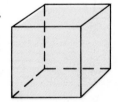

   7.

Which is a model of a rectangular prism? A cylinder? A cube?
A sphere? A cone? A triangular prism?

1.

2.

3.

4.

5.

6.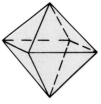

7. Copy and complete the table.

Number of faces				
Number of vertices				
Number of edges				

Volume

The cubic centimeter is
a unit of volume. It is
used to measure solids.

1 cm

1 cm

1 cm

1 cubic centimeter
1 cm³

▶ The number of cubic units in a solid
is called its **volume.**

The volume of this rectangular
prism is 8 cubic centimeters.
It is written 8 cm³.

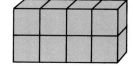

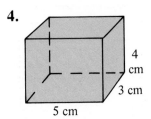

A. We can find the volume of a rectangular
prism without counting.

1. How many cubes in the lower layer?

THINK   length is 4, width is 2.

$$4 \times 2 = \underline{\quad?\quad}$$

2. How many layers of cubes
will fill the prism?

THINK   Height is 3.

3. What is the volume?

THINK $4 \times 2 \times 3 = \underline{\quad?\quad}$

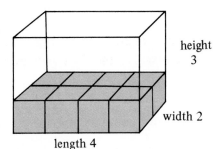

height
3

width 2

length 4

▶ The volume of a rectangular prism is the product of
the length, width, and height. $V = l \times w \times h$

B. Find the volume of each rectangular prism.

4.

4
cm

3 cm

5 cm

5.

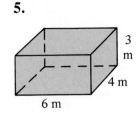

3
m

4 m

6 m

	Length	Width	Height
6.	7 cm	5 cm	2 cm
7.	8 m	6 m	4 m
8.	9 cm	5 cm	3 cm

Find the volume of each rectangular prism.

1.

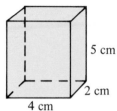

5 cm
2 cm
4 cm

2.

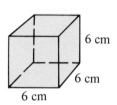

6 cm
6 cm
6 cm

3.

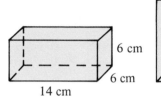

6 cm
6 cm
14 cm

4.

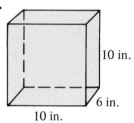

10 in.
6 in.
10 in.

	Length	Width	Height
5.	6 cm	2 cm	4 cm
6.	8 cm	3 cm	2 cm
7.	5 cm	5 cm	5 cm
8.	8 in.	2 in.	5 in.
9.	9 ft	4 ft	4 ft
10.	7 yd	4 yd	3 yd

Solve.

11. Suzie's lunch box is 20 cm long, 15 cm wide, and 19 cm high. What is the volume?

★ **12.** Jerome's fish tank is 40.1 cm long, 25.2 cm wide, and 30.0 cm high. What is the volume?

Find Out!
Calculator Activity

Find the volume of each rectangular prism. Then double each dimension and find the volume again.

	Length	Width	Height	Volume	Double each dimension			
					Length	Width	Height	Volume
1.	6	2	5					
2.	5	4	3					
3.	8	3	4					

What happens to the volume of a rectangular prism when each dimension is doubled?

Find the areas. *(322, 324)*

1.

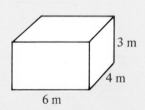

7 cm

7 cm

2.

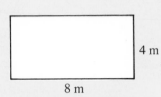

4 m

8 m

3.

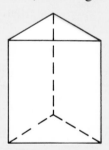

5 cm

8 cm

Name a model for each figure. *(326)*

4.

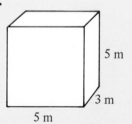

5.

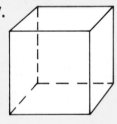

6.

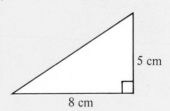

Give the number of faces, vertices, and edges for each figure. *(326)*

7.

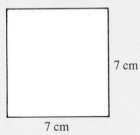

8.

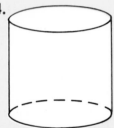

9.

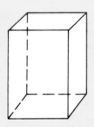

Find the volume of each rectangular prism. *(328)*

10.

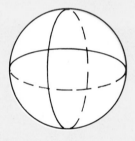

5 m

3 m

5 m

11.

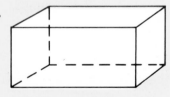

3 m

4 m

6 m

	Length	Width	Height
12.	4 cm	7 cm	2 cm
13.	6 cm	9 cm	3 cm
14.	10 cm	5 cm	4 cm

Keeping Fit

Divide.

1. $6\overline{)72}$
2. $4\overline{)56}$
3. $6\overline{)246}$

4. $4\overline{)328}$
5. $5\overline{)265}$
6. $3\overline{)198}$

7. $8\overline{)99}$
8. $7\overline{)85}$
9. $5\overline{)168}$
10. $2\overline{)159}$

11. $4\overline{)5,548}$
12. $6\overline{)8,214}$
13. $3\overline{)3,769}$
14. $5\overline{)7,128}$

15. $7\overline{)99,715}$
16. $4\overline{)85,712}$
17. $6\overline{)85,429}$
18. $2\overline{)54,513}$

19. $6\overline{)3,522}$
20. $8\overline{)3,432}$
21. $9\overline{)6,818}$
22. $7\overline{)2,643}$

23. $7\overline{)41,888}$
24. $8\overline{)31,112}$
25. $6\overline{)51,870}$
26. $5\overline{)23,780}$

27. $4\overline{)4,832}$
28. $6\overline{)8,436}$
29. $4\overline{)1,632}$
30. $8\overline{)5,672}$

31. $4\overline{)44,296}$
32. $3\overline{)84,222}$
33. $9\overline{)45,612}$
34. $8\overline{)52,056}$

35. $20\overline{)4,780}$
36. $30\overline{)6,510}$
37. $40\overline{)9,690}$
38. $50\overline{)7,640}$

39. $17\overline{)51}$
40. $23\overline{)92}$
41. $32\overline{)69}$
42. $28\overline{)55}$

43. $34\overline{)952}$
44. $27\overline{)783}$
45. $19\overline{)842}$
46. $22\overline{)314}$

47. $26\overline{)9,334}$
48. $35\overline{)4,655}$
49. $18\overline{)8,935}$
50. $31\overline{)4,314}$

51. $48\overline{)288}$
52. $58\overline{)522}$
53. $46\overline{)245}$
54. $92\overline{)578}$

55. $62\overline{)1,612}$
56. $24\overline{)1,824}$
57. $52\overline{)1,894}$
58. $37\overline{)1,967}$

59. $26\overline{)66,794}$
60. $41\overline{)97,129}$
61. $39\overline{)76,349}$
62. $65\overline{)88,341}$

63. $53\overline{)50,668}$
64. $28\overline{)21,084}$
65. $67\overline{)29,581}$
66. $41\overline{)38,997}$

67. $23\overline{)184}$
68. $34\overline{)238}$
69. $37\overline{)2,559}$
70. $63\overline{)2,839}$

71. $47\overline{)38,681}$
72. $29\overline{)25,926}$
73. $47\overline{)92,063}$
74. $35\overline{)69,088}$

75. $3\overline{)\$4.68}$
76. $7\overline{)\$8.05}$
77. $4\overline{)\$92.92}$
78. $2\overline{)\$31.56}$

79. $21\overline{)\$5.46}$
80. $18\overline{)\$5.94}$
81. $35\overline{)\$39.55}$
82. $26\overline{)\$82.16}$

Problem Solving

A rectangular playground is 50 m long and 30 m wide. How much fencing is needed to fence the playground?

PLAN   **Step 1**   Draw a picture.
            Step 2   What must you do
                      to solve the problem?

SOLVE Perimeter $= 50 + 30 + 50 + 30$
                       $= 160$ m

So, 160 m of fencing is needed.

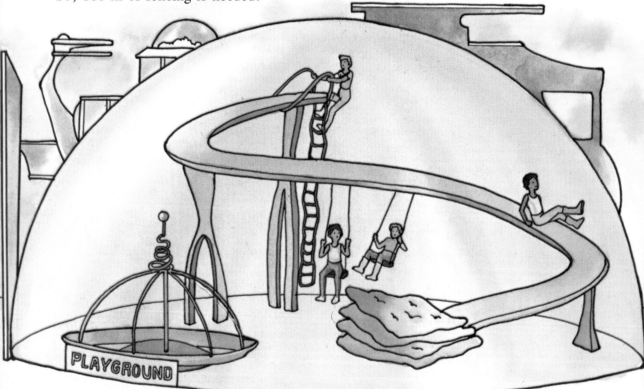

A. Solve. Draw a picture for each problem.

1. Bill wants to frame a playground sign 50 cm long and 80 cm wide. How much wood does he need?

2. Viola mows the lawn in the playground. It is 20 m by 15 m. How many square meters is this?

Solve.

1. Mrs. Schwartz had a 6-m strip of outdoor carpeting. She used 2.52 m on the steps and 2.75 m near the slide. How much is left?

2. David, Rod, and Betty shared a pie equally. David gave $\frac{1}{2}$ of his piece to Kichiko. What part of the pie did Kichiko get?

3. Joe wants to fence a yard 50 m long and 80 m wide. How much fencing does he need?

4. Ellen weeds a flower bed 4 m long and 5 m wide. How many square meters is this?

5. Susan drew pictures of 4 out of 20 children. One-half of her drawings were in charcoal. How many was that?

6. Mr. Eng walks 10 km to the park. He walks $7\frac{3}{4}$ km and then rests. How far does he still have to walk?

★ 7. One play area is 9 m long and 4 m wide. A second play area is a square with the same area as the first. What are the dimensions of the second play area?

Scale Drawings

Here is a scale drawing of a dog. The drawing is $\frac{1}{6}$ the size of the dog. The dog is 6 times the size of the drawing. The ratio used is 1 to 6.

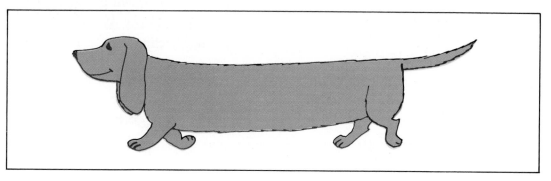

Size of drawing	*Actual Size*
Head 2 cm	Head 12 cm (2 × 6 = 12)
Body 7 cm	Body 42 cm (7 × 6 = 42)
Tail 2 cm	Tail 12 cm (2 × 6 = 12)

A. Here is a scale drawing of a room. The drawing is $\frac{1}{12}$ of the actual size.

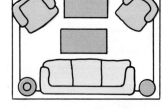

1. What is the ratio used?

2. Measure the length. What is the actual length?

3. Measure the width. What is the actual width?

B. This scale drawing of a snail is twice the actual size.

4. What is the ratio used?

5. Measure the diameter of the snail. What is the actual diameter?

▶ A scale drawing of an object is the same shape as the object, but the size may be different.

Practice

This scale drawing of a bug is 5 times the bug's actual size.

1. What is the ratio used?

2. Measure the length of the bug.

3. What is the actual length?

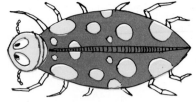

The scale drawing of the floor of a doll house is $\frac{1}{8}$ the actual size.
Complete the table.

Living room	Dining room	Kitchen
Master bedroom	Bath	Child's bedroom

		Size in drawing	Actual size
	Length of living room	4 cm	32 cm
4.	Width of living room		
5.	Width of dining room		
6.	Length of kitchen		
7.	Length of master bedroom		
8.	Width of bathroom		
9.	Length of child's bedroom		

★ **10.** Make a scale drawing of your desk, $\frac{1}{4}$ the actual size.

Map Reading

The map scale shows that 1 cm on the map stands for 100 km of actual distance.

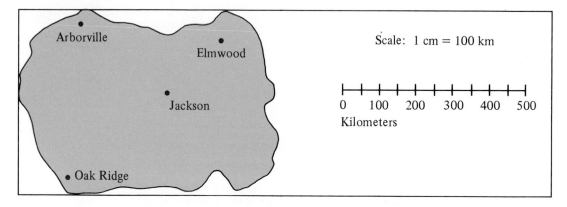

A. We can use a piece of string and the scale of kilometers to find the approximate distance between cities.

    1. Place the end of your string at Elmwood. Stretch the string to Jackson. Mark the distance on your string.

    2. Place the end of the string at 0 on the scale. Read the scale at the place where you marked the string.

    3. What is the approximate distance from Elmwood to Jackson?

B. Find the approximate distances between the cities. Use the steps listed above.

    4. Jackson to Oak Ridge

    5. Oak Ridge to Arborville

C. On this map, a map distance of 1 cm means an actual distance of 3 km. Use your ruler to find the approximate distance between the houses.

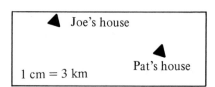

D. On the map in part C, what map distance would you use to show two houses that are 12 km apart?

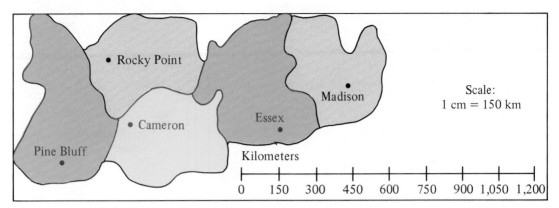

Use a piece of string and the scale of kilometers to find the approximate distances between the cities.

1. Pine Bluff to Rocky Point

2. Pine Bluff to Madison

3. Rocky Point to Essex

4. Cameron to Madison

Use your ruler to find the approximate distances.

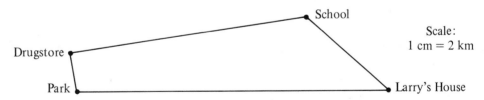

5. Larry's house to school

6. Park to drugstore

7. Drugstore to school

8. Jill lives 14 km from Larry. What map distance will show this?

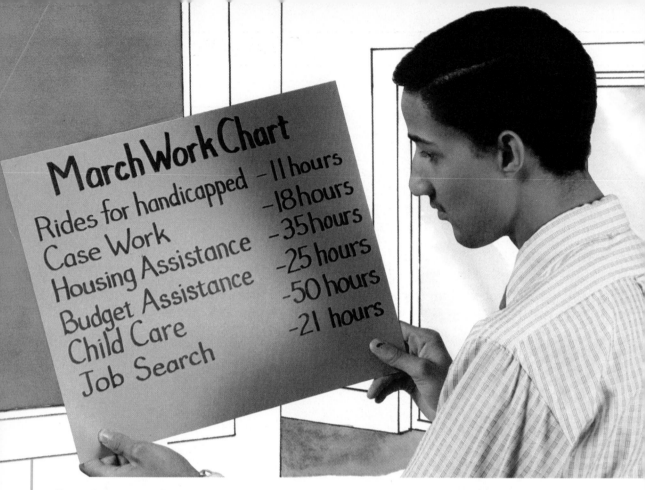

March Work Chart

Rides for handicapped	– 11 hours
Case Work	– 18 hours
Housing Assistance	– 35 hours
Budget Assistance	– 25 hours
Child Care	– 50 hours
Job Search	– 21 hours

Problem Solving • Social Service Aides

1. On what job did Chris spend the least time? [HINT: Look at the chart.]

2. On what job did he spend about $\frac{1}{2}$ as much time as housing assistance?

3. On what job did he spend twice as much time as budget assistance?

4. How many hours did he work in March?

5. In February, Chris worked 17 hours less than in March. How many hours did Chris work in February?

6. Chris worked 4 weeks in March. What was the average number of hours he worked each week?

7. In one week, the agency spent $774 for salaries and $325 for rent. Estimate the total amount spent on salaries and rent.

8. The office building has 110 workers on each floor. There are 10 floors. About how many workers are there in all?

Find the areas. *(322, 324)*

1.

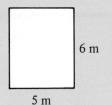

6 m

5 m

2.

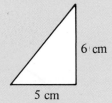

3 cm

8 cm

3.

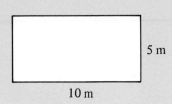

5 m

10 m

4.

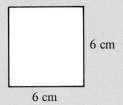

6 cm

6 cm

5.

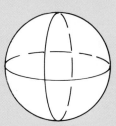

6 cm

5 cm

6.

5 cm

10 cm

Name the figures. *(326)*

7.

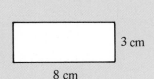

8.

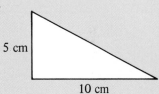

9.

10. Give the number of faces, edges, and vertices for the rectangular prism. *(326)*

11. Find the volume of the *(328)* rectangular prism.

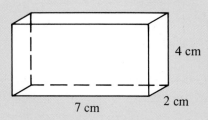

4 cm

7 cm

2 cm

Solve. *(332, 336)*

12. How many square meters of carpet will cover the floor of a room 7 m long and 9 m wide?

13. On a map, 1 cm represents 25 m. What is the actual distance for 7 cm on the map?

Find the areas. *(322, 324)*

1.

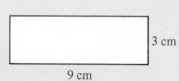

3 cm

9 cm

2.

6 m

7 m

3.

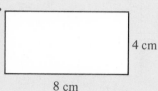

4 cm

8 cm

4.

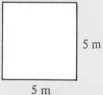

5 m

5 m

5.

5 cm

9 cm

6.

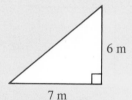

6 m

7 m

Name the figures. *(326)*

7.

8.

9.

10. Give the number of faces, edges, and vertices for the rectangular prism. *(326)*

11. Find the volume of the
(328) rectangular prism.

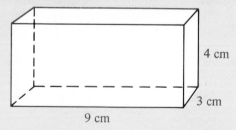

4 cm

3 cm

9 cm

Solve. *(332, 336)*

12. Tim's garden is 9 m long and 6 m wide. What is the area?

13. On a map, 1 cm represents 50 km. What is the actual distance for 8 cm on the map?

Basic Skills Check

1. Jill bought a book for $3.95, a writing pad for $0.59, and a pen for $0.89. What was her total bill?

   A $4.43   B $5.33

   C $5.43   D $5.63

2. Today is Friday. What day will it be 4 days from now?

   E Tuesday   F Wednesday

   G Sunday   H Monday

3. Mr. Lee wants to put a fence around his garden. His garden is 13 m by 20 m. How many meters of fencing are needed?

   A 260 m   B 66 m

   C 56 m   D 33 m

4. Find the volume.

   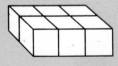

   E 2 ft³   F 4 ft³

   G 5 ft³   H 6 ft³

5. Janice bought 2 lbs of cheese. She used 7 ozs of it in a recipe. How much cheese is left?

   A 9 oz   B 1 lb

   C 1 lb 3 oz   D 1 lb 9 oz

6. How many minutes are there in 5 hours?

   E 360 minutes   F 300 minutes

   G 250 minutes   H 60 minutes

7. Barry wants to buy a used bicycle for $23.75. He has $20. How much more money does he need?

   A $16.25   B $7.75

   C $7.25   D $3.75

8. The graph below shows the number of games won by teams A, B, C and D. Which team won the most games?

   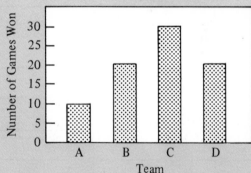

   E Team A   F Team B

   G Team D   H Team C

9. Miss Magin drove 268 km in her new car. She used 67 liters of gas. How many kilometers per liter does her car get?

   A 3   B 4

   C 7   D 18

Bar Graphs

Three students took a survey. They wanted to find out how many students had birthdays in January, February, March, and April. They showed the same information in different ways.

Judy used a tally.

BIRTH MONTHS

MONTH	TALLY
January	⊥⊦⊦⊦ ‖
February	‖|
March	⊦⊦⊦⊥
April	‖‖

Roberto used cards with students' names.

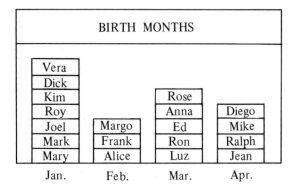

BIRTH MONTHS			
Vera			
Dick			
Kim		Rose	
Roy		Anna	Diego
Joel	Margo	Ed	Mike
Mark	Frank	Ron	Ralph
Mary	Alice	Luz	Jean
Jan.	Feb.	Mar.	Apr.

Liz used a bar graph.

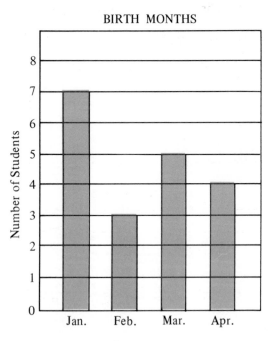

BIRTH MONTHS

1. Which month had the most birthdays?

2. How many birthdays were there in that month?

3. Which way makes it easier to find the information?

CHAPTER 13

GRAPHS AND PROBABILITY

This bar graph shows some of the favorite hobbies of some students.

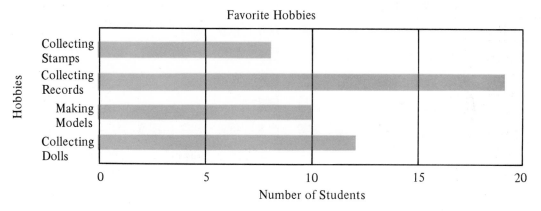

4. What is the title of the graph?

5. What is shown along the bottom?

6. What is shown along the side?

7. How many students make models?

8. Do more students collect dolls or stamps?

9. What is the most popular hobby?

This bar graph shows the number of pets some students have.

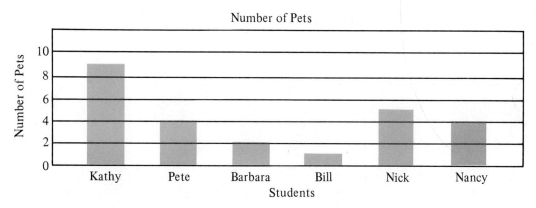

10. Who had the least number of pets?

11. How many pets did Nick have?

12. Which people had the same number of pets?

13. What was the total number of pets?

Pictographs

Pictographs use pictures to show information.
This pictograph shows how long some animals live.

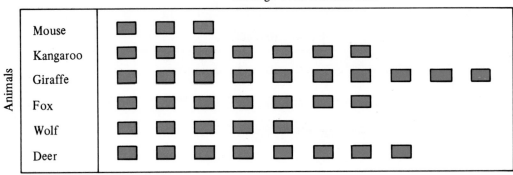

Average Years Animals Live

Animals		
Mouse	▪ ▪ ▪	
Kangaroo	▪ ▪ ▪ ▪ ▪ ▪ ▪	
Giraffe	▪ ▪ ▪ ▪ ▪ ▪ ▪ ▪ ▪ ▪	
Fox	▪ ▪ ▪ ▪ ▪ ▪ ▪	
Wolf	▪ ▪ ▪ ▪ ▪	
Deer	▪ ▪ ▪ ▪ ▪ ▪ ▪ ▪	

Each symbol ▪ stands for 1 year

A. Look at the graph.

1. What does the symbol ▪ stand for?

2. What is shown on the side?

3. How long does a kangaroo live?

4. Which animal lives the longest?

5. How would 12 years be shown?

Heights of Buildings

Buildings	
Sears Tower	▲ ▲ ▲ ▲ ▲ ▲ ▲ ▲ ◢
John Hancock Center	▲ ▲ ▲ ▲ ▲ ▲ ◢
Transamerica Pyramid	▲ ▲ ▲ ▲ ▲
World Trade Center	▲ ▲ ▲ ▲ ▲ ▲ ▲ ▲
Empire State Building	▲ ▲ ▲ ▲ ▲ ▲ ▲ ◢

Each symbol ▲ stands for 50 meters

1. What does the pictograph show?

2. What does each symbol ▲ stand for?

3. How tall is the Empire State Building?

4. Which building is the tallest?

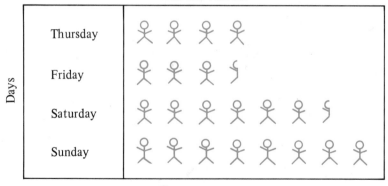

Museum Visitors

Days	
Thursday	☺ ☺ ☺ ☺
Friday	☺ ☺ ☺ ⸮
Saturday	☺ ☺ ☺ ☺ ☺ ☺ ⸮
Sunday	☺ ☺ ☺ ☺ ☺ ☺ ☺ ☺

Each symbol ☺ stands for 100 visitors

5. Which day did the museum have the least number of visitors?

6. How many visitors were there on Saturday?

7. On which day were there 350 visitors?

8. What was the total number of visitors during the four days?

Making a Bar Graph

Ralph made a bar graph to show how
much money he spent each day for
four days. He used this information:

Monday: $5.00
Tuesday: $3.00
Wednesday: $4.50
Thursday: $4.00

A. Ralph used graph paper, a pencil,
and a straightedge to make a
graph.

Step 1 Write a title.

1. What is the title of Ralph's
   graph?

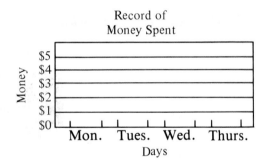

Record of
Money Spent

Step 2 Set up a side or vertical
scale. Start at zero.

2. What is shown along the
   vertical scale?

3. How did Ralph label the
   vertical scale?

Step 3 Set up a bottom or
horizontal scale.

4. What is shown along the
   horizontal scale?

5. Copy and complete the graph.
   Make the bars the same width
   and the same distance apart.

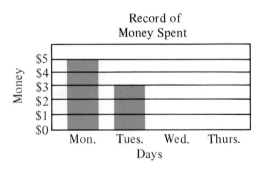

Record of
Money Spent

B. Make a graph using the information in the chart.

CINDY'S WALKING RECORD

Thursday	2 km
Friday	$1\frac{1}{2}$ km
Saturday	5 km
Sunday	$4\frac{1}{2}$ km

Practice

Make bar graphs using the information in the charts below.

1. FAVORITE SEASONS

Spring	7 votes
Summer	8 votes
Autumn	3 votes
Winter	5 votes

2. TEST SCORES

English	95
Math	100
History	80
Science	90

3. VISITORS DURING SCHOOL WEEK

Monday	20
Tuesday	42
Wednesday	35
Thursday	40
Friday	50

4. HOURS CLASS TEAM PRACTICED

1st week	5
2nd week	$6\frac{1}{2}$
3rd week	$4\frac{1}{2}$
4th week	5

Broken-line Graphs

Broken-line graphs are used to show change.
Mrs. Brown's class planted seeds. They kept a record of how
many plants they had at the end of each week.

A. Look at the graph.

   1. What is the title?

   2. What is shown along the bottom?

   3. What is shown along the side?

   4. How many plants were there at the end of the second week?

   5. Between the second and third weeks, was there an increase or decrease in the number of plants?

The Crafts Club made candles to sell.
They kept a record of how many candles were made in one week.

B. Look at the graph.

   6. How many candles were made on Wednesday?

   7. What is the difference between the number of candles made on Wednesday and Thursday?

   8. On which days did the number of candles made decrease from the day before?

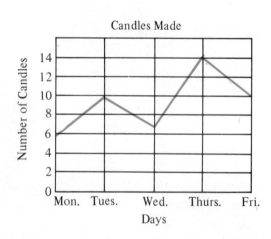

   9. What was the total number of candles made?

Look at the graph titled Temperature Record.

1. What was the highest temperature?

2. What was the lowest temperature?

3. What was the temperature at 10 am?

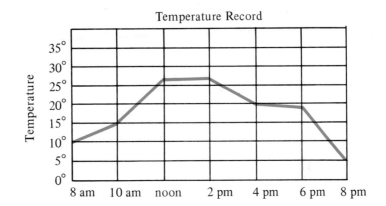

Temperature Record

4. Between what hours did the temperature remain the same?

5. Between what hours was the greatest increase?

Look at the graph titled Linda's Test Scores.

6. What was Linda's highest test score?

7. What was her lowest test score?

8. On which three tests did Linda have the same score?

9. What was her score on the second test?

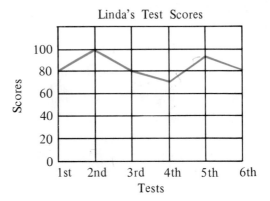

Linda's Test Scores

10. What was the difference between the scores on the second and fourth tests?

11. Which test showed the greatest decrease?

Circle Graphs

Jay's class voted for their favorite kinds of television shows. This circle graph shows the results.

A. Look at the graph.

    1. What kinds of television shows were voted on?

    2. What was the favorite kind of show?

    3. What was the least favorite?

    4. Which kind of show received about $\frac{1}{2}$ of all votes?

Favorite TV Shows

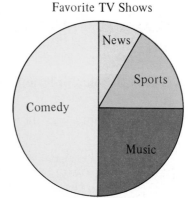

B. Theresa made this circle graph showing how she spent her allowance. She showed what fraction of the total she spent on each item.

    5. On what did Theresa spend the most money?

    6. On what two items did she spend the same amount?

    7. On what item did she spend $\frac{1}{4}$ of her allowance?

How Theresa Spent Her Allowance

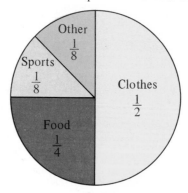

    8. Her allowance was $8. How much money did she spend on clothes?

    9. Add the fractions. What is their sum?

Look at the graph titled Favorite Sports.

1. Which sport received the most votes?

2. Which was more popular, hockey or basketball?

3. Which was more popular, football or baseball?

4. Which sports received about the same number of votes?

5. Which sport received about $\frac{1}{4}$ of the votes?

Favorite Sports

Club Members

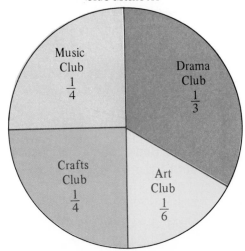

Look at the graph showing club members.

6. Which club had the most members?

7. Which club had the fewest members?

8. Which clubs had about the same number of members?

9. The total number of members in all of the clubs was 100. How many were in the Music Club?

10. Add the fractions. What is their sum?

1. What was the favorite subject?
(342)

2. What subject got 14 votes?

3. How many votes did reading get?

4. What was the total number of votes?

Number of Students in Each Grade

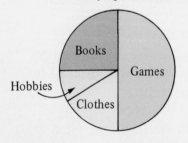

𝔁 stands for 20 students.

8. Which days had the same number
(348) of sales?

9. Which day had a decrease in sales from the day before?

10. How many toys were sold on Thursday?

How Betty Spent her Money

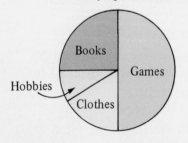

Favorite Subjects

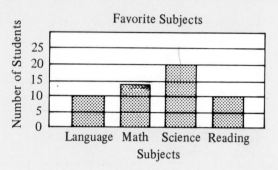

5. Which grade had the least number
(344) of students?

6. How many students were in the fourth grade?

7. Which grade had 100 students?

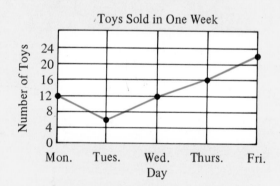

Toys Sold in One Week

11. What did Betty spend the least
(350) amount of money on?

12. What did she spend about $\frac{1}{2}$ of her money on?

13. Which did she spend more on, books or clothes?

Keeping Fit

Add.

1. 57
  + 35

2. 269
  + 107

3. 499
  + 512

4. 860
  + 413

5. 973
  + 219

6. 6,832
  + 2,741

Subtract.

7. 73
  − 44

8. 88
  − 36

9. 384
  − 159

10. 426
  − 282

11. 502
  − 427

12. 676
  − 300

13. 847
  − 698

14. 924
  − 567

15. 2,965
  − 1,786

16. 3,737
  − 2,671

17. 4,172
  − 388

18. 6,654
  − 4,656

Multiply.

19. 84
  × 6

20. 92
  × 7

21. 621
  × 8

22. 717
  × 11

23. 810
  × 19

24. 936
  × 28

25. 435
  × 23

26. 49
  × 37

27. 58
  × 43

28. 275
  × 29

29. 392
  × 47

30. 368
  × 164

31. 407
  × 111

32. 473
  × 213

Divide.

33. $20\overline{)160}$

34. $18\overline{)595}$

35. $10\overline{)1,600}$

36. $31\overline{)715}$

37. $66\overline{)548}$

38. $71\overline{)266}$

39. $53\overline{)4,134}$

40. $47\overline{)5,160}$

41. $62\overline{)6,698}$

42. $83\overline{)7,179}$

43. $77\overline{)8,312}$

44. $92\overline{)9,228}$

Rename in simplest form.

45. $\frac{14}{28}$

46. $\frac{16}{48}$

47. $\frac{18}{36}$

48. $\frac{27}{36}$

49. $\frac{9}{45}$

50. $\frac{3}{21}$

51. $\frac{12}{18}$

52. $\frac{4}{20}$

53. $\frac{12}{15}$

54. $\frac{17}{51}$

55. $\frac{30}{45}$

56. $\frac{40}{50}$

57. $\frac{5}{30}$

58. $\frac{32}{64}$

59. $\frac{8}{64}$

60. $\frac{11}{44}$

61. $\frac{3}{42}$

62. $\frac{56}{64}$

Find the product. Name in simplest form.

63. $\frac{3}{8} \times \frac{1}{2}$

64. $\frac{2}{3} \times \frac{3}{4}$

65. $\frac{1}{4} \times \frac{3}{5}$

66. $\frac{3}{4} \times \frac{8}{9}$

67. $\frac{1}{6} \times \frac{1}{8}$

68. $\frac{4}{5} \times \frac{1}{8}$

69. $\frac{5}{6} \times \frac{1}{2}$

70. $\frac{1}{3} \times \frac{9}{10}$

Problem Solving

Ramona bought 17 postcards for her collection. She now has 32. How many postcards did she have to start?

PLAN: Write a number sentence.
$$n + 17 = 32$$

SOLVE: $n + 17 = 32$
$$n = 15$$

So, Ramona had 15 postcards.

Write a number sentence for each problem. Solve.

1. Meredith's hobby is writing crossword puzzles. It takes her 2 hours to write one puzzle. Last month she spent 26 hours on her hobby. How many puzzles did she write?

2. The pieces for Aaron's model car kit came in 4 bags. There were 96 pieces in all. How many pieces were there in each bag?

Practice

Write a number sentence for each problem. Solve.

1. Phil gave away 68 of his trading cards. Now he only has 97. How many cards did he have to begin with?

2. Jack added 45 stamps to his collection this month. He now has 183 stamps. How many did he have before?

3. Maryanne sold 17 miniature cars from her collection. She has 45 cars left. How many cars were in her collection before she sold the 17 cars?

4. Jane likes to build model boats. It takes her 3 hours to build each one. She spent a total of 54 hours building boats. How many did she build?

5. Tim had a large shell collection. On a trip, he found 37 more shells. Now he has 175. How many shells did he have before his trip?

6. Andy gave 16 coins in his collection to his friends. He now has 84 coins. How many coins did he have to start with?

7. Rosa's hobby is making paper planes. She divided her collection into 12 squadrons. There were 14 planes in each squadron. How many planes did she make altogether?

8. Sarah divided her magazine collection among 7 of her friends. She gave each friend 14 magazines. How many did she have to start?

Graphing Ordered Pairs

A cat is in the window at Apartment 4, Floor 3. Another way to say this is (4, 3). To find the window with the cat in it, you must move across 4 and up 3.

(4, 3) is called an **ordered pair** of numbers.

A. Write the ordered pair to show which window has each.

    1. Red flowers   **2.** A boy   **3.** Green curtains   **4.** A girl

B. What is in the window described by each ordered pair?

    5. (3, 4)   **6.** (1, 1)   **7.** (2, 3)   **8.** (2, 1)   **9.** (3, 2)

C. Ordered pairs can be graphed.

A is at $(1, 2)$. *B* is at $(0, 5)$.

10. What is the ordered pair for *E*?

11. What is the ordered pair for *C*?

12. What letter is at $(2, 0)$?

13. What letter is at $(2, 4)$?

D. To mark $(4, 3)$ on graph paper, move across 4 and up 3. Use graph paper to mark these points.

14. $(1, 5)$ **15.** $(4, 0)$ **16.** $(3, 7)$ **17.** $(6, 6)$ **18.** $(0, 1)$

Practice

What letter is at each ordered pair?
Write the words.

1. $(2, 2)$ $(3, 7)$ $(5, 3)$ $(3, 3)$

2. $(3, 3)$ $(6, 0)$ $(7, 2)$ $(0, 5)$

3. $(1, 6)$ $(6, 0)$ $(7, 6)$ $(0, 1)$

4. $(7, 6)$ $(0, 1)$ $(0, 5)$ $(1, 6)$

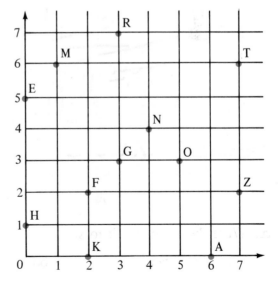

What are the ordered pairs for each letter?

5. tank   **6.** game

7. maze   **8.** fort

Use graph paper. Mark these points.

9. $(1, 1)$ **10.** $(0, 3)$ **11.** $(6, 1)$ **12.** $(5, 4)$ **13.** $(2, 7)$

14. $(4, 4)$ **15.** $(7, 3)$ **16.** $(4, 6)$ **17.** $(1, 0)$ **18.** $(2, 5)$

Probability

Lee had three pencils in his pocket.
One was red, one was yellow, and one was green.
Without looking, he took one pencil out.
The possible outcomes were a red pencil, a
yellow pencil, or a green pencil.
The probability of Lee's picking a red pencil
was 1 out of 3, or $\frac{1}{3}$.

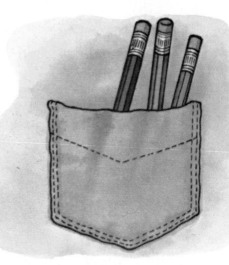

A. Lee put all three pencils back in his pocket.

   1. What was the probability that he would pick a green pencil?

   2. What was the probability that he would pick a yellow pencil?

B. Ellen tossed a coin.

   3. Name the possible outcomes.

   4. What was the probability that it would land on heads?

   5. What was the probability that it would land on tails?

C. Look at the spinner. The probability that the arrow will
   land on yellow is $\frac{2}{5}$.

   6. Name the possible outcomes.

   7. What is the probability that
   the arrow will land on red?

   8. What is the probability that it will land on blue?

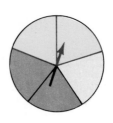

D. Sue picks one marble at a time
   without looking.

   9. What is the probability that
   she will pick a black marble?

   10. What is the probability that
   she will pick a green marble?

What is the probability of the arrow pointing to blue?

1. 　　**2.** 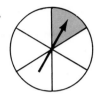　　**3.** 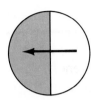　　**4.**

5. 　　**6.** 　　**7.** 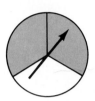　　**8.**

These cards are placed in a box. What is the probability of choosing each color?

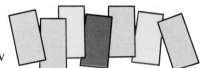

9. Blue　　　　**10.** Red　　　　**11.** Yellow

Ann, Carol, and Alberto each placed their name in the hat.

12. What is the probability of picking Carol's name?

13. What is the probability of picking a girl's name?

14. What is the probability of picking a boy's name?

Lynn will pick one block at a time without looking.

★ **15.** What is the probability of picking a red block?

★ **16.** What is the probability of picking a block?

★ **17.** What is the probability of picking a blue block?

★ **18.** What is the probability of picking a marble?

Probability Activities

Make a spinner like this one.

A. What is the probability of the arrow stopping on:

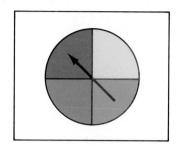

    1. Red?   **2.** Blue?

    3. Yellow?   **4.** Green?

Notice that each of these probabilities is the same. This means that the arrow should stop on each color about the same number of times.

B. Use your spinner to show this. Spin it 100 times. Keep a tally of the color it lands on.

Red	III
Blue	IIII
Yellow	IIII I
Green	III

    5. Did the arrow point to each color about the same number of times?

C. Make a spinner like this one.

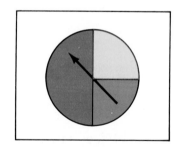

    6. What is the probability of the arrow stopping on each of the colors?

Now spin the spinner 100 times.

    7. What do you think will happen? Keep a tally of the color it lands on.

D. Knowing the probability helps us to predict a result.

    8. What is the probability of picking a red card? A white card? A green card?

If you picked a card 15 times, replacing it each time, you could expect these results.

Pick red: $\frac{1}{3} \times 15 = 5$ Pick white: $\frac{1}{3} \times 15 = 5$ Pick green: $\frac{1}{3} \times 15 = 5$

9. Put a red, white, and green card in a bag. Pick a card 30 times, replacing it each time. Predict about how many times you would pick each kind of card. Keep a tally. Did you predict correctly?

E. Now make 5 cards like these.

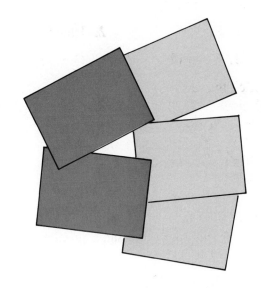

10. What is the probability of picking a red card? A blue card? Are the probabilities equal?

11. Put the cards in a bag. If you picked a card 45 times, replacing it each time, predict how many times you would pick a red card. Pick the cards. Did you predict correctly?

F. Make 4 cards like these. Put them in a bag. Pick one card 60 times, replacing it each time.

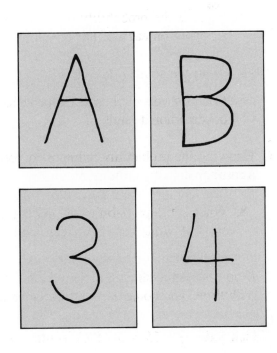

12. Predict how many times you would expect to pick the 4.

13. Predict how many times you would expect to pick the A.

14. Predict how many times you would expect to pick a letter.

15. Pick the cards. Keep a tally. How close were your predictions?

Problem Solving • Broadcast Technicians

1. Ms. Stewart is a broadcast technician. She and other technicians set-up and operated equipment during the Presidential election. Ms. Stewart usually works a 35-hour week. During the election week she worked 57 hours. For each hour worked over 35, she receives overtime pay. For how many hours did she receive overtime pay?

2. Three broadcast technicians earned $250, $180, and $278 respectively, one week. What was their average salary?

3. Mr. Mitchell earned $260.50 one week. There was $48.35 deducted from his paycheck for taxes and insurance. How much was his take-home pay?

4. More people are now buying color television sets. Approximately 15 million television sets were sold one year. Of these, about $\frac{3}{5}$ were color sets. How many color sets were sold that year?

5. In a recent year, there were 386 radio and television stations in Pennsylvania. There were 255 stations in Wisconsin, 48 in Hawaii, and 80 in Utah. How many radio and television stations were there in all four states?

1. Which week had the greatest
(342) number of sales?

2. During which week were 21
(342) bikes sold?

3. How many bikes were sold
(342) during the first week?

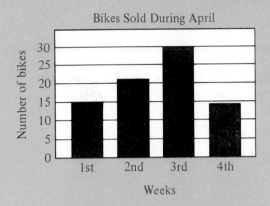

Bikes Sold During April

4. Which item had the most
(350) sales?

5. Which items had about the
(350) same number of sales?

6. Which item was about $\frac{1}{4}$ of
(350) the total sales?

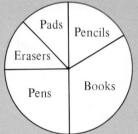

Items Sold at the Bookstore

Write the ordered pair for each point.
Use the graph at the right. *(356)*

7. A   **8.** B

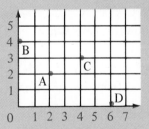

9. C   **10.** D

What is the probability of the arrow's stopping on red? *(358)*

11. 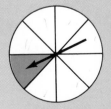   **12.** 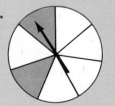   **13.** 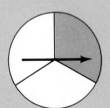   **14.**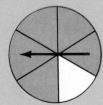

1. On which days was the
(348) snowfall the same?

2. Which day showed a
(348) decrease in the snowfall?

3. How many centimeters did it
(348) snow on Wednesday?

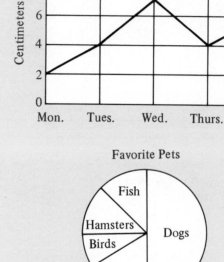

Record of Snowfall

4. Which pet got about $\frac{1}{2}$ of the
(350) votes?

5. Which pet got the least
(350) number of votes?

6. Which animals got about the
(350) same number of votes?

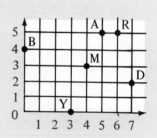

Favorite Pets

Write the letter that names each ordered pair.
Use the graph at the right. (356)

7. (0, 4)   **8.** (6, 5)

9. (3, 0)   **10.** (4, 3)

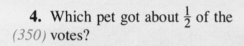

What is the probability of picking a blue marble? (358)

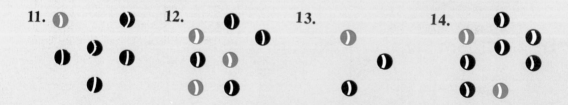

11.   **12.**   **13.**   **14.**

1. Carlos bought 3 apples for 11¢ each and 3 peaches for 18¢ each. How much did he pay for the fruit?

   A 87¢

   B 78¢

   C 77¢

   D 29¢

2. Juanita drove 604 km on the first day of her vacation, 312 km the second day, and 402 km on the third day. How many kilometers did Juanita drive in all?

   E 1,218 km

   F 1,318 km

   G 1,428 km

   H 2,220 km

3. How many cases of cookies did Jay sell?

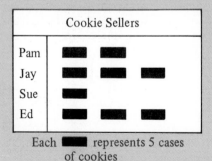

   Each ▬ represents 5 cases of cookies

   A 2 cases

   B 3 cases

   C 10 cases

   D 15 cases

4. One truck carried 1,173 kg of steel. Another carried 2,302 kg. How many more kilograms of steel did the second truck carry?

   E 1,129 kg

   F 1,131 kg

   G 3,475 kg

   H 3,485 kg

5. Three classes were going to the circus. Class A had 32 pupils, class B had 26 pupils, and class C had 36 pupils. Estimate about how many tickets were needed.

   A 70

   B 80

   C 90

   D 100

6. Len played 5 games of baseball. In which game did he have the most hits?

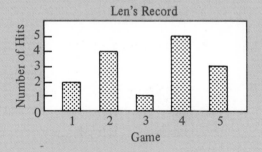

   E Game 1

   F Game 2

   G Game 3

   H Game 4

EXTRA PRACTICE

Add. *(Use with page 30.)*

1.	36 + 45	**2.**	93 + 48	**3.**	74 + 86	**4.**	784 + 94	**5.**	653 + 698	**6.**	743 + 92
7.	527 + 398	**8.**	787 + 956	**9.**	$ 4.85 + 0.73	**10.**	$ 9.71 + 6.39	**11.**	$ 4.32 + 7.64	**12.**	$ 7.85 + 3.94
13.	76 3 + 98	**14.**	65 78 + 94	**15.**	357 468 + 92	**16.**	781 375 + 648	**17.**	$ 3.45 7.98 + 0.56	**18.**	$ 9.78 2.19 + 3.86

★ Find the missing digits.

19. $83 + 3\square + \triangle 7 = 165$ **20.** $637 + 9\square 3 + \triangle 62 = 1,982$

Add. *(Use with page 38.)*

1. 9,364 + 2,875	**2.** 1,203 + 2,125	**3.** 6,875 + 2,093	**4.** 34,861 + 27,495	**5.** $ 384.77 + 899.99
6. 4,379 6,713 + 15,486	**7.** 6,721 1,158 + 3,212	**8.** 27,314 8,596 + 12,378	**9.** 33,149 8,675 + 24,123	**10.** $ 483.67 34.87 + 259.74
11. 38,162 21,235 + 29,145	**12.** 34,125 13,056 41,674 + 8,395	**13.** 6,875 9,341 5,067 + 984	**14.** $ 604.59 137.68 220.75 + 131.62	**15.** $ 153.41 78.92 364.78 + 35.64

★ Solve.

16. $156 + \square = 39 + 156$ **17.** $(\square + 87) + 35 = 98 + (87 + 35)$

Add. *(Use with page 40.)*

1. 135,246 + 532,271	**2.** 614,231 + 294,772	**3.** 753,864 + 8,394	**4.** 125,678 + 34,982	**5.** 738,975 + 246,108
6. 731,486 + 59,271	**7.** 45,167 + 374,198	**8.** $ 6,345.91 + 789.45	**9.** $ 1,567.98 + 3,694.59	**10.** $ 7,534.75 + 38.79
11. 736,591 941,873 + 418,964	**12.** $ 6,748.31 964.83 + 7,413.25	★ **13.** 62,164,389 4,873,123 + 96,486	★ **14.** 13,498,615 52,773,114 + 67,998,713	★ **15.** 76,183,452 9,487,267 + 38,145,362

Estimate the sum. *(Use with page 42.)*

1. 35 + 41	**2.** 37 + 32	**3.** 65 + 24	**4.** 184 + 637	**5.** 516 + 359	**6.** 3,503 + 1,641
7. 65 48 + 34	**8.** 71 39 + 55	**9.** 14 79 + 32	**10.** 47 38 + 31	**11.** 716 115 + 409	**12.** 145 286 + 153
13. 192 356 + 804	**14.** 775 659 + 321	**15.** 843 217 + 463	★**16.** 148 675 329 + 147	★**17.** 375 456 813 + 284	★**18.** 738 259 716 + 832

Round each addend to the nearest dollar. Estimate the sum.

19. $ 4.75 + 3.58	**20.** $ 3.64 + 2.49	**21.** $ 9.47 3.56 + 2.87	**22.** $ 5.55 3.48 + 2.09	★**23.** $ 48.16 29.56 + 34.18	★**24.** $ 36.89 41.73 + 2.56

Add. *(Use with page 45.)*

1. 7 5 + 3	**2.** 5 6 4 + 8	**3.** 1 3 9 6 + 4	**4.** 3 8 7 6 + 2	**5.** 9 6 1 8 4 + 3
6. 94 + 83	**7.** 645 + 384	**8.** 667 39 + 483	**9.** $ 3.49 0.73 + 2.86	**10.** $ 7.56 2.89 + 4.15
11. 6,783 + 2,145	**12.** 9,684 + 1,025	**13.** $ 16.89 + 64.73	**14.** 86,473 + 29,675	**15.** 75,867 + 32,493
16. $ 810.96 + 394.53	**17.** 12,736 58,692 + 1,735	**18.** 73,785 27,386 + 49,287	**19.** 65,187 98,413 + 14,562	**20.** 83,146 29,487 + 11,181
21. 14,873 29,671 13,487 + 36,109	**22.** 65,148 39,876 8,145 + 3,475	**23.** 14,863 2,458 6,329 + 38,475	**24.** 155,983 + 374,828	**25.** 632,871 + 286,498
26. 486,361 + 247,113	**27.** $ 5,986.18 + 3,241.86	**28.** $ 3,746.83 + 1,473.52	**29.** 538,674 153,186 + 15,918	**30.** 751,367 9,473 + 38,671

Subtract. *(Use with page 52.)*

1. 837 − 419	**2.** 354 − 129	**3.** 746 − 74	**4.** 985 − 392	**5.** $ 6.36 − 3.52	**6.** $ 7.64 − 4.28
7. 761 − 498	**8.** 417 − 98	**9.** $ 8.73 − 2.59	**10.** 9,473 − 2,184	**11.** 6,543 − 5,982	**12.** 7,364 − 3,983
13. 7,867 − 93	**14.** 6,242 − 135	**15.** 6,927 − 4,719	**16.** 5,643 − 2,471	**17.** $ 96.34 − 4.15	**18.** $ 54.78 − 23.67

★ Find the missing digits.

19. 836 − ?4? = 94

20. 783 − ?9? = 384

21. 2?9? − 1,468 = 1,325

22. 7?2? − 2,637 = 4,589

Subtract. *(Use with page 54.)*

1. 700 − 168	**2.** 600 − 235	**3.** 806 − 459	**4.** 980 − 357	**5.** 400 − 246	**6.** 306 − 299
7. 270 − 143	**8.** 908 − 246	**9.** 4,003 − 2,239	**10.** 5,060 − 4,905	**11.** 8,009 − 7,848	**12.** 7,007 − 6,839
13. 9,090 − 3,785	**14.** 6,000 − 3,489	**15.** 7,500 − 3,498	**16.** $ 60.05 − 39.47	**17.** $ 40.60 − 25.56	**18.** $ 90.00 − 37.95

★ Find the answer. Do the work inside the parentheses first.

19. 180 + (16 − 7)

20. 400 − (59 + 86)

21. 6,005 − (753 − 94)

Subtract. *(Use with page 56.)*

1. 65,543 − 13,629	**2.** 17,493 − 6,635	**3.** 45,319 − 26,456	**4.** 37,272 − 21,584	**5.** 64,539 − 37,869
6. 84,276 − 9,473	**7.** 45,820 − 26,845	**8.** 87,200 − 68,409	**9.** $ 850.00 − 674.79	**10.** $ 342.76 − 74.64
11. 346,189 − 147,206	**12.** 784,291 − 599,684	**13.** 476,291 − 92,674	**14.** 805,609 − 35,788	**15.** 900,601 − 568,793
16. 543,278 − 494,123	**17.** 912,700 − 36,483	**18.** 783,000 − 414,046	**19.** $ 4,168.75 − 487.93	**20.** $ 8,653.01 − 498.67
★ **21.** 6,643,189 − 3,157,263	★ **22.** 7,006,390 − 258,674	★ **23.** $ 63,450.91 − 35,671.98	★ **24.** $ 72,006.74 − 9,487.49	

Subtract. *(Use with page 69.)*

1. 48 − 27	**2.** 86 − 59	**3.** 56 − 37	**4.** 648 − 391	**5.** 736 − 587
6. 800 − 467	**7.** 903 − 286	**8.** $ 7.89 − 3.92	**9.** $ 8.00 − 6.75	**10.** 3,966 − 1,348
11. 7,431 − 2,372	**12.** 3,486 − 2,194	**13.** 4,000 − 2,073	**14.** $ 37.29 − 18.53	**15.** $ 80.03 − 24.56
16. 34,579 − 12,436	**17.** 83,147 − 12,899	**18.** 60,403 − 25,679	**19.** $ 740.00 − 238.75	**20.** $ 603.00 − 498.64
21. 367,482 − 159,394	**22.** 136,748 − 29,753	**23.** 900,473 − 286,592	**24.** $ 6,430.98 − 4,867.43	**25.** 674,281 − 357,673

Multiply. *(Use with page 76.)*

1. 80 × 3	**2.** 40 × 5	**3.** $70 × 9	**4.** 100 × 7	**5.** 300 × 8
6. $700 × 7	**7.** 5,000 × 3	**8.** 6,000 × 7	**9.** $8,000 × 5	**10.** 40,000 × 9
11. 30,000 × 7	**12.** $70,000 × 3	**13.** 9,000 × 4	**14.** 40 × 4	**15.** 600 × 3
16. 80,000 × 9	★ **17.** 100,000 × 5	★ **18.** 700,000 × 4	★ **19.** 300,000 × 8	★ **20.** 900,000 × 6

Multiply. *(Use with page 80.)*

1. 24 × 2	**2.** 81 × 5	**3.** 78 × 4	**4.** 89 × 6	**5.** 37 × 9	**6.** $96 × 8	**7.** $65 × 7
8. 324 × 2	**9.** 632 × 3	**10.** 148 × 2	**11.** 364 × 2	**12.** 608 × 7	**13.** $453 × 5	**14.** $789 × 6
15. 78 × 5	**16.** 486 × 3	**17.** 185 × 4	**18.** $37 × 2	**19.** 367 × 9	**20.** 874 × 3	**21.** $709 × 8

★ Complete.

22. ?4 × 3 ‾‾‾ 222	**23.** ?6? × 8 ‾‾‾ 4,528	**24.** 7? × 6 ‾‾‾ 450	**25.** 6?? × 7 ‾‾‾ 4,361	**26.** ??8 × 5 ‾‾‾ 2,840

Multiply. *(Use with page 82.)*

1. 3,420 × 3	**2.** 6,343 × 2	**3.** 2,173 × 8	**4.** 4,215 × 4	**5.** $6,249 × 8
6. 28,312 × 9	**7.** 16,925 × 6	**8.** 33,724 × 5	**9.** 59,312 × 3	**10.** $42,756 × 5
11. $14.35 × 7	**12.** $30.75 × 9	**13.** $864.98 × 5	**14.** $471.18 × 8	**15.** $300.49 × 6
16. 3,847 × 7	**17.** 98,765 × 3	**18.** 72,526 × 4	**19.** 4,720 × 3	**20.** 94,906 × 8

★ **21.** 34,806,274
     × 3

★ **22.** 14,896,006
     × 7

★ **23.** 45,711,362
     × 5

★ **24.** 86,940,300
     × 4

Multiply. *(Use with page 92.)*

1. 75 × 18	**2.** 36 × 24	**3.** 76 × 37	**4.** 39 × 47	**5.** $82 × 87	**6.** 95 × 74
7. 135 × 32	**8.** 427 × 42	**9.** 398 × 27	**10.** $876 × 94	**11.** 906 × 35	**12.** 547 × 89
13. 55 × 66	**14.** $8.73 × 29	**15.** $4.37 × 52	**16.** 84 × 65	**17.** 153 × 64	**18.** 307 × 99

★ Complete.

19. 43 × 6? ?709	**20.** 58 × 4? 2?68	**21.** 346 × 3? 1?802	**22.** 774 × 5? 44,8?2

Multiply. *(Use with page 94.)*

1. 388 × 123	**2.** 417 × 386	**3.** $374 × 285	**4.** 869 × 273	**5.** 712 × 153	**6.** 843 × 456
7. 343 × 298	**8.** 762 × 845	**9.** 476 × 287	**10.** $7.49 × 308	**11.** 491 × 707	**12.** 605 × 309
13. 487 × 208	**14.** $157 × 809	**15.** 337 × 706	**16.** 815 × 247	**17.** 763 × 898	**18.** 402 × 148
19. $3.49 × 471	**20.** 703 × 205	★ **21.** 3,426 × 184	★ **22.** 3,007 × 259	★ **23.** 7,641 × 302	★ **24.** 4,579 × 813

Solve. *(Use with page 98.)*

1. Sue bought 7 rolls of film for her camera. Each roll cost $4.98. How much did she pay in all?

2. José bought a coat for $49.95 and a hat for $7.75. How much did he spend in all?

3. Mrs. Brown drives 136 miles each week. How many miles does she drive in 52 weeks?

4. Tony bought a model for $7.98. How much change did he get back from a $20 bill?

5. Mr. Weiss sold 256 books in August, 387 books in September, and 189 books in October. How many books did he sell in all?

6. Jane swam 12 laps. Each lap was 35 feet. How many feet did she swim in all?

7. Mr. Thompson baked 7 dozen cookies and 5 dozen brownies. How many cookies and brownies did he bake in all?

8. Sarah made 157 paper roses. Don made 89. How many more roses did Sarah make than Don?

9. Jason made 24 piles of baseball cards. Each pile had 15 cards. How many cards does he have in all?

10. A farmer planted 145 seeds in each of 36 rows. How many seeds did she plant in all?

11. Jan ran for 38 minutes on Sunday, 27 minutes on Monday, and 46 minutes on Tuesday. How long did she run in all?

12. Jill bought a bat for $11.98, a glove for $9.99, and a ball for $6.75. How much change did she get from $50?

Multiply. *(Use with page 99.)*

1. 50×4	2. 600×6	3. $7,000 \times 8$	4. $30,000 \times 9$	5. $80,000 \times 7$
6. 34×2	7. 386×7	8. $1,543 \times 9$	9. $\$38.07 \times 6$	10. $73,004 \times 9$
11. 24×10	12. 75×60	13. 186×90	14. 736×100	15. 849×600
16. 34×23	17. 67×48	18. $\$39 \times 64$	19. 284×25	20. 356×78
21. $\$414 \times 87$	22. $\$1.74 \times 93$	23. 321×137	24. 624×238	25. 705×347
26. 137×209	27. $\$646 \times 131$	28. $\$8.53 \times 134$	29. $\$9.06 \times 257$	30. $\$7.36 \times 305$

Divide. *(Use with page 108.)*

1. 4)88 **2.** 6)96 **3.** 5)75 **4.** 8)96 **5.** 2)84

6. 6)96 **7.** 6)84 **8.** 7)84 **9.** 3)57 **10.** 2)76

11. 3)495 **12.** 4)896 **13.** 6)744 **14.** 7)966 **15.** 4)872

16. 4)184 **17.** 5)390 **18.** 6)252 **19.** 6)138 **20.** 8)608

21. 5)95 **22.** 4)868 **23.** 7)91 **24.** 8)768 **25.** 5)375

Complete.

26. 5)$\overline{?}$ (45) **27.** 8)$\overline{?}$ (63) **28.** 7)$\overline{?}$ (41) **29.** 3)$\overline{?}$ (146) **30.** 4)$\overline{?}$ (238)

Divide. *(Use with page 110.)*

1. 3)88 **2.** 4)95 **3.** 8)97 **4.** 5)86 **5.** 6)93

6. 7)86 **7.** 2)75 **8.** 4)85 **9.** 8)329 **10.** 7)299

11. 6)341 **12.** 6)449 **13.** 7)456 **14.** 3)221 **15.** 9)341

16. 9)649 **17.** 4)143 **18.** 9)431 **19.** 6)79 **20.** 6)215

21. 7)459 **22.** 5)163 **23.** 6)81 **24.** 9)650 **25.** 8)435

★ Complete.

26. 8)$\overline{?}$ (37 r 6) **27.** 6)$\overline{?}$ (15 r 5) **28.** 7)$\overline{?}$ (132 r 4) **29.** 2)$\overline{?}$ (436 r 1) **30.** 3)$\overline{?}$ (236 r 1)

Divide. *(Use with page 116.)*

1. 3)4,162 **2.** 6)7,189 **3.** 5)6,173 **4.** 8)9,175 **5.** 7)7,962

6. 2)5,139 **7.** 8)9,143 **8.** 7)8,619 **9.** 5)8,317 **10.** 6)9,675

11. 4)8,633 **12.** 7)8,389 **13.** 6)86,135 **14.** 3)98,165 **15.** 7)93,206

16. 3)64,280 **17.** 4)76,545 **18.** 5)85,743 **19.** 8)91,006 **20.** 7)78,461

21. 6)71,386 **22.** 3)93,487 **23.** 8)96,345 **24.** 5)93,424 **25.** 6)93,675

★ **26.** 5)634,189 ★ **27.** 3)416,209 ★ **28.** 5)6,310,141 ★ **29.** 8)9,345,874

Divide. *(Use with page 118.)*

1. $4\overline{)2,119}$ **2.** $3\overline{)1,175}$ **3.** $6\overline{)1,271}$ **4.** $5\overline{)1,213}$ **5.** $2\overline{)1,111}$

6. $8\overline{)5,149}$ **7.** $9\overline{)3,794}$ **8.** $7\overline{)1,328}$ **9.** $6\overline{)\$2,708}$ **10.** $7\overline{)3,756}$

11. $8\overline{)62,809}$ **12.** $6\overline{)\$21,473}$ **13.** $7\overline{)25,034}$ **14.** $9\overline{)58,942}$ **15.** $2\overline{)\$19,037}$

16. $4\overline{)14,793}$ **17.** $8\overline{)46,285}$ **18.** $3\overline{)25,280}$ **19.** $5\overline{)\$46,133}$ **20.** $9\overline{)71,348}$

★ **21.** $4\overline{)351,289}$ ★ **22.** $8\overline{)461,049}$ ★ **23.** $5\overline{)3,674,013}$ ★ **24.** $9\overline{)734,014}$

Divide *(Use with page 120.)*

1. $5\overline{)545}$ **2.** $3\overline{)625}$ **3.** $6\overline{)245}$ **4.** $2\overline{)960}$ **5.** $8\overline{)846}$

6. $3\overline{)1,223}$ **7.** $6\overline{)\$1,820}$ **8.** $9\overline{)1,807}$ **9.** $7\overline{)2,735}$ **10.** $5\overline{)\$6,543}$

11. $9\overline{)18,006}$ **12.** $7\overline{)42,028}$ **13.** $8\overline{)87,325}$ **14.** $5\overline{)65,347}$ **15.** $8\overline{)40,062}$

16. $4\overline{)3,635}$ **17.** $6\overline{)25,203}$ **18.** $8\overline{)\$7,124}$ **19.** $5\overline{)27,150}$ **20.** $6\overline{)\$72,045}$

★ **21.** $3\overline{)642,135}$ ★ **22.** $8\overline{)723,471}$ ★ **23.** $6\overline{)1,243,213}$ ★ **24.** $9\overline{)8,146,879}$

Divide. *(Use with page 127.)*

1. $5\overline{)0}$ **2.** $36\overline{)36}$ **3.** $8\overline{)160}$ **4.** $7\overline{)4,200}$ **5.** $8\overline{)64,000}$

6. $5\overline{)75}$ **7.** $8\overline{)\$936}$ **8.** $3\overline{)68}$ **9.** $7\overline{)936}$ **10.** $4\overline{)965}$

11. $8\overline{)9,413}$ **12.** $7\overline{)\$8,367}$ **13.** $4\overline{)56,481}$ **14.** $5\overline{)3,964}$ **15.** $8\overline{)62,374}$

16. $9\overline{)73,453}$ **17.** $5\overline{)1,043}$ **18.** $4\overline{)\$3,237}$ **19.** $8\overline{)48,373}$ **20.** $6\overline{)49,253}$

Divide. *(Use with page 132.)*

1. $30\overline{)56}$ **2.** $80\overline{)94}$ **3.** $20\overline{)73}$ **4.** $20\overline{)871}$ **5.** $40\overline{)387}$

6. $50\overline{)364}$ **7.** $70\overline{)148}$ **8.** $60\overline{)487}$ **9.** $40\overline{)8,712}$ **10.** $50\overline{)9,371}$

11. $80\overline{)9,712}$ **12.** $30\overline{)8,647}$ **13.** $60\overline{)4,839}$ **14.** $90\overline{)7,426}$ **15.** $70\overline{)3,480}$

16. $60\overline{)93}$ **17.** $40\overline{)674}$ **18.** $80\overline{)9,314}$ **19.** $60\overline{)3,777}$ **20.** $50\overline{)5,619}$

★ Complete.

21. $70\overline{)?}\ \ ^{8r61}$ **22.** $50\overline{)?}\ \ ^{37r28}$ **23.** $60\overline{)?}\ \ ^{143r25}$ **24.** $80\overline{)?}\ \ ^{49r36}$

Divide. *(Use with page 134.)*

1. $32\overline{)64}$ 2. $43\overline{)86}$ 3. $57\overline{)98}$ 4. $23\overline{)96}$ 5. $67\overline{)93}$

6. $47\overline{)631}$ 7. $32\overline{)769}$ 8. $54\overline{)819}$ 9. $72\overline{)866}$ 10. $52\overline{)785}$

11. $23\overline{)716}$ 12. $36\overline{)4,619}$ 13. $84\overline{)9,147}$ 14. $67\overline{)8,137}$ 15. $23\overline{)5,092}$

16. $41\overline{)8,897}$ 17. $32\overline{)7,556}$ 18. $24\overline{)3,144}$ 19. $26\overline{)5,841}$ 20. $56\overline{)9,371}$

21. $46\overline{)981}$ 22. $51\overline{)732}$ 23. $74\overline{)8,161}$ 24. $35\overline{)781}$ 25. $31\overline{)9,884}$

★ Complete.

26. $87\overline{)\,?}^{\,24r18}$ 27. $35\overline{)\,?}^{\,16r24}$ 28. $56\overline{)\,?}^{\,139r4}$ 29. $23\overline{)\,?}^{\,234r28}$

Divide. *(Use with page 136.)*

1. $43\overline{)156}$ 2. $87\overline{)375}$ 3. $42\overline{)259}$ 4. $53\overline{)497}$ 5. $97\overline{)238}$

6. $22\overline{)157}$ 7. $21\overline{)199}$ 8. $71\overline{)486}$ 9. $65\overline{)597}$ 10. $92\overline{)753}$

11. $33\overline{)2,741}$ 12. $84\overline{)7,813}$ 13. $52\overline{)1,887}$ 14. $73\overline{)5,296}$ 15. $64\overline{)2,375}$

16. $91\overline{)8,847}$ 17. $43\overline{)2,740}$ 18. $31\overline{)2,647}$ 19. $62\overline{)3,587}$ 20. $77\overline{)5,599}$

21. $52\overline{)248}$ 22. $41\overline{)314}$ 23. $62\overline{)3,549}$ 24. $83\overline{)634}$ 25. $72\overline{)2,748}$

★ Complete.

26. $65\overline{)\,?}^{\,9r43}$ 27. $32\overline{)\,?}^{\,8r15}$ 28. $43\overline{)\,?}^{\,37r26}$ 29. $74\overline{)\,?}^{\,84r65}$

Divide. *(Use with page 138.)*

1. $23\overline{)48,861}$ 2. $56\overline{)98,135}$ 3. $43\overline{)89,174}$ 4. $52\overline{)61,387}$

5. $42\overline{)96,871}$ 6. $34\overline{)76,183}$ 7. $81\overline{)94,374}$ 8. $73\overline{)86,153}$

9. $61\overline{)35,471}$ 10. $53\overline{)44,781}$ 11. $23\overline{)19,463}$ 12. $42\overline{)31,499}$

13. $71\overline{)48,763}$ 14. $84\overline{)39,983}$ 15. $34\overline{)20,877}$ 16. $62\overline{)41,873}$

17. $43\overline{)79,364}$ 18. $22\overline{)93,486}$ 19. $51\overline{)44,361}$ 20. $73\overline{)69,287}$

★ 21. $34\overline{)898,476}$ ★ 22. $51\overline{)243,672}$ ★ 23. $43\overline{)271,381}$ ★ 24. $71\overline{)346,814}$

Divide. *(Use with page 140.)*

1. 24)196 **2.** 59)368 **3.** 43)418 **4.** 83)571 **5.** 78)637

6. 95)6,374 **7.** 67)4,387 **8.** 57)4,567 **9.** 24)4,274 **10.** 86)4,873

11. 25)70,673 **12.** 78)14,361 **13.** 47)91,121 **14.** 65)12,136 **15.** 31)61,164

16. 18)273 **17.** 57)4,536 **18.** 61)48,311 **19.** 49)178 **20.** 55)5,111

★ **21.** 85)493,115 ★ **22.** 93)371,061 ★ **23.** 47)173,149 ★ **24.** 36)224,137

Divide. *(Use with page 144.)*

1. 5)$5.75 **2.** 7)$4.55 **3.** 8)$51.44 **4.** 3)$45.75

5. 6)$53.76 **6.** 9)$771.03 **7.** 8)$543.84 **8.** 5)$631.75

9. 14)$5.04 **10.** 30)$5.10 **11.** 52)$69.68 **12.** 67)$61.64

13. 73)$60.59 **14.** 29)$105.85 **15.** 45)$550.35 **16.** 83)$283.86

17. 8)$362.56 **18.** 36)$56.16 **19.** 7)$18.13 **20.** 42)$261.66

★ **21.** 8)$1,881.84 ★ **22.** 17)$4,000.27 ★ **23.** 41)$1,461.24 ★ **24.** 56)$5,897.92

Write too much or enough. Solve. *(Use with page 148.)*

1. Andy bought 5 books for $3.98 each. He already has 10 books. How much did he spend in all?

2. Mrs. Adler drove 1,440 miles in all. She drove 96 miles each day. How many days did it take?

3. Julio sold $1.55 worth of candy bars on Monday, $2.95 on Tuesday and $1.75 on Friday. How much did he sell in all?

4. Mr. Sands paid $99.60 for 24 fence posts. He also bought 156 feet of wire. How much was each post?

5. Ms. Olsen bought 5 pounds of meat at $3.75 a pound. She paid with a $20 bill. How much did the meat cost?

6. Sue paid $8.97 for a shirt. Pat paid $10.29 for the same shirt. How much more did Pat pay?

7. Betsy paid $26.25 for 7 movie tickets. She went with 10 friends. How much was each ticket?

8. Maria bought 4 dresses for $55.16. How much change did she receive from $60?

9. Mr. Bello makes $8.50 an hour. How much does he make in an 8-hour day?

10. Mrs. Chin makes $253 a week. Her son makes $179 a week. How much does Mrs. Chin make in a year?

Divide. *(Use with page 153.)*

1. $40\overline{)280}$
2. $80\overline{)320}$
3. $70\overline{)49,000}$
4. $60\overline{)54,000}$

5. $20\overline{)186}$
6. $90\overline{)374}$
7. $30\overline{)2,743}$
8. $80\overline{)6,348}$

9. $26\overline{)74}$
10. $56\overline{)871}$
11. $65\overline{)866}$
12. $45\overline{)8,736}$

13. $72\overline{)486}$
14. $22\overline{)159}$
15. $83\overline{)4,537}$
16. $53\overline{)3,478}$

17. $41\overline{)15,361}$
18. $33\overline{)20,489}$
19. $64\overline{)47,987}$
20. $81\overline{)63,477}$

21. $27\overline{)436}$
22. $65\overline{)3,648}$
23. $75\overline{)35,610}$
24. $24\overline{)46,180}$

25. $4\overline{)\$16.24}$
26. $26\overline{)\$10.14}$
27. $36\overline{)\$92.16}$
28. $54\overline{)\$143.10}$

Solve. *(Use with page 186.)*

1. Nancy is reading a book with 549 pages. She has read 398 pages so far. How many more pages does she have left to read?

2. Ms. Thomas earned $15,863 one year and $18,473 the next year. How much did she earn in all?

3. There are 24 rubber bands in a box and 5,400 in all. How many boxes are there?

4. Melba ran 225 meters a day for 14 days. How many meters did she run in all?

5. A typist can type 75 words a minute. How many words can he type in 15 minutes?

6. Al had $60. He bought skates for $39.98, a puck for $5.98, and gloves for $11.50. How much money was left?

7. A telephone book has 4 columns of names. There are 392 names on a page. How many names are in a column?

8. José collected 3,415 shells. Juan collected 2,186 shells. How many more shells did José collect?

9. Bill paid $1.98 a kilogram for 4 kg of grapes and $.87 a kilogram for 3 kg of plums. How much did he spend in all?

10. Ms. Wong has 9 cases of juice with 24 bottles in a case. Each bottle holds 2 liters. How many liters of juice does she have in all?

Solve. *(Use with page 197.)*

1. $\frac{1}{3} = \frac{?}{9}$
2. $\frac{3}{4} = \frac{?}{12}$
3. $\frac{2}{5} = \frac{10}{?}$
4. $\frac{1}{2} = \frac{8}{?}$
5. $\frac{5}{6} = \frac{?}{12}$

6. $\frac{1}{4} = \frac{?}{12}$
7. $\frac{2}{3} = \frac{?}{12}$
8. $\frac{3}{5} = \frac{?}{15}$
9. $\frac{1}{6} = \frac{3}{?}$
10. $\frac{4}{5} = \frac{?}{15}$

11. $\frac{1}{5} = \frac{4}{?}$
12. $\frac{2}{3} = \frac{?}{6}$
★13. $\frac{?}{8} = \frac{8}{64}$
★14. $\frac{4}{7} = \frac{?}{49}$
★15. $\frac{5}{12} = \frac{?}{60}$

Find the LCM. *(Use with page 200.)*

1. 4 and 6   **2.** 5 and 9   **3.** 2 and 10   **4.** 3 and 9

5. 3 and 6   **6.** 8 and 10   **7.** 9 and 18   **8.** 7 and 8

9. 2 and 12   **10.** 6 and 9   **11.** 8 and 9   **12.** 5 and 15

13. 6 and 14   **14.** 8 and 14   **15.** 7 and 9   **16.** 10 and 14

17. 3 and 12   **18.** 4 and 18   **19.** 5 and 8   **20.** 9 and 15

★ **21.** 2, 3, and 5   ★ **22.** 3, 4, and 6   ★ **23.** 4, 5, and 10

Compare. Use >, <, and =. *(Use with page 202.)*

1. $\frac{3}{6} \equiv \frac{5}{6}$ **2.** $\frac{7}{8} \equiv \frac{3}{8}$ **3.** $\frac{4}{5} \equiv \frac{3}{5}$ **4.** $\frac{2}{7} \equiv \frac{4}{7}$ **5.** $\frac{4}{9} \equiv \frac{3}{9}$

6. $\frac{3}{4} \equiv \frac{7}{8}$ **7.** $\frac{1}{2} \equiv \frac{5}{6}$ **8.** $\frac{2}{3} \equiv \frac{6}{9}$ **9.** $\frac{5}{6} \equiv \frac{3}{8}$ **10.** $\frac{4}{5} \equiv \frac{8}{10}$

11. $\frac{5}{8} \equiv \frac{5}{6}$ **12.** $\frac{4}{7} \equiv \frac{3}{5}$ **13.** $\frac{4}{6} \equiv \frac{2}{3}$ **14.** $\frac{3}{5} \equiv \frac{4}{6}$ **15.** $\frac{3}{4} \equiv \frac{9}{12}$

16. $\frac{2}{3} \equiv \frac{4}{5}$ **17.** $\frac{7}{8} \equiv \frac{4}{5}$ **18.** $\frac{5}{7} \equiv \frac{2}{3}$ **19.** $\frac{2}{5} \equiv \frac{4}{10}$ **20.** $\frac{5}{6} \equiv \frac{15}{18}$

21. $\frac{3}{5} \equiv \frac{2}{5}$ **22.** $\frac{6}{7} \equiv \frac{3}{7}$ **23.** $\frac{5}{8} \equiv \frac{2}{3}$ **24.** $\frac{7}{9} \equiv \frac{8}{9}$ **25.** $\frac{4}{7} \equiv \frac{1}{3}$

★ **26.** $\frac{5}{12} \equiv \frac{8}{15}$ ★ **27.** $\frac{8}{21} \equiv \frac{7}{12}$ ★ **28.** $\frac{9}{14} \equiv \frac{11}{21}$ ★ **29.** $\frac{7}{16} \equiv \frac{9}{20}$

Find the GCF. *(Use with page 204.)*

1. 9 and 45   **2.** 4 and 8   **3.** 8 and 16   **4.** 12 and 18

5. 6 and 21   **6.** 9 and 15   **7.** 2 and 10   **8.** 15 and 27

9. 14 and 20   **10.** 12 and 24   **11.** 6 and 9   **12.** 9 and 18

13. 10 and 20   **14.** 5 and 20   **15.** 7 and 21   **16.** 8 and 14

17. 15 and 25   **18.** 6 and 24   **19.** 12 and 36   **20.** 9 and 21

21. 14 and 21   **22.** 8 and 20   **23.** 9 and 27   **24.** 16 and 24

★ **25.** 9, 12, and 15   ★ **26.** 6, 24, and 30   ★ **27.** 10, 25, and 45

Simplify. *(Use with page 206.)*

1. $\frac{6}{9}$ 2. $\frac{10}{18}$ 3. $\frac{15}{21}$ 4. $\frac{9}{27}$ 5. $\frac{8}{16}$ 6. $\frac{21}{24}$ 7. $\frac{14}{28}$

8. $\frac{7}{14}$ 9. $\frac{12}{40}$ 10. $\frac{9}{33}$ 11. $\frac{6}{30}$ 12. $\frac{18}{21}$ 13. $\frac{12}{20}$ 14. $\frac{22}{44}$

15. $\frac{8}{36}$ 16. $\frac{6}{22}$ 17. $\frac{18}{27}$ 18. $\frac{14}{35}$ ★ 19. $\frac{36}{124}$ ★ 20. $\frac{234}{345}$ ★ 21. $\frac{184}{448}$

Add. *(Use with page 218.)*

1. $\frac{2}{5}$ $+\frac{1}{5}$ 2. $\frac{1}{7}$ $+\frac{4}{7}$ 3. $\frac{3}{8}$ $+\frac{4}{8}$ 4. $\frac{3}{11}$ $+\frac{4}{11}$ 5. $\frac{5}{9}$ $+\frac{3}{9}$ 6. $\frac{5}{12}$ $+\frac{2}{12}$

7. $\frac{2}{9}$ $+\frac{5}{9}$ 8. $\frac{5}{14}$ $+\frac{4}{14}$ 9. $\frac{2}{7}$ $+\frac{4}{7}$ 10. $\frac{2}{9}$ $+\frac{2}{9}$ 11. $\frac{1}{10}$ $+\frac{8}{10}$ 12. $\frac{6}{11}$ $+\frac{3}{11}$

13. $\frac{3}{7}$ $\frac{1}{7}$ $+\frac{2}{7}$ 14. $\frac{1}{12}$ $\frac{4}{12}$ $+\frac{2}{12}$ 15. $\frac{1}{11}$ $\frac{5}{11}$ $+\frac{3}{11}$ 16. $\frac{3}{8}$ $\frac{1}{8}$ $+\frac{3}{8}$ 17. $\frac{2}{9}$ $\frac{1}{9}$ $+\frac{4}{9}$ 18. $\frac{3}{14}$ $\frac{5}{14}$ $+\frac{1}{14}$

★ Complete.

19. $\frac{3}{8} + \frac{?}{8} = \frac{5}{8}$ 20. $\frac{?}{10} + \frac{3}{10} = \frac{7}{10}$ 21. $\frac{3}{14} + \frac{6}{14} + \frac{?}{14} = \frac{13}{14}$

Add and simplify. *(Use with page 220.)*

1. $\frac{3}{9}$ $+\frac{3}{9}$ 2. $\frac{3}{10}$ $+\frac{5}{10}$ 3. $\frac{7}{12}$ $+\frac{1}{12}$ 4. $\frac{2}{14}$ $+\frac{5}{14}$ 5. $\frac{5}{9}$ $+\frac{1}{9}$ 6. $\frac{7}{16}$ $+\frac{5}{16}$

7. $\frac{2}{8}$ $+\frac{4}{8}$ 8. $\frac{4}{15}$ $+\frac{1}{15}$ 9. $\frac{5}{10}$ $+\frac{1}{10}$ 10. $\frac{2}{12}$ $+\frac{1}{12}$ 11. $\frac{7}{14}$ $+\frac{5}{14}$ 12. $\frac{7}{15}$ $+\frac{3}{15}$

13. $\frac{3}{10}$ $\frac{2}{10}$ $+\frac{1}{10}$ 14. $\frac{3}{12}$ $\frac{1}{12}$ $+\frac{5}{12}$ 15. $\frac{3}{14}$ $\frac{2}{14}$ $+\frac{2}{14}$ 16. $\frac{2}{15}$ $\frac{7}{15}$ $+\frac{1}{15}$ 17. $\frac{3}{16}$ $\frac{7}{16}$ $+\frac{2}{16}$ 18. $\frac{5}{18}$ $\frac{3}{18}$ $+\frac{1}{18}$

★ 19. $\frac{17}{50}$ $+\frac{8}{50}$ ★ 20. $\frac{35}{125}$ $+\frac{40}{125}$ ★ 21. $\frac{33}{200}$ $+\frac{67}{200}$ ★ 22. $\frac{124}{288}$ $+\frac{44}{288}$

Add and simplify. *(Use with page 222.)*

1. $\dfrac{1}{3}$
$+\dfrac{1}{6}$

2. $\dfrac{1}{4}$
$+\dfrac{5}{12}$

3. $\dfrac{3}{8}$
$+\dfrac{4}{16}$

4. $\dfrac{3}{9}$
$+\dfrac{1}{4}$

5. $\dfrac{1}{8}$
$+\dfrac{1}{3}$

6. $\dfrac{5}{7}+\dfrac{2}{21}$

7. $\dfrac{2}{3}$
$+\dfrac{1}{6}$

8. $\dfrac{1}{5}$
$+\dfrac{2}{6}$

9. $\dfrac{1}{3}$
$+\dfrac{5}{12}$

10. $\dfrac{2}{8}$
$+\dfrac{1}{3}$

11. $\dfrac{2}{4}$
$+\dfrac{1}{6}$

12. $\dfrac{2}{8}+\dfrac{3}{10}$

13. $\dfrac{1}{2}$
$+\dfrac{2}{8}$

14. $\dfrac{1}{6}$
$+\dfrac{9}{30}$

15. $\dfrac{3}{10}$
$+\dfrac{2}{5}$

16. $\dfrac{3}{4}$
$+\dfrac{1}{8}$

17. $\dfrac{2}{8}$
$+\dfrac{3}{12}$

18. $\dfrac{3}{7}+\dfrac{2}{6}$

19. $\dfrac{2}{7}$
$\dfrac{3}{14}$
$+\dfrac{1}{28}$

20. $\dfrac{3}{8}$
$\dfrac{1}{4}$
$+\dfrac{1}{16}$

21. $\dfrac{1}{4}$
$\dfrac{3}{8}$
$+\dfrac{2}{16}$

22. $\dfrac{2}{4}$
$\dfrac{1}{6}$
$+\dfrac{1}{12}$

23. $\dfrac{5}{8}$
$\dfrac{1}{6}$
$+\dfrac{1}{24}$

24. $\dfrac{1}{5}+\dfrac{3}{10}+\dfrac{1}{20}$

★ 25. $\dfrac{1}{15}$
$+\dfrac{1}{48}$

★ 26. $\dfrac{8}{21}$
$+\dfrac{3}{18}$

★ 27. $\dfrac{3}{20}$
$+\dfrac{9}{24}$

★ 28. $\dfrac{5}{12}$
$+\dfrac{13}{42}$

★ 29. $\dfrac{5}{24}$
$+\dfrac{6}{18}$

★ 30. $\dfrac{1}{12}+\dfrac{5}{16}+\dfrac{3}{8}$

Add and simplify. *(Use with page 226.)*

1. $\dfrac{2}{3}$
$+\dfrac{3}{5}$

2. $\dfrac{7}{8}$
$+\dfrac{1}{2}$

3. $\dfrac{3}{5}$
$+\dfrac{4}{5}$

4. $\dfrac{6}{7}$
$+\dfrac{1}{2}$

5. $\dfrac{7}{8}$
$+\dfrac{3}{8}$

6. $\dfrac{1}{3}$
$+\dfrac{5}{7}$

7. $\dfrac{5}{6}$
$+\dfrac{3}{4}$

8. $\dfrac{11}{12}$
$+\dfrac{7}{12}$

9. $\dfrac{3}{4}$
$+\dfrac{1}{2}$

10. $\dfrac{4}{5}$
$+\dfrac{5}{6}$

11. $\dfrac{13}{14}$
$+\dfrac{5}{14}$

12. $\dfrac{3}{8}$
$+\dfrac{5}{6}$

13. $\dfrac{5}{8}$
$+\dfrac{6}{10}$

14. $\dfrac{2}{3}$
$+\dfrac{5}{8}$

15. $\dfrac{5}{9}$
$+\dfrac{7}{9}$

16. $\dfrac{5}{6}$
$+\dfrac{2}{3}$

17. $\dfrac{7}{10}$
$+\dfrac{3}{5}$

18. $\dfrac{4}{7}$
$+\dfrac{13}{21}$

19. $\dfrac{3}{4}$
$\dfrac{5}{6}$
$+\dfrac{1}{12}$

20. $\dfrac{1}{4}$
$\dfrac{3}{4}$
$+\dfrac{2}{4}$

21. $\dfrac{1}{3}$
$\dfrac{5}{6}$
$+\dfrac{1}{4}$

22. $\dfrac{1}{2}$
$\dfrac{3}{5}$
$+\dfrac{1}{10}$

23. $\dfrac{1}{3}$
$\dfrac{2}{7}$
$+\dfrac{11}{21}$

24. $\dfrac{2}{3}$
$\dfrac{1}{6}$
$+\dfrac{3}{4}$

★ 25. $\dfrac{9}{14}$
$+\dfrac{30}{42}$

★ 26. $\dfrac{11}{12}$
$+\dfrac{15}{30}$

★ 27. $\dfrac{19}{32}$
$+\dfrac{24}{48}$

★ 28. $\dfrac{18}{28}$
$+\dfrac{15}{40}$

★ 29. $\dfrac{3}{4}$
$\dfrac{7}{8}$
$+\dfrac{9}{16}$

★ 30. $\dfrac{5}{10}$
$\dfrac{7}{15}$
$+\dfrac{15}{25}$

Add and simplify. *(Use with page 230.)*

1. $8\frac{3}{4}$
   $+ 4\frac{2}{3}$

2. $3\frac{4}{5}$
   $+ 6\frac{3}{5}$

3. $9\frac{3}{7}$
   $+ 8\frac{11}{14}$

4. $1\frac{5}{6}$
   $+ 3\frac{7}{10}$

5. $7\frac{7}{9}$
   $+ 8\frac{5}{9}$

6. $3\frac{7}{12}$
   $+ 1\frac{8}{9}$

7. $9\frac{4}{5}$
   $+ 3\frac{3}{5}$

8. $5\frac{2}{3}$
   $+ 6\frac{4}{7}$

9. $7\frac{7}{10}$
   $+ 3\frac{4}{5}$

10. $12\frac{2}{3}$
    $+ 10\frac{2}{3}$

11. $15\frac{5}{6}$
    $+ 9\frac{7}{8}$

12. $8\frac{6}{11}$
    $+ 4\frac{9}{11}$

13. $10\frac{4}{7}$
    $+ 8\frac{9}{14}$

14. $26\frac{9}{10}$
    $+ 15\frac{2}{3}$

15. $11\frac{7}{9}$
    $+ 8\frac{5}{12}$

16. $21\frac{5}{6}$
    $+ 15\frac{3}{4}$

17. $4\frac{7}{8}$
    $+ 3\frac{7}{10}$

18. $13\frac{4}{5}$
    $+ 12\frac{5}{6}$

19. $3\frac{4}{5} + 9\frac{9}{10}$

20. $9\frac{8}{13} + 6\frac{9}{13}$

21. $15\frac{3}{8} + 21\frac{11}{12}$

★ 22. $3\frac{7}{12} + 1\frac{5}{12} + 8\frac{11}{12}$

★ 23. $7\frac{7}{8} + 3\frac{5}{16} + 4\frac{3}{32}$

★ 24. $10\frac{2}{3} + 9\frac{1}{4} + 12\frac{5}{6}$

Subtract and simplify. *(Use with page 234.)*

1. $\frac{7}{8}$
   $- \frac{1}{8}$

2. $\frac{7}{10}$
   $- \frac{3}{5}$

3. $\frac{11}{12}$
   $- \frac{3}{4}$

4. $\frac{8}{9}$
   $- \frac{1}{3}$

5. $\frac{3}{4}$
   $- \frac{2}{3}$

6. $\frac{5}{6}$
   $- \frac{1}{6}$

7. $\frac{4}{5}$
   $- \frac{2}{3}$

8. $\frac{4}{5}$
   $- \frac{2}{15}$

9. $\frac{7}{8}$
   $- \frac{2}{3}$

10. $\frac{1}{2}$
    $- \frac{3}{10}$

11. $\frac{9}{13}$
    $- \frac{4}{13}$

12. $\frac{7}{12}$
    $- \frac{1}{18}$

13. $\frac{7}{18}$
    $- \frac{1}{9}$

14. $\frac{8}{11}$
    $- \frac{3}{11}$

15. $\frac{4}{5}$
    $- \frac{3}{8}$

★ 16. $\frac{17}{36}$
    $- \frac{8}{24}$

★ 17. $\frac{25}{45}$
    $- \frac{21}{42}$

★ 18. $\frac{14}{21}$
    $- \frac{15}{24}$

Subtract and simplify. *(Use with page 236.)*

1. $8\frac{5}{6}$
   $- 2\frac{2}{3}$

2. $6\frac{4}{5}$
   $- 2\frac{3}{5}$

3. $5\frac{7}{8}$
   $- 3\frac{3}{4}$

4. $9\frac{2}{3}$
   $- 6$

5. $7\frac{7}{10}$
   $- 2\frac{1}{5}$

6. $3\frac{7}{10}$
   $- 2\frac{1}{6}$

7. $9\frac{7}{12}$
   $- 3\frac{1}{4}$

8. $5\frac{7}{9}$
   $- 2\frac{1}{6}$

9. $4\frac{7}{11}$
   $- 2\frac{3}{11}$

10. $6\frac{7}{8}$
    $- 2\frac{1}{5}$

11. $8\frac{2}{3}$
    $- 8\frac{1}{4}$

12. $7\frac{9}{10}$
    $- 2\frac{1}{4}$

13. $10\frac{7}{8}$
    $- 3\frac{1}{3}$

14. $6\frac{11}{12}$
    $- 3$

15. $4\frac{9}{14}$
    $- 3\frac{2}{7}$

★ 16. $3\frac{19}{24}$
    $- 2\frac{18}{36}$

★ 17. $9\frac{35}{36}$
    $- 5\frac{35}{42}$

★ 18. $7\frac{13}{14}$
    $- 2\frac{9}{42}$

Subtract and simplify. *(Use with page 238.)*

1. 6 $-4\frac{7}{8}$	**2.** 12 $-2\frac{3}{5}$	**3.** 15 $-3\frac{1}{6}$	**4.** 5 $-4\frac{3}{7}$	**5.** 7 $-2\frac{5}{6}$	**6.** 8 $-2\frac{4}{11}$
7. $8\frac{4}{7}$ $-3\frac{6}{7}$	**8.** $19\frac{3}{10}$ $-8\frac{7}{10}$	**9.** $11\frac{7}{12}$ $-3\frac{11}{12}$	**10.** $4\frac{1}{8}$ $-3\frac{7}{8}$	**11.** $6\frac{4}{9}$ $-2\frac{7}{9}$	**12.** $3\frac{4}{15}$ $-1\frac{11}{15}$
13. 9 $-3\frac{2}{5}$	**14.** $8\frac{5}{12}$ $-6\frac{7}{12}$	**15.** $3\frac{2}{5}$ $-1\frac{4}{5}$	**16.** $9\frac{3}{8}$ $-4\frac{7}{8}$	**17.** 24 $-13\frac{4}{9}$	**18.** $13\frac{3}{7}$ $-7\frac{4}{7}$
19. $18\frac{1}{6}$ $-3\frac{5}{6}$	**20.** $16\frac{7}{15}$ $-12\frac{9}{15}$	**21.** $7\frac{3}{10}$ $-4\frac{9}{10}$	**★22.** 34 $-8\frac{4}{39}$	**★23.** $6\frac{23}{54}$ $-\frac{47}{54}$	**★24.** $11\frac{13}{84}$ $-7\frac{23}{84}$

Subtract and simplify. *(Use with page 240.)*

1. $6\frac{1}{2}$ $-3\frac{7}{8}$	**2.** $9\frac{2}{3}$ $-5\frac{3}{4}$	**3.** $8\frac{2}{5}$ $-4\frac{5}{6}$	**4.** $35\frac{1}{6}$ $-7\frac{3}{8}$	**5.** $7\frac{1}{5}$ $-2\frac{7}{10}$	**6.** $3\frac{3}{10}$ $-2\frac{5}{8}$
7. $5\frac{1}{3}$ $-2\frac{3}{4}$	**8.** $6\frac{3}{8}$ $-1\frac{4}{5}$	**9.** $15\frac{2}{3}$ $-6\frac{3}{4}$	**10.** $11\frac{2}{9}$ $-3\frac{5}{6}$	**11.** $6\frac{1}{3}$ $-5\frac{1}{2}$	**12.** $7\frac{1}{3}$ $-2\frac{5}{6}$
13. $10\frac{5}{6}$ $-3\frac{8}{9}$	**14.** $15\frac{1}{10}$ $-4\frac{1}{2}$	**15.** $20\frac{1}{2}$ $-18\frac{9}{10}$	**16.** $7\frac{1}{3}$ $-2\frac{5}{6}$	**17.** $18\frac{1}{6}$ $-15\frac{2}{3}$	**18.** $24\frac{5}{12}$ $-15\frac{2}{3}$
19. $12\frac{4}{9}$ $-3\frac{4}{5}$	**20.** $19\frac{1}{10}$ $-6\frac{4}{5}$	**21.** $8\frac{5}{12}$ $-3\frac{3}{4}$	**★22.** $15\frac{2}{16}$ $-9\frac{15}{32}$	**★23.** $56\frac{3}{14}$ $-13\frac{10}{28}$	**★24.** $18\frac{3}{35}$ $-17\frac{26}{70}$

Multiply and simplify. *(Use with page 246.)*

1. $\frac{2}{3} \times \frac{3}{10}$ **2.** $\frac{3}{5} \times \frac{10}{21}$ **3.** $\frac{6}{7} \times \frac{7}{9}$ **4.** $\frac{8}{13} \times \frac{7}{12}$ **5.** $\frac{4}{5} \times \frac{5}{8}$

6. $\frac{7}{9} \times \frac{3}{5}$ **7.** $\frac{2}{3} \times \frac{4}{9}$ **8.** $\frac{5}{9} \times \frac{3}{10}$ **9.** $\frac{7}{8} \times \frac{4}{5}$ **10.** $\frac{3}{4} \times \frac{6}{11}$

11. $\frac{5}{8} \times \frac{2}{5} \times \frac{1}{3}$ **12.** $\frac{1}{3} \times \frac{6}{7} \times \frac{2}{5}$ **13.** $\frac{7}{8} \times \frac{2}{3} \times \frac{3}{5}$ **14.** $\frac{4}{9} \times \frac{3}{4} \times \frac{1}{8}$

★15. $\frac{8}{9} \times \frac{3}{4} \times \frac{4}{8}$ **★16.** $\frac{2}{3} \times \frac{6}{8} \times \frac{4}{5}$ **★17.** $\frac{3}{6} \times \frac{3}{4} \times \frac{2}{9}$ **★18.** $\frac{5}{6} \times \frac{3}{10} \times \frac{2}{5}$

Multiply and simplify. *(Use with page 248.)*

1. $\frac{1}{5} \times 6$ **2.** $8 \times \frac{1}{3}$ **3.** $9 \times \frac{1}{5}$ **4.** $\frac{3}{7} \times 7$ **5.** $\frac{2}{5} \times 10$

6. $7 \times \frac{3}{14}$ **7.** $\frac{5}{9} \times 3$ **8.** $4 \times \frac{1}{3}$ **9.** $8 \times \frac{3}{4}$ **10.** $\frac{4}{5} \times 15$

11. $\frac{7}{8} \times 16$ **12.** $\frac{3}{8} \times 10$ **13.** $\frac{5}{6} \times 12$ **14.** $\frac{4}{9} \times 6$ **15.** $\frac{7}{10} \times 8$

16. $\frac{4}{5} \times 10$ **17.** $\frac{4}{7} \times 14$ ★**18.** $3\frac{1}{4} \times 4\frac{1}{3}$ ★**19.** $1\frac{3}{5} \times 2\frac{1}{6}$ ★**20.** $4\frac{3}{8} \times 2\frac{1}{4}$

Solve. *(Use with page 252.)*

1. Mr. Rice sold 3,452 pigs in May and 5,129 pigs in June. How many more did he sell in June?

2. A book store has 288 books with 24 books in a carton. How many cartons are there?

3. Joe had $20. He bought 5 pens for $2.98 each. How much money was left?

4. Sal earned $49.50 for 18 hours of work. How much did he earn an hour?

5. Mrs. Shaw bought 25 yards of carpeting at $9.98 a yard. How much did she spend in all?

6. Jon scored 125, 98 and 115 in three games of bowling. What was his total score?

7. Beryl earned $168.75 in July and $259.85 in August. How much did she make in all?

8. Kim bought a car for $8,059 and she sold it 3 years later for $5,186. What was the difference in the value of the car?

Add and simplify. *(Use with page 253.)*

1. $\begin{array}{r} \frac{3}{8} \\ + \frac{3}{8} \\ \hline \end{array}$ **2.** $\begin{array}{r} \frac{3}{5} \\ + \frac{2}{10} \\ \hline \end{array}$ **3.** $\begin{array}{r} \frac{5}{4} \\ + \frac{2}{8} \\ \hline \end{array}$ **4.** $\begin{array}{r} 3\frac{4}{9} \\ + 2\frac{2}{9} \\ \hline \end{array}$ **5.** $\begin{array}{r} 8\frac{5}{6} \\ + 2\frac{7}{9} \\ \hline \end{array}$ **6.** $\frac{1}{12} + \frac{1}{3} + \frac{1}{4}$

Subtract and simplify.

7. $\begin{array}{r} \frac{9}{10} \\ - \frac{7}{10} \\ \hline \end{array}$ **8.** $\begin{array}{r} \frac{7}{8} \\ - \frac{1}{2} \\ \hline \end{array}$ **9.** $\begin{array}{r} \frac{9}{12} \\ - \frac{1}{6} \\ \hline \end{array}$ **10.** $\begin{array}{r} \frac{2}{3} \\ - \frac{1}{7} \\ \hline \end{array}$ **11.** $\begin{array}{r} 6\frac{5}{6} \\ - 3\frac{1}{6} \\ \hline \end{array}$ **12.** $\begin{array}{r} 5\frac{5}{8} \\ - 1\frac{1}{2} \\ \hline \end{array}$

13. $\begin{array}{r} 10\frac{6}{7} \\ - 3\frac{2}{3} \\ \hline \end{array}$ **14.** $\begin{array}{r} 14\frac{3}{8} \\ - 6 \\ \hline \end{array}$ **15.** $\begin{array}{r} 5\frac{7}{10} \\ - 3\frac{1}{5} \\ \hline \end{array}$ **16.** $\begin{array}{r} 7 \\ - 3\frac{3}{4} \\ \hline \end{array}$ **17.** $\begin{array}{r} 9\frac{2}{9} \\ - 3\frac{2}{3} \\ \hline \end{array}$ **18.** $\begin{array}{r} 8\frac{2}{5} \\ - 7\frac{2}{3} \\ \hline \end{array}$

Multiply and simplify.

19. $\frac{1}{3} \times \frac{1}{5}$ **20.** $\frac{4}{9} \times \frac{3}{4}$ **21.** $\frac{5}{6} \times \frac{4}{9}$ **22.** $\frac{1}{3} \times \frac{3}{7} \times \frac{7}{9}$ **23.** $\frac{3}{5} \times 3$

Write decimals. *(Use with page 290.)*

1. $\frac{3}{10}$ **2.** $\frac{7}{10}$ **3.** $\frac{4}{10}$ **4.** $\frac{1}{10}$ **5.** $\frac{2}{10}$ **6.** $7\frac{5}{10}$

7. $5\frac{6}{10}$ **8.** $96\frac{9}{10}$ **9.** $25\frac{8}{10}$ ★**10.** $\frac{13}{10}$ ★**11.** $\frac{29}{10}$ ★**12.** $\frac{65}{10}$

Write fractions or mixed numbers.

13. 9.6   **14.** 3.4   **15.** 8.1   **16.** 7.9   **17.** 15.5   **18.** 21.7

19. 37.8   **20.** 86.2   **21.** 74.3   **22.** 116.1   **23.** 814.6   **24.** 320.9

Write decimals. *(Use with page 292.)*

1. $\frac{8}{100}$ **2.** $\frac{6}{100}$ **3.** $\frac{2}{100}$ **4.** $\frac{17}{100}$ **5.** $\frac{46}{100}$

6. $\frac{83}{100}$ **7.** $\frac{30}{100}$ **8.** $\frac{96}{100}$ **9.** $3\frac{71}{100}$ **10.** $24\frac{57}{100}$

11. $2\frac{5}{100}$ **12.** $36\frac{83}{100}$ ★**13.** $\frac{123}{100}$ ★**14.** $\frac{306}{100}$ ★**15.** $\frac{498}{100}$

Write fractions or mixed numbers.

16. 0.05   **17.** 0.02   **18.** 0.09   **19.** 0.16   **20.** 0.28

21. 0.36   **22.** 0.94   **23.** 0.80   **24.** 1.73   **25.** 4.06

26. 3.67   **27.** 19.31   **28.** 57.80   **29.** 79.03   **30.** 62.67

Write decimals. *(Use with page 294.)*

1. $\frac{6}{1,000}$ **2.** $\frac{3}{1,000}$ **3.** $\frac{17}{1,000}$ **4.** $\frac{58}{1,000}$ **5.** $\frac{79}{1,000}$

6. $\frac{431}{1,000}$ **7.** $\frac{306}{1,000}$ **8.** $\frac{680}{1,000}$ **9.** $3\frac{4}{1,000}$ **10.** $8\frac{65}{1,000}$

11. $24\frac{71}{1,000}$ **12.** $15\frac{207}{1,000}$ ★**13.** $\frac{1,036}{1,000}$ ★**14.** $\frac{3,467}{1,000}$ ★**15.** $\frac{8,006}{1,000}$

Write fractions or mixed numbers.

16. 0.007   **17.** 0.004   **18.** 0.056   **19.** 0.090   **20.** 0.038

21. 0.367   **22.** 0.403   **23.** 0.860   **24.** 3.143   **25.** 9.016

26. 7.003   **27.** 8.147   **28.** 3.600   **29.** 2.037   **30.** 5.105

★**31.** 0.0005   ★**32.** 0.1063   ★**33.** 0.0136   ★**34.** 6.0056   ★**35.** 7.1008

Write as hundredths. *(Use with page 296.)*

1. 0.3 **2.** 0.7 **3.** 0.4 **4.** 0.9 **5.** 0.8 **6.** 0.5

Write as thousandths.

7. 0.03 **8.** 0.07 **9.** 0.09 **10.** 0.18 **11.** 0.45 **12.** 0.93

13. 0.87 **14.** 0.50 **15.** 0.66 **16.** 0.74 **17.** 0.62 **18.** 0.99

19. 0.70 **20.** 0.11 **21.** 0.26 ★**22.** 0.7 ★**23.** 4.38 ★**24.** 6.08

Compare. Use $<$, $>$ or $=$. *(Use with page 298.)*

1. 0.3 ▤ 0.8 **2.** 0.7 ▤ 0.9 **3.** 0.2 ▤ 0.3 **4.** 0.9 ▤ 0.7

5. 0.15 ▤ 0.09 **6.** 0.36 ▤ 0.45 **7.** 0.52 ▤ 0.25 **8.** 0.6 ▤ 0.60

9. 0.123 ▤ 0.213 **10.** 0.517 ▤ 0.361 **11.** 0.811 ▤ 0.764 **12.** 0.400 ▤ 0.310

13. 0.30 ▤ 0.3 **14.** 0.52 ▤ 0.431 **15.** 0.79 ▤ 0.9 **16.** 0.136 ▤ 0.63

17. 0.86 ▤ .709 **18.** 0.61 ▤ 0.6 **19.** 0.311 ▤ 0.43 **20.** 0.7 ▤ 0.78

★**21.** 0.4 ▤ 0.43 ★**22.** 0.387 ▤ 0.4 ★**23.** 0.567 ▤ 0.6 ★**24.** 0.3 ▤ 0.034

Add. *(Use with page 304.)*

1. 0.5
   + 0.4

2. 0.3
   + 0.6

3. 0.2
   + 0.6

4. 0.04
   + 0.03

5. 0.43
   + 0.56

6. 0.15
   + 0.68

7. 0.39
   + 0.08

8. 0.003
   + 0.007

9. 0.027
   + 0.063

10. 0.364
   + 0.289

11. 0.3
    0.1
   + 0.5

12. 0.56
    0.15
   + 0.23

13. 0.07
    0.48
   + 0.32

14. 0.346
    0.009
   + 0.067

15. 0.134
    0.258
   + 0.362

16. 0.3 + 0.5 **17.** 0.2 + 0.2 **18.** 0.32 + 0.47

19. 0.51 + 0.37 **20.** 0.379 + 0.148 **21.** 0.561 + 0.132

22. 0.46 + 0.19 + 0.21 **23.** 0.37 + 0.32 + 0.18

★**24.** 0.26 + 0.3 ★**25.** 0.564 + 0.2

★**26.** 0.4 + 0.23 + 0.156 ★**27.** 0.3 + 0.364 + 0.21 + 0.17

Add. *(Use with page 306.)*

1.   0.8
   + 0.5

2.   6.7
   + 2.9

3.   5.6
   + 8.4

4.   17.3 cm
   + 19.6 cm

5.   0.49
   + 0.86

6.   3.48
   + 6.53

7.   15.75 m
   + 38.96 m

8.   0.673
   + 0.489

9.   2.713
   + 4.881

10.   9.712 m
   + 5.831 m

11.   2.6
    1.8
   + 3.5

12.   0.56
    0.37
   + 0.94

13.   5.13 m
    2.87 m
   + 6.91 m

14.   7.316
    8.149
   + 6.076

15.   9.811 cm
    7.152 cm
   + 1.832 cm

16. 0.73 + 0.94

17. 18.91 + 25.47

18. 13.436 + 19.871

19. 0.116 + 0.894

20. 0.16 + 0.24 + 0.98

21. 3.516 + 8.152 + 1.871

★ **22.** 0.4 + 6.98

★ **23.** 4.4 + 3.91 + 7.113

★ **24.** 6.348 + .7 + 1.41

Subtract. *(Use with page 310.)*

1.   0.7
   − 0.4

2.   0.9
   − 0.6

3.   0.8
   − 0.3

4.   0.09
   − 0.03

5.   0.46
   − 0.15

6.   0.73
   − 0.68

7.   0.85
   − 0.37

8.   0.83
   − 0.79

9.   0.738
   − 0.364

10.   0.135
   − 0.129

11.   0.650
   − 0.475

12.   0.749
   − 0.658

13.   0.506
   − 0.283

14.   0.136
   − 0.085

15.   0.986
   − 0.378

16. 0.6 − 0.2

17. 0.56 − 0.37

18. 0.483 − 0.379

★ **19.** 0.39 − 0.2

★ **20.** 0.473 − 0.37

★ **21.** 0.9 − 0.376

Subtract. *(Use with page 312.)*

1.   3.7
   − 0.3

2.   5.8
   − 3.9

3.   9.3
   − 8.5

4.   2.46
   − 1.29

5.   8.59
   − 3.78

6.   7.63
   − 7.47

7.   4.67
   − 2.98

8.   6.55
   − 5.98

9.   6.349
   − 4.126

10.   8.137
   − 2.486

11.   1.689
   − 1.398

12.   9.137
   − 2.483

13.   8.763
   − 7.949

14.   7.364
   − 6.987

15.   5.247
   − 5.239

16. 7.3 − 6.5

17. 3.86 − 1.97

18. 5.136 − 4.987

★ **19.** 3.21 − 1.143

★ **20.** 7.56 − 2.4

★ **21.** 8.3 − 6.984

Multiply. *(Use with page 314.)*

1. 0.3 ×6	**2.** 0.7 ×9	**3.** 0.5 ×6	**4.** 0.8 ×3	**5.** 0.4 ×0.2	**6.** 0.6 ×0.1	**7.** 0.9 ×0.8
8. 0.7 ×0.6	**9.** 6.3 ×2	**10.** 8.7 ×5	**11.** 9.6 ×4	**12.** 7.3 ×9	★**13.** 1.4 ×3.6	★**14.** 2.7 ×4.8

Solve. *(Use with page 316.)*

1. The snowfall for 3 days was 16.4 cm, 19.6 cm, and 17.8 cm. What was the total snowfall?

2. Pat ran a race in 27.86 seconds. Sara ran it in 28.48 seconds. What was the difference in the time?

3. Ken bought 4 poles each 1.4 m long. How long are they in all?

4. Al's pail holds 3.7 L and Jan's holds 1.9 L. How much more does Al's hold?

5. Sue has 5 cakes each weighing 1.7 kg. How much do they weigh in all?

6. Two cats weighed 8.64 kg and 5.79 kg. How much do they weigh together?

7. It rained 4.53 cm on Monday and 3.17 cm on Tuesday. How much more did it rain on Monday?

8. Mr. Jones bought 9 stamps each weighing 0.8 oz. How much did they weigh in all?

Write decimals. *(Use with page 317.)*

1. $\frac{3}{10}$ **2.** $4\frac{5}{10}$ **3.** $\frac{7}{100}$ **4.** $\frac{39}{100}$ **5.** $\frac{8}{1,000}$ **6.** $\frac{743}{1,000}$

Write fractions or mixed numerals.

7. 0.9 **8.** 7.8 **9.** 0.93 **10.** 0.06 **11.** 0.143 **12.** 0.079

Compare. Use <, > or =.

13. 0.37 ≡ 0.73 **14.** 0.346 ≡ 0.791 **15.** 0.47 ≡ 0.4 **16.** 0.563 ≡ 0.65

Add or subtract.

17. 0.5 + 0.4	**18.** 3.47 + 1.98	**19.** 0.486 + 0.325	**20.** 0.761 + 0.439	**21.** 3.716 + 4.871
22. 0.9 − 0.6	**23.** 0.86 − 0.79	**24.** 0.679 − 0.598	**25.** 2.56 − 1.39	**26.** 8.764 − 7.983

Multiply.

27. 0.3 ×2	**28.** 0.4 ×0.2	**29.** 0.5 ×0.3	**30.** 7.2 ×3	**31.** 8.3 ×4

Table of Measures

Metric

Customary

Length

1 centimeter (cm) = 10 millimeters (mm)
1 meter (m) = 100 centimeters
1 kilometer (km) = 1,000 meters

1 foot (ft) = 12 inches (in.)
1 yard (yd) = 3 feet
1 yard = 36 inches
1 mile (mi) = 5,280 feet
1 mile = 1,760 yards

Mass/Weight

1 kilogram (kg) = 1,000 grams (g)
1 metric ton (t) = 1,000 kilograms

1 pound (lb) = 16 ounces (oz)
1 ton = 2,000 pounds

Liquid

1 liter (L) = 1,000 milliliters (mL)

1 pint (pt) = 2 cups
1 quart (qt) = 2 pints
1 gallon (gal) = 4 quarts

Time

1 minute (min) = 60 seconds (s)
1 hour (h) = 60 minutes
1 day = 24 hours
1 week = 7 days
12 months = 1 year
1 decade = 10 years
1 century = 100 years

GLOSSARY

This glossary contains an example, an illustration, or a brief description of important terms used in this book.

Addends   Numbers that are added. (page 24)
Example $3 + 8 = 11$
3 and 8 are addends.

Angle   A figure formed by two rays with a common endpoint. This is $\angle ABC$ or $\angle B$. (page 258)

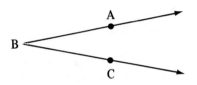

Area   The number of square units in a surface. The area of this figure is 8 square units. (page 320)

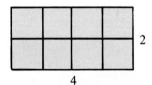

Associative property of addition   When three numbers are added, the sum is the same, no matter which two are added first. (page 25)
Example $(7 + 3) + 4 = 7 + (3 + 4)$

Associative property of multiplication   When three numbers are multiplied, the product is the same, no matter which two are multiplied first. (page 75)
Example
$2 \times (4 \times 10) = (2 \times 4) \times 10$

Average   The result of dividing the sum of several addends by the number of addends. (page 147)
Example The average of 8, 4, and 3 is 5.
$8 + 4 + 3 = 15$ and
$15 \div 3 = 5$.

Chord   Any line segment with its endpoints on a circle. (page 265)

Circle   A simple closed curve with all points the same distance from a point called the center. (page 256)

Closed curve   A curve that ends where it starts. (page 272)

Common factor   3 is a common factor of 6 and 9 because it is a factor of both numbers. (page 122)

Common multiple   18 is a common multiple of 6 and 9 because it is a multiple of both numbers. (page 89)

Commutative property of addition   The sum of two numbers is the same, regardless of the order they are added. (page 25)
Example $3 + 5 = 5 + 3$

Commutative property of multiplication   The product of two numbers is the same, regardless of the order they are multiplied. (page 75)
Example $2 \times 6 = 6 \times 2$

Compass   A tool used to draw circles. (page 256)

Composite number   A number with more than itself and 1 as factors. (page 124)
Example 8 is a composite number.

Cone   A figure in space. A funnel is a model of a cone. (page 326)

Congruent   Figures with the same size and shape. (page 283)

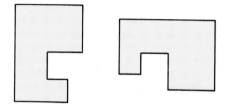

Cube   A figure in space of this shape. Each of its 6 faces is a square. (page 326)

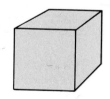

Cubic measure   Cubic measure is used to find the volume of a figure in space. It is the number of unit cubes that will fit inside a figure. (page 328)

Cylinder   A figure in space. A can is a model of a cylinder. (page 326)

Decimal   A number, such as three tenths, may be shown in fraction form $\left(\frac{3}{10}\right)$ or in decimal form (0.3). (page 290)

Degree   A unit of temperature or of angle measure. (page 260)

Denominator   In $\frac{3}{5}$, 5 is the denominator. (page 191)

Diagonal   In a rectangle, a line segment from one corner to the opposite corner. (page 277)

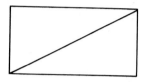

Diameter   A line segment going through the center of a circle and having both endpoints on the circle. $\overline{AB}$ is a diameter. (page 265)

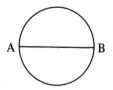

Difference   The answer in subtraction. (page 51)
Example $5 - 3 = 2$
2 is the difference.

Digit   Any of the individual symbols used to write a numeral. In the base-ten system, the digits are 0, 1, 2, 3, 4, 5, 6, 7, 8, 9. (page 4)

Distributive property   A property that relates addition and multiplication. (page 75)
Example
$3 \times (4 + 5) = (3 \times 4) + (3 \times 5)$

Dividend   The number that is to be divided. (page 102)
Example $45 \div 9$
45 is the dividend.

Glossary

Divisible A whole number is divisible by a counting number when the remainder is 0. (page 121)
Example 12 is divisible by 3, but is not divisible by 5.

Divisor The number that is used to divide by. (page 102)
Example $45 \div 9$
9 is the divisor.

Equal fractions Two or more names (numerals) for the same fraction. (page 194)
Example $\frac{2}{3} = \frac{4}{6}$

Equation A number sentence with an equals sign. (page 62)

Even number A number with a factor of 2. (page 121)
Example $6 = 2 \times 3$; thus 6 is an even number.

Expanded numeral A numeral that shows the value of each place in a standard numeral. (page 5)
Example $245 = 200 + 40 + 5$

Factors Numbers that are multiplied. (page 72)
Example $2 \times 4 \times 5 = 40$
2, 4, and 5 are factors.

Factor tree A form used for showing the prime factorization of a number. (page 124)
Example
$$45$$
$$9 \times 5$$
$$3 \times 3 \times 5$$

Flip The figures below show a flip. The figure does not change in size or shape. (page 280)

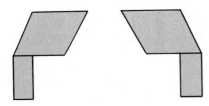

Flow chart An ordered list of steps. (page 36)

Fraction A number named by a numeral such as $\frac{3}{4}$, or $\frac{6}{1}$. (page 290)

Graph Information shown by use of pictures, dots, or bars. (page 342)

Greatest common factor The largest of the common factors of a pair of numbers. (page 204)
Example For 8 and 12, 4 is the greatest common factor.

Hexagon A polygon with 6 sides. (page 272)

Inequality A number sentence that contains $<$ or $>$. (page 66)

Intersect When two lines or line segments have a point in common, we say they intersect. (page 259)

Least common denominator The least common multiple of the denominators of two or more fractions (page 222)
Example 8 is the least common denominator of $\frac{1}{4}$ and $\frac{3}{8}$.

Least common multiple The smallest of the common multiples of two or more numbers. (page 200)
Example For 6 and 8, 24 is the least common multiple.

Line A line goes straight in two directions and has no end. This is $\overleftrightarrow{AB}$. (page 258)

Line of symmetry A line of folding so that the two halves of a figure match. (page 282)

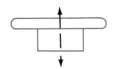

Glossary

Line segment   A part of a line. This is $\overline{AB}$. (page 256)

Mixed number   A numeral such as $4\frac{2}{3}$, $6\frac{1}{2}$. (page 224)

Multiple   The product of a given number and another number. (page 88)
Example 6 is a multiple of 2 because $2 \times 3 = 6$.

Number line   A line on which numbers are matched to points. (page 14)

Number sentence   An equation or inequality. (page 34)
Examples $n + 6 = 9$ or $3 \times 2 < 8$

Numeral   A name for a number. (page 2)

Numerator   In $\frac{4}{5}$, 4 is the numerator. (page 191)

Odd number   A whole number that is not an even number. (page 121)
Examples 1, 3, 5, . . .

Opposite operations   Addition and subtraction are opposite operations, as are multiplication and division. One operation undoes the other. (page 150)

Ordered pairs   A pair of numbers where the order of the numbers is important. (page 356)

Parallel lines   Two lines that do not intersect. (page 274)

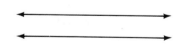

Parallelogram   A quadrilateral with both pairs of opposite sides parallel. (page 274)

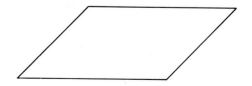

Parentheses   These marks, ( ). In arithmetic the parentheses tell us to work inside them first. (page 25)
Example $3 + (5 + 8) = 3 + 13$

Pentagon   A polygon with five sides. (page 272)

Perimeter   The distance around a figure. The perimeter of this figure is $3 + 4 + 1 + 3 + 2 + 7$, or 20 units. (page 278)

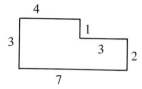

Periods in numerals   The groups of three digits set off by a comma in a numeral. (page 4)

Perpendicular lines   Two lines that intersect so that each angle they form measures 90°. (page 262)

Point   A point is a location in space. (page 256)

Polygon   A simple closed curve made up of line segments. (page 272)

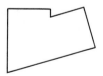

Prime factor   A factor that is a prime number. (page 124)
Example 2 is a prime factor of 10.

Prime factorization $2 \times 3 \times 3$ is a prime factorization of 18, because 2 and 3 are prime numbers. (page 124)

Prime number   A number that has exactly two factors, itself and 1. (page 124)

Probability   The ratio of the number of favorable outcomes to the number of possible outcomes. (page 358)

Product   The answer in multiplication. (page 72)
Example 4 × 6 = 24
24 is the product.

Property of one for multiplication   The product of 1 and any number is that number. (page 75)

Property of zero for addition   The sum of zero and any number is the number itself. (page 25)

Protractor   A device for measuring angles. (page 260)

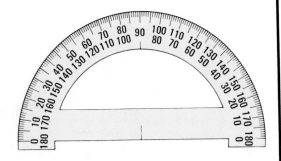

Quadrilateral   A polygon with four sides. (page 272)

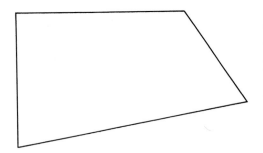

Quotient   The answer in division. (page 102)
Example 8 ÷ 2 = 4
4 is the quotient.

Radius   A line segment from the center of a circle to a point on the circle. (page 264)

Ratio   The comparison of the numbers by division. (page 210)

Ray   A ray has one endpoint and is unending in one direction. This is $\overrightarrow{AB}$. (page 258)

Rectangle   A parallelogram with four right angles. (page 276)

Rectangular prism   A figure in space of this shape. Each of its 6 faces is a rectangle. (page 326)

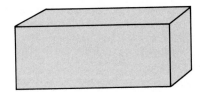

Related sentences   Related sentences use the same number and the same or opposite operation. (page 150)

Remainder   In the division 17 ÷ 5, the quotient is 3 and the remainder is 2. (page 102)

Rhombus   A parallelogram with all sides the same measure. (page 276)

Right angle   An angle whose measure is 90°. (page 262)

Right triangle   A triangle with a right angle. (page 324)

Simple closed curve   A curve that ends where it begins and never crosses itself. (page 272)

Slide   These figures show a slide. The figure does not change shape or size. (page 280)

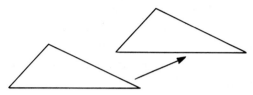

Solution   A replacement number that makes a number sentence true. (page 66)

Sphere   A figure in space. A ball is a model of a sphere. (page 326)

Square   A rectangle with all sides the same measure. (page 276)

Standard numeral   The usual or common name for a number. The standard numeral for twelve is 12. (page 2)

Sum   The answer in addition. (page 24)
Example $3 + 5 = 8$
        8 is the sum.

Trapezoid   Any quadrilateral that has one pair of parallel sides. (page 274)

Triangle   A polygon with three sides. (page 272)

Turn   These figures show a turn. The figure does not change shape or size. (page 280)

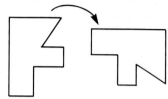

Vertex   The common endpoint of the sides of an angle. (page 260)

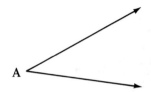

Volume   The measure of the interior of a space figure. (page 192)

Whole numbers   The numbers 0, 1, 2, 3, and so on. (page 2)

Glossary

SYMBOL LIST

		Page
$=$	is equal to	12
$>$	is greater than	12
$<$	is less than	12
$\overline{AB}$	line segment AB	258
$\overleftrightarrow{AB}$	line AB	258
$\overrightarrow{AB}$	ray AB	258
$\angle ABC$	angle ABC	258
$180°$	one hundred eighty degrees	260
$30°C$	30 degrees Celsius	174

INDEX

G means the word is listed in the Glossary.

A

Activity
discovering 1 L of water has a mass of 1 kg, 169
estimating length, 160
finding fractions, 201
making a liter container, 164
measuring to the nearest centimeter, 156–157
measuring to the nearest millimeter, 161

Addends, 24–25, **G**

Addition
associative property of, 25
basic facts, *see* Addition facts
checking subtraction by, 52
column, 28–29
commutative property of, 25
of decimals, 304–307
of 5-digit numbers, 38–39
of fractions, 218–223, 226–227
Keeping Fit, 67, 79, 113, 166, 229, 267, 271, 353
of mixed numbers, 228–229; with renaming, 230–231
of money amounts: 3-digit, 30–31; 5-digit, 38–39; 6-digit, 40–41
with a nomograph, 24–25
patterns in, 59
renaming in, 30–31, 176–177, 226–229
of 6-digit numbers, 40–41
solving word problems using, 44
of units of time with renaming, 176–177
using sums of 10, 28
zero property of, 25

Addition sentences
as multiplication sentences, 72–73
subtraction sentences related to, 150

Aid to Memory, 27, 85, 163

Angle(s), 258–259, **G**
acute, 262–263
congruent, 283
drawing and measuring with a protractor, 260–261
obtuse, 262–263
right, 262–263
of triangles, 272–273
vertex of, 260

Area, 320–321, **G**
of a rectangle, 322–323
of a right triangle, 324–325

Associative property of addition, 25, **G**
in solving equations by inspection, 241

Associative property of multiplication, 75, **G**

Average, 146–147, **G**

B

Bar graphs, 342–343
making, 346–347

Basic Facts Review, 3, 8 15, 19

Basic Skills Check, 23, 47, 71, 101, 129, 155, 189, 217, 255, 287, 319, 341, 365

Brainteaser, 35, 57, 91, 93, 112, 123, 151, 171, 181, 195, 232, 249, 251, 259, 263, 265, 273, 295, 300, 323

Broken-line graphs, 348–349

C

Calculator Activity, 89, 142, 175, 211, 247, 281, 295, 329

Capacity, units of, 164–165, 170, 182

Career
broadcast technicians, 362
floor covering installers, 252
librarians, 20
physical therapists, 186
social service aides, 338

Centimeter (cm), 159–160, 162–163, 170
cubic (cm³), 328–329
on map scale, 336–337
measuring to the nearest, 156–157
square (cm²), 320–321
tenths of, 288–289

Century, 178–179

Chapter Review, 21, 45, 69, 99, 127, 153, 187, 215, 253, 285, 317, 339, 363

Chapter Test, 22, 46, 70, 100, 128, 154, 188, 216, 254, 286, 318, 340, 364

Chart, using information in a, 20

Circles, 256–257, **G**
center and radius and diameter of, 264–265

Circle graphs, 350–351

Common factors, 122–123, 204, 205, 206, **G**

Commutative property of addition, 25, **G**
in solving equations by inspection, 241

Commutative property of multiplication, 75, **G**

Comparing numbers, 12–13

Composite numbers, 124–125, **G**
Computation skills with decimals: addition,
Computation skills
  with decimals: addition, 304–307; multiplication, 314–315; subtraction, 310–314
  with fractions: addition, 218–223, 226–231; multiplication, 244–251; subtraction, 234–235
  with whole numbers: addition, 3, 26, 28–31, 38–41; division, 19, 104–111, 116–120, 130–139; multiplication, 15, 75–78, 80–83, 90–97; subtraction, 8, 50–55
Congruent figures, 283, **G**
Consumer Skills
  change from a purchase, 126
  computing with money amounts, 30–31, 38–41, 82–83, 144–145
  estimating with money amounts, 42–43, 60–61, 96–97
  finding the better buy, 214
  making change, 68
  multiple step problem with money amounts, 86–87
Coordinates, 357
Customary system, 180–185
  cubic units, 328–329
  cup, 182
  foot (ft), 180–181
  fluid ounce (fl oz), 182
  gallon (gal), 182
  inch (in.), 180–181
  mile (mi), 180–181
  ounce (oz), 183
  pint (pt), 182
  pound (lb), 183

  quart (qt), 182
  square units, 322–323
  ton, 183
  yard (yd), 180–181

D

Day(s), 176–177
  between two given days or dates, 178–179
Daylight savings time, 179
Decade, 178–179
Decimal name for a number, 290, **G**
Decimal point, 304, 306, 310, 312
Decimals
  addition of: with sums greater than 1, 306–307; with sums less than 1, 304–305
  comparing, 298–299
  equivalent, 296
  estimating sums, 308–309
  multiplying, 314–315
  renaming, 296–297
  rounding to the nearest whole number, 308–309
  subtraction of: with differences greater than 1, 312–313; with differences less than 1, 310–311
  writing, 290–297
Denominators, 191, 196, **G**
  common, 202
  least common, 222, 226
Diagnostic review, *see* Basic Facts Review; Keeping Fit
Diagonals, 277, **G**
Differences, 51, **G**
  estimating, *see* Estimating differences
Digit(s), 4–7, **G**
Distributive property of multiplication, 75, 85, **G**

Dividend, 102–103, **G**
Divisibility of numbers, 121, **G**
Division
  basic facts, 19, 104
  finding factors by, 122–123
  with the first estimate too large 140–141
  Keeping Fit, 166, 267, 331, 353
  of a 2-digit number: by a 1-digit divisor, 110–111; no remainders, 108–109; by a 2-digit divisor, 134–135
  of a 3-digit number: a 1-digit divisor, 110–111; no remainers, 108–109; by a 2-digit divisor, 134–135, 136–137
  of a 4-digit number: by a multiple of 10, 132–133; by a 2-digit divisor, 136–137; by a 3-digit divisor, 134–135
  of a 4- or 5-digit number by a 1-digit divisor: with a 4- or 5-digit quotient, 116–117; with a 3- or 4-digit quotient, 118–119
  of a 5-digit number: by a 2-digit divisor, 138–139; with zeros in the quotient, 120; of money amounts, 144–145
  patterns in, 106–107, 130–131
  of a whole number by 1 or itself, 105
  of zero, 105
  Review, 19, 104
Division sentences, 102–103
  multiplication sentences related to, 150
Divisor, 102–103, **G**

Index

Index

Index

interpreting a flow chart
with a loop, 36–37
selecting an object which
is the opposite, 171
Remainder, 102–103, **G**
Renaming
in addition, 30–31, 176–
177, 226–229
decimals, 296
fractions, 297
in length measurement,
180–181
mixed numbers, 237, 238
in multiplication, 80–83
in subtraction, 48–49,
51–57, 176–177
whole numbers as mixed
numbers, 237
Right triangle, area of,
324–325, **G**
Roman numerals, 18–19
Rounding
decimals to the nearest
whole number, 308–
309
mixed numbers to the
nearest whole number,
233
money amounts to the
nearest ten cents and
dollar, 14–15
numbers, 14–17
Keeping Fit, 33, 67, 113,
199
Ruler, 156–157

S

Scale drawings, 334–335
Sequences, completing, 59
Special Topic
copying line segments,
270–271
customary measurement,
180–185
designs with circles,
256–257
factor trees, 124–125
flow charts, 36–37
game with number cube, 9

graphing ordered pairs,
356–357
inequalities, 66
making a balance scale,
167
metric measurement, 158
multiplication, 250–251
multiplication properties,
74–75
number puzzle game, 84
probabilities, 360–361
properties of addition,
241
related number sentences,
150–151
renaming fractions, 297
rounding decimals and
estimating 308–309
scale drawings, 334–335
slides and turns and flips
of figures, 280–281
Standard time, 179
Subtraction
basic facts, 8, 50
checking, by addition, 52
of 4-digit numbers, 52–55
of 6-digit numbers, 56–
57
of fractions, 234–235
Keeping Fit, 79, 113,
166, 229, 267, 271,
353
of mixed numbers, 236,
238–240
sentences, 150
patterns in, 59
renaming in, 48–49, 51–
57, 176–177
of decimals, 310–313
of units of time with
renaming, 176–177
with zero, 54–55
Sum, 24–25, **G**
Symmetry, lines of, 282

T

Temperature measurement
on the Celsius (°C) scale,
174–175

on the Fahrenheit (°F)
scale, 184–185
Time
am and pm, 176–177,
181
calendar, 179
elapsed, 178–179
units of, 176–177
years: centuries,
decades, 179

V

Vertex, G
of an angle, 260
of a solid figure, 326–
327
of a triangle, 272–273
Volume, 328–329, **G**

W

Weight measure, 183
Whole number, G, *see also*
Computation skills with
whole numbers
renaming a, as a mixed
number, 237
rounding decimals to the
nearest, 308–309
rounding a mixed number
to the nearest, 233
Word names for numbers
decimals, 290–295
whole numbers, 2–3, 6–7
Word problems, *see*
Problem-solving
application; Problem-
solving skill

Y

Year, 178–179

Z

Zero
property of: for addition,
25; for multiplication,
75
in quotients, 120
subtraction with, 54–55

Index

ANSWERS TO THE LEARNING STAGE

This section contains answers to learning stage items only.

CHAPTER 1
PAGE 2
A. 1. three thousand, five hundred
2. four thousand, eighty-five
3. six thousand, one
4. eight thousand, two hundred, four
5. nine thousand, two hundred eighteen
B. 6. 755   7. 6,071
C. 8. twenty   9. thirty-three
10. one hundred fifty-six
11. one dollar and eighty-nine cents
12. two dollars and fifty-cents

PAGES 4–5
A. 1. 117   2. 1   3. 8
B. 4. ten thousand, ninety-two
5. twenty-five thousand, five hundred four
6. one hundred four thousand, six hundred fifty-five
C. 7. four hundred fifty-two thousand, seven hundred ninety-four
8. thousands   9. ten thousands
10. hundred thousands   11. thousands
D. 12. 1,000   13. 600   14. 20,000
15. 900,000

PAGE 6
A. 1. one millions
2. one thousands
3. one thousands
4. one billions
B. 1. one hundred seventy-five million, three hundred eighty-seven thousand, three hundred ninety-two
2. four hundred two million, three hundred one thousand, five hundred
3. two hundred sixty-three billion, nine hundred twenty-eight million, six hundred ten thousand
4. seven hundred forty-nine billion, two hundred eight-one million, one hundred thirty-one thousand, thirty-nine

C. 5. 12,000,000   6. 64,000,000
7. 90,000,000
8. 46,000,000,000   9. 673,000,000,000
10. 1,000,000,000
11. 97,425,000
12. 4,740,000,056

PAGE 10
A. 1. addition   2. $3.56 + 1.36 = \square$
B. 3. $9 \times 3 = \square$ 4. $24 - 12 = \square$

PAGE 12
A. 1. yes   2. no   3. 25,342
B. 4. >   5. <
C. 6. >   7. <   8. =   9. <
10. >   11. >

PAGE 14
A. 1. 80   2. 90   3. neither
B. 4. 20   5. 20   6. $0.60
7. 70   8. $0.70
C. 9. 200   10. 600   11. $6.00
12. 900   13. $9.00
D. 14. 2,000   15. 3,000   16. 6,000
17. 8,000   18. 10,000

PAGE 16
A. 1. 50,000   2. 90,000
3. 30,000   4. 90,000
5. 170,000   6. 260,000
7. 380,000   8. 430,000
9. 600,000   10. 630,000
11. 790,000   12. 800,000
B. 13. 300,000   14. 700,000
15. 700,000   16. 800,000
17. 1,300,000   18. 1,900,000
19. 2,400,000   20. 3,800,000
21. 4,000,000   22. 5,500,000
23. 6,800,000   24. 8,000,000
C. 25. 3,000,000   26. 6,000,000
27. 8,000,000
28. 17,000,000   29. 21,000,000
30. 29,000,000
31. 32,000,000   32. 39,000,000
33. 56,000,000

PAGE 18
A. 1. 100 + 5 + 3 or 108
2. 1,000 + 300 + 50 + 10 + 1 or 1,361
3. 2,000 + 1 or 2,001
4. 3,000 + 200 + 30 or 3,230

B. **5.** 90   **6.** 400
C. **7.** 274   **8.** 709   **9.** 942
D. **10.** DCIV   **11.** MDLXV
   12. MMCMLXXIX
   13. MMMCDXXXIII

CHAPTER 2
PAGE 28
A. **1.** 24   **2.** Betsy added up.
   3. Mark looked for sums of 10.
B. **4.** 19   **5.** 15   **6.** 27   **7.** 23   **8.** 29
PAGE 30
A. **1.** 8   **2.** 13   **3.** 1, 3   **4.** 4   **5.** 438
B. **6.** $4.73   **7.** $8.18   **8.** $10.93
   9. $12.03   **10.** $11.24   **11.** $4.87
C. **12.** 71   **13.** 361   **14.** $7.81
   15. 1,339   **16.** 837   **17.** 477
PAGE 34
A. **1.** 1,219
   2. 853
   3. addition
   4. $1,219 + 853 = n$
B. **5.** 4,172
   6. 3,309
   7. subtraction
   8. $4,172 - 3,309 = n$
PAGE 38
A. **1.**
$$\begin{array}{r} \overset{1}{}\$\,92.35 \\ +\ 24.06 \\ \hline 116.41 \end{array}$$
2.
$$\begin{array}{r} \overset{1\ 1}{62{,}842} \\ +\ 79{,}321 \\ \hline 142{,}163 \end{array}$$
3.
$$\begin{array}{r} \overset{1}{14{,}922} \\ +\ 30{,}455 \\ \hline 45{,}377 \end{array}$$
   4.
$$\begin{array}{r} 83{,}910 \\ +\ 1{,}650 \\ \hline 85{,}560 \end{array}$$
5.
$$\begin{array}{r} \overset{1\ \ \ 1}{27{,}406} \\ +\ 3{,}517 \\ \hline 30{,}923 \end{array}$$
B. **6.**
$$\begin{array}{r} 43{,}651 \\ 29{,}327 \\ +\ 1{,}420 \\ \hline 74{,}398 \end{array}$$
7.
$$\begin{array}{r} 48{,}296 \\ 345 \\ +\ 6{,}728 \\ \hline 55{,}369 \end{array}$$
C. **8.** 6,347   **9.** $1,066.99   **10.** 68,707
   11. $778.38   **12.** 87,682
PAGE 40
A. **1.**
$$\begin{array}{r} \overset{1\ 1}{245{,}346} \\ +\ 100{,}587 \\ \hline 345{,}933 \end{array}$$
2.
$$\begin{array}{r} \overset{1\ 1}{349{,}902} \\ +\ 114{,}364 \\ \hline 464{,}266 \end{array}$$
   3.
$$\begin{array}{r} \overset{1\ 1\ 1}{275{,}463} \\ +\ 38{,}621 \\ \hline 314{,}084 \end{array}$$
4.
$$\begin{array}{r} \overset{1\ \ 11}{596{,}031} \\ +\ 822{,}589 \\ \hline 1{,}418{,}620 \end{array}$$

5.
$$\begin{array}{r} \overset{121\ 11}{789{,}543} \\ 142{,}679 \\ +\ 459{,}346 \\ \hline 1{,}391{,}568 \end{array}$$
6.
$$\begin{array}{r} \overset{11\ 11}{504{,}388} \\ 140{,}847 \\ +\ 27{,}341 \\ \hline 672{,}576 \end{array}$$
7.
$$\begin{array}{r} \overset{111\ \ 1}{728{,}400} \\ 65{,}796 \\ +\ 23{,}241 \\ \hline 817{,}437 \end{array}$$
8.
$$\begin{array}{r} \overset{21\ \ \ 1}{826{,}302} \\ 8{,}468 \\ +\ 29{,}723 \\ \hline 864{,}493 \end{array}$$
B. **9.** $2,023.99   **10.** 781,820
   11. 1,283,876   **12.** 11,244.59
   13. 677,988   **14.** 1,791,293
   15. $12,632.54   **16.** 747,257
PAGE 42
A. **1.** 300   **2.** 700   **3.** 1,000
   4. 1,032   **5.** yes
B. **6.** yes
C. **7.** 70   **8.** 800   **9.** 800
   10. 3,900   **11.** 1,500   **12.** $13.00

CHAPTER 3
PAGE 49
A. **1.** 12
B. **2.** $\overset{3\ 19}{4\cancel{9}}$ **3.** $\overset{7\ 17}{8\cancel{7}}$ **4.** $\overset{8\ 12}{9\cancel{2}}$
   5. $1\overset{3\ 16}{4\cancel{6}}$ **6.** $2\overset{4\ 15}{8\cancel{8}}$
C. **7.** $\overset{2\ 16}{3\cancel{6}5}$ **8.** $\overset{3\ 10}{4\cancel{0}7}$ **9.** $7\overset{6\ 19}{\cancel{9}6}$
   10. $\overset{4\ 14}{\cancel{1}{,}\cancel{5}42}$ **11.** $2{,}\overset{7\ 10}{\cancel{8}09}$
PAGE 51
A. **1.** 3   **2.** 13   **3.** 8
   4. 1   **5.** 183
B. **6.** 47   **7.** 48   **8.** 708
   9. 135   **10.** 193
PAGE 52
A. **1.**
$$\begin{array}{r} 697 \\ -\ 284 \\ \hline 413 \end{array}$$
2.
$$\begin{array}{r} \overset{8\ 13}{7\cancel{9}\cancel{3}} \\ -\ 356 \\ \hline 437 \end{array}$$
3.
$$\begin{array}{r} \overset{3\ 14\ 12}{4\cancel{5}\cancel{2}} \\ -\ 165 \\ \hline 287 \end{array}$$
   4.
$$\begin{array}{r} \overset{2\ 11\ 4\ 14}{3{,}\cancel{1}\cancel{5}\cancel{4}} \\ -\ 249 \\ \hline 2{,}905 \end{array}$$
5.
$$\begin{array}{r} \overset{4\ 11\ 15\ 11}{\cancel{5}{,}\cancel{2}\cancel{6}\cancel{1}} \\ -\ 3{,}478 \\ \hline 1{,}783 \end{array}$$
B. **6.** $1.85   **7.** $98.18   **8.** $73.86
   9. $4.04   **10.** $9.69
C. **11.** 63   **12.** 5,438   **13.** 2,923
   14. $7.81   **15.** $38.77

PAGE 54

A. **1.** $\begin{array}{r} {\scriptstyle 3\ 10} \\ \cancel{4}\cancel{0}\,8 \\ -\ \ 4\,7 \\ \hline 3\,6\,1 \end{array}$ **2.** $\begin{array}{r} {\scriptstyle 5\ 9\ 15} \\ \cancel{6}\cancel{0}\cancel{5} \\ -\,2\,4\,9 \\ \hline 3\,5\,6 \end{array}$ **3.** $\begin{array}{r} {\scriptstyle 2\ 9\ 10} \\ 6,\cancel{3}\cancel{0}\cancel{0} \\ -\,1,2\,7\,8 \\ \hline 5,0\,2\,2 \end{array}$

B. **4.** $\begin{array}{r} {\scriptstyle 7\ 9\ 13} \\ \cancel{8}\cancel{0}\cancel{3} \\ -\,4\,5\,8 \\ \hline 3\,4\,5 \end{array}$ **5.** $\begin{array}{r} {\scriptstyle 4\ 9\ 9\ 16} \\ \cancel{5},\cancel{0}\cancel{0}\cancel{6} \\ -\,4,4\,2\,9 \\ \hline 5\,7\,7 \end{array}$

6. $\begin{array}{r} {\scriptstyle 6\ 9\ 9\ 10} \\ \cancel{7},\cancel{0}\cancel{0}\cancel{0} \\ -\,3,1\,4\,5 \\ \hline 3,8\,5\,5 \end{array}$ **7.** $\begin{array}{r} {\scriptstyle 3\ 9\ 9\ 10} \\ \cancel{4},\cancel{0}\cancel{0}\cancel{0} \\ -\,2,0\,8\,3 \\ \hline 1,9\,1\,7 \end{array}$

C. **8.** 870 **9.** 222 **10.** 5,818
11. 331 **12.** 2,454

PAGE 56

A. **1.** $\begin{array}{r} {\scriptstyle 7\ 16\ 14\ 8\ 10} \\ 2\,\cancel{8}\,\cancel{7},\cancel{4}\,\cancel{9}\,\cancel{0} \\ -\ \ 6\,9,7\,1\,3 \\ \hline 2\,1\,7,7\,7\,7 \end{array}$ **2.** $\begin{array}{r} {\scriptstyle 8\ 14\ 14\ 12\ 16} \\ 4\,\cancel{9}\,\cancel{5},\cancel{5}\,\cancel{3}\,\cancel{6} \\ -\,1\,2\,6,7\,9\,8 \\ \hline 3\,6\,8,7\,3\,8 \end{array}$

3. $\begin{array}{r} {\scriptstyle 6\ 13\ 12\ 10\ 12} \\ \$\,\cancel{7},\cancel{4}\,\cancel{3}\,\cancel{1}.\cancel{2}\,1 \\ -\ \ 6,7\,8\,7.5\,0 \\ \hline \$\ \ 6\,4\,3.7\,1 \end{array}$

B. **4.** 421,978 **5.** 63,677 **6.** 54,845
C. **7.** 43,332 **8.** $147.31
9. 129,207 **10.** 335,807
11. 835,519 **12.** 591,835
13. 150,883 **14.** 329,807

PAGE 59

A. **1.** 17, 26, 35, 44
2. 67, 73, 64, 70
B. **3.** 78, 75, 72, 69
4. 69, 75, 81, 87
5. 102, 93, 103, 94

PAGE 60

A. **1.** 300 **2.** 200
3. 132 **4.** 100
5. yes
B. **6.** $\begin{array}{r} 400 \\ -\,200 \\ \hline 200 \end{array}$ **7.** $\begin{array}{r} 8,000 \\ -\,7,000 \\ \hline 1,000 \end{array}$
C. **8.** $4.00
D. **9.** 500 **10.** 200 **11.** $4.00
12. 3,000 **13.** 5,000

PAGE 62

A. **1.** 42 **2.** 56
3. 8 **4.** 24
5. 20 **6.** 86
B. **7.** 26 **8.** 8 **9.** 19
10. 110 **11.** 348 **12.** 5

PAGE 64

A. **1.** 328
2. 119
3. How many more people are on the first plane than on the second plane?
4. subtraction **5.** $328 - 119 = n$
6. 209 **7.** people
8. 209
B. **9.** 85 empty seats

PAGE 66

A. **1.** > **2.** < **3.** >
4. < **5.** > **6.** >
B. **7.** 7, 8, 9 **8.** 0, 1, 2, 3, 4, 5, 6, 7
9. 3, 4, 5, 6, 7, 8, 9
10. 0, 1, 2, 3, 4, 5

CHAPTER 4
PAGES 74–75

A. **1.** 3 **2.** 6 **3.** 7
B. **4.** 2 **5.** 4
C. **6.** 5 **7.** 24 **8.** 1
D. **9.** 0 **10.** 0 **11.** 0
E. **12.** 3 **13.** 3 **14.** 5 **15.** 4

PAGE 76

A. **1.** 50,000 **2.** 6,000; 60,000
3. 900; 9,000; 90,000
B. **4.** 3 **5.** 3 **6.** 3 **7.** 30,000
C. **8.** 240,000 **9.** 15,000; 150,000
10. 5,600; 56,000; 560,000
D. **11.** 6 **12.** 6 **13.** 6 **14.** 60,000
E. **15.** 30 **16.** 180 **17.** 400
18. $18,000 **19.** 280,000

PAGE 80

A. **1.** 12 **2.** 1 **3.** 8 **4.** 9 **5.** 92
B. **6.** 16 **7.** 3 **8.** 8
9. 13 **10.** 257

PAGE 82

A. **1.** $\begin{array}{r} {\scriptstyle 3\ 12} \\ 1,925 \\ \times\ \ 4 \\ \hline 7,700 \end{array}$ **2.** $\begin{array}{r} {\scriptstyle 1\ 32} \\ 3,243 \\ \times\ \ 7 \\ \hline 22,701 \end{array}$ **3.** $\begin{array}{r} {\scriptstyle 2\ \ \ 1} \\ 28,325 \\ \times\ \ \ \ 3 \\ \hline 84,975 \end{array}$

4. $\begin{array}{r} {\scriptstyle 3\,4} \\ 14,968 \\ \times\ \ \ 5 \\ \hline 74,840 \end{array}$ **5.** $\begin{array}{r} {\scriptstyle 22\ 13} \\ 45,629 \\ \times\ \ \ \ 4 \\ \hline 182,516 \end{array}$

B. **6.** 14,682 **7.** 24,648 **8.** 175,357
9. 379,230 **10.** 58,365
C. **11.** $57.92 **12.** $4.13 **13.** $489.90
14. $665.46 **15.** $2,341.05

PAGE 86
1. $7.95
2. $8.95
3. $20
4. Find how much change she received.
5. $16.90
6. $3.10
7. Mrs. Coleman received $3.10 in change.

PAGES 88–89
A. 1. 3　2. 6　3. 9
B. 4. 6, 10
　5. 12, 18, 30, 36
　6. 8, 16, 24, 32, 40, 48
C. 7. 6, 12, 18　8. 6, 12, 18　9. 12, 24, 36

PAGE 90
A. 1. 4,700　2. 15,000　3. 14,400
B. 4. 6　5. 6　6. 6
C. 7. 23,600　8. 80,000　9. 72,200
D. 10. 18　11. 18　12. 18
E. 13. 210　14. 760　15. 800
　16. 5,000　17. 6,000
　18. 12,000　19. 30,000　20. 280,000
　21. 250,000　22. 630,000

PAGE 92
A. 1. 765　2. 1,856　3. 4,444
　4. 55,251　5. 14,875
B. 6. 7,998　7. 21,164　8. 29,850
C. 9. 1,440　10. 2,666　11. 1,947
　12. 2,088　13. 23,808
　14. 14,712　15. 10,767　16. 3,132
　17. $33.32　18. $138.38

PAGE 94
A.
1.
```
     341
  × 526
    2046
    6820
  170500
  179,366
```
2.
```
     878
  × 163
    2634
   52680
   87800
  143,114
```
3.
```
     409
  × 733
    1227
   12270
  286300
  299,797
```
4.
```
     558
  × 237
    3906
   16740
  111600
  132,246
```
5.
```
     629
  × 455
    3145
   31450
  251600
  286,195
```
B. 6. 127,617　7. $265,174　8. 174,798
　9. 481,076　10. $3,011.82

PAGE 96
A. 1. 400　2. 400　3. 160,000　4. yes
B. 5. $15.00
C. 6. 800　7. 18,000　8. 2,000
　9. 6,300　10. 90,000

CHAPTER 5
PAGE 105
A. 1. 8　2. 25　3. 39　4. 0　5. 0
　6. 0　7. 0　8. 1　9. 1　10. 1

PAGE 106
A. 1. 1; 1
　2. 10; 10
　3. 100; 100
　4. 1,000; 1,000
B. 5. 7; 7
　6. 70; 70
　7. 700; 700
　8. 7,000; 7,000
C. 9. 10　10. 100
　11. 1,000　12. 10,000
　13. 8　14. 80
　15. 800　16. 8,000
　17. 700　18. 5,000
　19. 20　20. 80

PAGE 108
A. 1. 4　2. tens　3. 42
B. 4. 32　5. 132　6. 122
　7. $32　8. 73

PAGE 110
A.
1.
```
   12 r 3
 6)75
   6
   15
   12
    3
```
2.
```
    5 r 4
 5)29
   25
    4
```
3.
```
  122 r 1
 3)367
   3
   6
   6
   7
   6
   1
```
4.
```
  164 r 1
 4)657
   4
   25
   24
   17
   16
    1
```
5.
```
   68 r 1
 4)273
   24
   33
   32
    1
```
B. 6. 22 r 1　7. 19 r 1　8. 11 r 7
　9. 7 r 3　10. 7 r 3
　11. 211 r 3　12. 145 r 1　13. 117 r 7
　14. 51 r 2　15. 72 r 2

PAGE 114
A. 1. multiplication
　2. $8,726.25
B. 3. $1,175.00

PAGE 116

A.

1.
```
    2,841
3)8,523
  6
  2 5
  2 4
    12
    12
     3
     3
```

2.
```
    1,528 r 2
5)7,642
  5
  2 6
  2 5
    14
    10
    42
    40
     2
```

3.
```
    24,135
4)96,540
  8
  16
  16
   5
   4
   14
   12
   20
   20
    0
```

4.
```
    1,877 r 3
4)7,511
  4
  3 5
  3 2
   31
   28
   31
   28
    3
```

5.
```
    1,248
7)8,736
  7
  1 7
  1 4
   33
   28
   56
   56
```

6.
```
    12,466 r 1
5)62,331
  5
  12
  10
  2 3
  2 0
   33
   30
   31
   30
    1
```

7. 1,144   8. 1,121 r 1
9. 2,489 r 1   10. 1,152 r 3
11. 42,157   12. 15,542
13. 13,162 r 5   14. 26,317 r 2

PAGE 118

A.

1.
```
    594 r 1
4)2,377
  2 0
   37
   36
   17
   16
    1
```

2.
```
    349
7)2,443
  2 1
   34
   28
   63
   63
```

3.
```
    9,368 r 1
6)56,209
  54
  2 2
  1 8
   40
   36
   49
   48
    1
```

4.
```
    5,148
4)20,592
  20
   5
   4
   19
   16
   32
   32
```

B.
5. 588   6. $583
7. 564   8. 238 r 3
9. 8,563   10. 4,125
11. $5,137   12. 6,641 r 4

PAGE 120

A.

1.
```
    $1.01
4)$4.04
  4
  04
  04
```

2.
```
    1,026
9)9,234
  9
  23
  18
  54
  54
```

3.
```
    906
2)1,812
  1 8
   12
   12
```

4.
```
    30,870 r 2
3)92,612
  9
  2 6
  2 4
   21
   21
    2
```

B.
5. 103 r 1   6. $1,205
7. 13,066 r 2   8. 2,400 r 3

PAGE 121

A. 1. 2, 4, 5   2. 3, 6
B. 3. odd   4. even   5. odd
6. even   7. odd   8. even
C. 9. yes   10. no   11. yes
12. yes   13. no

PAGE 122

A. 1. 18   2. 9   3. 6   4. 3, 6, 9, 18
B. 5. 3, 4, 6, 12   6. 1, 2, 4, 5, 10, 20
C. 7. 1, 2, 4, 8, 16   8. 1, 2, 3, 4, 6, 12
9. 1, 5, 25   10. 1, 2, 11, 22
11. 1, 5, 7, 35
D. 12. 1, 2, 5, 10   13. 1, 7
14. 1, 5   15. 1, 2, 8

PAGE 124

A. 1. 1, 13   2. prime
B. 3. 2, 4   4. 2 × 2 × 2
C. 5.
```
      18
     /  \
    2 × 9
   /    / \
  2 × 3 × 3
```
6.
```
      18
     /  \
    3 × 6
   /    / \
  3 × 3 × 2
```
D. 7.
```
      30
     /  \
    5 × 6
   /    / \
  5 × 3 × 2
```
8.
```
      28
     /  \
    2 × 14
   /    / \
  2 × 2 × 7
```
9.
```
        24
       /  \
      2 × 12
     /    /  \
    2 × 2  × 6
   /    /  \  \
  2 × 2 × 2 × 3
```
10.
```
        45
       /  \
      3 × 15
     /    /  \
    3 × 3  × 5
```
11.
```
        16
       /  \
      2 × 8
     /    / \
    2 × 2 × 4
   /    /  \  \
  2 × 2 × 2 × 2
```

PAGE 132

A. **1.** .4 **2.** 42r17

B. **3.** 2r9 **4.** 8r8 **5.** 31r3

  6. 31 **7.** 32r35

PAGE 134

A. **1.** 2

  2. There are 0 23's in 11.

  3. 205

B. **4.** 2r8 **5.** 11r6 **6.** 10r11

  7. 3 **8.** 170r25

PAGE 136

A. **1.** 5r3 **2.** 6 **3.** 33 **4.** 52r4

B. **5.** 9 **6.** 6r4 **7.** 54r8 **8.** 50r34

PAGE 138

A. **1.** 7 yes **2.** 1,070r2

B. **3.** 3,124 **4.** 847

  5. 807r1 **6.** 1,170r57

C. **7.** 700r6 **8.** 2,102r31

  9. 4,532r7 **10.** 626

PAGE 140

A. **1.** no **2.** 1 **3.** 1,752

B. **4.** 7r2 **5.** 15r34

  6. 69r23 **7.** 814r53

C. **8.** 18r26 **9.** 18r16

  10. 61r5 **11.** 2,719r17

PAGE 144

A. **1.** $0.39 **2.** $8.50 **3.** $146.91

  4. $0.52 **5.** $7.42 **6.** $7.34

B. **7.** $1.04 **8.** $7.41 **9.** $133.23

  10. $0.08 **11.** $0.75 **12.** $5.90

PAGE 146

A. **1.** 140 **2.** 140

B. **3.** 80 **4.** 55¢ **5.** 6

  6. 400 **7.** $4.02

PAGE 148

A. **1.** You must know how much he pays
     for each rose and how much he
     sells each for.

  2. no

B. **1.** Too much $5.50 **2.** Enough $60.00

PAGE 150

A. **1.** 7 **2.** 8 **3.** 6

B. **4.** 15 **5.** 24 **6.** 8 **7.** 19

C. **8.** 9 **9.** 8 **10.** 32

  11. 45 **12.** 8 **13.** 13

CHAPTER 7

PAGES 156–157

A. **1.** 10 cm **2.** 12 cm

B. **3.** 8 cm **4.** 10 cm

C. **5.** 7 cm **6.** 3 cm **7.** 13 cm

  8. 2 cm **9.** 5 cm **10.** 12 cm

PAGE 159

A. **1.** 300 **2.** 6

B. **3.** 9,000 **4.** 7

PAGE 162

A. **1.** 60 **2.** 90 **3.** 2 **4.** 8

B. **5.** 2,000 **6.** 8,000 **7.** 4 m **8.** 6

C. **9.** cm **10.** cm **11.** m

  12. cm **13.** mm **14.** km

PAGE 165

A. **1.** 2,000 **2.** 6

B. **3.** mL **4.** L **5.** mL

PAGE 168

A. **1.** 4,000 **2.** 8 **3.** 5,000 **4.** 6

B. **5.** t **6.** g **7.** kg

  8. t **9.** kg **10.** g

PAGE 170

A. **1.** km, m, cm, mm **2.** cm

B. **3.** g, kg, t **4.** g

PAGE 172

A. **1.** 40 kg

  2. unknown

  3. How much more is the hog
     than the piglet?

  4. No. Not enough information is
     given.

B. **5.** 5 years

  6. unknown

  7. How old is Harriet?

  8. No. Not enough information is
     given.

C. **9.** enough **10.** not enough

PAGE 174

A. **1.** 0°C

B. **2.** cool

C. **3.** cool

D. **6.** 14°C

E. **9.** 12°C

F. **10.** 15°C **11.** 5 **12.** −8°C

PAGE 176

A. **1.** 48 **2.** 180 **3.** 90 **4.** 150

B. **5.** 7:20 am **6.** 11:45 am

C. **7.** 7, 34 **8.** 20

D. **9.** 2, 25 **10.** 3, 35

PAGE 178

A. **1.** Monday **2.** January 14 **3.** Monday

B. **4.** 7 **5.** 12

PAGE 180

A. **1.** 48 **2.** 15,840 **3.** 72 **4.** 3

  5. 2 **6.** 3 **7.** 12 **8.** 3,520

B. **9.** 2 **10.** 16

C. **11.** 6 ft 4 in. **12.** 3 ft 8 in.

Answers to learning stage items only **405**

Answers to the Learning Stage

PAGE 182

A. **1.** 4 **2.** 4 **3.** 1 **4.** $3\frac{1}{2}$

B. 24 fl oz

C. 3 cups; 5 cups

PAGE 183

A. **1.** 32 **2.** 2

3. 6,000 **4.** 5

5. 1 lb 2 oz **6.** 36

B. **7.** 8, 8 **8.** 1,000, 1,000

PAGE 184

A. **1.** 32°F **2.** 78°F **3.** −4°F **4.** hot

B. **5.** 38°F **6.** 50°F **7.** 78°F

8. rise of 22°

C. **9.** warm **10.** no

CHAPTER 8

PAGE 192

A. **1.** $\frac{3}{8}$ **2.** $\frac{5}{8}$

B. **3.** $\frac{1}{2}$ **4.** $\frac{1}{2}$

C. **5.** $\frac{3}{5}$ **6.** $\frac{2}{3}$ **7.** $\frac{1}{4}$ **8.** $\frac{6}{7}$

D. **9.** $\frac{4}{6}$ **10.** $\frac{1}{6}$ **11.** $\frac{8}{6}$

PAGE 194

A. **1.** $\frac{3}{5}$ **2.** $\frac{3}{5}$

B. **3.** $\frac{2}{8}$

C. **4.** 2 **5.** 6

D. **6.** $\frac{6}{12}, \frac{3}{6}, \frac{1}{2}$ **7.** $\frac{8}{16}, \frac{4}{8}, \frac{1}{2}$

PAGE 197

A. **1.** $\frac{1}{3}, \frac{2}{6}, \frac{3}{9}, \frac{4}{12}, \frac{5}{15}$ **2.** $\frac{2}{5}, \frac{4}{10}, \frac{6}{15}, \frac{8}{20}, \frac{10}{25}$

3. $\frac{3}{4}, \frac{6}{8}, \frac{9}{12}, \frac{12}{16}, \frac{15}{20}$ **4.** $\frac{2}{7}, \frac{4}{14}, \frac{6}{21}, \frac{8}{28}, \frac{10}{35}$

5. $\frac{5}{8}, \frac{10}{16}, \frac{15}{24}, \frac{20}{32}, \frac{25}{40}$ **6.** $\frac{1}{10}, \frac{2}{20}, \frac{3}{30}, \frac{4}{40}, \frac{5}{50}$

B. **7.** 3 **8.** 12 **9.** 8 **10.** 10

PAGE 198

A. **1.** 24 **2.** 25 **3.** no

B. **4.** true **5.** false **6.** true **7.** true

PAGE 200

A. **1.** 12, 24, 36 **2.** 12, 24, 36 **3.** 10, 20, 30

B. **4.** 6 **5.** 8 **6.** 36

C. **7.** 14 **8.** 20 **9.** 6

10. 16 **11.** 33 **12.** 18

PAGE 202

A. **1.** 10, 9

2. >

B. **3.** < **4.** <

5. < **6.** <

PAGE 204

A. **1.** Factors of 12: 1, 2, 3, 4, 6, 12

Factors of 36: 1, 2, 3, 4, 6, 9, 12, 18, 36

2. 1, 2, 3, 4, 6, 12

3. 12

B. **4.** 1, 2, 3, 4, 6, 12 **5.** 6

C. **6.** 6 **7.** 3 **8.** 3 **9.** 4

PAGE 205

A. **1.** 1, 3 **2.** 1, 2 **3.** 1, 2, 3, 6

4. 1, 2, 4 **5.** 1, 3

B. **6.** yes **7.** no **8.** yes

9. yes **10.** no

PAGE 206

A. **1.** $\frac{2}{3}$ **2.** $\frac{2}{3}$

B. **3.** $\frac{1}{2}$ **4.** $\frac{2}{3}$

C. **5.** $\frac{4}{7}$ **6.** $\frac{3}{4}$ **7.** $\frac{3}{5}$

8. $\frac{3}{5}$ **9.** $\frac{5}{8}$ **10.** $\frac{3}{4}$

11. $\frac{1}{3}$ **12.** $\frac{3}{4}$ **13.** $\frac{8}{21}$

PAGE 210

A. **1.** 3 to 2

B. **2.** 4 to 1 **3.** 1 to 4

4. 7 to 4 **5.** 4 to 7

C. **6.** 3 for 80¢ **7.** 2 for 25¢

PAGE 212

A. **1.** $\frac{6}{5}$ **2.** $\frac{3}{8}$ **3.** $\frac{1}{7}$ **4.** $\frac{5}{2}$

B. **5.** 1 to 8 **6.** 4 to 3

7. 7 to 10 **8.** 3 to 5

C. **9.** 4 to 12, $\frac{4}{12}$ **10.** 5 to 9, $\frac{5}{9}$

11. 9 to 4, $\frac{9}{4}$ **12.** 12 to 4, $\frac{12}{4}$

CHAPTER 9

PAGE 219

A. **1.** 6 **2.** 10 **3.** 7 **4.** 5 **5.** 15

B. **6.** $\frac{4}{9}$ **7.** $\frac{5}{7}$ **8.** $\frac{12}{13}$ **9.** $\frac{5}{6}$ **10.** $\frac{9}{11}$

PAGE 220

A. **1.** 2 **2.** 2, 2 **3.** 4, 4, 2

4. 1 **5.** 2 **6.** 1

B. **7.** $\frac{1}{3}$ **8.** $\frac{1}{3}$ **9.** $\frac{3}{4}$

10. $\frac{2}{5}$ **11.** $\frac{1}{6}$ **12.** $\frac{1}{2}$

13. $\frac{2}{3}$ **14.** $\frac{2}{3}$ **15.** $\frac{1}{3}$ **16.** $\frac{1}{2}$ **17.** $\frac{2}{3}$

PAGE 222

A. **1.** 4, 8, 12, 16, 20, 24

2. 8, 16, 24

3. 12, 24

4. 24

5.

$$\frac{1}{4} = \frac{6}{24}$$
$$\frac{3}{8} = \frac{9}{24}$$
$$+ \frac{3}{12} = \frac{6}{24}$$
$$\overline{\frac{21}{24} = \frac{7}{8}}$$

B. **6.** $\frac{7}{8}$ **7.** $\frac{13}{20}$ **8.** $\frac{1}{2}$ **9.** $\frac{11}{18}$ **10.** $\frac{7}{8}$ **11.** $\frac{11}{18}$

PAGE 224
A. **1.** 10 **2.** 13 **3.** 13 **4.** 5
B. **5.** $\frac{31}{6}$ **6.** $\frac{13}{5}$ **7.** $\frac{14}{3}$
8. $\frac{80}{7}$ **9.** $\frac{53}{4}$ **10.** $\frac{55}{3}$

PAGE 225
A. **1.** 3 **2.** $\frac{1}{2}$
B. **3.** $1\frac{4}{5}$ **4.** $4\frac{3}{4}$ **5.** $4\frac{2}{3}$ **6.** $3\frac{3}{7}$ **7.** $2\frac{1}{8}$
8. $4\frac{1}{2}$ **9.** $2\frac{1}{2}$ **10.** $9\frac{1}{2}$ **11.** $5\frac{1}{2}$ **12.** $4\frac{1}{3}$

PAGE 226
A. **1.** 1 **2.** 1 **3.** $1\frac{3}{7}$ **4.** 3
B. **5.** 1 **6.** $1\frac{1}{3}$ **7.** $2\frac{1}{8}$ **8.** $2\frac{1}{4}$
C. **9.** $1\frac{5}{24}$ **10.** $1\frac{13}{30}$ **11.** $1\frac{1}{4}$ **12.** $1\frac{1}{2}$

PAGE 228
A. **1.** $5\frac{2}{3}$ **2.** $6\frac{4}{5}$ **3.** $4\frac{3}{8}$
4. $12\frac{1}{3}$ **5.** $14\frac{2}{3}$
B. **6.** 3, 11 **7.** 2, $6\frac{1}{2}$ **8.** 8, 10, $7\frac{5}{6}$
C. **9.** $10\frac{5}{7}$ **10.** $7\frac{5}{8}$ **11.** $8\frac{13}{20}$ **12.** $59\frac{14}{15}$
13. 9 **14.** $26\frac{7}{20}$
15. $24\frac{2}{3}$ **16.** $8\frac{2}{9}$

PAGE 230
A. **1.** $6\frac{4}{9}$ **2.** $6\frac{19}{30}$ **3.** $9\frac{1}{2}$
B. **4.** 19, 1 **5.** 15, 5, $10\frac{1}{2}$
C. **6.** $8\frac{1}{2}$ **7.** $10\frac{3}{8}$ **8.** $8\frac{4}{15}$
9. $45\frac{8}{15}$ **10.** $35\frac{5}{24}$
11. $14\frac{2}{5}$ **12.** $22\frac{7}{12}$ **13.** $21\frac{1}{4}$
14. $23\frac{1}{4}$ **15.** $61\frac{11}{42}$

PAGE 233
A. **1.** 5, 5 **2.** 5
B. **3.** 9 **4.** 9 **5.** 17 **6.** 2 **7.** 13
PAGE 234
A. **1.** 3 **2.** 1 **3.** 3, 1 **4.** 2 **5.** 3, 1
B. **6.** 1 **7.** 2, 1 **8.** 16, 8
C. **9.** $\frac{1}{2}$ **10.** $\frac{1}{5}$ **11.** $\frac{1}{4}$ **12.** $\frac{1}{2}$ **13.** $\frac{2}{15}$

PAGE 236
A. **1.** 5 **2.** 1 **3.** 3, 1
B. **4.** $3\frac{1}{3}$ **5.** $6\frac{1}{2}$ **6.** $2\frac{1}{2}$ **7.** $2\frac{4}{9}$ **8.** $8\frac{1}{4}$
PAGE 237
A. **1.** 5 **2.** 4 **3.** 2 **4.** 8
B. **5.** 4 **6.** 17
C. **7.** 7 **8.** 14 **9.** 15 **10.** 16
PAGE 238
A. **1.** $2\frac{4}{5}$ **2.** 8, $2\frac{3}{8}$
B. **3.** 4, $2\frac{2}{3}$ **4.** 11, $4\frac{1}{2}$ **5.** 7, 2, $1\frac{1}{3}$
C. **6.** $4\frac{5}{7}$ **7.** $\frac{3}{5}$ **8.** $2\frac{3}{4}$ **9.** $8\frac{1}{3}$ **10.** $3\frac{3}{5}$

PAGE 240
A. **1.** 15 **2.** 9, $2\frac{2}{3}$
B. **3.** $4\frac{5}{6}$ **4.** $7\frac{3}{4}$ **5.** $1\frac{5}{6}$ **6.** $4\frac{1}{2}$
PAGE 241
A. **1.** $\frac{2}{3}$ **2.** $\frac{6}{7}$ **3.** $\frac{13}{100}$ **4.** $\frac{11}{12}$
B. **5.** $\frac{4}{7}$ **6.** $\frac{2}{8}$ **7.** $\frac{3}{10}$ **8.** $\frac{2}{15}$
PAGE 242
A. **1.** 2, 4
2. addition
3. 11, $6\frac{1}{10}$
B. $17\frac{1}{6}$ skeins
PAGE 244
A. **1.** 1 **2.** 24 **3.** $\frac{1}{24}$
B. **4.** $\frac{1}{10}$ **5.** $\frac{1}{12}$ **6.** $\frac{1}{48}$ **7.** $\frac{1}{35}$
8. $\frac{1}{63}$ **9.** $\frac{1}{1,000}$ **10.** $\frac{1}{60}$ **11.** $\frac{1}{42}$
PAGE 246
A. **1.** 5 **2.** 48 **3.** $\frac{5}{48}$
B. **4.** $\frac{6}{35}$ **5.** $\frac{3}{32}$ **6.** $\frac{15}{32}$ **7.** $\frac{10}{21}$
C. **8.** $\frac{5}{12}$ **9.** $\frac{3}{10}$ **10.** $\frac{1}{8}$ **11.** $\frac{1}{2}$
12. $\frac{3}{5}$ **13.** $\frac{2}{15}$ **14.** $\frac{5}{12}$ **15.** $\frac{1}{10}$
PAGE 248
A. **1.** $\frac{7}{1}$ **2.** 7 **3.** 8 **4.** $\frac{7}{8}$
B. **5.** $\frac{4}{5}$ **6.** $\frac{3}{8}$ **7.** $1\frac{1}{11}$ **8.** $\frac{10}{11}$
C. **9.** 4 **10.** 6 **11.** $\frac{3}{4}$ **12.** $1\frac{1}{2}$
13. $\frac{4}{5}$ **14.** $4\frac{1}{2}$ **15.** $1\frac{1}{10}$ **16.** $\frac{1}{2}$
PAGE 250
A. **1.** $\frac{7}{3}, \frac{21}{24}, \frac{7}{8}$ **2.** $\frac{7}{4}, \frac{35}{32}, 1\frac{3}{32}$
B. **3.** $\frac{4}{5}$ **4.** $1\frac{7}{20}$ **5.** $1\frac{21}{32}$ **6.** $2\frac{20}{27}$

C. 7. 119, 19   8. 32, 21
D. 9. $3\frac{3}{14}$ 10. $3\frac{35}{36}$ 11. $32\frac{16}{25}$ 12. $15\frac{13}{27}$

CHAPTER 10
PAGE 258
A. 1. line segment   2. line
3. line segment
4. $\overline{EF}$, $\overline{FE}$; $\overleftrightarrow{BC}$, $\overleftrightarrow{CB}$; $\overline{DX}$, $\overline{XD}$
B. 5. P
C. 6. $\overrightarrow{AC}$ 7. ∠EFG, ∠GFE
8. ∠XYZ, ∠ZYX

PAGE 260
A. 1. 125°
B. 2. 35°   3. 120°

PAGE 262
A. 1. right   2. obtuse   3. acute
B. 4. no   5. yes   6. no

PAGE 264
A. 1. $\overline{PR}$, $\overline{PS}$, $\overline{PT}$, $\overline{PU}$
2. All radii are equal in length.
B. 3.

E •————• D ————• F

C. 4. $\overline{DX}$, $\overline{CD}$ 5. 1 cm   6. 2 cm
7. The length of the diameter is twice the length of the radius.
D. 8. 8 m   9. $2\frac{1}{2}$ cm

PAGE 272
A. 1. pentagon   2. triangle
3. quadrilateral
4. hexagon   5. octagon
★6. quadrilateral
B. 7. 3, XY, YZ, ZX   8. Y, Z   9. ∠Y, ∠Z

PAGE 274
A. 1. yes   2. yes   3. no
B. 4. 4   5. The sides are parallel.
6. The sides are not parallel.
C. 7. The sides are parallel.
8. The sides are parallel.
D. 9. trapezoid   10. quadrilateral
11. parallelogram

PAGE 276
A. 1. $\overline{GH}$ 2. $\overline{EH}$ 3. right   4. 4
B. 5. yes
6. All sides are equal in length.
C. 7. All sides are equal in length.

PAGE 277
D. 8. $\overline{OM}$
9. 2 diagonals. $\overline{WY}$, $\overline{XZ}$

PAGES 278–279
A. 1. 5   2. 23
B. 3. 21 cm   4. 24 m   5. 25 m
C. 6. 30 cm
D. 7. 20 cm   8. 20 cm
9. 8 + 8 + 8 + 8 = 32 cm, 4 × 8 = 32 cm

PAGE 280
A. 4. no
B. 7. no
C. 10. no
D. 11. flip   12. slide   13. turn

PAGE 282
A. 1. yes   2. yes   3. no
B. 4. 4

PAGE 283
A. 1. yes   2. no   3. yes
B. 4. yes   5. yes   6. no

CHAPTER 11
PAGE 290
A. 1. 0.2   2. 0.8   3. 0.6
B. 4. 0.8   5. 0.4   6. 0.2   7. 0.1
C. 8. $\frac{1}{2}$ 9. $\frac{1}{5}$ 10. $\frac{2}{5}$ 11. $\frac{3}{10}$
D. 12. 1.6   13. 8.5
14. 4.2   15. 6.1   16. 12.9   17. 27.3
E. 18. $7\frac{1}{10}$ 19. $3\frac{4}{5}$ 20. $16\frac{7}{10}$ 21. $48\frac{1}{5}$

PAGE 292
A. 1. 0.07   2. 0.03   3. 0.15   4. 0.6
B. 5. $\frac{4}{100}$ 6. $\frac{8}{100}$ 7. $\frac{52}{100}$ 8. $\frac{90}{100}$
C. 9. 0.03   10. 8.16
D. 11. 6.18   12. 4.02
13. 16.25   14. 72.04
E. 15. $5\frac{3}{100}$ 16. $8\frac{27}{100}$
17. $6\frac{80}{100}$ 18. $23\frac{91}{100}$

PAGE 294
A. 1. 0.005   2. 0.017
3. 0.374   4. 0.600
B. 5. $\frac{2}{1,000}$ 6. $\frac{56}{1,000}$
7. $\frac{139}{1,000}$ 8. $\frac{508}{1,000}$
C. 9. 0.001
10. 7.002
11. 5.104
12. 22.674
D. 13. 6.002   14. 4.032
15. 9.185   16. 18.020
E. 17. $10\frac{1}{1,000}$ 18. $3\frac{97}{1,000}$
19. $17\frac{139}{1,000}$ 20. $16\frac{50}{1,000}$

PAGE 296
A. **1.** 0.20   **2.** 0.70   **3.** 0.90   **4.** 0.40
B. **5.** 0.340   **6.** 0.750
C. **7.** 0.060   **8.** 0.080
   9. 0.230   **10.** 0.810

PAGE 298
A. **1.** yes   **2.** yes   **3.** no   **4.** 0.426
B. **5.** <   **6.** <   **7.** >   **8.** =   **9.** <   **10.** >
C. **11.** >   **12.** <   **13.** <   **14.** =   **15.** >   **16.** >

PAGE 304
A. **1.** 0.7   **2.** 0.66
   3. 0.857   **4.** 0.605   **5.** 0.940
B. **6.** 0.9   **7.** 0.6
   8. 0.86   **9.** 0.53
   10. 0.922   **11.** 0.963

PAGE 306
A. **1.** 1.3   **2.** 1.2   **3.** 1.6   **4.** 14.3
   5. 14.58   **6.** 7.313
   7. 36.4 cm   **8.** 14.428
B. **9.** 1.08   **10.** 1.354
   11. 18.24   **12.** 29.03
   13. 39.5   **14.** 10.348

PAGE 308
A. **1.** 3   **2.** 5   **3.** 5   **4.** 36
B. **5.** 4   **6.** 29
   7. 42.4   **8.** 43
   9. yes
C. **10.** 12   **11.** 47   **12.** 62
   13. 89   **14.** 94

PAGE 310
A. **1.** 0.3   **2.** 0.6   **3.** 0.03   **4.** 0.45
   5. 0.08   **6.** 0.012   **7.** 0.134   **8.** 0.287
B. **9.** 0.33   **10.** 0.29
   11. 0.086   **12.** 0.735

PAGE 312
A. **1.** 0.9   **2.** 2.2   **3.** 0.9 cm   **4.** 5.69
   5. 0.71   **6.** 7.85
   7. 0.829   **8.** 3.615
B. **9.** 2.9   **10.** 1.9
   11. 5.64   **12.** 1.8
   13. 2.532   **14.** 4.639

PAGE 314
A. **1.** 0.4   **2.** 0.8   **3.** 5.4   **4.** 4.0
B. **5.** 0.09   **6.** 0.06   **7.** 0.35   **8.** 0.42
C. **9.** 14.8   **10.** 48   **11.** 1.26   **12.** 6.00

CHAPTER 12
PAGE 322
A. **1.** 7   **2.** 3   **3.** 21   **4.** 21
B. **5.** 16 cm²   **6.** 35 m²   **7.** 20 cm²
   8. 35 m²   **9.** 32 cm²   **10.** 54 m²
   11. 24 m²   **12.** 40 cm²   **13.** 49 m²

PAGE 324
A. **1.** 40 cm²
   2. right triangles
   3. yes
   4. 20 cm²
B. **5.** 24 cm²   **6.** 21 m²   **7.** 18 m²
   8. 21 cm²   **9.** 18 cm²   **10.** 12.5 cm²
   11. 6 cm²   **12.** 25 cm²
   13. 28 cm²   **14.** 27 cm²

PAGE 326
A. Answers may vary.
  sphere: basketball
  cone: ice cream cone
  rectangular prism: box
  cube: die
  triangular prism: pup tent
B. edge — rectangular region
  vertex — line segment
  face — point
C. **5.** 6 faces   **6.** 6 faces
     12 edges   12 edges
     8 vertices   8 vertices
  7. 5 faces
     9 edges
     6 vertices

PAGE 328
A. **1.** 8   **2.** 3   **3.** 24
B. **4.** 60 cm³   **5.** 72 m³   **6.** 70 cm²
   7. 192 m³   **8.** 135 m³

PAGE 334
A. **1.** 1 to 12   **12.** 48 cm   **3.** 36 cm
B. **4.** 2 to 1   **5.** 1.5 cm

PAGE 336
A. **3.** 200 km
B. **4.** 350 km   **5.** 400 km
C.   9 km
D.   4 cm

CHAPTER 13
PAGE 344
A. **1.** 1 year
   2. animals
   3. 7 years
   4. giraffe
   5. 12 squares

PAGES 346–347
A. **1.** Record of Money Spent
   2. money
   3. Money
   4. days

B.

Cindy's Walking Record

D.

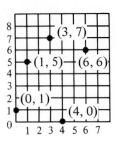

PAGE 348

A. 1. Number of Plants   **2.** weeks
    3. number of plants   **4.** 15   **5.** increase

B. 6. 7   **7.** 7
    8. Wednesday, Friday   **9.** 47

PAGE 350

A. 1. comedy, news, sports, music
    2. comedy   **3.** news   **4.** comedy

B. 5. clothes   **6.** sports, other
    7. food   **8.** $4   **9.** 1

PAGES 356–357

A. 1. (4, 2)   **2.** (2, 4)
    3. (2, 2)   **4.** (3, 3)

B. 5. yellow flowers   **6.** bird in cage
    7. empty   **8.** green plant
    9. orange curtains

C. 10. (3, 3)   **11.** (4, 2)   **12.** D   **13.** F

PAGE 358

A. 1. $\frac{1}{3}$ **2.** $\frac{1}{3}$

B. 3. heads or tails   **4.** $\frac{1}{2}$ **5.** $\frac{1}{2}$

C. 6. red, yellow, blue   **7.** $\frac{2}{5}$ **8.** $\frac{1}{5}$

D. 9. $\frac{4}{7}$ **10.** $\frac{3}{7}$

PAGE 360

A. 1. $\frac{1}{4}$ **2.** $\frac{1}{4}$ **3.** $\frac{1}{4}$ **4.** $\frac{1}{4}$

B. 5. yes

C. 6. $\frac{1}{2}$ red; $\frac{1}{4}$ yellow; $\frac{1}{4}$ blue
    7. red about 50 times, yellow about
    25 times, blue about 25 times

D. 8. $\frac{1}{3}, \frac{1}{3}, \frac{1}{3}$
    9. red: 10 times white: 10 times
    green: 10 times

E. 10. $\frac{2}{5}, \frac{3}{5}$, no   **11.** 18 times, yes

F. 12. 15 times   **13.** 15 times   **14.** 30 times

PHOTO CREDITS

ART CREDITS

Answers to the Learning Stage

$$
\begin{array}{r}
1\ 1\ 1\ 1 \\
238,074 \\
69,946 \\
472 \\
\hline
308472
\end{array}
$$

$$
\begin{array}{r}
1\ 1 \\
345,461 \\
51,654 \\
2,342 \\
\hline
399,457
\end{array}
$$

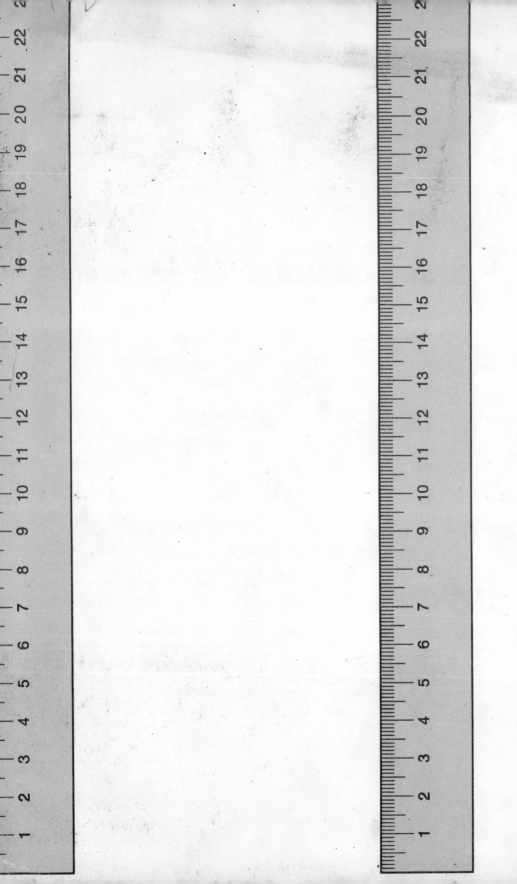